LEFT IN THE

DARK

Film Reviews and Essays 1988–2001

STUART KLAWANS

FOREWORD BY BEN SONNENBERG

NATION
BOOKS

Copyright © 2002 by Stuart Klawans
Foreword © 2002 by Ben Sonnenberg

Published by
Thunder's Mouth Press/Nation Books
161 William St., 16th Floor
New York, NY 10038

Nation Books is a co-publishing venture of the Nation Institute and Avalon
Publishing Group Incorporated.

Library of Congress Cataloging-in-Publication Data is available.

ISBN 1-56025-365-7

9 8 7 6 5 4 3 2 1

Printed in the United States of America
Distributed by Publishers Group West

"A.I. Artificial Intelligence," "An Angel at My Table," "Caro Diario," "Moulin Rouge,"
"The Puppetmaster" and "Sink or Swim" are published here for the first time.

"That Void in Cyberspace Looks a Lot Like Kansas" and "Pietro Germi"
© 1999 by the New York Times Co. "The Political Ethnography of the Academy of
Motion Picture Arts and Sciences" and "How the First World War Changed the Movies" ©
2000 by the New York Times Co. "Ousmane Sembene" © 2001 by the New York Times
Co. Reprinted by permission.

"Mute and Glorious Miltons" and "Koker Trilogy" © 1997 and 2001 by Parnassus: Poetry
in Review. Reprinted by permission.

"Francesco Rosi" © 1995 by the Film Society of Lincoln Center (Film Comment).
Reprinted by permission.

"The Great White Hype" © 1996 by Common Quest. Reprinted by permission.

"Shined Shoes (The Band Wagon)" was first published as "Shined Shoes" in *O.K. You
Mugs: Writers on Movie Actors* (Pantheon Books, 1999), edited by Luc Sante and Melissa
Holbrook Pierson. © 1999 by Stuart Klawans.

All other reviews and essays originally appeared in *The Nation*.

For Bali and Jacob

Contents

Foreword

by

Ben Sonnenberg

'<br>'ve known Stuart Klawans for fourteen years—as a friend, as a fan, as his editor at Grand Street. He's one of a rapidly vanishing breed, a very good writer who is also a first-rate critic and a hilarious entertainer. This selection of his movie reviews shows him to be a worthy successor to those earlier *Nation* critics, James Agee and Manny Farber. *Left in the Dark* will take its place next to *Agee on Film* and Farber's *Negative Space*.

The Stuart Klawans of *Left in the Dark* is an intoxicated movie-goer, impatient to tell of his dislikes and eager to share his enthusiasms. My favorite of his put-downs is the antic review on page 322 of Steven Spielberg's *The Lost World: Jurassic Park 2*, which calls up Stuart's alter-ego, Rabbi Simcha Feffeferman, spiritual leader of Congregation Anshe Tsurres. Readers unfamiliar with Stuart's work should turn to this page first. The Rabbi makes another appearance on page 314 in Stuart's lethal notice of Oliver Stone's *Natural Born Killers*, a "tour through Oliver Stone's empty head." The Rabbi is a creation worthy of Fred Allen, of Richard Pryor, a reminder that James Thurber once (alas, only once) wrote a movie review for *The Nation*.

Stuart is at the top of his form in the section called "They Were Never Wrong, The Old Masters." I admire here his long review of Mikhail Kalatozov's *I Am Cuba*, "a work of cinematic delirium and great political ambition, of political delirium and great cinematic ambition—a fabulous beast of a movie, part white

vii

elephant and part fire-breathing dragon." Stuart's paragraph-long description of one of the movie's shots takes your breath away. One wonderful deft sentence epitomizes the movie: "At once, Kalatozov plunged into the sort of death-, convention- and gravity-defying camera excursion that characterizes *I Am Cuba*."

I admire even more Stuart's deep and moving essay on page 216 on Renoir's *Grand Illusion*. Here Stuart performs that most treacherous of critical tasks: praising a masterpiece. Stuart says that "*Grand Illusion* taught me that great acting is a mystery." He shows us a still greater mystery: the workings of tragicomedy.

> An "antiwar film" would try to remain within the pastoral. Or, more sardonically, it might go full circle, returning Maréchal [the character played by Jean Gabin] to his original setting. Instead, *Grand Illusion* leaves Maréchal in a field of snow, where he's seen in long-shot with a friend he'd never dreamed of having [the character of the Jew Rosenthal, played by Marcel Dalio]. Each finely balanced element of the film has shifted, subtly but decisively, yielding an ending that's wide open.

Somewhere in these pages Stuart refers to the shutting down of art movie houses all over America. (Fortunately, they seem to be coming back.) Reading Stuart is like living within reach of one of those movie houses. He gives us Gianni Amelio, say, much as Dan Talbot's New Yorker Theater used to give us Fassbinder or the Thalia used to give us Rossellini and much as today Film Forum and Lincoln Plaza give us Claire Denis and Wong Kar-wai.

Stuart is a truly profound critic, one of the scant handful able to discern from among the many phosphorescences of modern movies the few real flames which, to paraphrase Louis MacNeice in his poem "The news-reel," do not last but happen often enough:

> To give us hope that fact is a façade
> And that there is an organism behind
> Its brittle littleness, a rhythm and a meaning,
> Something half-conjectured and half-divined,
> Something to give way to and so find.

BEN SONNENBERG is the founding editor of *Grand Street*, and the author of *Lost Property, Memoirs & Confessions of a Bad Boy*.

Introduction

Left in the Dark: This refers to my inability to follow a plot.

People who have gone to the movies with me may be recognized by the self-inflicted palmprints on their foreheads, left there after I'd asked who stole the briefcase, and wasn't the killer nanny really the girl's aunt in disguise? I suppose my incapacity results from some miswiring in the brain, combined with the prejudices born of a rabbinical and Modernist education. I learned to read not long after mid-century, at a time when "literature" had not yet been dissolved into "cultural studies"; and since the two books on which I practiced the most were the Torah and *Ulysses*, I didn't much care whether the action rose or fell.

For a movie reviewer, an indifference to plot has its advantages. Instead of wondering about what happens next, you notice what's on the screen and the soundtrack right now. I don't claim this kind of attention adds up to a critical method; but while I've been busy misunderstanding events, the things I've seen and heard have been so amazing that I once wrote a whole essay on the subject, "The Cluelessness Manifesto," which wasn't worth including in this book.

What *is* worth the ink and paper? To answer that question, I first have to own up to a feeling of dread that strikes all movie reviewers. We come to understand, sooner or later, that the running time of the world's annual film production far exceeds the hours for watching. Ignorance is inevitable; and the shafts of light that do enter the mind tend to play haphazardly, since the whims of distributors, the vagaries of screening schedules and the demands of deadlines all limit our decisions about what to review.

This, too, is part of the meaning of *Left in the Dark*. If you should wonder why you find a review of Atom Egoyan's *The Sweet Hereafter* but none of *Exotica*, you should know that I don't necessarily prefer the first; I just never got around to writing much on the second. Other notable omissions, of which I'm sure there are many, betray the outright gaps in my filmgoing. I would hope that *Left in the Dark* conveys something of the range of international cinema at this moment; I would also hope that it helps bring attention to any number of worthwhile but lesser-known movies. But no collection, this one included, can comprehend world cinema from 1988 to 2001. "Nothing is yet known about film," said Henri Langlois; and now, more than ever, he's right.

That said, I will own up to the political meaning of the title. If this collection coheres at all, it's because the great majority of these pieces were first published in that old, contentious, proudly out-of-step and deeply democratic magazine, *The Nation*.

I started reviewing for *The Nation* just when the death of cinephilia, and of cinema itself, was being proclaimed. On that subject, I strongly disagree, for reasons that might be called political, and that run through all of the pieces in this book. I intend to elaborate on those reasons. But first, for the sake of context, I must admit that there's some truth to the naysayers' argument. By the time I began writing about movies, American studios had perfected the arts of dullness.

Acting more as venture capitalists than as producers, today's studios generally release pictures that were packaged by independent outfits. These companies, in their turn, may get start-up funds from still other groups. That's why, when the budget rises above a certain level, you have to watch three different computer-animated logos at the start of the movie and read the names of eight executive producers. Each of them needs to exercise due diligence—that is to say, act important by finding something to fiddle with. And so, when all the parties are done protecting their investments, the opening credits are the most interesting thing left to see.

No matter. Above a certain budget level, the movie becomes the Product of the Week, helping to sell newspapers and magazines, attracting viewers to TV shows, moving merchandise through hamburger shops, supplying Op-Ed columnists with some ready-made zing. The result: We live among fantastically lucrative movies that everybody knows about and nobody enjoys, the prime example of which, in this book, would be *Star Wars: Episode One—The Phantom Menace*.

At this point, the death-of-cinema folks may conclude their argument. And yet there's more, and worse.

The period covered by this book also saw the American independent film become an institution. This wasn't simply a matter of "Sundance" and "Miramax" entering the common vocabulary. The distribution and marketing of independent films, and even their financing to a certain extent, became organized as never before, with a handful of companies dominating a newly defined market niche. Many of these companies are subsidiaries of major studios—Miramax is a part of Disney, for example—which means that the movie business has developed a modern equivalent of the studio system. In the past, during the age of industrial capital, each studio's assembly line cranked out a balanced line of products: so many superproductions, A pictures, B pictures, programmers and shorts. Today, in the venture capital era, the assembly line is gone; but the balance is established by other means. Superproductions and A pictures come out with the Warner Bros. label, while B pictures (a category of budget and marketing, not of merit) bear the label of Fine Line, an AOL Time Warner Company.

Readers who think this analysis too vulgarly Marxist to be credible might contemplate the fate of The Shooting Gallery: a New York outfit that began life in the early 1990s as a scrappy production company and then, under the guidance of a Wall Street type, expanded and diversified. It leased real estate, made TV commercials and music videos, bet heavily on an Internet business and by the end of the decade had merged with a bigger company, which previously had invested in gold mining ventures. By the time this corporate master declared The Shooting Gallery bankrupt, its identity as an independent film company was no more substantial than the fragment of a peanut shell spat off of somebody's tongue.

So much for American filmmaking, high-end and low. As for the fortunes in the United States of foreign-language pictures, they make the death-of-cinema folks sound like prophets.

And yet, while going to the movies in my haphazard way, I've found a world of vitality in the dark. Every country harbors talented people who feel the urge to make films, people who don't seem to know they should quit in despair. As a doctrinaire leftist, committed to the idea that labor is dignified and creative power universal, I've assumed my job is to help these filmmakers go on working. That's all a critic can do: tell people about the good work as it comes along, and keep the path free by clearing away the bad.

So most of this book, like most of my writing for *The Nation*, consists of advertisements for the good, a category that gets me into a lot of trouble. What's "a good movie"? Part of the answer might lie in the relationship the film proposes to have with you. I like movies that acknowledge themselves to be a part of a bigger world—movies that allow you to co-exist with them, as you live with buses and parks and friends. That's why, over the past dozen years, many of the films that have appealed to me have been fictions with a strong documentary impulse, or documentaries that play like fictions. These are works by artists whose imaginations operate through the real; and so the book begins with them. Readers who want to know why Iranian cinema has meant so much to certain audiences may want to consult this chapter. Readers who are seeking more of an explanation for my love for such borderline films may find it in the book's next chapter, "Polemics."

The sections that follow are full of praise: for American features, foreign features and documentaries of the last dozen years, and also for films of the past that have popped up again in theaters. Apart from wanting to promote good films as a leftist agenda, I assume people read reviews because they feel like going to the movies, and so most of my *Nation* articles have taken the form of recommendations. On the other hand, readers also enjoy displays of heartless cruelty. To sate such bloodlust, I have gathered my savageries in one convenient location, titled "Nothing Better Than They Deserve."

Those who grow queasy at the spectacle may calm themselves by consulting another section, called "Spiritual Guidance." In the belief that film reviews should serve the whole person, I have made religious instruction a regular feature of *The Nation*. Here are the most uplifting examples.

What do I hope readers will gain from this collection? Only what the movies have always promised us: entertainment. I have sometimes pointed out, to the more glum among *The Nation*'s readers, that when a work entertains you, it invites you in (as would a good host) and engages you in conversation—an *entretien*, as the film-mad French would say. Entertainment makes the world seem a bigger, more interlocutory place, at least for a couple of hours—and that, too, can be political in the broad sense.

I would be happy if readers were to discover such a spirit in this book, as well as in the films it discusses. There's fun to be had in being out of step; and nothing's more entertaining than democracy.

In the Business

The Other Sister
8mm
200 Cigarettes
Six Ways to Sunday
Dancemaker
The Howard Stern Show

M*onday.* Screening of Garry Marshall's *The Other Sister*, which seems to be about a goldfish. Whenever the characters have to make a decision, the film cuts to a close-up of the cute little fella swimming in his bowl. Since the picture was photographed by Dante Spinotti, the background pebbles are of a blue so luscious as to be edible. But distractions multiply, keeping me from entering into a meditative union with the fish. Snatches of pop music keep drifting onto the soundtrack and off again, as if someone on the set had been having trouble tuning a radio. And then there's the plot.

The Other Sister claims to be concerned with a plucky young woman named Carla (Juliette Lewis), who is determined to lead a full life despite being (in the current phrase) mentally challenged. While attending a technical college in San Francisco, she meets and falls in love with Danny (Giovanni Ribisi), who is similarly challenged. He also faces a second hurdle: Unlike Carla, whose family rolls in money, Danny is scraping by. I think this is a fine subject for a film—but by Fassbinder, not Garry Marshall. Given his emphatic style, you'd think Carla and Danny were not just the protagonists but also the intended audience. I wonder what they'd make of all those goldfish shots.

I also wonder what they'd think of the role of Carla's mom, which has been fixed on Diane Keaton like a curse. During the early scenes, Mom is so cold, commanding, heartless and manipulative, you keep expecting her to offer Carla a poisoned apple; and at the climax, when (for comic effect) she's doused by the sprinklers on the country club's golf course, the only thing missing is a strangled cry of "I'm melting!" Considering the movie's nonstop lectures about granting people their dignity, perhaps Marshall might have reined in his get-Mom urges. He also might have granted some dignity to the black people in the movie, who exist solely as background, except when they step forward, minstrel-style, to entertain Carla and Danny.

Instead of leaving with an inward promise to respect the mentally challenged, I go out brooding on the Return of the Strutting Negro.

Tuesday. Screening of *8mm.* The soundtrack throbs with Arab music, laid on to lend an atmosphere of spice and danger to what the press notes call the "garish red-light district in Hollywood." As the notes go on to say, "there is no such district." But what the hell—what are set designers and Arabs for, if not this?

I find I can mull over that question, watch Nicolas Cage stroll through entire basements full of Threatening Negroes, Mexicans and Filipinos, and still have plenty of leisure to review the history of film criticism. It was in the fifties, as I recall, that certain critics adopted the habit of interpreting films as the self-dramatizations of their directors. Where exactly would we discover Joel Schumacher in *8mm*?

There's a clue in those invaluable press notes. Nicolas Cage describes the character he plays, a private detective, as someone whose work "starts to trigger a darkness inside of him." Or, as a sidekick says to Cage in the film itself, "Dance with the devil . . . the devil changes you." Apparently, Schumacher told everyone that the movie is about someone who comes face to face with the evil inside himself—in which case, *8mm* can't be about the detective. He's just a guy who schleps from one grungy place to another. But if Schumacher is the true protagonist, and *8mm* his journey of self-discovery, then we know where he encounters the ugly truth about himself. It's in the character of Dino Velvet (Peter Stormare), the filmmaker known as "the Jim Jarmusch of S&M." Dino Velvet is tacky; he's self-infatuated; he dresses badly; he lives and works in a place that looks like an old-fashioned gay-sex paraphernalia shop on Christopher Street. And the worst thing about him is not that he killed a runaway girl on camera. The worst is, he let the producer keep all the money and took chump change as his fee.

The horror. The horror.

Wednesday. Screening of Risa Bramon Garcia's *200 Cigarettes.* Young white heteros bicker in New York's East Village on New Year's Eve 1981, while a black cabbie (Dave Chappelle) chauffeurs them around and pop hits of the year drift onto the soundtrack and off again. Was I in the East Village that evening? I can't remember. My memory seems to have stopped at Election Night 1980.

I remember that Keith phoned, saying, "I can't take this on my own. Can I come over?" He showed up fifteen minutes later with a bottle of Stolichnaya.

"Good," I said. "I've got Jameson. Let's mix them."

We poured equal measures over ice and got something that looked like a Stinger and tasted like sweetened antifreeze. "What should we call it?" I asked.

"Stoli and Jameson," Keith said. "It's an IRA."

After three of them, we still knew Reagan would be President, but we temporarily didn't care. But what about *200 Cigarettes*? It occurs to me that a movie has been unspooling. Evidently this, too, is something I don't care about—and the feeling in this case would seem to be permanent.

Thursday. Screening of Adam Bernstein's *Six Ways to Sunday*, a movie with subtle links to *200 Cigarettes*. Bernstein can claim to have directed more than seventy music videos, while *200 Cigarettes* is co-produced by MTV Films. Also, the soundtrack to *200 Cigarettes* features a number of tunes by Blondie, whose lead singer, Deborah Harry, has a lead role in *Six Ways to Sunday*, as the domineering mother of an up-and-coming gangster in Youngstown, Ohio.

So is *Six Ways to Sunday* merely a continuation of *200 Cigarettes* by other means? No—it's too weird for that. Based on Charles Perry's novel *Portrait of a Young Man Drowning*, the movie stars slit-eyed Norman Reedus as a severely repressed young man who discovers his métier—and his sexuality—while beating people up for the mob. Every time he whacks a victim, the screen explodes in a freakout montage of distorted faces, bloody colors, flashing lights. This is the normal part of the movie. The strange stuff has to do with the Yiddish-speaking, klezmer-loving gangsters for whom the boy works, the junk-shop decor of Mom's apartment, the allure of the limping maid (Elina Lowensöhn) who ministers to the chief hoodlum and (above all) the question of what we're to make of the people in this high-style freak show.

Are we to laugh? Mourn? Giggle in superiority? Or just use these people for thrills and move on, as Dino Velvet would do? Since the plot is a machine for eliminating the characters, one by one, the question is perhaps self-resolving. Once the remaining two have left Youngstown, in effect voiding the screen, we're simply free to get up and go as well. In a way, that makes *Six Ways to Sunday* the most coherent film I've seen all week—praise whose height you may judge for yourself.

Friday. I watch a videocassette of Matthew Diamond's *Dancemaker*, an Oscar-nominated documentary that will play in New York at the Film Forum. The subject is Paul Taylor and his dance company—which is different from saying it's about Paul Taylor (a man who gives away very little about himself) or his dances (which are discussed for the most part in surprisingly superficial interview snippets). What comes through is the peculiar form of master-slave relationship that's developed between Taylor as boss and choreographer and his dancers as employees and collaborating artists. A high point: archival footage from perhaps three sources showing Taylor himself dancing a classic solo, beautifully intercut with new footage of Taylor setting the same solo on a member of his current company. For the first time all week, I feel I've watched a movie. It's just not as deep and consistent a movie as I've been hungering for.

Saturday. While visiting my sister-in-law and brother-in-law, I watch Howard Stern's television program. Tonight, he's put together a travesty of *Hollywood Squares*, which he's titled *Hollyweird Squares*. The "celebrity contestants" include a mentally challenged young man called Gary the Retard, a damaged former drug addict called Crackhead Bob, an assertive black man called Angry Black, a truly powerful-looking female bodybuilder and a full-dress member of the Ku Klux Klan. This is an even bigger freak show than *Six Ways to Sunday*, a deeper look into the heart of darkness than *8mm*, a more truthful presentation of the mentally challenged than *The Other Sister*, a more troubling exploration of mutual exploitation than *Dancemaker*. In fact, the next time Bill Clinton talks about "what America looks like," he ought to refer to the tape of this show.

But that's just another way of saying the broadcast makes me feel as if I've been trolled through a sewer. Surely someone in film or television could find a way to engage with the craziest stuff America can offer, neither cheating on the details nor neglecting the side of the craziness that's genuinely uplifting.

2 REAL IMAGINATION

Hoop Dreams

Filmed by three white guys in Chicago from a script by God, *Hoop Dreams* is an epic of American life in the here-and-now. It's about the near-total divorce in our cities between black society and white; about the grind of poverty, by the day and by the year; about the various ways in which the impoverished respond—with courtliness, optimism, self-control or self-loathing—as they see dollars showered in frivolity all about them.

The hope that some of those dollars might float their way drives the people in *Hoop Dreams* onward; in the simplest terms, the film is about two young black men from the Chicago ghetto, Arthur Agee and William Gates, who are determined at all costs to become players in the National Basketball Association. We learn, in great detail, what the words "at all costs" might mean to such young men. We also learn the somewhat different meanings of those words to their families and friends, to coaches and teachers, to recruiters and broadcasters and the onlooking throng. As the film takes in this very broad sweep of American society, it also works up portraits of Agee and Gates, portraits that are unexpected—breathtaking—in their intimacy. It's this combination of the panorama with the close-up that makes *Hoop Dreams* a landmark film—that, and the valor of the film's subjects, the persistence of its filmmakers, the cunning of that scriptwriter who was working out of sight.

Some background: In 1986, Steve James, Frederick Marx and Peter Gilbert approached a distinguished documentary production company, Kartemquin Films, with a proposal to make a movie about schoolyard basketball players in Chicago. As the trio has since explained—with a laugh—they were envisioning a half-hour program for public television. Then, touring the playgrounds with a freelance scout named Earl Smith, they met Arthur Agee, a 14-year-old grammar-school kid from the Garfield Park neighborhood. Smith wanted to take Arthur to a tryout at St. Joseph, a nearly all-white, Roman Catholic high school in the sub-urbs. The filmmakers tagged along; and so they found themselves recording how the St. Joseph coach, Gene Pingatore, recruited Arthur, hooking his parents with talk of an eventual college education while dazzling the young player by intro-ducing him on-court to St. Joseph's most famous graduate, Isiah Thomas.

Pingatore was happy to acquire Arthur for the freshman squad; but his dreams of a state championship rested with another 14-year-old, William Gates, whom he had recruited from the Cabrini-Green housing project and put straight onto the varsity squad. With William's permission and that of his family, the filmmakers started following him as well.

Did they approach any other young basketball players? At a recent press con-ference at the New York Film Festival, the filmmakers explained that they had not; having started with $2,500 in their pockets, they barely had enough money at any one time to keep filming William and Arthur. But they did keep filming—for four and a half years, all the way through the young players' high school careers, until some 250 hours of footage had piled up. Once edited to a release length of a little over two and a half hours, *Hoop Dreams* turned out to have the insane shooting ratio of 100 to 1.

None of this would matter, of course, had James, Marx and Gilbert amassed 250 hours' worth of garbage. But life turned out to be marvelously accommo-dating, for the filmmakers if not for the subjects. As *Hoop Dreams* unfolds, William's story winds up complementing Arthur's almost point for point, giving the film a depth and completeness that are all the more thrilling for having been impossible to plan.

Born into a family of stolid, round-faced people, William sets to work at St. Joseph with a determination that's as quiet as it is joyless. Coach Pingatore tells him what to do; so does his older brother Curtis, whose own hoop dreams have failed; so, in her way, does the St. Joseph fan who helps pay William's tuition and gives him a summer job. William, soft-spoken and shy, mostly listens and obeys. He asserts himself with pleasure in two areas only: in the classroom, where he discovers that he can stand up to the white students academically, and at home, where he starts a family of his own by the time he's in the eleventh grade. It says something about William's needs and his character that he keeps this family hidden from his coach for as long as possible.

Singled out for success, relentlessly pressured and promoted, William is the type of player who soars on the court. Arthur, by contrast, is the type who scoots. Like his parents, Sheila and Bo, he's high-strung and rabbity. Like them, he can be vividly demonstrative or else shut out other people entirely, but he will not practice the guarded courtesy that William excels in, nor does he get the first-class treatment that William enjoys.

Having disappointed Coach Pingatore with his erratic play, Arthur somehow never encounters any tuition-paying fans. So, midway through his first semester of tenth grade, the school sends him packing. His mother, suffering from a bad back, has had to give up her job and cannot pay St. Joseph. As for Arthur's father, he has been laid off from a series of jobs by now and is settling into a period of unemployment, drug use and street crime. It's not clear in the film whether the drug habit caused the job losses or was caused by them. (It's not always clear in life, either.) To all of the Agees, though, it seems *very* clear that St. Joseph would have tolerated the debt had Coach Pingatore thought more highly of Arthur's skills. Marked a failure at 15 and still reading at the fourth-grade level, Arthur has to plunge at midterm into the metal-detector atmosphere of Chicago's Marshall High School, joining classmates and basketball players who are not used to having him around.

It would be hard to invent a more grating story of how white America uses and discards young black men; and if *Hoop Dreams* concluded at this point, it would be a memorably devastating picture (not to mention a much shorter one). But the filmmakers' virtue, like Arthur's, was to keep going. More reversals ensue, in Arthur's fortunes and in William's, enough of them for a whole novel. Meanwhile, as the subjects' lives arrange themselves into a pattern of Dreiserian irony, the movie fills up with multitudes of detail. To the average viewer, these particulars may seem repetitive, even downright exhausting; but only a fool would give them up.

It's important to see, for example, that the Agees and their community organize a ceremony to mark each change in life. Humble in tone, despite the participants' great care to look their best, these events usually involve a lot of unoccupied folding chairs and invariably feature a gospel singer, who rises above the pings and echoes of the hall's amplifier to perform a heartfelt solo. One such ceremony, incorporated into a film, would amount to local color. *Hoop Dreams* gives you three or four, so you can feel the cumulative rhythm in the Agees' lives of struggle and thanksgiving.

Other elements of *Hoop Dreams* also have their cumulative effect: the basketball games, with their rising intensity as each season wears on; the physical changes that overtake the subjects, as children grow to maturity and parents lose their teeth; the words—all those orders and counsels, blandishments and threats—that pour in a steady torrent over William and Arthur. Since Arthur has a way of going deaf around authority, a casual viewer might think him unaffected by the yak-yak, for good or ill. But the increasing steadiness of his play leads me to believe he must have paid some attention to his coach at Marshall, Luther Bedford, who as a black man has, shall we say, a different perspective from that of Gene Pingatore. We hear Bedford speak forcefully about the one-time hoop-dreamers who now stand on street corners in Chicago, owning nothing but the empty boast that they once played for Marshall. A vivid picture—though Pingatore seems strangely unfamiliar with it. His talk is all about the disappointment gnawing at Isiah Thomas's heart to this day, because he never led St. Joseph to a state championship. It does not surprise me that William Gates, after listening to this stuff for four years, said goodbye to Pingatore in one of the coldest scenes ever to be recorded on celluloid.

"I *have* to play basketball," William has said at one point to his girlfriend, Catherine. "It's my way out. It's the only way I'm ever getting to college." Her reply: "Well, *I'm* going to college, and I don't play basketball." By the end of the film, William seems to have learned what she already knew. He will go to college, but he will study as much as play, knowing he needs a life beyond basketball. (What will he study? Communications, he tells Pingatore—"so when you come asking me for a contribution, I'll know the right way to turn you down.") Arthur, too, is disillusioned; though still intent on a basketball career, he now pursues his goal with cold eyes.

By this time, Arthur has learned what he amounts to in the sports business, and in the society that business serves. If he's good—if he's very, very good—then he'll be what a coach in *Hoop Dreams* admits he's searching for:

"Professional meat."

Caro Diaro

S ummer in Rome: Nothing's showing, except Italian films, and so Nanni buzzes around on his Vespa, looking at the neighborhoods. I understand at once that I'm in the company of a reasonable man. Nanni sees that life is best lived as a change of pace from the movies.

Examples of architecture slide across the screen. Nanni is almost indiscriminate in his affection for buildings. Sometimes, though, it's not enough for him to view the facades. He wants to see the life of these places from within; and so, to talk his way into the apartments, he claims he's scouting locations for a movie. To enjoy a change of pace, it seems, Nanni needs recourse to the films in his head.

And what a head! It's mostly a crash helmet and dark glasses, with an undergrowth of auburn beard. "What kind of a movie are you making?" an apartment dweller might reasonably ask. "A musical," Nanni replies, shifting his lanky, T-shirted frame while searching the well-protected skull for an answer. "A musical, uhm, set in the 1950s, about a Trotskyite pastry chef."

Actually, that's not a bad idea for a movie, Nanni thinks as he drives away. Why not a Trotskyite pastry chef, in that era of conformity? I see the Vespa now from behind, now from in front, as it winds through streets and lanes, which unspool into the city like long strips of film. On the soundtrack (or is it in Nanni's mind?) a variety of traveling music plays, suitable for this sunny weather: African pop, a Leonard Cohen groove, salsa.

No, the salsa is being played in a park, where people are dancing. "I've always wanted to be able to dance well," Nanni reflects, watching the crowd from his Vespa. That's why he wants to make a musical; he wants to participate in this dance of life. He *will* participate. Suddenly, he's on the bandstand, still in his helmet and dark glasses, stepping up to the microphone to sing back-up.

Even so, I see that Nanni is a little too critical, or too odd, to blend in with other people. Stopped at an intersection, he turns to the driver who's pulled up next to him: a man in a business suit, driving a big convertible. "I've just now come to realize," Nanni announces, "that as much as I want to be a part of this society, I'm always going to feel at odds with it." The businessman is not unsympathetic: "Good luck," he says, before rolling away.

This is more or less the response Nanni gets from the film community, or the part of it represented by Jennifer Beals. There she is on the sidewalk, the actress whose *Flashdance* changed Nanni's life! She's the one who made him realize he had to dance—and she's walking along in the Roman afternoon! Beals tries to humor this excitable man who has zoomed up on a Vespa—he's easily offended, too— while considering out loud whether Nanni is best described as "off" or "crazy."

All right, so he won't get to make a musical with Jennifer Beals. Nanni still knows the difference between himself and the people in Italian films. He's recently visited one of those pictures, for lack of anything better to watch, and seen a bunch of middle-aged, middle-class characters slumped on sofas, mouthing long speeches about their disillusionment. Long ago, they recall with bitter smiles, we shouted violent slogans; and now, see how ugly we've become. "Speak for yourselves," Nanni says, sitting tall on his Vespa with the fresh air rippling his T-shirt. "I shouted all the *right* slogans, and I've become a splendid 40-year-old."

Me, too, I think. (Let's say this screening is in May 1994.) But I still feel the unease that tugs at Nanni, even though the weather outside my theater is as lovely as his afternoon in Rome. I go willingly on his long ride to the outskirts of Rome, in search of the homely pile of concrete that serves as a monument to Pasolini. "I think of him more and more," Nanni says before setting out, as he leafs through a scrapbook. He doesn't need to say why. In this era when the self-proclaimed ugly deride their "illusions of '68," it's enough to glimpse the newspaper clippings about Pasolini's murder and think about what died with him. We ride out to the site, listening to Keith Jarrett build a piano solo out of mere noodling, as Nanni's improvised cinema-of-the-outdoors unreels a flat landscape of low buildings, wire fences, scrubby fields. A desolation? No—but Nanni has driven for the moment into sadness and loss.

Chapter Two: Nanni goes on vacation.

Here's an old friend, Gerardo (actually an actor, Renato Carpentieri), who is

LEFT IN THE DARK

short and round and makes Nanni look that much more linear. Gerardo has been working for years on a study of James Joyce's *Ulysses*. Who could be a better companion for a voyage around Mediterranean islands? It will be a working voyage, of course. Gerardo lugs along a briefcase with his books, and Nanni (who intends to piece together a screenplay) brings part of his vast collection of newspaper clippings.

On this odyssey, the perils turn out to be purely sociological. First, understandably, Nanni and Gerardo make the mistake of landing on the Island of Vacationers. They can't possibly work in such a bustling place. So they sail on: to the Island of Affluent Parents (where each couple is tyrannized by its single child), the Island of Party People (where everyone is surgically improved and lives for cocktails), the Island of Cinema History (or Stromboli, where the mayor launches cultural initiatives that the other residents scorn), the Island of Grim Rectitude (whose inhabitants, in their intellectual rigor, repudiate all forms of modern corruption, including the electric light).

Needless to say, no work gets done. The critical Nanni, who will always be at odds with most people, can't write his screenplay in a society of routine busyness and bourgeois self-enclosure and trash-brained partying and groundless "cultural" boosterism. But then, when Nanni overindulges in criticism—when he feels himself slipping into an attitude of quasi-monastic disapproval of everything and everybody—he wants to run screaming back to the day-by-day.

In fact, Gerardo *does* run screaming. He's been undergoing a transformation on this voyage. He, too, had a touch of Grim Rectitude when he started out. ("You know what Enzensberger writes about television? I agree with him.") But after watching part of a TV program while on a ferry, Gerardo wants to see more, and more, until he concludes that Enzensberger is wrong. TV does *not* transmit nothingness. TV transmits stories, and meanings. Our children dream with their eyes open! Gerardo leads the way off the final island—this terrible place without television!—and Nanni follows, a self trotting behind its undone superego.

Chapter Three: Doctors.

Apparently, no work will get done in this movie. The splendid 40-year-old, back in his usual surroundings, still can't make a film or participate fully in life because he's now undergoing treatment for cancer. Here's a video of his final chemotherapy session. Once again, that remarkable head is helmeted, this time by a surgical cap. I am three years older than Nanni. Already, in 1994, three of my friends have died of cancer.

In this final section of the movie, Nanni doesn't go on any airy tours of Rome, or voyage laughingly through allegorical islands. He makes the round of doctors, who for the longest time fail to understand his problem. He's devel-

14

oped a maddening itch, he tells them, which gets worse at night and prevents him from sleeping. Each doctor has a different diagnosis and a different set of prescriptions. Pills and syrups and salves pile up, along with the accusations against Nanni himself. If he doesn't get better, then he's an uncooperative patient; he must be the source of his own unease.

By now, the comically irritable Nanni has vanished, to be replaced by an angry man. He loathes the way these princes of medicine lord it over him, with potentially fatal consequences; but he doesn't call them murderers. Still less does he claim to be a second Pasolini. Yet here he is, a leftist Italian filmmaker for whom death has now come into plain sight.

Once again, the movie threatens to drive itself into desolation; and once again, it does not. The final image is of the living, stripped-down Nanni—no helmet, no sunglasses, no surgical cap. He looks knowingly at the camera and straight into my eyes.

I have been watching *Caro Diario* (*Dear Diary*), a 1994 film written and directed by Nanni Moretti, starring Moretti, Jennifer Beals, Renato Carpentieri and a lot of people who impersonate doctors. It is a film about the way we live with movies and movies live with us; and so, in a way, it's also about being a critic. It shows us things as they are; it keeps believing they can be better.

Caro Diario dreams with its eyes open.

A Moment of Innocence

When people label a film "great," the usual effect is to close off a discussion that ought to be opening. But when the film was made in Western Asia, cheaply and under threat of censorship, by a guy with so marketable a name as Mohsen Makhmalbaf, a critic has no need to be delicate. Let the discussion begin with the obvious: *A Moment of Innocence* is a great film.

I'm even tempted to say it's one of the key artworks of our time. Half documentary and half conjuring trick, *A Moment of Innocence* transforms a past act of political violence into a present-day vision of generosity, in which gifts are offered, veils are removed and jaws drop all around. This is as much magic as any film can work—and it seems to be done right before your eyes, as you watch the movie being made.

At the film's core is a bit of autobiography. In 1974, when he was 17 and working to overthrow the Shah of Iran, Mohsen Makhmalbaf helped organize an attack on a police station. He planned to stab a cop and make away with his gun; but in the event, he accomplished only the first half of his goal. Makhmalbaf spent the next five years in prison, gaining release when the Ayatollah Khomeini took power.

Two decades later, the man whom Makhmalbaf had stabbed reappeared in his life. Mirhadi Tayebi, no longer a cop, came to the open casting call that

Makhmalbaf held for his 1994 documentary *Salaam Cinema*. If you've seen that picture, you've watched a snippet of Tayebi's screen test. He's the man with the mug like Frankenstein's monster, who earnestly asks to play romantic leads.

At the start of *A Moment of Innocence*, Makhmalbaf transposes his re-encounter with Tayebi into the realm of fiction. You see the ex-cop come trudging unannounced to Makhmalbaf's home in search of a film career, only to have his knock answered by the director's young daughter. She cracks the door just enough to peer up at the stranger, tell him her father isn't home and then engage Tayebi in a rambling conversation he doesn't want, about homework. Seen from the middle distance—the camera, unmoving, is set far enough back to show both figures in full—the man who once aroused hatred and fear in Makhmalbaf now appears as a supplicant, deferring with all the patience he can muster to a little girl.

Out of this droll encounter grows the project Makhmalbaf "documents" in *A Moment of Innocence*. At a distance of twenty years, he will make a film about his attack on the policeman. Tayebi won't get to act in this film; but he will serve, in effect, as an assistant director, hired to coach the young man chosen to play him.

Immediately, Tayebi takes offense and stalks away. Having imagined himself being played by a big, handsome kid, he's hurt when Makhmalbaf instead casts gangly young Ammar Tafti. With more difficulty than he'd expected, Makhmalbaf coaxes Tayebi to come back, to get Ammar outfitted in an old-style cop's uniform and begin teaching him the drill. The uniform is a bit of a problem. The only available cap is too big; it bobbles on Ammar's head while he's trying to march. Even so, Tayebi takes a liking to the quiet, solemn boy, who seems eager to please, or perhaps terrified.

Makhmalbaf, meanwhile, is busy selecting a 17-year-old to play himself. We see the casting call—or, rather, the group interview—at which the director tests various young men by asking if they hope to change the world. No, says one. The world is a big place; it's plenty just to lead a decent life and keep things going. Makhmalbaf dismisses that candidate. He chooses Ali Bakhshi, who says he feels called to help everyone and make life better. Soon Ali is driving around Teheran in Makhmalbaf's car, soaking up monologues about prerevolutionary times and helping the director cast the third major role.

It seems there was also a young woman involved in the attack. She had the job of distracting Tayebi, so Makhmalbaf could sneak up with the knife. Who can Makhmalbaf recruit for the part? His first choice won't even come out of the house to talk with him. (In the days of the Shah, women fought for the Islamic revolution. Today, they hesitate to appear on camera.) But eventually Makhmalbaf finds Maryam Mohamadamini, who not only consents to appear

17

in the film but even lets the camera follow her around after school, as she walks through the market chatting goofily with her sort-of-boyfriend.

Now everything is in place for a rehearsal of the attack—and everything falls apart. These young people! Ali turns out to be so tenderhearted that he breaks down during the first run-through. Makhmalbaf has to shout at him: "You say you want to make the world better? Then you have to stab! Stab!" In a parallel scene, Ammar takes instruction in violence from Tayebi, who has learned something unexpected about the long-ago attack and is now enraged. As Ammar goes white-faced, Tayebi demonstrates very convincingly how to empty his gun, and into whom.

Such is the uncontrollable mess in Makhmalbaf's hands as filming begins. Cameras follow the young people through covered streets as they make their way toward an encounter that either will or will not duplicate an older generation's murderous grudges. What you see at this point is wholly real, wholly fictive and completely unpredictable. Only a miracle could resolve the tension—and that's precisely how the film ends, with cloths whipped back in a flourish and a vision of astonishment revealed.

Actually, it's just a tableau, with three kids playing dress-up. But that gawkiness, or innocence if you will, is part of the world of hope that's summed up in the final shot—a world of hunger satisfied, love ventured, women emerging into the light. Write to me at once if you see another film with so urgent and complete an image of people's hurts, fears, needs and dreams at the end of our bloody century.

Don't even write. Come straight to my door and knock.

Taste of Cherry

Written, produced, edited and directed by Abbas Kiarostami, *Taste of Cherry* is a masterpiece—and masterpieces, like strange dogs, should not be approached in haste. I will take my cue from the author himself, who lets twenty-three minutes go by in this ninety-five-minute film before he reveals his subject matter. Let's talk about something else. Let's talk about dogs.

Kiarostami's first film, made in 1970, was a short titled *Bread and Alley*, concerning a small boy confronted on his errands by a lean and growling mutt. How is the boy to carry home the bread of the title, so long as the mutt blocks the way? Ten minutes into the picture, a solution dawns: The boy tears off a corner of the bread and tosses it to the side, then scoots ahead while his assailant is busy eating. Music up; end of the fable of the cleverly generous boy.

And yet it's not the end. The camera lingers in the alley long enough to follow the now-jaunty dog around a corner. The dog waits. A second boy approaches, carrying bread, and the dog darts into sight, teeth bared. Music up again; end of the fable, which now is about a cleverly greedy dog.

You can learn a lot about Kiarostami from this little film. You see, for example, how the things he chooses to put in his viewfinder remind him of many other things, which he left out. At the start of his career, he pointed up this exclusion simply by letting a movie run on for what seemed an extra minute. The result: a different story than you'd expected, focusing on a different protagonist. Later on, his methods became more elaborate. There is an "accidental" loss of sound in his feature-length documentary *Homework* (1989), for which Kiarostami interviewed the boys in an elementary school in Teheran. The silence, strategically placed, echoes with a thousand thoughts and feelings that the boys have choked down in the rest of the film. Or consider *Through the Olive Trees* (1994), the third film in the so-called Earthquake Trilogy. The picture consists almost entirely of events that take place on- and off-camera while "Kiarostami" (played by an actor) shoots a scene for the second Earthquake film, *And Life Goes On* (1992).

Let me state the obvious, since that's what a masterpiece demands: Kiarostami has his reasons for stretching and folding and poking holes in film. Those reasons have little to do with polysyllables: alienation effect, post-structuralism, postmodernism, de-marginalization. We might get closer to his purpose were we to think instead of the ever-restless aesthete who plays "Either" to Kierkegaard's "Or"—but only slightly closer, since Kiarostami does not despair, even in *Taste of Cherry*.

But I've almost blurted the subject of the film. Let's talk about chance encounters.

Recent Iranian films are so full of them that I've decided to make up a category: the recruitment trope. Boys come down an alley, and a dog recruits them to be its feeders. Or: A director auditions nonprofessionals to act in his new movie. (So begins *Through the Olive Trees*, not to mention Mohsen Makhmalbaf's *Salaam Cinema* and *A Moment of Innocence*.) Or: A boy walks to a neighboring village, where he asks for directions. (Such is the scheme of the first Earthquake film, made in 1987, *Where Is the Friend's Home?*) Or: "Kiarostami" asks for directions, as he drives along ruined roads from Teheran to a northern village. The film built upon this latter scheme, *And Life Goes On*, also makes use of smaller-scale recruitment tropes, beginning with the first shot. We see a toll booth; the view remains fixed as one car after another pulls up, until finally the camera chooses a subject—"Kiarostami"'s car—out of the multitude passing by.

And now, let's speak of the motorist-recruiter in the new film, *Taste of Cherry*. He's the first thing we see: a man of about 50, who sits behind the wheel of a white Range Rover and peers toward the camera. What is he looking for? His eyes are smudged. His bruise-colored lips pout beneath magnificent nostrils, which lift as if he were a wine-taster and the world a dubious vintage. A reverse shot gives us his point of view: a street corner in Teheran, bustling in clear morning light. Close by the Range Rover's windows stand day laborers wanting to be hired. "Need a worker?" asks one. We cut back to the recruiter, who looks away and drives on. Now, perhaps, we notice that his princely head needs barbering. Dark curls, untended, tumble down his nape into a little clump, perhaps hinting at some greater disorder. When more day laborers crowd forward, he waves them off and proceeds out of town, across a river valley and into the hills: in search of what?

At a hilltop construction site where huge pipes are piled on the ground and high-tension wires march into the distance, he accosts a young man at a telephone booth. "You have money problems," says the recruiter. "I can help you." No, comes the reply; and when the recruiter presses his offer, the young man warns him to drive off or get his face smashed. Apparently, the young man thinks he's being propositioned for sex. Is that what the driver wants?

The light has turned dusty; shadows now draw closer to their owners. The driver halts at the edge of a ravine, where a scavenger roots through garbage. What's that you're collecting? How much does it bring you? Would you like to do something that pays a lot? The scavenger begs off, as if perplexed that a man in a good car should pay him such attention.

We are ten minutes into the film. The credits roll. Half a day seems to have gone by, and we still don't know the man's goal, or even his name.

By the time the credits end, the film has jumped forward to five in the afternoon. The light is golden; shadows are long, as they will be throughout the main body of *Taste of Cherry*. Taking into account the interludes—views of the landscape, briefer moments of human contact—we might say this core amounts to three long dialogues, carried out between the recruiter and the men who agree to ride with him.

The first is a teenage soldier, who is hitchhiking back to his barracks. He is an isolated figure: a Kurd who seems to know almost no one in Teheran and shows no sign of having bonded with army life. The second rider is similarly cut off from social ties. A man in his late 20s or early 30s, he is a student at an Islamic seminary—an Afghan who came to Iran because of war and admits to feeling at loose ends. The third rider is exceptional in that he is older than the driver and does the bulk of the talking. But he, too, is a loner: a Turk (if I understand correctly) who works in a lowly capacity at the natural history museum, and who is struggling to care for a sickly child.

But what does the driver want from these solitary men?

Just at the moment when the mystery has become maddening, when the young soldier yells "I want to get out!" and the audience, having been shut in the car for twenty minutes, might feel the same way; just when the camera cuts away from a seemingly endless round of close-ups to present one of Kiarostami's super-extra-long landscape shots, which shrink human beings to the scale of ants, though their voices continue to ring in our ears; at this point of maximum tension, which functions as Kiarostami's equivalent of Hitchcockian suspense, the car stops for a rare medium shot, and the driver reveals his purpose. Mr. Badii—at last we get his name—intends to kill himself.

But that, of course, is no purpose at all; it's the stopping of all purpose. And why has Mr. Badii spent the whole day driving around, looking for lonely men who are short of money? Though he wants to commit the ultimate act of self-isolation, he also wants to be buried—a social nicety, for which he requires one final human relationship.

You will now understand my hesitation in naming the subject matter of *Taste of Cherry*. Once you say what the film's about, you can't say anything more. But this point, at which description falters and analysis fails, is precisely where *Taste of Cherry* begins. That's why it is a masterpiece.

It is the second masterpiece Kiarostami has made on the impossible theme, "Is life worth living?" *And Life Goes On . . .* was the first: a journey into an area of Iran where thousands had just been struck dead in an earthquake. Bringing his camera into this region while the survivors were still digging out of the rubble, Kiarostami called up a wordless answer to the question he couldn't state; or rather he evoked a hundred answers, seen in faces and gestures, heard in tones of voice and felt in the unfolding of the landscape, which together gave a deep, great, silent response.

And Life Goes On . . . allowed Kiarostami to satisfy Randall Jarrell's definition of a poet: someone who spends a lifetime standing out in the rain in the hope of being struck by lightning. I know, I'm misquoting—but only slightly, and only to point out that Kiarostami, having succeeded once, wasn't obliged to try for a second flash. But apparently he continues to mull over the things he's left out of the frame. Perhaps that's why he chose to make *Taste of Cherry*, a film that once more asks, "Is life worth living?" but now voices the "no" as well as the "yes."

Both answers come through with tremendous cumulative force, though not through any particular line of dialogue. After the subject has been announced, the characters spend seventy-two minutes in discussion, without saying anything more clever than would you or I, had we been the ones recruited for this mysterious trial.

The most powerful argument advanced in favor of life is the entirely homely question that gives the film its title: Is Mr. Badii really prepared never again to taste a cherry? You feel the justice of the image not because it's original but because it comes out in a gruff voice, spoken by a baggy looking man with a bushy mustache (Abdolhossein Bagheri, as the Turk), while the 6 o'clock shadows grow ever longer and a turn in the road takes the Range Rover into greener fields. You also feel the insufficiency of the argument—the fact that it's addressed to a man who has lost his taste buds—not because of any eloquence but because by this hour a stubble has sprouted on the cleft chin of Mr. Badii (Homayoun Ershadi), because his hair looks even oilier, because he's abandoned his pushy, sophistical speech and lapsed into a pained silence.

Of course, you want to know what this has to do with politics. When *Taste of Cherry* won the Palme d'Or at the 1997 Cannes festival, reports circulated about Kiarostami's problems in making the film. Most focused on the Islamic prohibition against suicide; in these accounts, Iranian authorities had been unhappy with Kiarostami because of his choice of subject. I suppose some government official, concerned about Iran's image on the international circuit, also might have objected to the world built up in the movie: a society that consists entirely of displaced persons and menial laborers, plus one middle-class man who doesn't want to live. Unfortunately, no one in power in Iran has yet taken me into his confidence, so I can't reliably address the reasons for censorship, or even confirm that it was attempted.

I would prefer to talk about the suppression of Kiarostami's work in another nation, the United States, where I have some experience. In 1992, I had the happiness of serving on the selection committee for the New York Film Festival. On a split decision (you may guess how I voted) we invited Kiarostami to show *And Life Goes On . . . .* Many of the reviews were casually dismissive; audiences, less than wild. Apparently, films from Iran were, by definition, of no interest. Two years later, the New York Film Festival showed *Through the Olive Trees,* which received only a slightly more engaged response. Miramax picked up the U.S. distribution rights but seemed baffled by the property it had acquired and soon withdrew it from the market.

So Kiarostami joined that cinematic Olympus whose gods are barred (though unofficially) from American screens. You may know this pantheon—Hou Hsiao-hsien, Manoel de Oliveira, Chantal Akerman, Souleymane Cissé; great filmmakers all, whose works rarely if ever make it into our commercial movie houses. Adrian Lyne's *Lolita?* The mark of someone who hasn't really been following movies is that he, or she, thinks its absence from America is a big deal.

I'll tell you what's a big deal. A scrappy company of American cinephiles, Zeitgeist Films, is distributing *Taste of Cherry.* You will be able to see this one without having to search out a one-time-only festival screening. Buy a ticket and tell your friends to do the same. Your reward, other than the experience of political virtue, might be the discovery of another reason to live.

Koker Trilogy (Earhquake Trilogy)

Time moves forward and then spirals back on itself in Abbas Kiarostami's Koker trilogy—*Where Is the Friend's Home?* (1987), *And Life Goes On . . .* (1992) and *Through the Olive Trees* (1994)—as the village that gives the series its name is defined, reapproached (though not reached) and remade. These complex and sophisticated motions become possible through even headier shifts of perspective. The third film in the trilogy is a fiction about the making of the second, and the second is a fictionalized documentary about the director and performers of the first. However dizzying it might be to think about these changes of state, which take you back and forth continually between reality and invention, they feel serenely unforced on the screen—no less natural, and no less wondrous, than the ocean's water being sublimated into clouds, the clouds condensed into rain.

But maybe I should choose a rougher metaphor. The natural event that intervened between the first and second films was the earthquake that struck northern Iran in June 1990, killing multitudes. It was Kiarostami's response to this devastation that transformed the small, charming *Where Is the Friend's Home?* into the first film in a trilogy, and that changed him from an admirable filmmaker into a great one.

Where Is the Friend's Home? begins in a one-room village school in Koker, where young Ahmed (Babek Ahmed Poor) and Nematzadeh (Ahmed Ahmed

Poor) endure the usual pedagogical tyranny. The trial is more severe for Nematzadeh, because he has neglected to write his homework in the proper notebook, as required, and will be in big trouble should he fail again. So a heavy responsibility drops upon Ahmed's shoulders, when he comes home from school and discovers he's accidentally walked off with Nematzadeh's notebook. For Ahmed to return the book, he will have to run up a switchback path, over a hill, to the neighboring village of Poshteh, which he has never before visited. Once there, he realizes that he has no idea where Nematzadeh lives—and the grown-ups are no help at all.

By the time he made this picture, Kiarostami was already expert at shooting on location with a non-professional cast. He also had acquired considerable experience in making light, ingenious films about the ways in which children solve problems and negotiate right and wrong. (In 1969, he had left a career in graphic art and advertising to establish the film division of Iran's Institute for the Intellectual Development of Children and Young Adults.) *Where Is the Friend's Home?* is the perfect fruit of all the skill and generosity of spirit that Kiarostami had developed through this work.

It is also an early summary of traits that would soon be recognized as his signature. For example, the story takes place almost entirely outdoors and is structured through repetition. (Ahmed keeps returning to Koker, then running back up that switchback path over the hill. And when he's in Poshteh, he has to ask the same question over and over.) Also, the goal of the journey, though pursued single-mindedly, turns out to be less important than the encounters along the way, which sketch out for Ahmed a whole range of life's possibilities. Kiarostami was to use these narrative devices many times, always with a marvelous (and hard-won) air of simplicity, in both the future films he directed himself and in those he wrote (such as Jafar Panahi's *The White Balloon*).

Yet nothing in *Where Is the Friend's Home?*, with the possible exception of the hints of physical violence against children, could have foretold the astonishing turn Kiarostami's art would take over the next years. To account for the change, I can point to a pair of dramatic shifts, of which the earthquake was the second. The first was the breakdown of the barrier between fiction and documentary represented by the 1990 film *Close Up*.

In this picture, Kiarostami recounted and reinvented the true story of a man who had gone about impersonating another great Iranian filmmaker, Mohsen Makhmalbaf. Was the impostor a con artist, a deeply needy fan, or some combination of the two? Kiarostami left the question unanswered—even in courtroom scenes that seem to be documentary footage (until the accused turns toward the camera to explain himself), even when the impostor is at last introduced to his model, who says, "I'm tired of being Makhmalbaf. You do it for a while."

Close Up puts a filmmaker (albeit a fraudulent one) at the center of a picture in which it's hard to tell the difference between staged scenes and spontaneous events. For Kiarostami, this turned out to be good preparation for the catastrophe to come. After the 1990 earthquake, when he realized that Koker sat in the midst of the destruction, he decided to take a small crew back to northern Iran, to show how people were coping with their loss and to dramatize the search for survivors. An actor named Ferhad Kherdamend played the role of a director who had made a picture titled *Where Is the Friend's Home?* Driving with him in a little car was a boy, Buba Bayour, to play the role of the director's son, Puya.

And Life Goes On . . . follows the director (unnamed in the film) and Puya over broken roads, through villages reduced to rubble, across a harshly beautiful mountain landscape full of newly visible rifts, as father and son make their slow way toward the seemingly unreachable Koker. The director at first is brusque, even peremptory, with the people he meets along the way; he demands road directions, shows photographs of the two boys from his film (perhaps to emphasize his own importance) and then drives off in a hurry. He's also overbearingly protective of Puya. But the more the director drives (with the camera unfolding those grand landscape shots that are another of Kiarostami's signatures), the more he realizes that there's no way to hurry. He begins to pause along the way, having no alternative, and starts to let Puya wander out of his sight for more than a few seconds. Father and son begin to relax with one another; and through their conversations with the earthquake's survivors, who despite terrible loss have started to rebuild, the two come to understand a truth that seems a mere cliché when spelled out in the film's title, but becomes a profound, lived experience in the film.

Two examples may illustrate how Kiarostami rescues something urgent and essential from the status of platitude. In the opening shot, the camera watches a toll booth as cars stop and go. The car with the director and Puya is only one drop in the stream of traffic; but that's the drop the camera decides to follow. So, from the start, you understand that the characters you're observing are part of a much bigger whole; and in the closing shot, they're reabsorbed into that totality. The director (or rather his car) is last seen in the longest of long shots, as little more than a dot on a mountain road. The shot is held patiently, for a very long time, as the car tries to climb almost straight up the hill, stalls and slips back. It's not certain that this road would lead the driver to Koker, even if his car could crest the hill; but, having failed once, he reverses himself, picks up a pedestrian (whom he'd neglected to help in the previous shot) and tries again. The film ends with the car all but disappearing into the landscape.

And Life Goes On . . . is so direct in emotional impact, so startling in documentary power and yet so carefully framed as fiction that I feel I'm violating the picture by pinning a paraphrasable meaning to it, or even tossing laudatory adjectives in its direction. One thing I can say, though, is that the film's themes include education—in particular, the lesson that a modern urbanite can learn from rural folk. For the last of his trilogy, Kiarostami turned this theme around, showing what rural folk can learn from city people.

Through the Olive Trees begins with the well-known actor Mohamad Ali Keshavarz introducing himself, to explain that he is present to play the role of a film director. The story you are about to see shows how this director makes a film titled *And Life Goes On . . .* What follows is a comedy of errors, beginning with a casting call in which the director and his crew (including Ferhad Kherdamend, the "director" from *And Life Goes On . . .*) are swamped by villagers wanting to appear in the film. Some are cast, only to drop out or prove unworkable. And then, when two likely performers are found for a brief scene, the problems really start.

The scene (which really was a part of *And Life Goes On . . .*) is a minor domestic exchange between husband and wife on the balcony of their damaged two-story house. Hossein Rezai, a bricklayer who lost his home in the earthquake, is hired to play the husband, and a young woman named Tahereh Ladania is recruited to play the wife. In making these choices, the filmmakers unfortunately do not consider the possibility that Hossein might actually love Tahereh and want to marry her. In fact, before the earthquake hit, he had proposed to her and been rejected by her family on the grounds of his being lower-class and illiterate. Now her parents are dead; and though Hossein does not want to belittle this tragedy, he would like to point out that the future lies open before her. Thrown together with Tahereh on a film set, he renews his suit—passionately, abjectly, volubly, tirelessly—with disastrous results for the film crew, who find themselves going through take after take of the smallest action.

For anyone who was fooled by the apparent ease of *And Life Goes On . . .*, *Through the Olive Trees* provides an hilarious lesson in the pitfalls of location shooting. The filmmakers go from exasperation to exasperation. Meanwhile, their presence enables Hossein to speak as never before, helping him dare to love Tahereh, however silent and inscrutable she may be. This drama goes unremarked by the filmmakers, even though it's happening right in front of them, even though they've constructed the stage on which it's played. Only the audience knows—and then, at the end, we become as ignorant as the film crew.

In an extreme long shot that echoes the final image of *And Life Goes On . . .*, Hossein pursues Tahereh into the distant landscape, presumably talking all the way, until both figures all but vanish. Until this point, we have gleefully enjoyed a perspective on Hossein and Tahereh that was denied the "film crew." Now we lose our privileged knowledge—which means that our point of view has at last been joined with the filmmakers'. As this happens, another gap closes as well, the one between the characters and their world. No longer isolated as objects of special interest, Hossein and Tahereh become two features of the living landscape.

We usually associate humor of a certain kind with irony. But here, contrary to all expectation, laughter bubbles up when the irony is released, and Tahereh turns toward Hossein. We have few reasons to project our hopes into this moment; our only promptings toward optimism are the music by Vivaldi, the greenness of the scenery and the fact that Tahereh (or any Iranian woman) has finally said something. It's impossible to see facial expressions or hear words. And yet, with so many aspects of the film now coming together—the distance between viewpoints closed, the rift between figure and ground healed—it seems inevitable that Tahereh and Hossein, too, might soon embrace.

With that, a sense of joyful release unites the viewers and the view, and the Kokier trilogy ends, in a long shot that's as emotionally vivid as any close-up.

Sink or Swim

F or a film that's as simple as ABC, Su Friedrich's *Sink or Swim* gets more mysterious the more times you watch it.

Even on first viewing, you catch onto the plan. *Sink or Swim* will consist of 26 brief segments, each headed by a title card that announces a topic. The first to come up is "Zygote"—a natural enough beginning—followed by "Y Chromosome," "X Chromosome" and so on. The alphabetical order (zeewyexical?) is perfectly clear, or seems to be; and its hint of whimsy matches the deadpan humor of the opening shots. "Zygote" is illustrated with black-and-white footage that might have been borrowed from a Surrealist's high-school science film. An ovum floats onto the screen, as majestic as a full moon; spermatozoa wriggle eagerly in a school. "Y Chromosome" is a handful of white fluff, opening in slow motion into the wind; "X Chromosome," an elephant's foot and rooting trunk.

So far—and at this point you've barely had time to settle in the dark—the only puzzle is why you should be moving backward through the alphabet. But as you progress, or regress, beyond ZYX you can feel the complications beginning to gather.

If you're familiar with the avant-garde in general and feminist cinema in particular, you might think that *Sink or Swim* will be a confessional work. How right you'd be. *Sink or Swim* belongs to the genre of "Memoirs of a Catholic

Girlhood in 1950s America." And yet the voice on the soundtrack neither belongs to Su Friedrich nor claims to speak about her. Instead, you hear a child-like narrator telling you about some third party, called The Girl. The stories about this character are full of local color and private detail; but the order in which they're told soon turns out to be as impersonal a structure as the alphabet.

Look at the titles: "Witness," "Virginity," "Utopia," "Temptation." *Sink or Swim* is taking you from creation to a state of innocence to the fall, followed by adventures in a post-lapsarian world. By around the fifth minute, you're reading backward not only into the life of The Girl but also (as the voiceover suggests) into the stories of very old and outsize characters: Athena, Aphrodite, Atalanta. These three were among the mythological figures introduced to The Girl by her father, a professor of anthropology and linguistics otherwise known as Zeus.

This much of the film's beginning is paraphrasable; it's information pieced together from language. Meanwhile, the early images are off in their own world of zoology and show business. You see caged jungle animals and prancing horses, showgirls, acrobats and circus fliers, the grinning competitors in a women's bodybuilding contest. I'd call these pictures a delirium, except that they somehow jibe, in an unhurried way, with the words. Running on at their own pace, and often framed with apparent casualness, these black-and-white pictures might be likened not to a fever dream but to home movies—although that comparison fails, too, unless these are the Home Movies of the Gods. In their perfectly modulated light, where the range of greys is wide and rich, whatever glimmers may occur dance across the surface of things like rumors of the supernatural.

As the homely yet uncanny pictures move out of the timeless realm of natural history and displays of physical prowess, into the social world of the streets and alleys of Brooklyn, you begin to notice that the lights most often do their dancing on water. More on that later—much more.

More, too, on the curious fact that Z could stand for Zeus, just as easily as zygote. Maybe you'd like to ponder that overflow of meaning, which makes the contents of the pattern spill over from the very first box. Maybe, if you remember your basic biology, you're also wondering if Friedrich goofed with her puffy Y chromosome and ponderous X. Or did she intend to reverse genetic expectations?

But the time for those questions may already be past. "Seduction" is now before you, to be followed (naturally enough) by "Realism." There can be no better heading under which to ask: What's going on here?

What's really going on, I suppose, is that Su Friedrich is unburdening her-

self about her father, who was terrifying when he bullied her and even more terrifying when he walked away. Or maybe she's explaining how The Girl became
Su Friedrich. She seems to be doing both; and there, perhaps, lies the mystery
that runs through this brief and orderly film. Before Friedrich can look straight
into the mirror, she has to wind her way into her father's mind. To purge herself
of the pain he inflicted, she has to play his scholar's game and turn her life into
a diagram. So she's devised her brilliant *Sink or Swim*, a film that's deviously
straightforward and dispassionately harrowing.

The harrowing parts, which are so strong that I've heard them make a whole
audience suck in its breath, take us straight into the meaning of the title. When
The Girl wanted to learn to swim, we hear, Zeus took her to a pool, offered a
few words of advice and tossed her into the deep end. This was "Realism."

As the child on the soundtrack informs us, The Girl responded well to this
harsh pedagogy; she came to love swimming. (We see girls splashing in a city
pool.) Only when we get to the sections titled "Memory" and "Loss" do we
plummet, with The Girl, beneath the sparkling surface. It seems the father had
a beloved sister who drowned as a child, and for whose death he had felt responsible. (We see more home movies, not godlike this time but grainy and flickering.) The Girl, like the audience, knew nothing of that history when the father
first risked her in deep water. But the information is available, and horrible in
its implications, by the time we learn how Zeus disciplined his daughter when
she was wild. He filled the bathtub, then forced down her head.

There's more, and worse. How strong Friedrich must be—how much like her
father—to resist simply blurting it out. I've lived through none of these events,
except in screenings, and yet I'm tempted to recount them all. But then, by doing
so, I would betray Friedrich's canniness, wit and ceaseless intelligence, which are
the qualities she seems to have rescued from childhood, as Athena bore away her
father's shield and thunderbolt. Does Friedrich show us a flailing, sputtering girl
during the tale of the bathtub? No—the images are of children in white, going
to their first communion at a Brooklyn church. The surface remains cool; the
topics continue to move along in order, unperturbed and quietly deceptive.

We're roughly halfway through the alphabet—so we know we're in the center
of the film—when the little girl's voice temporarily drops off the soundtrack and
the music starts. It's Schubert: "Gretchen at the Spinning Wheel." Why this
song? For now, there's no clue. Why have the images abruptly flown away from
New York City, to scenes of trains, desert highways, birds wheeling over palm
trees, two women making love in the shower? We seem to have entered, without
transition, into the filmmaker's adult life, and again we don't know why, since
the section's title, though suggestive, gives no immediate help. What we now see
and hear ostensibly represents "Kinship."

Kinship to whom, or what? We will get the answers—Friedrich withholds nothing—but not where we'd expect to get them; and that's because the pattern of *Sink or Swim* is as deceptive, even as treacherous, as what we call the normal order of life. "Gretchen at the Spinning Wheel" was the song the mother listened to over and over, weeping, after her divorce. Kinship was the topic the father was studying at the time he left his family—that is, his first family. And so, at the core of *Sink or Swim*, we have this enigmatic passage that looks like a diary film but isn't; this nexus of themes that are laid out for us in rational fashion, but elsewhere and under the wrong titles. (An episode about the divorce, that might well be called "Loss," has been displaced to "Journalism"; material that deals with kinship, and is labeled as such, is shifted to "Discovery.") It's impossible to watch this middle piece, this travelogue of the emotions, and not feel that an urgent confession is in progress; and yet, when you know all that *Sink or Swim* has to tell you, it's also impossible to say exactly what's been confessed. Maybe that's because the kinship works both ways. Maybe Friedrich sometimes feels as emptied out as her mother, and at the same time wonders if she makes love like her father.

But now I've yielded to the film's treachery. I'm talking about Su Friedrich, when I ought to speak of The Girl, or Athena, Aphrodite, Atalanta—and that's as it should be.

The astounding feat that Friedrich performs in *Sink or Swim*—defying death more thrillingly than any circus flier—is to persuade you that you're getting the raw facts of her life, as you no doubt are, even as you're being drawn into a territory of ghosts. That a haunting of sorts is in progress can't be denied. As you move past the era of childhood, with its footage lifted from 1950s television shows—the only non-ironic use I've ever encountered of *Make Room for Daddy* and *Father Knows Best*—you see Friedrich herself in the present, a handsome and big-boned woman but glum, who stalks the margin of things. She presents herself as someone who spends her days clacking away at a typewriter in a low-rent apartment, staring at weedy lots through chain-link fences, soaking in that ever-dangerous bathtub, always with a cigarette burning close at hand, always with a beer bottle stuck to her lips. Some Greek goddess.

But if you cast your mind back to the beginning of *Sink or Swim*, following the film's underground currents, you'll recall that you've seen Friedrich's beer bottle before. In a scene of kids playing dress-up, it lay in the dancing waters of a gutter, which The Girl (so we're told) used to pretend was the River Nile.

You might think that Athena, wised up, left that bottle behind as her marker. How right you'd be. And yet—this is the simple, mysterious, death-defying part—The Girl wasn't all wrong.

D'Est

A snow-crusted road scrolls across your field of vision, like a line of text asking to be read. Behind it stand blocky compounds that soften into twilight, or twilit market stalls or vistas of other roads—mute presences, such as gather behind the simplest sentence. We're in Russia as seen by Chantal Akerman. Here, space doesn't recede into the background; it pushes forward, subtly pressuring the line that's moving by. Along it are strung the letters: men and women bundled up in fur hats or stocking caps, in plump overcoats or baggy jackets—clumps, bunches and crowds of women and men, each of whom is somehow isolated among the others, silent, irreducible, urgent with meaning but illegible.

To Akerman, this is a "foreign land that was not altogether foreign." Born in 1950 in Belgium, the daughter of refugees from Poland (her maternal grandparents died in Auschwitz), she decided in 1991 to undertake a "grand journey" into Eastern Europe. Was she hoping to explore, or to reclaim? If we may judge from her preparatory notes, she wanted nothing less than the vision of a second life, the one she and her family hadn't led: "I'd like to shoot everything. Everything that moves me. Faces, streets, cars going by and buses, train stations and plains, rivers and oceans, streams and brooks, trees and forests. Fields and factories and yet more faces. Food, interiors, doors, windows, meals being prepared." This is a pretty good inventory of *D'Est*, the film Akerman shot on a trip that took her from the former East Germany to Moscow.

33

The title is usually translated as "From the East," suggesting a common origin for the film and Akerman's family. Considering the direction actually taken by the production, perhaps we'd do better to say "Of the East" or "About the East." But then, there's the matter of the missing article: not *De l'Est* but *D'Est*, "east" as an adjective. An east *what?* Francophones tell me there's an audible gap in the title, which Akerman must have intended. It silently echoes all the other absences built into her film: "Eastern [rule]."

The most notable of these gaps is the lack of human interaction. *D'Est* plays as if it were in three large movements; only in the first do people pay attention to one another. We begin in summer in a prosperous city where the sidewalks are crowded, then in a resort town where the beach and band shell are well used. A middle-aged couple, glimpsed through the window, is playing cards; they don't speak, but their gestures suggest a sense of ease with one another, or at worst a slight boredom. For the second movement, we travel farther east, into farmland. Late-model cars give way to horse-drawn carts and old trucks. In a field, barrel-like women advance toward the camera, stooping and straightening as they pull beets from the ground and drop them into buckets. They work as a unit but never speak, never glance at one another.

Then comes the great third movement, set in Russia in the depths of winter. For some of the scenes, the camera remains still, fixed on one or two figures: a young woman cutting sausage in her kitchen, a fortyish man playing the piano while his child watches television, an older woman giving a cello recital at a concert hall. But the scenes that haunt the memory are those shot in and around bus stops and tram stations, near offices or factories at closing time, along a sidewalk where people offer for sale whatever objects they might own. People spread out in such places, arraying themselves in a band, if not a line: so in effect they're already posed, dozens and dozens of them. Akerman saw these subjects were waiting for her. All she had to do was drive past very slowly or walk by with the camera, perhaps casting a little extra light across the road, perhaps varying her speed to suit the scene that was unfolding. And there they were: groups arranged more beautifully than if they'd been directed, individuals standing patiently as if for their portraits to be made, sociological types, unassimilable persons—history and subjects of history, revealed together in a single sweep of the camera.

D'Est is now on view in New York at The Jewish Museum (it's playing through May 27), where it's being presented as a touring installation from the Walker Art Center, in association with the San Francisco Museum of Modern Art. I give all the affiliations out of a sense of guilt. Having been overwhelmed by *D'Est* when I saw it a couple of years ago, I resisted the notion of the film's being changed into a museum show, even though the changing was done by Akerman herself. I now see I should have trusted her.

At the Jewish Museum, you first have a chance to watch the film projected on a gallery wall. (The screenings are continuous, so you don't have to worry about show times.) Then you enter a second gallery, where Akerman has set up eight banks of video monitors, with three monitors to a bank. Scenes from the Russian section of *D'Est* fill the room, staggered so that a single moment might play on two of three monitors, or be repeated from one bank to the next. Someone, though not I, should write a dissertation about the resulting shock. The film has drawn you into the illusion of travel, of one thing following the next; and suddenly the video installation plunges you into an experience of simultaneity. You might also say the film, projected continuously, is like the flow of history; whereas the monitors, arrayed through the gallery, seem like the people who stand along the roads of *D'Est*.

One room remains. There, on a single video monitor, an enigmatic, almost abstract image plays across the screen: scenes of lights going by at night on a Moscow street. While the lights come out of the darkness and disappear again, you hear Akerman, in a throaty voice, read a brief text. Some of it, in English, consists of notes written in preparation for *D'Est*. Some, in Hebrew, is a biblical injunction: "Thou shalt not make unto thee any graven image, or any likeness of any thing that is in heaven above, or that is in the earth beneath. . . ." A strange confession—not of sin, perhaps, but of the camera's inadequacy. Maybe *D'Est* doesn't qualify as a "likeness" because so much that's important in it remains silent and invisible: the memory of a past annihilation, the awareness of an oblivion to come. Between those voids stands the world of *D'Est*. If this isn't a masterpiece, tear the word from your dictionary.

The Puppetmaster

P uppet shows and the Chinese opera are raucous affairs, played to the accompaniment of gongs and firecrackers for an audience that tends toward the peripatetic. Something exciting must always be in progress; whereas in Hou Hsiao-hsien's *The Puppetmaster*, the camera can profitably sit still for minutes on end, while two people in the middle distance play a silly, drunken game.

It's an absorbing game, for them. They've just launched a flirtation—he's the performer of the title, she's a prostitute in a southern Taiwanese town—and so they've repaired to her brothel to get to know one another. They do so by sitting close at a table and passing a lighted cigarette back and forth, no hands. Should you ever want to try this method of getting acquainted, you should know the hard part is the cigarette's intermediate stop beneath the man's nose. He has to cradle it in the curl of his upper lip, then catch it in his mouth—no easy trick when a buddy is killing time at the same table, heckling him while awaiting a girl of his own.

Shadows veil the left and right sides of the screen. In the middle, a cone of light spreads downward from a single bulb, casting a protective, deep-colored aura around the new lovers, their irritating pal and the swirls of smoke that define the air. Compared with the popular entertainments that fetch a living for Li Tienlu (Lim Giong), this leisurely scene has no action at all. There are no swordfights or mystical feats, no daring robberies or prodigies of weather. People just go on living.

How amazing, to look at a screen and see people living.

After years of merely admiring Hou Hsiao-hsien, I became a convert to his films when I fell headlong into this scene. I forgot the actors, forgot the set, even forgot that this episode from the late 1930s had been shot in 1992. I might as well have been watching a documentary, filmed with the aid of a time machine.

Then the real, octogenarian Li Tienlu came on screen to tell his own story, as he periodically does, and I remembered with a thrill that I actually was watching a documentary of sorts. *The Puppetmaster* is a faithful realization of Li's childhood and early adult years—or, to be more precise, of his way of thinking about those times. In *The Puppetmaster*, an intensely detailed physical reality is fused with a far more magical reality of the mind.

Li's memoirs, from infancy through the end of World War II, are full of fortunes told, bargains made with the gods, inexplicable curses, medicinal frogs. From the moment he's born—we see him brought in to a beaming but cheapskate grandfather—he's swaddled in thought patterns that were common only a few decades ago, yet seem wondrous to the present-day viewer. They change even the most basic relationships into something strange—as when, to ward off the boy's harsh fate, Li's family teaches him that his father is "uncle" and his mother "aunt."

Does Li today put faith in such dodges? It's enough to see him chatting away behind sunglasses, hands shaping his recollections with a pro's skill, to know he's an old show-biz character of practical bent. "If you believe in these things," he says, "they'll soon enough come true." So the answer is no, as you'd expect of a man who has spent much of his life behind a curtain, manipulating puppets. Illusions are for other people. Then again, even the most up-to-date minds indulge in magical thinking, and so the answer is also yes: "You can't escape your fate."

Out of this double vision comes the spirit of grave goofiness that pervades *The Puppetmaster*. The most immediate irony, of course, arises from our alternating views of the puppet plays, which Hou first shows head-on, as they're meant to be seen, and then from the backstage side. Beyond that, Hou contrasts the plays with real events, as when a show that involves the festival of the dead follows closely upon the early death of Li's mother. The gap between the two experiences is poignant, delicate, perhaps subtly humorous—and unsettling, too, since Hou also expands such ironies into a narrative scheme. Again and again in *The Puppetmaster*, some faintly puzzling action will occur in an unannounced locale. Only at the end of the sequence does Li's voiceover come in to explain what you've been watching, just in time for a new mystery to begin.

You slip from disorientation to disorientation; and yet that sense of physical presence always brings you back to earth. Long use has settled every object into its spot; every person, however deep in the background, carries a load of custom and character. The air itself has weight, made visible by moisture, smoke or the breeze. You feel you're in the real world, which Hou renders with such nuance that other filmmakers seem like kids making mud pies. This is also the world as Li has known it—meaning it's as whimsically elegant as his puppets.

The cigarette scene is one example of the way time can stretch in Hou's film, or rather in Li's memory. Like all of us, Li can dwell on some minor incident—such as the time he shared a bowl of pig knuckle noodles with his lover—while forgetting almost everything about a major turning point in his life. Li's grandfather steps onto a staircase, tumbles downward out of the frame and then disappears forever, in a scene that lasts about five seconds. In a similar blink of an episode, Li's first child is born off-screen, while people mill about in a courtyard and his wife screams, unseen.

At times these solemn yet silly, magically out-of-proportion events reveal someone's character, just in passing. Li's father shows himself to be the gruff, hot-headed type when he drops in momentarily on an early scene, in which Japanese officers visit the grandfather's house. "We've come to tell you to cut off your pigtails," say these agents of modernity in their crisp white uniforms. "And then we're inviting you to the opera. Are these enough tickets?" Although Dad grudgingly shows up for pigtail inspection, he doesn't see the humor in the situation. "If I want to go to the opera, I'll go on my own," he mutters, stalking into the room and right out again.

So we touch upon politics, as lived by Li Tienlu. *The Puppetmaster* begins in the early years of the 20th century, shortly after Japan occupied Taiwan, and ends in 1945 with Japan's withdrawal. As a participant in this history, Li takes his place in a great line of myopics, which starts with Fabrizio in *The Charterhouse of Parma* and runs through Pierre in *War and Peace*. Like these characters, who set out to witness great battles but see only haphazard running-around, Li experiences World War II principally as a time when outdoor shows are banned. He has to find work in a stage company (which is how he comes to southern Taiwan) or else join a Japanese propaganda troupe. It's thanks to the latter job that we're treated to the film's only battle: a puppet show, featuring tiny but bestial Yanks, a doomed toy airplane and the glorious raising of the Imperial flag, which is roughly as big as your thumb.

Does Li also know death and privation? Of course. By the end of the picture, the people around him are literally falling into coffins. I can't laugh away this pain, which runs through *The Puppetmaster* as it does through all of Hou's work. (He is, after all, the man who made *A City of Sadness*.) But neither can I ignore the fullness of Li's world, as Hou has realized it for us.

I think of a view of the grandfather's house: a shot through a second-floor doorway toward the head of a stair. The camera lingers on this setting, letting you gaze into a space where volumes of darkness and planes of light recede, one after another, into the far depths. For the moment, you can't say that people are living on screen. No creature is in sight. And yet, as the seconds pass, you sense the touch, the breath, the memory of everyone who has inhabited this place.

In *The Puppetmaster*, everything is a flimsy play, and nothing is empty.

Lamerica

Gianni Amelio's *Lamerica* opens with scenes from a Fascist newsreel and ends with the re-enactment of a much-publicized episode from 1991. What happens in between is also based on documented reality—yet the film's events all seem to happen a few feet off the ground. A rotund woman, her hair done up in a rag, sings happily to herself in a debris-strewn factory as she hauls armloads of shoe leather off the floor. No one else is on the assembly line; there seems to be nothing to do with the material except throw it back where it came from. On a bridge over a narrow river, policemen haul dozens of ragged men off a bus, beating them and firing guns, maybe into the air, maybe not; as if losing interest in the attack, the camera pans left, discovering still more of the men running far below along the gravel bank. A reedlike girl, about 5 years old, dances Michael Jackson–style in the hallway of a derelict hotel, her eyes closed, her blond curls shaking as if in sexual rapture; to a passing stranger, her mother says cheerfully, "You like the girl? Take her. Put her on Italian TV." And in the shelter of a half-ruined pier, sitting before a bonfire, yet another little girl gives a language lesson to a circle of children. She stares as if blind as she intones, "Flower, shoe, ship, sea," then slowly smiles at the sound of the last word.

These are Albanians of the post-Communist era, most of them determined to sail to Italy, though they have neither documents nor money nor any idea of what might await them, other than what they've seen on TV. *Lamerica* is the story of how a young Italian businessman steps into this potentially lucrative situation, only to find himself on the road with these thousands of refugees-in-the-making. That's the up-to-the-minute, documentary side of the film—which, strangely enough, is the side that seems most fantastic. *Lamerica* is also the story of how the businessman becomes bound to an addled old man, whose destination is as elusive as that of any of the other travelers but even more pathetic. That side of the film is mythic in character, yet utterly down to earth. The old man wants to return to a home that vanished fifty years ago.

Gino shows up in Albania wearing shades and driving a green Suzuki. Though his get-up differs from that of the Fascist troops that took over in 1939, Gino's attitude seems strikingly similar. His purpose: to set up an Italian-owned shoe factory, using Albanian labor and raw materials. Not that he expects to make any shoes—just profits, of the sort that come with wonderful ease when post-Communist economies meet with foreign capital. Only one obstacle stands before him and his partners. He must find a suitable Albanian to act as president of the enterprise, "suitable" meaning silent and just literate enough to sign on a dotted line. In a former labor camp, a scene of rubble and crisscrossing metal chutes and bunk beds lined up in airless rows, Gino finds his man: the 70-year-old Spiro, said to have been jailed for opposing the Communist regime. When first seen, caked with coal dust and wearing a gray, quilted uniform, Spiro is so withdrawn that he won't even lift his head to meet Gino's eyes. Asked his age, he replies by holding up his finger—once, twice. The answering grin on Gino's face is too moist and knowing for mere greed. Lust would be more like it.

Of course the scheme goes wrong. Old Spiro takes off, with Gino in pursuit; and that's when *Lamerica* itself lifts off, as these two travelers, who constitute a society of their own, get swept up with the countless people on the road, moving with them and yet remaining separate and apart. During their journey, the film becomes a succession of CinemaScope panoramas—washed-out tans and browns under the glare of a pale blue sky—alternating with Caravaggesque interiors, where a few rays of light cut through the murk, isolating some characteristic feature of a face. To put it another way: *Lamerica* is a film of landscapes and multitudes, but it's also an extraordinary cinematic portrait gallery.

The most frequently encountered faces, naturally, are those of Gino and Spiro. The former is played by the remarkable young actor Enrico Lo Verso, who looks like Palermo's answer to Jeff Goldblum. His is a face of extensions; the ears fan to the side, the long, thin nose pokes down, the lips push forward. Only the eyes hang back, dark and sheltered under a ruler-straight brow. Though he's a product of classical training, Lo Verso has the gift of leaving artifice behind in his acting. There's something naked about his performance here; you feel you're seeing everything about Gino, from his rich-boy petulance to his insecurity to his would-be caginess, and it's all made visible on the surface, moment by moment. Spiro, on the other hand, is played by a nonprofessional who looks and acts like what he is—a onetime fisherman, laborer and janitor. His is a squared-off face, thin-lipped and hollow-cheeked—a stone facade, over which lies a curtain of lanky gray hair. But even though it's impassive by nature, Spiro's face can open with a kind of serene optimism. That happens when he encounters children, and it happens as well when he feels he's speaking to a friend, as he mistakenly does with Gino.

I am glad to report that the young urban hustler, when put into the company of a fatherly peasant, learns next to nothing. Brutally selfish from first to last, Gino alternately pushes the old man around and sweet-talks him, so long as Spiro is needed. As soon as he's not, Gino treats him like a wad of gum that's gotten stuck on his shoe. The audience, naturally enough, longs to see Gino pay for his misbehavior. And so he does, being progressively stripped of his possessions, his privileges and finally his identity. Embarrassed by Spiro, uneasy at the thought of having anything in common with him, Gino ends up having everything in common with the refugees crowding their way toward Italy.

In conversation, Gianni Amelio has revealed a personal source for this story of a wandering father figure and an uncomprehending young man. His own father emigrated from Calabria in 1947, when Amelio was 2 years old. By the time the family was reunited, some sixteen years later, the father had become a stranger. Amelio has said that he always wanted to make a film about such economic refugees and their families, but he didn't want to set the story in the past. Only with the collapse of Albania and the flood of immigrants into Italy did he see a chance to make his film—which explains how reportage got mixed with character study and the myth of homecoming, but not how Amelio integrated them all so movingly.

Not once in this deeply personal film does Amelio hint at his own emotions. It's as if he's transferred all those feelings to the public sphere, where everything (especially if it's a political statement) is keyed up one tone higher than usual. And yet there's a reticence about *Lamerica*. I've rarely seen a film with so many *non*-virtuoso tracking shots. They're fluid but discreet, never calling attention to themselves. The same might be said for Franco Piersanti's musical score, which creeps into scenes like a memory or a heartbeat, welling up fully only at the film's very end.

Is *Lamerica* a great movie? I can't say; I'm not all that sure what "great" means. All I can tell you is that I've now seen *Lamerica* three times, and despite a stern anti-lachrymal policy I found myself weeping each time. I can think of no other current film that could be compared without blushing to the work of Rossellini and de Sica. I'm certain no other film released this year is better.

POLEMICS

Wild At Heart

A film projectionist nods off in his booth and starts to dream. Separating itself from his slumbering form, a twin rises, takes from the wall a twin of his hat and goes down into the movie house to stand in the aisle and watch the film the dreamer is projecting. Then the twin approaches the screen and walks into the film.

Buster Keaton's adventure in *Sherlock Junior* has served for over sixty years as a model of how people watch movies. Not that all pictures work on an audience this way; but films, perhaps more than any other artworks, tend to set up a running commentary on their own unreality. They are like dreams in which one is aware of dreaming.

Many of the best movies balance this tendency with other characteristics of film: its unsurpassed ability to document the world; its forcefulness as a medium for argument; its rhythmic play of light and shadow, sound and silence, which allows it to border on the plastic arts. I'm thinking at the moment of Renoir's *The Crime of Monsieur Lange* and Fassbinder's *The Bitter Tears of Petra von Kant*, which played recently in New York at the Public Theater and the Bleecker Street Cinema. You may supply examples of your own, but they won't be many. Fully realized, four-dimensional films are rare. What you see most often are movies in which the tendency toward self-conscious fantasy predominates—which brings us to David Lynch.

Like a creature that has developed a single, oversized organ at the expense of the rest of its withered body, Lynch is a misshapen talent, oddly evolved to fit an odd cultural niche. He hasn't the slightest interest in the world around him. His images invariably seem to emerge from a soundstage, even when shot on location. His actors reveal only the gestures and turns of phrase of other actors. You will never feel the shock of recognition in a Lynch film, only shock itself. Nor is there a purpose to the jolt. Though Lynch's abundant stock of absurdities, incongruities and asides sometimes teases the viewer with a hint of profundity, nothing adds up in his pictures. He is as incapable of argument as of documentation. What he *can* do—and he does it supremely well—is draw the viewer into that mood of willful oneirism, using visual effects that are both dazzling and indelible.

Wild at Heart is his latest foray into the land of waking dreams. Based on a novel by Barry Gifford and photographed by Lynch's longtime collaborator Frederick Elmes, it is the story of young lovers on the run, from a Carolinas town called Cape Fear to New Orleans to a hellhole known as Big Tuna, Texas. Nicolas Cage plays Sailor, Laura Dern plays Lula. But the names don't really matter, since the characters are generic. They're the guy who dreams he's Elvis and the girl who's haunted by her past.

The proceedings get started with a bang. Immediately after the credits, there's an uncommonly bloody killing, which lands Sailor in jail. On his release—effected with a simple title card, announcing that time has passed—Lula picks him up in a black Thunderbird convertible. Cool cars, sunglasses and plenty of rock music are essential to a filmmaker of Lynch's aspirations. So, too, is dialogue that sounds like *Cliffs Notes* for the movie. Such is Sailor's comment when Lula hands him his beloved snakeskin jacket: "For me, it is a symbol of individuality and my belief in personal freedom." Then it's off for some hot sex, more rock and roll, more hot sex, a few flashbacks of violence. What can the lovers possibly do for a follow-up, except leave the state and break Sailor's parole?

What follows is mannered, arch, empty, labored, expertly made and intermittently thrilling. Though scene flows effortlessly into scene—no one is better than Lynch at transitions—I remember the events in pieces. A man on fire runs through a suburban living room. A young woman, injured in a car wreck, pokes uncomprehendingly at the bloody hole in her scalp. Lula, undergoing an abortion, lies under a doctor's magnifying lamp, her face appearing outsized while her tiny arms thrash helplessly. Many of the shots are enthralling, even when they're without incident—for example, the view of the roadside at night, seen as a horizontal band of shadowy green, rushing past beneath impenetrable blackness. There are also a few sequences, full of incident, that pull you all the way into the dream. The best of them, the great set piece of *Wild at Heart*, is a confrontation in a motel room between Lula and Bobby Peru (Willem Dafoe), Big Tuna's incarnation of evil. It's so intense an encounter that I could all but feel the breath coming through Bobby's rotten teeth.

Then Bobby left. He had shown his power over Lula; and Lynch had demonstrated much the same thing to me. Once more, he had proved he could push my buttons, and once more he'd turned out to have no good reason for pushing them. I felt used. I also felt that this scene, like certain episodes of *Blue Velvet,* exposed the vacuum in Lynch. In its own sick way, *Wild at Heart* is as much a brainless, heartless spectacle as *Indiana Jones and the Temple of Doom.* The difference is that Spielberg engineered his movie-as-rollercoaster for a general audience. Lynch constructs his for an audience that wants to feel wised-up, decadent, better than the Spielbergian middle class.

At this point, Lynch's fans, most of my friends among them, might object that his dreams are so troubled that one's complicit enjoyment of them is itself an act of culpability. By taking to a personal extreme the oneiric and plastic qualities of film, he draws the audience into a more conscious engagement with its desires. It sounds plausible; and if movies are indeed commentaries on a dream rather than mirrors of reality, what more can they honestly offer? So let me suggest a counterexample: Brian De Palma's *Blow Out,* a film so self-enclosed that *The Village Voice*'s J. Hoberman has likened it to a Möbius strip.

Blow Out is, in fact, a circular story with a twist, and it's all surface. Based explicitly on Antonioni's *Blow-Up,* with an added debt to Coppola's *The Conversation,* the picture is at every level a film about film. The protagonist lives within movies. His setting, too, is made up: a mythical city named Philadelphia, central to the history of an imaginary nation called the United States. In this never-never land, the women all have to sell their bodies in one way or another to survive, while the men make a living selling each other pictures of the women. You realize, of course, that this is a fantasy; and De Palma tells you as much in every way he knows how. Still, you leave the theater devastated for these phony characters in their invented country, and for yourself and your own nation as well. For all its artifice, *Blow Out* has weight, purpose, moral power. It's not a balanced film, but it's a great one.

Wild at Heart, on the other hand, is not only lopsided and brilliant but utterly cynical as well. That's a striking conjunction, given the way Lynch's work has been received. His best-known production, *Twin Peaks,* made its mark by providing just what we all want from television—sex, violence and easy laughs—delivering them more amply than the competition and with greater style. So why don't people just say that *Twin Peaks*—and *Wild at Heart* and *Blue Velvet*—are cheap thrills in expensive wrappers? (To take one example out of many: *The New York Times* puffed *Wild at Heart* just before its release by lauding the "unsettling vision" of David Lynch, "the reigning master of locating the bizarre, the surreal and the disturbing in American life.") You'd think, for all the hype, that Lynch's pictures were works of pioneering artistry, suitable to be stuck on a museum wall right next to *Un Chien Andalou*. More likely, though, they're empty artifacts of that cultural niche I mentioned at the beginning of this piece, the milieu of the institutional avant-garde.

Whenever you hear the words *disturbing, transgressive* and *subversive* tossed around, whenever rules are supposedly being broken and authorities challenged, you may assume you're in avant-garde territory. You're among the institutional avant-garde when the transgressors have M.F.A. degrees from good schools and are on a first-name basis with at least three arts administrators. This is the setting in which the avant-garde becomes avant-gardism, one more item in a repertory of styles—an approved, accredited part of the curriculum, to be studied in academies and practiced for the approbation of one's fellow professionals. If Lynch is a pioneer, it's because he has converted this outrage-by-the-numbers avant-gardism into mainstream, commercial success. Think of him as the boy voted Most Likely to Succeed, in a school where the other class notables include Robert Mapplethorpe and Karen Finley.

We might as well forgive the average tourist from Mars for assuming that the names I've just brought together represent America's greatest contemporary artists. Is that entirely a function of notoriety—sought-after and profitable in one case, unwanted in the others, who had their fame thrust upon them by a cabal of sleazoid politicians and Bible-thumpers? Or is there a real resemblance among these classmates?

Before answering, let me assure the reader that I am far from wanting to blame anyone for falling victim to Jesse Helms. More than that: I endorse the right of all artists to as much government money as they can grab, no strings attached. By all means, let the institutional avant-garde join with the Metropolitan Museum and the Metropolitan Opera to rejoice in the National Endowment for the Arts' $171 million a year. Better still, why not give the institutional avant-garde its own savings and loan? If James Fail could acquire the Bluebonnet Savings Bank along with $1.85 billion in federal subsidies after putting up just $1,000 of his own money, then surely we can do as much for Karen Finley and her friends.

Nevertheless, if we can bear for a moment to forget public policy and think about art, we might notice a powerful odor of bad faith arising from the vicinity of the institutional avant-garde. It's the smell of subversion that wants to be risk-free. First comes the self-validating gesture of declaring that all works of art should aspire to the condition of avant-gardism, if they're to be taken seriously; then comes the refusal to play out the consequences. For example: It's shabby to complain that performance artists, those descendants of the Dadaists, will soon have nowhere to perform, given that all the major venues receive government funds. Think of the *real* Dadaists in Berlin, who staged their events not in art galleries or at the local equivalent of Lincoln Center but in churches and bars and cafes, especially the ones where they weren't welcome. Think of the Berlin Dadaist Franz Jung, who in 1923 chose to express himself by hijacking a German freighter in the Baltic and taking it to Petrograd, where he turned the ship over to the Soviet authorities. There's an avant-gardist I can respect.

What I can't respect is work that denies all of the traditional, nontransgressive functions of art while simultaneously turning away from the risks of engagement with the world. Sometimes, on the excuse of favoring strong content over mere style, the artists and their flacks turn against the notion of formal skill. Sometimes, as with David Lynch, formal skill is all the artist provides. In either case, the presumed assault on bourgeois order is safely contained—in an art gallery, at a performing arts center, on the screen. The danger of the image is assumed; the image of danger is all that's demanded.

I came out of *Wild at Heart* feeling sick of images, sick of irony, sick of a copycat avant-garde that's addicted to money and applause. The poor get locked out of their jobs, get tossed out of their homes, get shot by stray bullets at the rate of one a day; and the college-educated play at wanting to be disturbed.

Tourists from Mars, wherever you travel next, try to speak kindly of us. The truth is too great a shame.

"Mute and Glorious Miltons: On 'Cinematic Poetry' and Its Critics"

W hat do people mean when they call a film "poetic?"

"It seems to have exploded directly from the filmmaker's psyche, a gonzo-poetic head trip about America's escalating culture of ultra-violence."

Thus a professional movie critic, Owen Gleiberman, writing on Oliver Stone's *Natural Born Killers*. Since the review is highly enthusiastic, we may conclude that it is good for a film to be "poetic," at least when modified by "gonzo."

"A feverish visual poem centering on the enigma of pregnancy."

Gleiberman again. But this time he's writing about Godard's *Hail, Mary*, which he finds dull and meaningless. The poetic must therefore be something bad, at least when modified by "feverish."

A couple more examples should help to muddy the issue. Here's Roger Ebert on a film full of unabashed sentimentality, *Field of Dreams*: "the movie depends on a poetic vision to make its point." And here's Peter Travers on a film full of gloating ugliness, *Wild at Heart*: It "resonates with a ghostly, poetic terror." One critic is glad to have been mindlessly uplifted by poetry; the other to have been mindlessly downtrodden. I wonder which poems these people have been reading.

Usually, it's impossible to tell. That's why I perked up recently when another critic, Caryn James, hinted at specificity in a review of two videos by Francisco Ruiz de Infante. His works "turn basic images into poetic dramas," she wrote. "A close-up of a plant being watered looks like a flood. . . . A washed-out image of a rotting apple turns into an apple in flames, which turns out to be the image of a planet."

Now we're getting somewhere. The images she describes are calamitous and surprising; one seems to flow into the next allusively, associatively, so that paraphrasable meaning splashes playfully in the wake of metaphorical invention. Has James been reading Ashbery? I wouldn't put it past her. And yet the passage above provides only one instance of her use of poetry as a metaphor. Within three paragraphs that discuss Ruiz de Infante, she employs the figure twice more, referring to "enigmatic poetic images" and asserting that they, "like written poetry," demand "repeated attention." By this point, her own repetition of "poetic" and "poetry" has begun to sound incantatory. Maybe Ashbery isn't the model after all; maybe James has been reading Kurt Schwitters, or Lord Dunsany.

So far, it would seem that "poetry" connotes incoherence, and the "poetic" in film is the stuff you don't understand. (Ruiz de Infante's video is "not the most accessible work," according to James; it is "tough to grasp . . . in one viewing.") Either you admire this incoherence because it seems artistic (Ebert) or else you hate it for the same reason (Gleiberman). As a corollary, poetry is the stuff that rescues filmmakers from judgment. In the old days, critics used to call sex scenes "poetic" in the hope of warding off the district attorney. (Unlike porn, poetry is not expected to be exciting; a poetic sex scene, by definition, cannot be actionable.) Today, when it's become possible to complain that a *Striptease* isn't dirty enough, a critic who described sex scenes as poetic would risk sounding genteel. But writers such as Travers and Gleiberman still must defend their right to enjoy a bloodbath, and so in today's culture it's more often violence that becomes poetic—partaking of a higher but indefinite meaning, which places the film beyond the reach of censors, and of those critics who think the splatterfest in question is simply a mess.

And what of those who continue to read poetry—that having-a-fit audience, and few? They might be tempted to write off the metaphor of "poetic film," at all times and in all cases, as one more abuse of language. I would like to suggest that this is not necessarily so. Looking back over the past three-quarters of a century, we may find that the precedents for this usage are honorable; and though the meaning of the phrase has changed over the years, so, too, have the contents in that mental anthology we title *Poetry*.

Historically, the concept of cinematic poetry is inseparable from that of film as fine art; so we must begin by asking how people over the years have distin-guished commercial moviemaking from supposedly higher endeavors.

Film historians generally agree that the first self-conscious effort to elevate the movies was undertaken in France by the Film d'Art company, founded in 1907 with the intention of putting famous performers from the Comédie Française and the boulevard theaters into respectable dramas, which might attract an elite audience. The company held the premiere of its first production, *L'Assassinat du Duc de Guise*, in November 1908, with an orchestra playing a score composed for the film by Camille Saint-Saëns. The company's best-known production, made in 1912, remains *Les Amours de la Reine Elisabeth*, starring Sarah Bern-hardt. The years have not dealt kindly with these films. Alan Williams makes a case for them in his excellent history of French cinema, *Republic of Images*, pointing out that they had a pervasive influence on the "tradition of quality" in France. They also left their mark on the American industry; the origins of Para-mount Pictures lie in an attempt to imitate the Film d'Art. But the possibility of associating the word "industry" with these productions reveals the shortcom-ings of the Film d'Art project from the viewpoint of people with a ready-made notion of high culture. Whatever the merits of this or that movie, as an ensemble these works are the cinematic forebears not of poetry but of middle-brow good taste, where the genteel meets the unintentionally risible.

That understood, film historians tend to agree on a second proposition: that the more advanced artistic possibilities of film were first appreciated by the Sur-realists. Here it is conventional to mention the popular serials made by Louis Feuillade—*Fantômas* (1913–14), *Les Vampires* (1915–16), and *Judex* (1916)—as found objects that helped to open the Surrealists' eyes. A later figure, Alain Resnais, recalling his own early enthusiasms, spoke in 1962 of how he found in these breathless, quasi-paranoid crime thrillers "this prodigious poetic instinct that allowed [Feuillade] to fashion Surrealism as easily as he breathed." Resnais added, "I could have been made a member of SAF, that imaginary Society of the Friends of Fantômas which was founded before 1914 by Guillaume Apollinaire and Max Jacob."

In such accounts—and there are many—a small, advanced clique of artists in France recognized the inherent poetry of film just as World War I broke out, "poetry" being understood (in their new definition) as a kind of delirium, in which elements of the absurd and the uncanny might erupt within the most blandly "normal" of settings. After the war, that absurd, uncanny eruption, came the first Surrealist films, which gave birth to the experimental cinema: Man Ray's *Le Retour à la raison* (1923), Léger's *Ballet mécanique* (1924), René Clair's *Entr'acte* (assisted by Francis Picabia, Erik Satie, Man Ray, Marcel Duchamp, and others, 1924), and Duchamp's *Anemic Cinema* (1926). The series of Surrealist productions then reached its climax with two collaborative works by Luis Buñuel and Salvador Dali: *Un Chien andalou* (1929) and *L'Age d'or* (1930).

I see a couple of problems with this account. First, when Apollinaire sang the praises of *Fantômas* in the journal *Soirées*, he seems not to have meant Feuillade's serials but the stories by Pierre Souvestre and Marcel Allain, which had been published monthly since October 1911. That, at least, is the opinion of Roger Shattuck in *The Banquet Years*, and it's a plausible one, despite the enormous popularity of Feuillade's films. Apollinaire called the *Fantômas* stories "classics" in a literary context, also praising Edgar Allen Poe, Jules Verne, H. G. Wells, and the pulp-fiction adventures of Nick Carter.

A second difficulty arises. It is true that the Surrealists made films in the 1920s and, more generally, indulged happily in movie-going. (Robert Desnos reviewed films for *Paris Journal*, Louis Aragon wrote of Sade's *Justine* as an admirable subject for the cinema, and André Breton liked to pretend that movie theaters were essentially public parks, suitable for the enjoyment of a picnic.) Nevertheless, I believe the Surrealists, like Apollinaire, were far more interested in literature and the traditional visual arts than they were in film. Breton's *Manifesto of Surrealism* (1924) bristles with the names of writers and painters and sculptors, past and present, who were inherently Surrealist or self-consciously Surrealist; but not a single filmmaker is mentioned. And though he composed the *Second Manifesto of Surrealism* (1930) in the wake of *Un Chien andalou*, Breton came up in the text with just one example of a cinematic Surrealist: Charles Chaplin.

I propose that the Surrealists might take a lesser place in the tradition of "artistic" filmmaking and also in the discourse that finds certain films "poetic." Although its glamour will always dazzle and its films continue to amuse, Surrealism has been only one among several competing ways of thinking about art in film. In fact, it cannot even claim to have originated the case for film poetry. That distinction, I believe, goes to a writer who was genuinely eccentric: an American, Vachel Lindsay, who first revealed his vision of a cinematic Parnassus in 1915.

He has lapsed into such obscurity that I might be forgiven for introducing some biographical notes. Born in Springfield, Illinois, in 1879, Lindsay grew up with a firm belief in the gospels of Abraham Lincoln and Jesus Christ, whose preachings he sought to infuse into the arts of his time. Toward that end, he dropped out of college at twenty to study painting, first in Chicago at the Art Institute and then in New York under Robert Henri. When the limits of his talent became unmistakable, Lindsay turned his energies from painting to poetry; and when he failed to find a publisher for a volume of his illustrated verse, he printed copies of two poems, at his own expense, and took to the streets, selling his work out of his overcoat pocket. Later, in the years 1906 through 1912, he hit the road, walking from Florida to Kentucky, from New York to Ohio, and from Illinois to New Mexico, knocking at farmhouse doors to offer his volume *Rhymes to Be Traded for Bread*.

By 1915, Lindsay was famous. That year, he published *The Art of the Moving Picture*. Its theories met with immediate and widespread approval (D. W. Griffith, Gordon Craig, and the *New Republic*'s Francis Hackett were early admirers), and in 1922 Lindsay issued a revised edition, incorporating material he had delivered in public at the new Denver Art Museum.

Lindsay's theories seem crucial to me because they discovered art (including poetry) within films as they *actually existed*. Lindsay did not see the need to import the trappings of another, more traditional medium into the nickelodeon (as the Film d'Art producers had done); nor did he foresee the need to remake tradition (as the Surrealists would do) using film as one of several handy tools. Instead, Lindsay looked closely at the commercial cinema of his day and found that it already shared the best qualities of Byron and Tennyson, Botticelli and Rembrandt. The appreciation of film as a popular art—of film as poetry, in the fullest sense—perhaps began here.

Proceeding in Aristotelian fashion, Lindsay surveyed the various works that filmmakers had produced, noting which ones seemed able to move the viewer. He asked about the source of their power. Then, having carried out this descriptive inquiry, he went on to categorize. This yielded a three-part scheme: chase pictures, melodramas, and spectacles (the latter encompassing both the historical epic and the fairy tale). Each of these categories was susceptible of further elaboration. Thus the chase picture (or "photoplay of action"), having been raised to a higher level in certain Westerns, became Sculpture-in-Motion. The melodrama (or "intimate photoplay"), attaining excellence in *The Rose of the Rancho* starring Bessie Barriscale (and hinting at a similar potential in the performances of Charles Chaplin), became Painting-in-Motion. As for the "photoplay of splendor," it aspired to become Architecture-in-Motion, as witnessed (according to the book's later edition) in *The Cabinet of Dr. Caligari*.

Lindsay's scheme is impressive as an abstract of the genres that had evolved in film by 1915; but it is even more impressive as an attempt to specify *why* those genres were successful, finding the answers in certain practical, fundamental aspects of the medium. The chase picture is basic to filmmaking, Lindsay says, not only because it gratifies "the incipient or rampant speed-mania in every American," but also because the camera is uniquely able to show us the object of the chase, clearly and as it really exists. The melodrama works because the film set (unlike the stage of a theater) is already, in reality, an intimate space. Spectacle films work because the camera can show us "the sea of humanity, not metaphorically but literally: the whirling of dancers in ballrooms, handkerchief-waving masses of people in balconies, hat-waving political ratification meetings, ragged glowering strikers, and gossiping, dickering people in the market-place."

Of course, some filmmakers (notably D. W. Griffith) were better than others at employing these special properties of the camera, just as some artists were better than others at using oil paints and a brush. The important point, to Lindsay, was that film, as practiced, was already an art form, which needed only to realize more fully its own integrity. Moreover, this new art was of a piece with world culture as a whole, including (needless to say) poetry.

Although the three basic genres, raised to perfection, might be said to become painting, sculpture, and architecture in motion, another way to classify their higher reaches would be "to use the old classification of poetry: dramatic, lyric, epic. The Action Play is a narrow form of the dramatic. The Intimate Motion Picture is an equivalent of the lyric. . . . And obviously the Splendor Pictures are the equivalent of the epic."

Thanks to this division, and to the names of writers that pepper his text, we can say with certainty which poems Lindsay had been reading. They were the writings that, taken together, made up the entire history of literature as he knew it. In his own poetry, of course, and in his wanderings as a Johnny Appleseed of American verse, Lindsay owed a special debt to Whitman, who received due acknowledgment in *The Art of the Moving Picture.* "We must have Whitmanesque scenarios," Lindsay wrote, "based on moods akin to that of the poem By Blue Ontario's Shore."

> The possibility of showing the entire American population its own face in the Mirror Screen has at last come. Whitman brought the idea of democracy to our sophisticated literati, but did not persuade the democracy itself to read his democratic poems. Sooner or later the kinetoscope will do what he could not, bring the nobler side of the equality idea to the people who are so crassly equal. . . . There is not a civilized or half-civilized land but may read the Whitmanesque message in time, if once it is put on the films with power.

But as the reference to dramatic, lyric, and epic poetry makes plain, Lindsay's culture was too broad for partisanship. He wanted some films to be like Whitman's poems, but others to resemble the works of Milton, Keats, Blake, Poe, Tennyson, Matthew Arnold, Yeats, Masefield, and Ezra Pound.

Like D. W. Griffith and many of the other early filmmakers, Lindsay was in large measure an autodidact, with a worldview formed in the late 19th century.

He seems to have thought of "art" as a global phenomenon, congruent with that sphere of moods and aspirations that may be called the human spirit. Within that sphere, each particular art has its own means of expression; but all are part of the larger enterprise. So it is that a film—even a one-reeler at the nickelodeon—may be analogous to a poem, whether "Enoch Arden" or "The Battle Hymn of the Republic."

Poor Lindsay. He died in Springfield in 1931, about a year after an aging and isolated Griffith, out of step with his times, flopped with his final picture, *Abraham Lincoln.* Though similarly old-fashioned, Lindsay managed to hold on in the anthologies for a few decades; but then the Civil Rights movement turned his best-known podium piece, "The Congo," into an embarrassment, and today he seems not to be read at all. Certainly his film theory has dropped out of general discussion. And yet, as we shall see, certain elements of his thought, subtly disguised, still come into play whenever people seriously consider poetry and film.

The disguise is French. To see through its trappings, we will have to jump ahead to the next major effort to put forth a poetics of filmmaking, which was not the Surrealist project but the strain in French film called "poetic realism."

A trend that took hold in the 1930s, poetic realism may perhaps be summed up in the title of Dudley Andrew's recent study of the subject, *Mists of Regret.* Anyone familiar with classic French cinema can supply the accompanying images: They emerge from Renoir's *La Nuit du carrefour* (1932) and *La Bête humaine* (1938), Grémillon's *Gueule d'amour* (1937), Duvivier's *Pépé le Moko* (1937), Carné's *Le Quai des brumes* (1938) and *Le Jour se lève* (1939). These and related pictures were a minority among French productions of the 1930s; but they were an influential minority, and worthy of our attention as the only group of popular films ever to have been tagged, explicitly, as "poetic."

The term—first used, according to Andrew, in a review in *Cinémonde* in 1933—was intended to assert artistic distinction, the only type the French could then hope for in the world market. Before World War I, the French had dominated international film; by the 1930s, they were struggling for survival, all but helpless before the conquering power of Hollywood. So began a polemic, which was addressed not only to domestic audiences but also to moviegoers abroad: American films were soulless products of the assembly line, whereas French films were the one-of-a-kind expressions of living, breathing artists. As a strategy for gaining a niche in the export market, this polemic achieved notable success; the films that were made, more or less deliberately, in accord with this line gained a reputation for artistic merit.

But what was the particular character of this artistry? Andrew gives this summary:

One finds an interpenetration of characters and what is best termed their "milieus." Often to the detriment of plot logic, or even thematic consistency, such films layer their characters with multiple, often contradictory values, signified not just in their verbal and gestural range but in a variety of accompanying imagistic registers. These include lighting, props, composition, and rhythm. . . . This intense representation of feelings that are seemingly independent of dramatic purpose must have been what prompted critics to adduce the term "poetic" in relation to such films, for compared to narrative fiction, poetry in our day is considered the genre of passion (with its connotation of "passivity"), lyrical meditation, reaction, and symbolic reading. It is also the genre that is conventionally thought to traffic in the realm of the imaginary. . . . Critics identified films of "atmosphere" as appealing to viewers sensitive to the pervasive, undifferentiated tone that in poetic realist works spreads across individual scenes or blankets an entire film.

We have abandoned the broad field of dramatic, lyric, and epic poetry and entered into a narrow band of the lyric—just as we are no longer surveying film production as a whole but concentrating on a particular set of films, made with a quasi-artistic, quasi-commercial agenda. Might the filmmakers and their critic/promoters have had any specific poems in mind? Andrew provides little documentary evidence, but he convincingly points to a tradition of Orientalism, languorous sensuality, and pessimism in French verse, running from Alfred de Musset and Baudelaire through the Symbolists.

This tradition entails more than the formal predominance of atmosphere over action and argument; it also involves a set of social and political themes, having to do with colonialism (many of the poetic realist films are set in Africa), the fate of the working class (doomed, one by one), and sexual ambiguity (the poetic realist film is often a melodrama, with a bulky male figure, usually Jean Gabin, substituted for the suffering female). We are far from Surrealism's gleeful sarcasm, burlesque sexuality, exuberant disobedience, and cult of violence.

Only one notable figure shared in poetic realism and Surrealism alike: Jean Cocteau. As a filmmaker whose principal subject was poetry—or, perhaps more accurately, the projection of himself as a poet—Cocteau has defined "poetic cinema" for half a century; and so it's telling that his work tends toward the misty side of French film, more than the uncanny and violent. To quote Cocteau's biographer Francis Steegmuller on *Le Sang d'un poète*, completed in 1930 and first shown to the public in 1932,

It is not, to use the term in a doctrinaire way, a Surrealist film (the Surrealists typically branded it as a poor imitation of one): dreams and unlikely juxtapositions are not its chief matter, although they play their roles in a poet's inspiration. Cocteau said that he tried to film poetry, as deep-sea explorers photograph submarine life; he called the picture "a realistic documentary of unreal happenings." It is an allegory of a poem's origin in assorted realities and unrealities (in so far as those can be differentiated); and despite certain crudities and benefiting from others, it achieves the status of a poem itself.

The contrast with Surrealism appears even greater, once we consider that the same aristocrats who financed *L'Age d'or*, Charles and Marie-Laure de Noailles, also paid for *Le Sang d'un poète*. The difference between the two films cannot be written off simply to the latter's narcissism. (To call Cocteau narcissistic is like complaining that grass is green.) Buñuel, at his worst, could seem arbitrary: a game-player more than a provocateur. But Cocteau was a man capable of fraternizing with the Nazi sculptor Arno Breker—this in the midst of the Occupation—and promoting his work. Whatever one thinks of this act as politics, as a matter of taste it was deplorable, in a way that carried over to Cocteau's filmmaking. Steeped in the same liquor as the poetic realists, in the same extract of evil flowers, Cocteau could lapse from startling, anguished brilliance into moodiness and kitsch. His weaknesses, when they occur, are the summation of "poetic filmmaking" when the term is used as an insult, meaning mushy, precious, and self-important. In much the same way, the weaknesses of the poetic realists, once their "tradition of quality" entered its degenerate era, could be summed up in a mocking phrase: "Daddy's movies." How comfortable poetry could become; how much like the Film d'Art.

It would seem that we already have accounted for all the connotations first encountered in our consideration of "poetic film": self-indulgence, loftiness, mystery, incoherence, psychic violence, and sentiment. Did nothing change from 1932 till now?

The common definition of poetry certainly changed; it continued to narrow, especially in America. Here, for example, is Stan Brakhage, looking back on the literary scene of the 1950s and its refusal to honor the poet and filmmaker James Broughton: "We were all under the shadow of T. S. Eliot's "The Waste Land" then, and if not that, certainly under the huger and more authentic shadow of Ezra Pound's *Cantos*. . . ." Brakhage is right: The prestige of Modernism was so great that people tended to ignore anything outside its canon. What's more, that canon itself became abbreviated. One of the advantages of reading Eliot and Pound was that they freed you from having to work your way through a couple of thousand years of writing; whatever you needed was now conveniently packed in Modernist boxes, in handy fragment form. And if that didn't satisfy you? The response (as Brakhage also notes) was very often a revival of Romanticism and the *faux-naif.* That was the sort of poetry James Broughton wrote—a sincere, nostalgic, myth-obsessed lyricism, countering the ironic, pessimistic, myth-obsessed lyricism of the Modernists:

> On the long outskirts of a dismantled city
> toward the final flicker of dusk
> I entered the nave of an unfinished cathedral
> and sought Mary Magdalene cooking up a stew . . .
> Have a sip of chowder, sir, said she,
> I've been stirring and poking this pot for years,
> it won't cure at all, nor is it lethal,
> it's rich in folly and savors of rue
> but it sometimes helps in the middle of the night.

Like Blake (and, for that matter, Allen Ginsberg), Broughton insisted he had been visited by an angel; the spirit's abiding presence allowed Broughton to live and dream as a poet and to rejoice in his love of men. Forgive me if I sound flippant; I don't mean to be, since nothing about Broughton's project was easy in 1950s America, least of all his openness about gay sex. But, having paid my respects, I also must note that Broughton's West Coast version of film poetry did not stray all that far from Cocteau's. It mostly gave Cocteau an American accent and a broader sense of humor and let him ramble somewhat, as anyone might in our landscape.

Or consider the New York-based filmmakers, poets, critics, and performers who wrote for *Film Culture* in the mid-1960s, putting their own stamp on the idea of film poetry. The Spring 1964 issue of the magazine, now lying on my desk, is as good as a time capsule: Open it, and out pops a rhapsody by Michael McClure, "In Defense of Jayne Mansfield"; poems by Ron Padgett, Gerard Malanga, and Ted Berrigan inspired by a brand-new Andy Warhol picture, "Sleep"; a letter from Samuel Fuller to Andrew Sarris, describing how he'd shot the opening scene of his latest production, *The Naked Kiss*; an interview with Jack Smith, the creator of *Flaming Creatures*, all of four lines long; and another rhapsody, this one by Carolee Schneemann, on Kenneth Anger's *Scorpio Rising*.

Just from this partial list of contents, it should be obvious that *Film Culture*, despite its sometime reputation as a partisan enterprise, was anything but single-minded. But it's also obvious that Jack Smith and Kenneth Anger were on the magazine's collective mind. The Spring 1964 *Film Culture* includes a second article on *Scorpio Rising*, this one confessing that the critic ought to have stated more explicitly his admiration for the film at an earlier date. The cover image is a photo of Anger on the set of *Scorpio Rising*, and the lead editorial, which explains everything, details the recent seizure of *Scorpio Rising* by the Los Angeles vice squad and the arrests—two of them—suffered by the magazine's editor and publisher, Jonas Mekas, whose crime was to have projected *Flaming Creatures* and Jean Genet's *Un Chant d'amour* on screens in New York.

Getting arrested does provide thrills of a sort, as well as an opportunity for self-promotion, as cynics often say; but these advantages are rated highly only by people who have never experienced them. In the Spring 1964 *Film Culture*, Mekas gave a more reasonable explanation for his having risked arrest: "We refuse to accept the authority of the police to pass judgment on what is art and what is not art. . . . No legal body can act as an art critic. There is an image in the minds of the people that cinema is only entertainment and business. What we are saying is that cinema is also art. And the meanings and values of art are not decided in courts or prisons."

Everywhere in *Film Culture*, the writers appealed to art as their highest value—an art that encompassed film, painting, sculpture, poetry, and dance. The writers also were committed, most of them, to a film art that would be avant-garde. That was the catch. On the one hand, the community represented in *Film Culture* felt an urgent need for novelty, experimentation, and radicalism, which the average spectator, doped by Hollywood and dulled by work, could not be expected to appreciate. (Let one quote, from Gregory Markopoulos, stand for many: "The spectator does not allow himself to accompany the filmmakers through the facades and holy places to which their courageous spirits wander and return to implant the motion picture with ideas. The spectator is afraid of ideas. . . . He sees a new code of film-making bursting before his eyes . . . . and he turns away.") On the other hand, the *Film Culture* writers needed to affirm that art existed on a higher plane than ordinary life, that it was above the cops, at any rate.

A familiar contradiction; and it was nowhere more evident than in the case of *Scorpio Rising*. Homoerotic, violent, visually disjunctive, and awash in popular culture, *Scorpio Rising* was about as thick a slice of outrage as anyone had yet attempted to stuff down the public's throat. It was also a compendium of every high-flown myth that its author could think of, a layering of symbolic (and explicitly lyrical) imagery, a hermetic exercise in art for art's sake. Its black-jacketed motorcyclists came not so much from the streets of 1960s America (or even *The Wild One*) as from Cocteau's *Orphée*. Its tone, certain later critics notwithstanding, fully justified the film's being included in Jonas Mekas's category of "the Baudelairean Cinema."

In its time, *Scorpio Rising* enjoyed successful runs in real (though small) movie houses; so, for that matter, did Broughton's *The Bed,* much to the encouragement of those avant-gardists who believed they could break through to a popular audience. Today, those films are confined within museums and universities, as if to confirm that they really were poetry, all along. The New American Cinema achieved a lot, not least of which was its contribution to sexual liberation, gay and straight alike; but for all its emphasis on individuality, its productions tended to occupy that familiar borderland between poetic realism and Surrealism. If we are going to find a newer meaning for "film poetry," we will have to look elsewhere.

Luckily, we don't have far to go. In that same issue of *Film Culture*, we come across a few perceptive notes about the films of Alfred Hitchcock, written by François Truffaut. In his way of thinking about film—and by Truffaut's way, I mean the entire school associated with the *auteur* theory, on both sides of the Atlantic—"film poetry" took on one of its more forceful meanings, one that still holds for many of the more thoughtful critics today.

Truffaut wasn't one to talk loosely about "poetry"; he had read too widely for that. When he did use the word, it was significant, perhaps nowhere more so than in a little piece he wrote in 1974, after the death of John Ford. Truffaut praised the apparent naturalness of Ford's style—his refusal to draw attention to his camera, or to himself; his desire, first and foremost, to reveal the characters to the audience, and to do so as directly as possible. Of course, other critics have felt that Ford was among the most mannered of directors; but that hardly refutes Truffaut. The important point was that, given a sympathetic viewer, Ford's images could *seem* transparent. Truffaut summarized Ford's achievement in these words: "Ford was an artist who never said the word 'art,' a poet who never mentioned 'poetry.'" We might even say that for Truffaut, Ford was a poet *because* he never mentioned poetry.

To the writers associated with *Cahiers du Cinéma* in the 1950s, this reticence (whether apparent or real) was one of the great virtues of the American film industry and a primary reason for considering certain of its products to be art. Again, let's choose just one quotation. This is Eric Rohmer, writing in *Cahiers* in 1955:

And then came the day when, in the shape of Claudette Colbert and Clark Gable, the cinema held up to me, under the most favourable lighting, a face without artifice, unpolished but not rough. It spoke to me in a language that was open, yet without a hint of coarseness in its tone. It behaved like the most civilized of creatures, yet without diminishing any of its naturalness. . . . If I had to characterize the American style of cinema, I would put forward the two words *efficacy* and *elegance*. I know that Hollywood has its share of the precious, but as a rule it does not smother itself in as many flourishes as our cinema does. Its filmmakers have more confidence in the power of what they show us than the angle they choose to show it from.

Perhaps the first point to be made is that Rohmer and his colleagues were committing treason. True, the *Cahiers* writers believed in the artistry of maverick, expatriate filmmakers such as Charles Chaplin and Orson Welles, who had proved too unruly for the American industry; they also took the part of self-consciously literary, avant-garde filmmakers in their midst, such as Cocteau and Resnais. But the praise they gave to seemingly ordinary Hollywood movies was an affront to a French industry that had prided itself on the individuality of its productions. Beyond that, the *Cahiers* writers insulted common sense. The Hollywood productions they liked weren't even the respectable ones but stuff like *Kiss Me Deadly, Johnny Guitar, The Girl Can't Help It,* and *Run of the Arrow.*

Setting aside the special frisson of treason, what might have been the merit of writing favorably about Hollywood? We might say the *auteurists* took up where Vachel Lindsay had left off: They were surveying the entire field of film production, without condescension, in order to speculate on what was artful about motion pictures. We might also say that their conclusions had a lot in common with Lindsay's theories. He had insisted that the basis of film art lay in the medium's inherent realism. The object of the chase was shown clearly, as it really was; the melodrama took place in a setting that really was intimate; the movie epic really showed a sea of humanity. In much the same way, the *Cahiers* critics admired Hollywood filmmakers for the simple, direct way in which they approached their subjects; the *what* was more important to them than the *how*.

To people concerned with complexity as a guarantor of value, this seeming artlessness might have argued against Hollywood. But the *Cahiers* writers generally followed their senior figure, André Bazin, in arguing that a sense of realism is basic to film. Even though we know that movies are full of artifice, we also know that something must have been physically present before the camera in order for the images to be recorded. For Bazin, as for Lindsay, film is most artful when it is most true to its own nature, building upon our desire to see the world *as it is.*

The difference between Lindsay and the *Cahiers* writers was that the latter had grown up listening to the polemic against assembly-line filmmaking. For

Lindsay, genres could be interesting in themselves, even if the director of this or that production was a bore. But the *auteurists* were set on discovering the director's personality. To them, film at its best became the outpouring of an individual spirit—meaning that if directors were poets, they were creators of a lyric art, even when their works were epic in their scope and ostensible subject. If the director had ties to the period of poetic realism (as did Renoir), then it was self-evident that his personality would suffuse his films. And if the director was an American such as John Ford or Howard Hawks? Then he removed himself from his own lyric, concentrating so fully on showing things as they were that he attained a kind of impersonality.

Perhaps this artistic ideal will sound paradoxical, but only if one has forgotten the sweet, cold plums eaten out of the icebox. American lyric poetry in this century has often made words into something tactile and matter-of-fact, as if the writer, for all of his or her idiosyncracies, might lay a hand not merely on the parts of speech but on the world itself. The great insight of the *auteurists,* an insight that helped bring about a worldwide revolution in taste, was that we might discover a similar poetry in films by Ford or Hawks. Since their works are made for a big screen, which is expected to address five hundred people at a time, their cold, sweet plums tend to be monumentalized. But that should not blind us to the nature of the artistic impulse, which I would say these filmmakers shared with William Carlos Williams (though they might never have read him). In their movies, we witness a movement toward directness, simplicity, clarity of vision.

Looking back from the viewpoint of *Cahiers* in the 1950s, we might find that this aesthetic had been gaining strength throughout the nineteenth century, especially after the invention of photography. The still camera, with its power to stop time, opened up an entire visual world, which had always existed around us and yet had been inaccessible to our eyes. The example everyone uses is Muybridge's studies of animal locomotion, which froze the stages of a horse's gallop, revealing for the first time the true positions of the hooves. But the oddly composed, silently portentous photographs that Degas took on the street will also do as examples; so, for that matter, will the snapshots taken by anonymous tourists with the first Kodak Brownies. The still camera turned up surprising new details of the world everywhere you pointed it. In so doing, it accustomed people to the notion that the world might be aesthetically interesting all on its own—that a work of art did not always have to be made but could sometimes be found.

There is a sense in which the Surrealists participated in this discovery of the mundane. The images they called up through automatism, though jarring, were supposed to arise without effort, much as the junk that would be used in collages simply presented itself to the alert artist. Anything might show itself as belonging to a work of art. Or, to put the emphasis on the maker rather than the made, anyone might turn out to be a poet, if only for a few moments. The long revolution of which Raymond Williams spoke—the realization, century by century, that a creative faculty is present in everyone—also sent its ripples through the *Manifesto of Surrealism,* a document that democratically recommends that *everyone* go crazy. From the point of view of the long revolution, all that was missing from Breton's text was the acknowledgment that observation might prove to be as revivifying as imaginative disturbance; just as everyone already has a poetic faculty, so might the world already be poetic, if only we saw it clearly.

Looking forward from *Cahiers* in the fifties to the present day, we may judge how quickly that possibility was abandoned. Hardly a decade after auteurism became dogma, a host of new theorists rose up, proclaiming the Author to be a romantic fiction and unmediated perception to be impossible. Correct. Yet who are the most vital of our contemporary filmmakers? I might begin the list with Hou Hsiao-Hsien, Abbas Kiarostami, Ousmane Sembene, Chantal Akerman, artists who are still trying to use the camera as a tool to show us the world: gangsters and dreamers in the smoky, neon-lit bars of Taipei; young children in the schoolrooms and houses clustered on the slopes of Northern Iran; schemers and strivers debating on the roads between Dakar and the villages of Senegal; the faces, dozens and dozens of them, of people on the streets of Eastern Europe, from Berlin clear east to Moscow. Although these filmmakers differ greatly from one another—although they sometimes differ from themselves, from one work to the next—they are all drawn toward that unchartable border region lying between fiction and documentary, imagination and perception.

The absence of their films from American movie houses (and from most of American intellectual discourse) in no way lessens their achievement. It merely underscores the change for the worse in the American film industry. Today, a writer who adhered to the old *Cahiers* standards would have a hard time finding Hollywood movies to praise. And yet, though Nicholas Ray is dead, world cinema persists—and the best of its practitioners are poets who never mention poetry.

The most poetic film I ever saw? I recall a screening presented half a dozen years ago by Ken Jacobs, one of the old guard of New York's avant-garde, a man who had been arrested with Jonas Mekas in that fabled spring of 1964. For an event at the New York Film Festival, Jacobs got his hands on some of the travelogue footage shot for the Lumière brothers, who in the late 1890s had dispatched their cameramen to picturesque spots around the world. Of course this footage seemed quaint, touching, fascinating. At a distance of a hundred years, you got to witness the banks of the Nile as seen from a riverboat, the rooftops of Vienna as photographed from an elevated train. But there was more: Jacobs had figured out that a cheap little strip of colored plastic, if held against one eye, would give this footage an illusion of depth. The Lumière cameramen had recorded more than they had known. These were 3-D movies, only no one had realized it.

Jacobs called his program "Opening the Nineteenth Century." I will never forget the sense of wonder I felt as these old views, which might otherwise have seemed archaeological, all at once became new and immediate. Snow fell in silence over a dark, gray city, and it looked as if I could have walked into that snowfall, which streaked past projecting eaves that might have come from a child's pop-up book; they were that magical, and they were *real*. Using the most simple and mechanical of methods, Jacobs had restored to those images the power they'd originally had, when the Lumière brothers' first audiences had jumped at the sight of an oncoming train.

People often compare films to dreams. And poems, too, have been said to arise as if their figures were a series of dream images. In poems and dreams, Nietzsche wrote, "we enjoy an immediate apprehension of forms, all shapes speak to us directly, nothing seems indifferent or redundant." And yet, he added, "Despite the high intensity with which these dream realities exist for us, we still have a residual sensation that they are illusions. . . ." In the highest film poetry, we find something that is different from a dream. We enjoy an immediate apprehension of forms, all shapes speak to us directly, nothing seems indifferent or redundant. At the same time, we know the wonderful pictures are more than an illusion. So it was with that snowfall, which somehow had become present to me after the passage of a hundred years. The images moved, but time stood still.

The Rage: Carrie 2

My friend Dennis Paoli says there are two kinds of horror movies, and since his screenwriting credits include *Re-Animator*, I treat his categories with respect. Either you organize a movie around nine decapitations, he says, spacing them at ten-minute intervals, or else you work up to a single big decapitation at the end.

Carrie is a notable example of the latter type: a movie with a long, long buildup, culminating in general slaughter. The big question, then, is, "What happens on the way to the bloodbath?" In the case of *Carrie*, the answer is, "Not much." If you watch the picture today, twenty-three years after its release—and you should, to get the most out of Katt Shea's *The Rage: Carrie 2*—you will be struck by its lack of incident. The fatal prom takes up a full twenty-five minutes of the film; another fifteen or twenty are devoted to the bloodshed in the prom's aftermath, and to the coda and closing credits. Nearly half the movie is payoff, and that half is realized at the pace of an adagio, so that Brian De Palma may demonstrate what his studies of Hitchcock have taught him.

It is not enough for De Palma to set a bucket of pig's blood over the spot where Carrie will stand. He also must track the course of the attached rope, starting from the lair of the pranksters and craning slowly to the rafters. Then, for good measure, he retraces the route, following it through the eyes of good-girl Amy Irving. I doubt the mechanics of a practical joke have ever been so exhaustively demonstrated—especially when the response to the joke will defy the laws of physics. And what is Sissy Spacek's Carrie doing, while this minimal plot device is being put into place? She's getting wet, literally and figuratively. From the opening credit sequence (a montage of autoeroticism in the shower) to the prom itself, where Carrie deliquesces in the arms of her date, De Palma keeps his protagonist moist with anticipation, though for a climax other than the one she gets.

To give a more general answer to the question posed above: On the long road toward a horror movie's bloodbath, we learn why revenge will be taken. In *Carrie*, the explicit reason for the rampage is that the protagonist has been mocked and ostracized. The implicit reason: She's been denied sexual pleasure. And then there's a third justification, which may be imputed not to the character but to De Palma himself. As master revenge-taker, he humiliates and destroys Carrie because she's the girl who won't put out. Take it from someone who is close to De Palma's age and can recall the sexual mythologies of the sixties and seventies: All women were supposedly begging for it. Unfortunately, too many of them were repressed and wouldn't come through.

That this notion wouldn't occur to Katt Shea, the director of *The Rage: Carrie 2*, might be obvious merely from her credits. We first encounter her as an actress, whose career intersects in an interesting way with De Palma's. She appeared in the role of Woman at Babylon Club in his 1983 *Scarface*. Other notable roles of the era included an appearance as a mud wrestler in *My Tutor* and as Dee Dee (a name at last!) in *Hollywood Hot Tubs*. Hired to be decorative and willing to do the job, Shea could not have felt that prudishness was the main problem in her life. Nor would she have seen herself as cowering before her sexuality, as De Palma imagined Carrie to do. A woman who can command money and attention through her body is someone whose power, however hampered, is real.

From actress to director and writer: With the occasional addition of the surname Ruben to her credits, Katt Shea began to make pictures of her own, beginning with the 1987 *Stripped to Kill* (the title, in itself, responds to De Palma) and continuing with movies that included the 1989 *Stripped to Kill II* (also known as *Live Girls*) and the gorgeously lurid *Poison Ivy* (1992). These pictures were remarkable for their disquieting themes (which had a lot to do with the possibilities and limits of a woman's sexual power), for their style (which was bold, fluent and varied) and for being released at all. Over the past dozen years, only five or six American women besides Shea have managed to turn out a comparable number of commercial features.

With that in mind—not to mention the low budgets, the genre trappings, the seven-year gap between *Poison Ivy* and now—I will pose my questions yet again. What happens on the way to the bloodbath? What wrong must be avenged? Or, to put it another way: Does *The Rage* merely re-enact *Carrie*, as we'd expect of a sequel? Or does Shea's movie exact a new punishment of its own?

The film starts: A brush, shown in close-up, dips into thick red paint and begins to trace a band across the walls of a shabby living room. We are back in the original *Carrie*'s atmosphere of overwrought religiosity, with candles burning everywhere and Mom (J. Smith-Cameron) huskily warning the devil away from her daughter. But already Shea has let the situation get out of control in a way that De Palma would not. His preacher-mom was a half-sly, half-sadistic Jesus-shouter, offered up for the audience's contempt. Shea's Mom is crazy. She paints her protective band heedlessly, smearing it over anything that gets in the way: furniture, windows, photos on the wall. What's more, when Mom is carted away, her little daughter feels devastated. For young Rachel, *The Rage* opens on a note of bewilderment and loss.

An overhead shot and a circling camera transform this child into the teenage Rachel, played by Emily Bergl. Note the baby-fat cheeks, the tidy nose, the Betty Boop lips over neat rows of little teeth. Were it not for the unmanageability of her dark curls and her funereal taste in nail-polish color, Rachel might seem half-infantile. But as Shea and Bergl conceive her (aided by screenwriter Rafael Moreu), Rachel is not only young but also guarded, defiant, alert, sympathetic and chatty by turns. When she feels the need, she will speak as if sunk two miles beneath her own surface. But unlike Carrie, who could barely meet anyone's eye, Rachel is also capable of bantering on the school bus with her best friend, Lisa (Mena Suvari). The topic is sex; and far from shying away from Lisa's tale of adventure, Rachel shares it eagerly, then responds by flashing a friends-forever sign: a view of the tattoo on her left arm, showing a heart encircled by ivy.

But for Rachel, forever does not last long. Lisa is already dressed like Ophelia, in trailing weeds. Within minutes (as you'll know if you've seen the trailer) she dives off the roof of Bates High School, having learned that her virginity meant nothing to the football hero to whom she'd given it. The trailer does not tell you where Shea will position the camera. (The choice, let's say, is made for maximum impact.) Nor will you understand, all at once and free of effort, the implications of the death. Yes, Lisa's suicide sets off Rachel's first big telekinetic blowout. But it's only upon reflection, and with the playing out of the film, that you appreciate the intensification of the theme. Whereas De Palma in *Carrie* kept going over the mechanics of his set, Shea doubles back on emotions. First there's the loss of the mother, then the loss of the girlfriend.

So the film sets out on the long road toward its preordained bloodbath. Here, the way is full of incident, which makes *The Rage* a far richer, more absorbing film than *Carrie*. But, more important, it's a film that does not cheat on its chosen theme of abandonment—even during the lighter moments, even when Rachel finds new companionship by falling in with Jesse (Jason London), the high school's only sensitive football hero. (In a reminiscence of the meet-cute between Claudette Colbert and Rudy Vallee in *The Palm Beach Story*, Rachel introduces herself to Jesse by shattering a strategic piece of glass.) The best thing about this deepening romance is that it actually deepens—which means that Jesse, estranged from the football brotherhood, becomes a virtual girl. (Trust me on this. It's a question of the haircut.) But contrary to the fantasies perpetuated by single-decapitation horror movies, some losses are irreparable. Amy Irving, returned from the original film as the sole survivor of the Bates High School prom, keeps pursuing Rachel, pressing offers of help on her and trying to expiate her own guilt about Carrie. You will see from the climactic bloodbath how well these things can be made up.

Why does Rachel kill everybody? The explicit reason is that she's been mocked and ostracized. The implicit reason is that her girlfriend died and her mother was driven crazy. And then there's the third reason, which emerges when the film's master revenge-taker, Katt Shea, appears on the screen. She has cast herself in *The Rage* as an assistant district attorney, who briefly attempts to prosecute the high school's football heroes for using and discarding young women. To her disgust, she learns the job can't be done: The boys' club is too widespread, its power too entrenched.

Twenty-three years after De Palma joined the boys' club, scoring his definitive hit with *Carrie* in those golden, innovative seventies, who can pretend that the girls' ongoing loss is reparable? Look at the beauty and terror that Katt Shea can achieve, and ask whether there's motivation today for *The Rage*.

The Way We Laughed

In Phillip Lopate's wonderfully unsentimental memoir about youthful cinephilia, "Anticipation of *La Notte*"—you can find it in a new collection of his pieces on film, *Totally Tenderly Tragically*—he calls the early sixties "the 'heroic' age of moviegoing." You know the song; any number of middle-aged critics have warbled it recently, though few with Lopate's sense of irony and self-knowledge. Back then, goes the tune, the world took cinema seriously. Back then, we fiery young people sprinted toward the box office (we could still sprint) for the first screening of the new Antonioni or Bresson. And how we argued over it! How sad the world has become, now that kids just drop cassettes into a VCR, never thinking to debate anything more vital than the extent of Tarantino's borrowings.

In his memoir, Lopate dumps a bucket of usefully cold water on all these wheezing songbirds. (Perhaps we'd forgotten the many disappointments toward which we raced. Perhaps we'd like to forget the painful gap between the passions we adored on the screen and the lives we led.) But Lopate also affirms something that is most likely true: "It does seem to have been my luck to have come of age during a period of phenomenal cinematic creativity."

I hereby attest (as our favorite French critics of the time would have written), I assert, I insist, that even though this period has ended, individual creativity has not. I further declare that gods and heroes still walk among us. If they seem to be scattered sparsely through a much-diminished landscape, it's precisely because we choose to ignore them. Betrayed by our memories, we in turn betray cinema.

Gianni Amelio is being betrayed. Strange to say so, after his new picture, *The Way We Laughed*, just won the top award at the Venice Film Festival. You might expect an honor of some kind would go to the director of *Lamerica* and *Stolen Children* when he shows his new picture in his own country. But in reporting from Venice, *Variety* declared the film to be a "disappointment." (Translation: An American distributor probably would not want to acquire the rights.) Among critics and programmers at the Toronto International Film Festival, where I saw the picture, the response was lukewarm; and *The Way We Laughed* will not be shown in this year's New York Film Festival, thereby losing a potential point of entry into the U.S. market.

I hope you will forgive me if I now describe a film that might not make it to a theater near you. The general failure to appreciate Gianni Amelio's new work seems to me symptomatic of the waywardness of our time, and much more urgent a topic of discussion than the merits of *Antz*.

In outline, *The Way We Laughed* sounds much like *Rocco and His Brothers* (that masterpiece from the heroic age of moviegoing), and its story spans the years of *Rocco*'s release. A Sicilian laborer named Giovanni (played by Amelio's favorite actor, the great Enrico Lo Verso) steps off the train in Turin one January day in 1958. He has come to visit his beloved little brother Pietro (Francesco Giuffrida), who unlike Giovanni has been taught to read and is now enrolled in a school.

With immense pride, Giovanni tells anyone who will listen that Pietro is going to be a teacher. He strenuously ignores the mounting evidence that Pietro might be less than ideal as a student and a brother. Has Pietro failed to show up at the train station, leaving Giovanni to find his own way through Turin, without being able to read the street signs? Giovanni berates himself for his own stupidity; he should have remembered that Pietro must be studying at this hour. Do the relatives with whom Pietro boards accuse the boy of theft? (A significant sum is missing from the household cache, and Pietro has begun to wear sharp new clothes.) Giovanni angrily changes the subject. Their apartment is a pigsty, he says, unfit for a student. Instead of visiting for a few days, Giovanni will remain in Turin and make a home for his brother.

All this time, Amelio's camera has also been following Pietro, who is as infuriating—and as heartbreakingly confused—as any poor teenager from the sticks trying to pass as a bourgeois in the city. In the suit and raincoat he bought with stolen money, he looks as if he's playing dress-up, all the while fearing (or hoping) that he might be stripped of the imposture. Although he fled from Giovanni at the train station, he can't help encountering another newly arrived Sicilian illiterate—there are so many—whom he consents to guide through Turin, perhaps out of a transferred sense of duty, perhaps out of guilt, perhaps to have someone to whom he can safely talk down. It takes a full twenty-four hours for Pietro to go back to the train station and allow Giovanni to meet him: to permit the embrace with which a more conventional movie would have opened, and which in this film already bears a frightening weight.

Amelio narrates the rest of *The Way We Laughed* in five similar segments, each showing the events of a single day, at intervals from 1959 through 1964. It's a rigorous structure, and a shapely one. The sixth day, like the first, begins and ends at a train station. Sections two and five deal with events surrounding Pietro's failure and then success at school (and with the singing of "La Mer"). The middle parts, numbers three and four, dramatize the rupture between Giovanni and Pietro and the brothers' absence from each other. I emphasize this symmetry only to demonstrate that any moviegoer who can watch and think simultaneously ought to be able to intuit the form of *The Way We Laughed*. It's absolutely clear—unlike the feelings that overflow the framework. The structure ordains reticences and gaps;w the film's emotional substance is liquid, ambiguous and unruly, as true to the flesh and as full of suggestive shadows as the Rembrandtesque lighting.

As Giovanni embarks on an increasingly successful but unhappy career (ostensibly for Pietro's sake), as Pietro forces himself to become what Giovanni wants him to be (a process that is at once self-fulfilling and self-destructive), Amelio gives us a number of scenes that ought to be instantly recognizable as classic. What were the movies invented to do, if not show us Pietro's botched attempt to invite his brother to dinner at a fancy restaurant; or to take us into the bars and employment offices where Giovanni dispenses favors as a "president" of a delicately titled "cooperative"; or to bring us into a crowded engagement party where Pietro makes himself known to Giovanni after a long separation? I choose these moments almost at random; I might just as well mention the labor strike and Communist rally that take place in the background of one sequence, while Giovanni wanders through the foreground, thinking of nothing but the way Pietro has vanished. Everywhere in *The Way We Laughed*, Amelio's flawless and self-concealing technique is put at the service of nothing less than the impossible thing: telling the truth about our emotions, as we live them in a particular time and place.

If you think human feelings and their historical context are worth caring about, if you believe artists can aspire toward something we might call honesty (to speak in shorthand), if you long for a cinema that is formally intelligent and socially aware and at the same time accessible to a wide audience, then *The Way We Laughed* ought to be an exemplary film. You, too, would be appalled to read in *Variety* that the picture is "problematically structured, overly protracted and lacking in narrative fluidity"—lies, all lies—and that the film's "dramatic short-comings" may be summed up in Pietro's responses to his brother, which "for most of the film remain annoyingly unclear" (meaning fully human). And had you, too, been present at the Toronto festival, you might have shuddered to hear the yawns at Gianni Amelio's work, compared with the gasps of excitement at Tom Tykwer's *Run Lola Run*, a film whose ratio of style to substance is incalculable, division by zero being undefined. "Rich in humor, rhythm, energy and inventiveness," wrote *Variety* of Tykwer's film, in a review that set off a feeding frenzy among US distributors, caused a jam at the press screening and momentarily got Bernard Weinraub of the *New York Times* to notice a foreign-language film.

What *Run Lola Run* had, what Amelio's film lacked, was buzz. Ye tinseled insects! I hereby declare, assert, insist, that *The Way We Laughed* is a buzzing world on film. A hero made it, and anyone who seeks it with a pure heart will become worthy of heroism.

The rest is *Antz*.

HOPE FOR AMERICA

Unforgiven

People often assume that westerns are about America; and people are often right. It's logical to think that Sergio Leone, in *Once Upon a Time in the West,* used the pioneer period to represent all of U.S. history. Yet the film he called *Once Upon a Time in America* is set in New York City. I advise caution when it comes to this "about" business.

On the screen right now we have *Unforgiven*, directed by Clint Eastwood from a screenplay by David Webb Peoples. It is a western, one that is so rich in its themes, so brooding and intense in its manner, that I suspect it will outlast us all. *Unforgiven* may turn out to be a classic. But is it a classic about America?

The answer is certainly yes, at least during two sequences, the lesser of which concerns a hired killer called English Bob. Played with sleazy grandiloquence by Richard Harris, English Bob rides into the town of Big Whiskey, Wyoming, accompanied by his very own biographer, who is eager to record Bob's exploits. For his part, Bob seems eager to stir up a few. He struts around, braying insults to the Americans on the subject of the recent assassination of President Garfield. When the head of state is a royal personage, Bob explains, a sense of awe will stay the murderer's hand. "With a President—well, why *not* kill him?" Before anyone foolishly and fatally takes offense at this slur on democracy, the town's sheriff disarms Bob. Then, presumably acting on behalf of the audience (and the director), the sheriff whales the daylights out of him.

The audience around me squirmed some at this beating. It went beyond expectations; it hinted that the keeper of the peace would be capable of even worse savageries in the name of law. Even so, the sheriff, Little Bill Daggett, was played by Gene Hackman, who'd been drawing on a formidable stock of shrugs, drawls and eye twinkles to make his character likable. In a spirit approaching gaiety, we received the movie's first allegorical lesson: Though nobody, even the President, is safe in this county, anyone who blames excessive violence on our precious liberty deserves to have the hell kicked out of him.

The second allegorical lesson of *Unforgiven* comes at the end of the film and is considerably less inspiring. Before us looms a man who's a lapsed everything—child killer, woman killer, horse abuser, drunk. At the start of the movie, he was reformed. Now he's done something damnable again, and he knows it. It's night-time. Rain is pouring down, and the man's deathly face is lit only by a flickering torch. In a mixture of rage and self-loathing, he utters this bone-chilling threat: that he will return, if he has to. The man, of course, is Clint Eastwood. Behind him hangs an American flag.

If Clint Eastwood represents America in *Unforgiven*, then America is a drunk who can't stay on the wagon, a killer who can't resist one last murder. Among this figure's other attributes: He idealizes women but apparently can't live with them; loves children but abandons them to fend for themselves. When Eastwood's character goes straight, he insists he's an ordinary man. (We hear an echo, perhaps, of English Bob's tirade on democracy.) But when the character reverts to type, he becomes a man apart—a killer so cold-blooded that he alone of all the badmen has outperformed his own legend. I thought of William Tecumseh Sherman. (Eastwood bears more than a slight likeness to photographs of him.) Having posited an absolute division between peace and war, Sherman concluded with terrible clarity that warfare must be made unendurable. That's the America Eastwood seems to represent—either stuck in a posture of rigid moralism or else descending into a frenzy of total war.

No doubt you could spend many profitable hours figuring out how the second allegorical lesson jibes with the first. They clearly represent key moments in *Unforgiven*—and yet, taken together, these sequences account for no more than ten minutes of the film's two hours. So much for the parts of *Unforgiven* that are explicitly about America. Let's start again, and this time take the film's events as they come.

Unforgiven begins with a prostitute in Big Whiskey who can't hide her amusement at the size of a cowboy's dick. The cowboy takes revenge by slashing the prostitute's face. The sheriff storms in; and all at once the characters settle into an argument, in which they reckon justice in the most concrete terms. What would be the appropriate repayment for a face slashing—a whipping, or a fine of seven ponies? The brothel's senior prostitute, Strawberry Alice (Frances Fisher), is unsatisfied with either proposed exchange, so she soon makes a reckoning of her own. The cowboy slasher and one of his buddies must die. Whoever does the killing will receive $500 for each life taken.

Another two themes come into play. In the first, a man resorts to violence to maintain his sense of superiority over a woman. That's common enough in our country, though I doubt it could be called characteristically American. Nor is it peculiar to Americans to treat justice as a question of exchange. Eye for eye, tooth for tooth, burning for burning—that's the law sheriff Daggett is trying to enforce, and the one that Strawberry Alice oversteps (with no small justification). There's even something biblical in the sheriff's cadences as he repeatedly orders the cowboys to bring their payment, the ponies having been reckoned the suitable recompense.

Are we in Big Whiskey, Wyoming, in the 1880s or in the spiritual landscape of Genesis and Exodus? If the answer is Wyoming, then we should recall that this territory granted women the vote in 1869. By 1872, a prostitute in Wyoming could even have imagined herself campaigning for President, in the person of Victoria Woodhull. No—by showing women being treated as chattel, Eastwood and Peoples have bypassed local history altogether, in favor of those biblical images of patriarchy that we all carry in the back of our heads.

It's an atavism, which the whole tone of the production helps to reinforce. Much of the time Eastwood shows the actors in long shot, outlined against the endless landscape; or else he shoots them in close-up at night, their faces floating in the deep gloom that he and his cinematographers love so much. Like Old Testament characters, the actors in *Unforgiven* stand out starkly against a background that seems like eternity.

What Erich Auerbach wrote about Genesis might serve to describe *Unforgiven* as well. In both, we see

> the externalization of only so much of the phenomena as is necessary for the purpose of the narrative, all else left in obscurity; the decisive points of the narrative alone are emphasized, what lies between is nonexistent; time and place are undefined and call for interpretation; thoughts and feeling remain unexpressed, are only suggested by the silence and the fragmentary speeches; the whole, permeated with the most unrelieved suspense and directed toward a single goal . . . remains mysterious and "fraught with background."

Only by specifying a time and place does *Unforgiven* depart from these stylistic traits; and even then, "Wyoming 1880" means little more than "once upon a time." That's precisely what makes the western a useful genre for Eastwood. It's his stepping-off point to the supernatural.

He's been even more explicit about this otherworldliness in previous westerns, such as *High Plains Drifter* and *Pale Rider*. Here, by contrast, he evokes the uncanny rather than presenting it. (He also reins in the grotesquerie that runs loose in those earlier pictures. In keeping with the mood of its central character, *Unforgiven* often proceeds with the solemn deliberation of someone who badly wants a drink.) Still, it should be obvious that Eastwood means the title to be taken seriously. If this movie is about America, it's also about a longing for redemption that antedates our Republic by 2,500 years.

So much for "about." Let's move on now to a more fruitful question: What is the western good for?

During the first twenty years of film history, the answer was simple: action. Moving pictures needed to move. They thrived on chase scenes, fight scenes, hairbreadth escapes and hurtling vehicles. Though the modern city could and did serve as a setting for such thrills, the West seemed more fitting. It was more manageable, too. In a period when many pictures were still filmed on location, rural California simply interfered less with shooting than did New York City. Not only was it easier to get the job done, but with so much less stuff in the landscape, there were fewer extraneous details on the screen to distract audiences from narrative sensation.

You can gauge how useful the West proved by watching, say, *The Girl and Her Trust,* a 1912 film by D.W. Griffith. It comes from the cinematic equivalent of the fifth century B.C., when Griffith, like the Greek sculptors of the classical period, seemed to have glimpsed in a flash all the possibilities of his medium and then developed them to perfection before breaking for lunch. Is there anything Griffith *didn't* do in that film? Yes—he neglected to tell us anything at all about the West. Even the date of the story seems uncertain—does it take place in the recent past, or the present? The answer, of course, doesn't matter. All Griffith wanted from the West was a train, two bad guys and a stretch of open country sufficiently large that it would take time for help to arrive. Anything else—history, economics, politics, manners—he saved for his social-issue dramas, where such information belonged.

To rephrase my first answer: The western was originally good for making pure cinema. If we keep that in mind, we'll also understand how the western became good for all sorts of other things as well. Some directors—John Ford, above all—were so persuasive in their use of the genre that they made it seem as if the vessel of the western had meaning in itself. What really mattered, though, was the vessel's void, into which filmmakers could pour whatever they wanted.

In Ford's case, he poured in nostalgia, a bittersweet fatalism, a code of personal and civic ethics. The western was especially useful to him on the latter count, since he could pretend that his values came straight from the sacred text of American history. When we speak loosely of the western as being about America, that's usually the aspect of the genre we have in mind. But try finding a sense of sacred history in *Red River, Rio Bravo* or *El Dorado*. To Howard Hawks, the West often seemed to be nothing more than a convenient place where men could hang around and pretend to fight, though they really were in love with each other. As for Nicholas Ray, Budd Boetticher, Anthony Mann, Sam Peckinpah, Don Siegel—

I'll stop. My point is simply that Clint Eastwood's westerns are distinctive, and that *Unforgiven,* as the most fully realized, is the most distinctive of all. It's true that Eastwood makes use of some conventions—how could he not? He fills the picture with talk about the old days and how they're passing, with interplay between a brash kid and sadder, wiser men. And as I said at the start, Eastwood does allegorize American history, a little. But if there's any picture in which he makes the West into a vision of America, it would be his 1980 romantic comedy *Bronco Billy,* which is set in the present and has him playing a shoe salesman from New Jersey. When Eastwood makes a real western, everything looks a lot darker—literally.

Just compare the richly toned murk of his cinematography to Ford's floods of sunlight, his highland settings to Ford's Monument Valley, his controlled-migraine performances to John Wayne's swagger (even when Wayne was at his most driven or doubtful). To sum up with a reductive but handy opposition: John Ford made Hellenic westerns, and Eastwood makes Hebraic ones. Come to think of it, maybe that's why women matter so much in Eastwood's pictures, why in *Unforgiven* he goes so far as to identify with the slashed-up prostitute. Though it's true that the patriarchs in Genesis have the power, the matriarchs all have wills and voices of their own.

Yes, *Unforgiven* is about America. Mostly, though, it's the story of a man with the suggestive name of Munny, who was expected to murder his wife but did not. See it twice.

To Sleep With Anger

The assembly of the halfhearted may now adjourn. After months of Yes, buts and Well, maybes, of mumbled praise and endorsements ending with a shrug, we finally have an American film that can be called flat-out wonderful. *To Sleep With Anger*, the latest film written and directed by Charles Burnett, is droll, visionary, alarming, ironic and deeply moving, all at the same time—and so far, I'm talking only about the images under the opening credits.

Imagine a powerfully built, middle-aged black man, somewhat gone to fat, dressed in a suit that looks too flashy for churchgoing but too cheap for high times. He sits in a room that's bare except for an old photograph on the wall and a bowl of fruit on the table. A fire burns in the bowl. While Sister Rosetta Tharpe sings "Precious Memories" on the soundtrack, while the man twiddles his thumbs and nods and dozes, the fire spreads, burning everything, consuming nothing.

This is Gideon (Paul Butler), who now resides in Los Angeles but has deep roots in the South. He's a man who has set his house in order, and with such a firm hand that to this day his son Sam (Richard Brooks) can't get anyone to call him by name. Although Sam is himself a homeowner and father, he is still known to everyone, including his wife, as Babe Brother.

Into this setting of old-fashioned warmth, intimacy and stifling virtue steps

Harry (Danny Glover), a friend from back home. Of course Gideon and his wife (Mary Alice) invite him to stay—and so they open their door to everything they have tried for years to shut out. For all his charm and exaggerated courtesy, Harry turns out to be the embodiment of corn liquor and hot music, of knife fights and whoring and gambling with marked cards. He is, above all, the spirit of suppressed rage, focused on white people but directed against safer targets, closer to hand.

What's wonderful about all this—flat-out wonderful—is the lightness of touch with which Burnett transforms his naturalistic characters and setting into the stuff of fable. The plot proceeds as if by sympathetic magic, until it reaches a moment of bloodletting during a thunderstorm, under a full moon; but all the while, every turn of phrase in the dialogue, every teacup in the decor, brings with it the delight of recognition. On the side of realism, *To Sleep With Anger* offers as thick a slice of African-American life as anybody has put on the screen, ever. On the side of the supernatural, it has Danny Glover, who can barely contain his joy in the role Burnett has written for him.

Since this column must revert in a moment to the mode of Yes, but, let me linger just enough to note a second great pleasure of *To Sleep With Anger*. Besides being a thoroughly good movie, it is a breakthrough for Burnett, who has spent some twenty years on the film-festival circuit. All that time, he suffered for want of an adequate budget and a cast capable of realizing his ideas; and even now, with those conditions satisfied, he has found a distributor only after the industry delayed unconscionably. That's why, at the end of *To Sleep With Anger*, I felt a triple sense of relief. Gideon's family had been exorcised; I had been allowed an entire film's worth of pure enjoyment; and Charles Burnett, an artist of immense talent, had just possibly been freed at last.

Commom Quest, Fall 1996

The Great White Hype

Back when the world's most famous boxer was named Daniel Mendoza, who fought as "Mendoza the Jew"—this was two centuries ago, in England—the stereotypes under which Jewish men labored were much like those heaped upon black men today. Popular literature was full of them: brutish, dirty, criminal, ignorant, indigent, oversexed Jews. Only if the "criminal" part paid off did anything change. Then "indigent" and "dirty" dropped away, and the Jew became showy and tasteless instead, with the remaining insults holding constant.

The interchangeability of the social masks assigned to blacks and Jews—an intuition of their interchangeability, anyway—provides one of the teasing pleasures of *The Great White Hype.* Directed by Reginald Hudlin from a script by Tony Hendra and Ron Shelton, and released all-too briefly in spring 1996, the film celebrates entrepreneurial cunning as embodied in a showy, tasteless, oversexed, criminal boxing promoter known as the Reverend Fred Sultan (Samuel L. Jackson). The Rev. Fred dresses in sequined turbans with matching scarves, cavorts in motel rooms with Girl Scout troops, greets creditors with professions of love in lieu of payment, and renders his partners docile with a reminder that even his cigar lighter is shaped like a gun. Except for this latter characteristic—the threat of physical violence having faded away from anti-Semitic stereotypes since the days of Daniel Mendoza—one almost might imagine the Rev. Fred to be a rich Jew.

I think the possibility of Judaicizing the Rev. Fred is worth considering, since social masks and expectations are the very substance of *The Great White Hype*. The plot turns on the readiness of a great portion of the American public to imagine that a bum might turn into a heavyweight contender, provided he's melanin-deprived. The bum in this case is Terry Conklin (Peter Berg), a one-time club fighter who now enjoys demigod status in Cleveland by virtue of singing in a band called Massive Head Wound. The name vividly suggests what Conklin might suffer should he climb into the ring with any professional, let alone the Rev. Fred's champion, James "The Grim Reaper" Roper (Damon Wayans). But to millions of Americans—not one of whom is a racist, you understand—Conklin somehow seems a wonderfully plausible challenger, once the Rev. Fred signs him to a contract.

Thus does the Rev. Fred spread his veil of illusion across the minds of white supremacists. And who are his principal assistants in this deception? Jews, of course. Within the film's clever scheme, Jews are dealers in imagery who mediate between the Rev. Fred's black world and white America. Such is the conflict-laden role assumed by the Rev. Fred's public-relations agent and flunkie, Sol (Jon Lovitz), and his self-appointed nemesis, a crusading journalist named Mitchell Kane (Jeff Goldblum).

For our purposes, the film's most revealing moment comes in the wake of a press conference at which the Rev. Fred has sprung Terry Conklin upon an eyeball-rolling corps of boxing reporters. One of these skeptics—a white man—follows the Rev. Fred right out of the conference room and down the hall of the MGM Grand in Las Vegas, protesting all the way, until the wily promoter wheels on him. Unloosing a flurry of accusations that are as multi-directional as a champion's punches, the Rev. Fred calls the sportswriter every-thing from a racist to an Uncle Tom. "I can't be an Uncle Tom," the writer objects. "I'm a Jew."

"Sol," says the Rev. Fred to his employee. "Can Jews be Uncle Toms?"

Says Sol to the man who signs his checks, "Sho we can."

A marvel of concision. In three words, the movie acknowledges that money, more than skin color, defines social position in America today. In those same three words, the movie also acknowledges that skin color, and other marks of caste, continue to matter. Yes, Jews can be Uncle Toms—unlike, let's say, white Presbyterians.

Should this interpretation of the dialogue sound too much like op-ed pun-ditry, then consider the casting of this little joke. The Jew who is so well pre-pared to Tom is played by Jon Lovitz, a comic actor who came to prominence on *Saturday Night Live* in the role of a pathological liar. One look at his fleshy features—the eyes perpetually scanning for threats of exposure, the nose turned sharply toward any advantage, the rubbery lips twisting readily around the most improbable statements—and the audience not only expects insincerity from Lovitz but longs for it. His lies are his trademark; so, by agreeing to be an Uncle Tom, the Lovitz character doesn't deny anything essential about himself (such as his Jewishness) but confirms his essence as the guy who goes along to get along. If it's possible to rescue some virtue from Tomming—the traditional weapon of hard-pressed but unheroic people—then Lovitz at that moment carries off the trick.

As for Samuel L. Jackson: before he took on the role of the Rev. Fred, he forever fixed himself in moviegoers' minds as the Bible-quoting hitman of *Pulp Fiction.* Everybody knows that Samuel L. Jackson will cheerfully request a bite of your Big Kahuna burger and congratulate you on its tastiness, just before he blows off your head. So, in *The Great White Hype,* nobody has to present evidence of the Rev. Fred's rumored depredations; it's enough for the actor to smile in order for the character to lower your blood temperature. Like state power, economic power rests upon an ultimate threat of murder, which is why Jon Lovitz (or anybody) jumps to play Tom. But in *The Great White Hype,* the threat rises to the surface, because economic power here is colored—literally—by violence. The Rev. Fred is not merely a boss but also a black stereotype: in the words of *Pulp Fiction,* a Bad Motherfucker.

And yet, though the Rev. Fred may seem bad to the Jewish Uncle Tom, he is himself something of a Tom to the white world at large. "What would happen," the Rev. Fred asks at one point, as he watches films of black fighters drubbing white men, "what would happen if politics was decided by fighting ability?" To which the whitest man on screen, the hotel owner (Corbin Bernsen), replies smoothly, "We'd learn how to fight." A nicely barbed answer—because the Rev. Fred knows that his empire, though real enough, is only an island within white America. In fact, that's the point of the film: the Rev. Fred can get away with promoting Terry Conklin as a heavyweight contender only because white America is so powerful, powerful enough to fantasize ruling every corner of the world, even one so small as a boxing ring.

The Rev. Fred makes his profit by flattering several million white bosses; this is Tomming done with flair, with grandeur, which is perhaps the reason why Sol's "Sho we can" rings with a note of pride. Sol knows he has something in common with his boss. And the other main Jew in the film, the one played by Jeff Goldblum? He, too, imagines sharing an aspect of the Rev. Fred's "black" character—not his inner Tom, but his outward badness.

Compared to Lovitz's persona, which grows out of the image of the wheedling ghetto Jew, Goldblum's brings together some of the more volatile, and attractive, images of the modern Jewish man, as found in America and

Israel. Goldblum is tall and rangy; physically powerful enough to have performed acrobatics in *The Fly*; handsome enough to have been linked with a goddess such as Geena Davis (on and off the screen), wiggy enough to have posed a physical threat (in the company of Laurence Fishburne) in *Deep Cover*. Often cast as someone who is brainy but impractical, Goldblum may play a goof on screen, but a goof who can rise to heroics (as in *Independence Day*, in which, accompanied by Will Smith, he flies a spacecraft smack into the hold of an alien mother ship). This persona could have become current only after the Six Day War; which means, in domestic terms, after the battles between blacks and Jews in New York over control of the schools, after white flight and the thuggery of Meir Kahane.

Following a certain moment in the late 1960s, certain Jews both attacked black people (using a moralistic tone) and tried to imitate a stereotype about them (their physical daring). In *The Great White Hype*, Goldblum recapitulates that history. The character he plays first crusades against the Rev. Fred, then is seduced into joining him, then (overestimating his own toughness) tries to supplant the Reverend. This being a comedy, the character merely undermines himself, as do all of the Rev. Fred's antagonists. This being a comedy directed by a black man, the Rev. Fred's triumph symbolically reproduces that of Reginald Hudlin, who has carved out a cinematic realm of his own amid the white producers and distributors.

Directed by someone who successfully lives between two worlds, *The Great White Hype* is about another black man who is a go-between success—about him, and about his conflicts and harmonies with Jews who are themselves intermediaries. They are secret sharers, all. But of course, that's only part of the story.

Do the Right Thing

n the days of the Harlem Renaissance, when Langston Hughes was being attacked in some quarters for writing about black America's lower classes, Carl Van Vechten remarked jestingly to the poet, "You and I are the only colored people who really love *niggers.*"

As it was with Hughes, so it has been with Spike Lee. He began his career only half a dozen years ago with the remarkably accomplished student film *Joe's Bed-Stuy Barbershop: We Cut Heads.* No one who saw it could ignore either Lee's talent or his love for the common citizens of the Brooklyn ghetto—not just the upward-striving, the politically involved, the gifted, but the whole range of street-corner society. In *She's Gotta Have It,* Lee himself portrays the fast-talking Mars Blackmon, who won't let anything so small as sexual jealousy come between him and a fellow African-American. In *School Daze,* the entire film depends on the conflict between black people who are plainly, emphatically black and those who are wannabes—that is, who want to be white. Now, in *Do the Right Thing,* you can still hear the echoes of Mars Blackmon's sentiment in the catch-phrase of Buggin Out (Giancarlo Esposito), whose standard parting line is, "Stay black."

A love like that separates loyalists from sellouts. It also animates certain troubled characters with a talent for making themselves unpopular. Jesters mock and receive favors in return; satirists love, and that seems to be Spike Lee's hard fate.

Do the Right Thing is Lee's most complex, heartfelt and disturbing film to date, a drama about racism that is more shockingly outspoken than any I've seen since David Mamet's great, and neglected, *Edmond*. Needless to say, the film depicts white bigotry with all due contempt. The best of the white characters—who seems a very good man indeed—is still ready to scream "nigger" when all else fails; the worst are willing to kill. The melanin-impaired will therefore feel uncomfortable with this film, and with good reason. But so, too, might the black community. Lee loves his fellow African-Americans, but he also portrays them as political good-for-nothings, long on talk and short on action, except when their actions are misguided. In *Do the Right Thing*, nobody does.

Set on a single block in Bedford-Stuyvesant, *Do the Right Thing* follows about two dozen characters through a very hot summer's day, from a morning when interracial civility is already strained to a night when all hell breaks loose. The structure is episodic; brief, seemingly self-enclosed dramas follow one another rapidly, with two characters helping to frame and judge the action. The first of these is Mister Señor Love Daddy (Sam Jackson), disc jockey of an extremely local radio station, who observes the neighborhood through his living-room window and broadcasts what he sees, along with the finest in black music. The second framing character is Da Mayor (Ossie Davis), an old gentleman who rambles up and down the block all day. Da Mayor is courtly and kindhearted; he's also a drunk. To some of the younger people, he is a figure of fun. To Mother Sister (Ruby Dee), the block's reigning older woman, he is a contemptible bum. It is Da Mayor who enunciates the sentiment of the title, "Always do the right thing," in addressing his neighbor Mookie (Spike Lee). And in fact, Mookie tries hard to follow that advice. The effort he makes, and the degree to which he fails, will be the subject of debate for everyone who sees the film.

When we first see him, Mookie is at home with his sister Jade (Joie Lee), who is running out of patience with him as an unpaying roommate. As far as she is concerned, Mookie should get an apartment of his own, preferably with his girl-friend, Tina (Rosie Perez), and his infant son. Apparently, Mookie lays eyes on Tina only when he wants to do the nasty. Then, pleading the need to work, he disappears again from her life, proceeding in the general direction of his place of employment, Sal's Famous Pizzeria.

The whole neighborhood seems to meet at Sal's, and has done so for twenty-five years. In the words of Sal himself (Danny Aiello), "These people grew up on my food. And I'm very proud of that." Bearlike and bluff, Sal enjoys his business, enjoys his customers (most of them) and treats Mookie with the same combination of amused tolerance and restrained sarcasm that Mookie uses with him. There's even a grudging respect between Sal and his deliveryman—and that is a problem for Mookie. He can deal with Sal's son Pino (John Turturro), an outspoken bigot who spends the day urging honest labor on Mookie while avoiding his own work. Since Pino has declared himself an enemy of all black people, Mookie can respond in kind, with a clear conscience. But Sal is not simply the enemy. He's humane enough to command some loyalty from Mookie, who then is caught between his white boss and his black friends and neighbors.

Mookie's conflict begins with a visit from Buggin Out, owner of the fastest mouth and strangest hairstyle on the block. In search of a fresh shot of adrenaline, Buggin Out picks a fight with Sal over the pizzeria's Wall of Fame: a display of photographs of celebrated Italian-Americans. Where are the photos of black people? Has Sal never heard of Malcolm X and Michael Jordan? Buggin Out blusters; Sal boils over; Mookie gets the unhappy task of escorting his friend outside. Mookie tries to keep the incident on a personal level, complaining that Buggin Out is giving him trouble at his job. Buggin Out absolves Mookie but says goodbye with a meaningful "Stay black."

The conflict worsens with the appearance in the pizzeria of Radio Raheem (Bill Nunn). Powerfully built, inarticulate, able to peel the paint off walls with a single glare, Raheem takes his nickname from his constant companion, the biggest boom-box in Brooklyn. He stalks the neighborhood on a single-minded mission: making sure that every resident of Bed-Stuy hears the soothing tones of "Fight the Power" by Public Enemy. This is the only song he will play—in fact, the only one he will allow anyone to hear. With a heart-stopping glower and the push of a lever on his mighty box, Raheem drowns out all other music in the neighborhood. Sal threatens to throw him out of the pizzeria.

Now there are two people on the block with a grudge against Sal. A third joins their ranks when Pino gratuitously insults Smiley, the neighborhood idiot (Roger Guenveur Smith). Ordinarily, Smiley goes about preaching love and selling hand-decorated photographs of Martin Luther King Jr. and Malcolm X. Once he's been chased down the block, though, Smiley, too, is ready to take action against Sal's Famous.

Consider Mookie's dilemma. On one side, there are the protesters—his own people, even though they can't agree on what they're protesting, even though Mookie actually likes only one of the three. On the other side, there is Sal. Though Mookie *almost* likes him, he is white, he's the boss, and he is backed by a police force that's willing to kill black people. As the long, hot day comes to a boil, Mookie is given one moment to decide how to do the right thing. And that's the moment when Sal announces his own, antithetical philosophy: "You do what you gotta."

So *Do the Right Thing* comes down to an argument between morality and necessity—or rather, alleged necessity. It is a film about conflicting loyalties and evaded responsibilities; about the way our society values a white man's property over a black man's life; about the terrible gap between a community's need to mobilize itself and an individual's political acumen. To call these themes and their treatment inflammatory would be no more than the literal truth. More to the point, Spike Lee makes them lively and vivid, funny and exasperating as well.

His style is deliberately juiced-up. The editing is fast, with dialogue sometimes crosscut on each line; the acting is often more stylized than natural. When Sal and his family first appear, for example, they seem to use three hand gestures for each spoken word. As in the past, Lee often points his camera head-on to the actors and has them talk straight into the lens. When even that method seems too oblique, he begins the shot with a fast dolly, as if the camera were a speeding Pontiac, jolting to a stop before somebody who refuses to get out of the way. Add to all this the episodic structure and the tendency of some of the characters to act out, and the film at times takes on an almost cartoonlike quality.

In other words, the style closely matches the characters' thoughts, which tend toward big, simplified outlines—the contours of a Hanna-Barbera cartoon, rather than a Disney animation. *Do the Right Thing* is very smart about portraying politics at this very dumb level. On the street, as Lee knows, there is little reasoned argument but a lot of totemism. Everything depends on which song is coming out of your radio, which photo is on the wall of your shop, which brand of sneaker you're wearing. The mere presence of a Boston Celtics jersey on a Bed-Stuy street is an insult to the residents—and if you don't know that, you obviously don't belong on the street in the first place. This, may heaven help us, is real American politics—which explains the inclusion of simple-minded Smiley in the plot and his ghastly moment of triumph at the climax.

Many of the reactions to the film, I imagine, will be on Smiley's level. Already Lee has had to explain that *Do the Right Thing* is not based on the Howard Beach case—that is, on white vigilantism—but is instead about the background to police violence. In some quarters, official murder is always alleged, never real. In those same quarters editorialists will probably call Lee's film an incitement to riot. (Sure—and racism, as Reagan informed us, is caused by civil rights leaders.) Among more open-minded viewers, though, *Do the Right Thing* will be seen as an incitement to thought. I hope the sidewalks outside the movie theaters this summer will be filled with people arguing over the rights and wrongs of Mookie's actions and the meanings of the two texts—one by Dr. King, the other by Malcolm X—that close the film.

Crooklyn

S pike Lee's *Crooklyn* feels very much like a first film—which I mean as a compliment. Having long resisted the impulse to be sincere and autobiographical, Lee has now taken the risk, at rather an advanced age, of filming a rambling memoir about his family and neighbors in Brooklyn during the early 1970s. The author of the screen story is his sister, Joie Susannah Lee; the screenplay is by Joie Susannah, Spike and their brother Cinque. A cozy collaboration, you might think—certainly too cozy for the majority of film reviewers, who have greeted *Crooklyn* with a yawn and a puzzled question: "But what's it *about?*" Friends, readers, colleagues: *Crooklyn* is about emotional situations that should be familiar to a great many viewers, and that Spike Lee himself has brought up before, in *Mo' Better Blues*, a film that played out as one long evasion of the issue. In *Crooklyn,* though, he has opened up these feelings with an unforced honesty and warmth that not only set the picture apart from most others in the theaters today but also establish this movie as a new beginning.

Set on a block of row houses in New York's Bedford-Stuyvesant section, the film tells a common-enough story about lower-middle-class life grown tense from economic strain. We see the predictable moments: the quarrels between mother and father over who's paying the bills; the spats and pranks among the children, interspersed with the kids' cockeyed epiphanies about the adult world. As usual in these cases, the film devotes lavish attention to re-creating, with gape-mouthed fascination, the costumes of the era; to mocking the old television shows; to wallowing in the music. And yet, I believe Lee achieves the remarkable feat of making all this seem fresh—as if he were a chef serving up a revelatory plate of scrambled eggs, or were Thelonious Monk discovering that twelve bars of standard walking bass can become "Misterioso."

In part, the freshness comes from the film's subject matter, which is as new to the screen as the themes are old. True to its origins in Bed-Stuy, *Crooklyn* may be the first movie ever to link sexual awakening to shoplifting. It's also one of the very few films to evoke the mixture of love, fear and rebellion that may be instilled in African-American children by their mothers. We've seen plenty of black mammies on the screen before, not to mention black motherfuckers. *Crooklyn,* though, has the distinction of showing us a black mother, period— one whose strength is not the sentimentalized stuff of legend but *strength,* with all the difficulties that entails.

The story: It's summer, and 10-year-old Troy (Zelda Harris), the only daughter in the Carmichael family, hangs out with her friends on the block, studies the adults, gets into quarrels with her older brother Clinton (Carlton Williams) and worries about her parents. Her mother, Carolyn (Alfre Woodard), a schoolteacher, is getting worn out with work in and out of the house and especially with bringing home the family's only paycheck. In the past, her husband, Woody (Delroy Lindo), made a living as a pianist and composer; but the market for jazz has dried up, just as Woody reaches that stage when you either grow into an artist of lasting value or else remain a journeyman. Now he's desperate. So is Carolyn. The two of them love and understand each other, and yet their conflict is insoluble. That's what we see as adult viewers. As for Troy, she at first sees the conflict mostly as a parental dispute over what the children eat and how they should be disciplined. Then, in fits and starts, she begins to see more.

Crooklyn is fresh in what it shows to Troy (and to us); but it's also fresh in how it makes us see. Remember "Misterioso"? Monk's walking bass isn't *entirely* standard in that composition. There's a twist in it; and so too is there a twist in Spike Lee's work. He plays the modernist game (unknown to the great majority of current directors) of letting the film remind you of its own making. So, for example, the opening shot of *Crooklyn* begins with a kid helping his friends start a footrace. He calls "On your mark, get set," and on "go" the camera starts to move, as if cued by the actor on screen. Another example: For the scenes in which little Troy leaves Brooklyn to stay with relatives in Georgia, Lee switches from a normal camera lens to the type that's used for certain wide-screen processes. Because the film is not projected widescreen, everything comes out looking pinched and elongated. A perfect match: the character trapped in a strange social environment; the image caught in an alien mechanical environment. I could multiply examples, though the important point is not that Lee wants to play this modernist game but that he does it with such self-assurance. The trick with the anamorphic lens does become tiresome (because obtrusive) by the end of the Georgia sequence. Otherwise, though, these self-reflexive moments seem to come to Lee as if they were second nature, helping him to engage the audience in a single gesture with the surface of the story and its emotional depths.

The cinematographer for *Crooklyn* is Arthur Jafa (*Daughters of the Dust*), who gives the film softer colors and a dreamier look than you'd see from Lee's usual cameraman, Ernest Dickerson. The soundtrack of wall-to-wall *Soul Train* hits is filled out evocatively by composer Terence Blanchard. Woody's piano solo is played by Sir Roland Hanna. Woody himself is played as a thoughtful, sweet-natured man who is outwardly strong but inwardly uncertain—a marvelous creation by Delroy Lindo, till now best known for his portrayal of West Indian Archie in Lee's *Malcolm X*. Alfre Woodard, as ever, manages to fill every inch of the screen for every second she's in front of the camera. Just a blink from her hooded eyes or a deep murmur from her pursed lips, and Carolyn's whole life opens before you. A marvelous remission from acting—as is the case with young Zelda Harris, who carries on as Troy with miraculous self-abandon.

And yet the critics insist: "What's it *about*?" To them, and to you, I advise, "Go see *Crooklyn*." At first sight, you'll find it handsome to look at. Upon second thought, you'll realize that its meanderings are only apparent, concealing an elegantly constructed design. Then, after mulling it over for a day or two, you may begin to feel grateful for the self-confidence with which Spike Lee has directed *Crooklyn*, allowing the film to stand back slightly rather than jumping down your throat. You get the pleasure of discovering on your own what this movie is about.

Election

n *Variety*, where industry rumors congeal into analysis and analysis hardens to consensus, the news is bad for filmmakers like Alexander Payne. "Small Pix Perplex Big Studios," reads a headline in the May 31 issue. The pix in question are the few recent films that were made relatively cheaply (for less than $10 million) and then released by studios more habituated to handling $50 million products. According to *Variety*, the result has been disappointment: for Buena Vista over *Rushmore*, for Sony over *Go* and for Paramount over Payne's *Election*, all of which "grossed less than $18 million at the box office—well below expectations."

As a *Nation* reader, you will refuse to pity anyone who trifles with such sums. But then, as a self-interested moviegoer, you might take seriously the studios' disappointment. Imagine yourself responsible for a production budget of, say, $8 million. Add the costs of advertising and promotion, and you might spend $15 million to release a clever little picture—with your cut of an $18 million box office amounting to some $9 million. That's why, as much as you might love *Election*, you probably would avoid the next project that reminded you of it.

So how are clever little pictures to reach an audience, if big studios shy away? *Variety*'s writer, Andrew Hindes, speaks for the consensus when he says the answer lies with "minimajors" such as Miramax (a division of Buena Vista/Disney). These companies market films more economically than do the studios; they also "are more oriented toward painstaking publicity-driven campaigns." But this is precisely where I begin to fear for Alexander Payne, knowing that his previous film, *Citizen Ruth*, was a Miramax release.

Miramax does well with uplifting fare, such as *Life Is Beautiful* (feel good about the Holocaust!), *Shakespeare in Love* (feel good about Shakespeare!) or *Kids* (feel good that you're not one of those rotten kids!). The company seems less comfortable when it sets about marketing something like *Citizen Ruth*. That film is a nails-on-blackboard comedy about one of the undeserving poor who does not hesitate to sell her body to the highest bidder. Even worse: The part of her body that interests the bidders is her fetus. The protagonist, having stumbled into the midst of pro-choice and antiabortion activists, discovers she can play them against one another for money—which is, in Alexander Payne's shocking view, the commodity of most use to a poor person.

I saw *Citizen Ruth* during the first week of its New York run and can recall being accosted at the multiplex door by a Miramax representative who was handing out audience survey forms. "We know this film is controversial," she told us as we entered. "Please give us your opinion, so we can know how to tell other people about *Citizen Ruth*." Such was the puzzle that Miramax had posed for itself; and I don't believe it ever figured out the answer.

I dredge up this history not to berate the company but to suggest that, mounds of publicity to the contrary, "Miramax" is not the equivalent of "Abracadabra." It's merely the name of a business, run by people with particular tastes and talents. Yet when this one firm is made into the paragon of the "independent" distributor (as it tends to be, in the *New York Times* as much as the trade papers), its preference for the cheerful, the sentimental, the just-slightly-daring begins to turn into an industry standard, to be emulated by the former October, Fine Line, Fox Searchlight and Screen Gems (divisions, respectively, of Universal, Time Warner, Twentieth Century Fox and Sony).

Citizen Ruth did not fit that mini-major standard. Now, it seems, Payne's new film, *Election*, has failed to fit the standard for big studio releases. It has received some excellent reviews and is becoming fodder for Op-Ed writers; but *Variety* says the picture is a disappointment, and so (to the industry) it must be.

By a curious coincidence (as Truffaut used to say), Payne's dilemma is mirrored within *Election*. This comedy of resentment, based upon a book by Tom Perrotta and written for the screen by Payne and Jim Taylor, happens to concern a young woman's relentless striving to be number one (like Coca-Cola, to use her own analogy). It's also about the growing desperation of one of her high school teachers, as he understands he'll never even be Pepsi.

As you may already know, the film's bootstrapper is eleventh grader Tracy Flick (Reese Witherspoon), who in her self-improving, self-advancing drive is determined to become the next school president. She's a girl who can't leave herself alone, or anyone else for that matter. You'll notice she's always changing her hairstyle, pushing it toward some never-to-be-attained ideal. She busies herself similarly with people, who must perpetually be rearranged into props for Tracy Flick's career.

I've noticed that most commentators on *Election* have dwelt on Tracy's awfulness—a quality that does, in fact, echo throughout the picture like the twang of a rubber band, or the Nebraska accent that Reese Witherspoon affects. But *Election* also acknowledges the anxiety that lies beneath Tracy's enameled pertness. You get a sense of the trouble when she's collecting nominating signatures for her candidacy, using as bait a bowl filled with sticks of chewing gum. When a kid grabs a handful in passing, Tracy suddenly drops her bright smile to chase the miscreant halfway down the hall. "It's one per customer!" she shouts—and if you've been paying attention, you understand she's angry because she couldn't afford more than that. This campaign has stretched her budget to the limit.

The dirty secret of *Election* is that Tracy has every right to bear a grudge. She knows there is no such thing as fairness at George Washington Carver High School (how's that for a striver's name?)—particularly because the civics teacher and student government adviser, Jim McAllister (Matthew Broderick), treats her as if she were something that sticks out and so must be pounded down.

The film is not too delicate to point out that the thing that really demands pounding lies between McAllister's legs. But out of a frustration he can't even admit to, this man who no longer notices his wife (or the dusty Ford he drives, or the shirts that will disintegrate with two more washings) chooses Tracy as the symbol of all evil. He decides to rig the election against her. To begin, he recruits an opponent: the school's football hero, a young man from a wealthy family, who radiates a bland beneficence. Why not? He already enjoys, without effort, everything Tracy is scrambling to get.

I will not dwell on the identity and motives of the third candidate in the election (the teen lesbian anarchist to whom *Election* gives its heart). Nor will I detail Payne's unerring sense of place (which was evident before in *Citizen Ruth*, with its landscape of power lines, sheds and chain-link fences) or his use of the garbage can as visual motif. My purpose is to address the realistic basis of Tracy's rage to succeed, and the corresponding realism of McAllister's rage against her.

Translate a student-government presidency into film-industry terms. It might be likened to a distribution deal with Miramax. That's what Tracy (considered as a filmmaker) would want at this stage in her career: validation by a mini-major, with a shot later on at the big time. And what in *Election* represents the big time? It's the worldly goods of the football hero—goods that ostensibly can be earned, but that more often are attained by accident of birth. Let's say *Election* is the story of how Tracy, against considerable odds and at great cost to her soul, gets her Miramax contract. By the end, she might even be set to nail down a deal with a major.

And here's Alexander Payne, who has gone the same route—though Miramax, for him, must have offered little satisfaction, and to Paramount (it seems) he's no football hero. Caught in between, he's now given us a howling comedy that passes itself off as a high school pageant. Laugh if you dare.

Rushmore

Max Fischer stands five feet three inches tall, weighs 112 pounds and is 15 years old. Those figures don't give us his true measure, but we might keep them in mind, since they're offered by no less a personage than a millionaire. He is Herman Blume (about six one, 200 pounds, maybe 50 years old)—a man who issues that description of Max in order to have him arrested. Max had been Blume's only friend.

That's what can happen in October, when the people in *Rushmore* suddenly find themselves facing the wrong way, as if turned about by a nasty gust. Characters spy on one another in the autumn chill, send poison-pen letters, snitch to bosses about workers, to wives about husbands. Blume's car loses its brakes (that's Max's doing), and Max is assaulted—stoned by kids dressed up as wizards and pirates. Tricks temporarily beat out treats. But in a work of art as wholly imagined as *Rushmore*, something fresh is always about to blow in, with a force as impersonal as the weather, in a pattern as human as fingerprints.

As you've guessed by now, the eye of the storm and prime generator of whorls is Max, who begins the film as a tenth grader at the elite Rushmore Academy. There he is, amid the high-budget oaks and bricklayer's Gothic, unalterably outfitted in a blue blazer, tie and khaki slacks. He looks so much like a prep-school prig that Blume, on first meeting him, can't bear to admit he sees through the act.

Blume must feel out of place in the world, because he spots a similar oddness in Max. In a glance, he takes in the laboriously relaxed gait, which makes Max resemble a teenage Jack Benny; he notes the genial patter, as hollow as a stiff's at the Yale Club, when he asks for a "dividend" on his drink. Then there's the hair. Max wears it brushed low on his forehead—as if he weren't a kid, but a 40-year-old who's pretending to youth. Were Blume to think deeply about the hair, he might realize that Max isn't, as he claims, the son of a neurosurgeon. His dad is a barber (one who's homey enough to be played by Seymour Cassel), and Max is a scholarship student who has begun the term on "sudden-death academic probation."

Though Max identifies with Rushmore so thoroughly that he leads, manages or fronts for every student activity, he's about to flunk out—a problem he doesn't seem able to address through conventional means, such as study. Stuck in his big-man-on-campus pose, he knows only how to lose himself in further distractions. So he spends September writing and directing his own theatrical version of *Serpico*, presented by The Max Fischer Players, meanwhile falling in love for the first time. Maybe his choice of love object reveals Max's deeper needs. He fixes on a kindergarten teacher.

Her name is Rosemary Cross (Olivia Williams), and, like Blume, she manages not to laugh at Max, despite the solemn manner that helps conceal his braces. Perhaps Miss Cross is so generous because she'd been looking for a Max. A smooth-faced young woman who was recently widowed, she came to teach at Rushmore because that's where her late husband went to school. Now she's picked up a trace of him, in a would-be grown-up with a 15-year-old's body.

Not that *Rushmore* would put the matter so bluntly. Directed by the astonishingly talented Wes Anderson and written by him with Owen Wilson, the film has been thought through so completely that it can afford to proceed through hints and ellipses, momentary acts of misdirection and accompanying sleights-of-hand. What are we to make of the hideous family portrait that's displayed with the opening credits? It shows a bilious Blume (Bill Murray) in the company of two grimacing teenagers and a pinch-faced wife. Many minutes pass before we see that painting again. It flashes across the screen momentarily when Blume, drunk at home, shuts his eyes. Now we know how he sees his life; now we've solved another piece of the film's puzzle.

It took me two viewings to appreciate how intricately the parts were fitted together. At first, *Rushmore* seemed to me an amiable but slight coming-of-age story, animated by two memorable performances. As Blume, Bill Murray acts even with his eyelids; every blink suggests untold convolutions of thought, which emerge only after being pursed back by the lips. Is there such a thing as a helium balloon with *gravitas*? Then that would be Murray, who achieves poignance without once cadging sympathy, who gives off a radiance of drollery not by striving to be funny but by sharing with us his amusement at Max. The latter is played by young Jason Schwartzman in an act verging on self-sacrifice. Only someone who is still dangerously close to adolescence could show us Max's vulnerability: how, without warning, the 10-year-old in him can querulously break through his impersonation of a middle-aged stockbroker. Schwartzman is willing to put himself through such a moment on camera; he's willing to inhabit every pomposity of Max, and to take them all seriously, though he knows they're funny. And he's willing to wait till the very end of the film, when Olivia Williams briefly lifts off his thick, black-framed glasses, to let us glimpse an unguarded face that might be his own—or Max's, when he grows up a little more. Williams, by the way, is pretty good herself; but Murray and Schwartzman make such strong impressions that maybe I can be forgiven for passing over her performance, as I first passed over the complexities of *Rushmore*.

Then came that second viewing, when curtains began to draw back in my mind, as they do on screen to introduce the passing months. With a theatrical flourish, we're in September, then October, and so forth into the new year, when the weather becomes brisk but clement, and The Max Fischer Players put on a stirring new production. A dozen of Max's friends and acquaintances get together for the show. Where did they come from? How did Wes Anderson introduce them so effortlessly in the earlier sequences, individuate them so clearly, unite them for a climax as natural as the coming of January? Awakening at last, I looked at all those characters dancing and chatting in a high school auditorium and understood *Rushmore* wasn't slight at all.

Unlike its name, the film isn't monumental. But big forces run through it: class envy, ambition, grief for the dead, yearnings for romance, the bitterest self-loathing and, most powerful of all, a healing conviviality, best represented by a beret-wearing little girl named Margaret Yang. What a wonder *she* is! I can't guess Margaret's height and weight, so you may have to see *Rushmore* yourself to judge her effect. But don't blink. When Max finally catches on to her, his reaction lasts only a second, recorded in a cutaway close-up. You can see the whole world shift in his face; and yet that moment, too, is only one more piece of the puzzle.

Matinee

One of my happiest childhood memories concerns *The Beginning of the End*, a movie about giant radioactive grasshoppers. Each looked to be as long as an eighteen-wheel rig; in a herd, they made a terrible racket and had a tendency to destroy civilization. The best thing about the grasshoppers, though, was their line of march, straight toward Chicago. When the Army officer who was monitoring them reported they had reached 71st and Jeffrey, I screamed, not out of fear but with pride. The bugs had smashed their way to *our* movie house!

So I recognize the excitement felt by young Gene (Simon Fenton) in *Matinee*, when he learns that a horror movie is going to have its premiere at *his* movie house in Key West. Even better, the debut of *Mant* ("Half Man . . . Half Ant . . . All Terror!!!") will feature a personal appearance by the producer himself, the self-appointed Master of Fear, Lawrence Woolsey.

Little things like that can make you feel your life has significance—especially in 1962, when the world might be overrun at any moment by radioactive mutants. But for Gene—and for the audience of *Matinee*—the real delight is that Lawrence Woolsey turns out to be a bigger personality than his own giant insect. He's played by John Goodman, who is perhaps the most likable man in America, as well as one of the few actors today who can fill a movie screen. I don't mean that he's fat; I mean that Goodman effortlessly projects large-scale emotions while making them seem intimate and naturalistic. He can enlist you on his side while admitting he's lying to you, sneak a handful of popcorn out of the box on your lap and make you feel he's just trying to be a good host. A middle-American Falstaff with no wars to fight and no Prince Hal to reject him, he's an infinitely reassuring presence—which is fortunate, in the context of *Matinee*.

As it turns out, the horror film within the film is opening in the midst of the Cuban missile crisis. Are the already jittery citizens of Key West primed for *Mant*? Or does the prospect of global nuclear destruction amount to unfair competition? That's about as far as Lawrence Woolsey gets in thinking through the relationship between his product and the bigger world. Happily, *Matinee* is ingenious enough to go a step or two further.

Written by Charles Haas—who also gave us the wonderfully funny screenplay for *Gremlins 2*—*Matinee* begins on an all too familiar note of nostalgic amusement. We see the American past as it's been re-created in *Grease* and *Happy Days*, as a site of lovable kitsch. Very quickly, though, reality intrudes. Young Gene learns that his father, a seaman, has been dispatched toward Cuba. The movie screen (in *Matinee*, not *Mant*) fills with the face of John Kennedy, declaring his willingness to blow up the world. For a long time—long enough to risk losing the lighter-minded members of the audience—*Matinee* baldly separates the subtext from the text of cold war horror movies, with an effect that is deliberately not funny. Soldiers take up positions on the beach; civilians rampage through the supermarket, as if hoards of food would do them any good. They can't seem to grasp the magnitude of the danger; hardly anybody can, except for Sandra (Lisa Jakub), a girl in Gene's school. She refuses to participate in an air-raid drill and is hustled off to the principal's office, screaming all the way.

It's easy to imagine Sandra today. She's in her mid-40s and is probably reading this magazine. In 1962, though, as imagined by Charlie Haas and the director, Joe Dante, she is still young enough that large chunks of her opinions sound borrowed from her parents. She's a solemn little broomstick of a girl, whose willingness to protest nevertheless comes off as admirable, and is further redeemed by her kindness. Though she has no use for the military, Sandra readily offers her sympathy to Gene, the Navy brat—which makes her a better person than most of the budding activists I knew back then.

In fact, like Sandra, most of the characters in *Matinee* turn out to be a little better than you'd expect, despite their being slightly ridiculous. Only a few are reduced to being the butt of a joke. The rest get to lead surprisingly full fictional lives—with the fullest, of course, being Lawrence Woolsey's. I like *Matinee* because at the end, Woolsey lets young Gene in on a secret: "Grown-ups are makin' it up as they go along, just like you do." That's a rare admission of uncertainty, in the current yay/boo era of American cinema. From my grown-up vantage point in 1993, it's almost as scary a thought as nuclear war.

A final note for really serious filmgoers: No, *Matinee* cannot hold up against *The Spirit of the Beehive,* though they've got a lot in common. Victor Erice's 1973 drama also re-creates a society and a political moment (that of Franco's Spain in 1940) as experienced by children under the influence of a horror movie. But the horror movie in Erice's film is *Frankenstein.* The mood is correspondingly eerie and brooding; the visual style varies from the quasi-documentary to an exquisite, almost bejeweled formality. Like most people who have seen it, I greatly admire *The Spirit of the Beehive.* But Erice doesn't know anything about guys dressed up in rubber antsuits. That kind of fun belongs to *our* culture—and, of course, to the Japanese.

The Addiction

On an ordinary New York street, on an ordinary evening, evil grabs Kathleen Conklin by the arm and hurls her into an alley. An alley? Not even that; just a crack between two buildings, a slit of space webbed by shadows, a cul-de-sac barely wide enough for the sleek shoulders of evil, who tonight is wearing a black cocktail dress and has her hair moussed to perfection. "Tell me to go away," says evil with a cocky smile, as Kathleen tries to walk backward through the wall. "Say it like you mean it." But Kathleen, nearly mute with terror and terminally polite, stammers "please." A fatal error; evil does not respect "please." That is the lesson of *The Addiction*, a useful and beautiful film, which tells how Kathleen, a typical N.Y.U. graduate student, abruptly becomes a vampire, with incalculable effects on her dissertation defense.

Written by Nicholas St. John and directed by Abel Ferrara, the team that made *China Girl* and *King of New York*, *The Addiction* is one of those rare films that see an idea through to its end. In this case, we might even speak of ideas, first among them the notion that a vampire's need resembles drug addiction. It's a familiar metaphor, which St. John and Ferrara dramatize with bracing literal-mindedness. They imagine that in the hours after the first bite, Kathleen would struggle against her changing nature, writhing and sweating and vomiting like a junkie in withdrawal. Later, giving in, she feeds her new habit by means of a syringeful of freshly collected blood, which she shoots up in the toilet. But if vampirism is a metaphor for drug addiction, what does addiction stand for? We come to the film's second idea: the notion that feelings of guilt may become self-perpetuating, insatiable, communicable. On an ordinary street in New York, where the poor in great numbers sprawl helplessly underfoot or else loom all too capably in one's face, an ordinary graduate student may discover plentiful opportunities to feel bad about her place in the world. If she's a graduate student in philosophy, who spends her time thinking about Calvinist doctrine and watching slide shows of My Lai, she might tremble with not just shock but also recognition when evil, in its cocktail dress, sneers at her, "Collaborator!"

A blood-drenched genre shocker about collective guilt and ethical relativism, The Addiction bears the characteristic marks of Abel Ferrara's contradictory sensibility. It's witty and calculating in its effects but at the same time unabashedly earnest, visually dynamic yet almost languorous in its appeal to the tactile and the atmospheric. Kathleen straggles (just like a junkie) through a black-and-white downtown Manhattan that's all shadows and spectral glow, where nothing happens until everything happens too fast. As played by the small, fierce Lili Taylor, Kathleen, too, is a bundle of contradictions—smug one moment, knotted in self-loathing the next, intelligent, ravenous, appalled at her helplessness but reveling in the power her abasement makes possible.

A great movie? No. But The Addiction is itself the product of need—of the filmmakers' obsessions and longings, more than of marketing strategies—and that alone makes it worth seeing and supporting. St. John and Ferrara are just crazy enough to propose that their protagonist is a moral being, that their audience is made up of people who are more than consumers, that vampire movies are thrilling because they talk about redemption. Strange hypotheses to put forth these days; worthwhile hypotheses.

Ulee's Gold

Y ou come to a moment in Victor Nunez's new film when Ulee Jackson—played by Peter Fonda in a K Mart shirt and purely functional wire-rim glasses—walks bone-tired into the kitchen of his little house to find his daughter-in-law puttering about. Her name is Helen (Christine Dunford), and it's been only a few days since Ulee unstrapped her from his bed. While he slept on the floor under the dining room table, Helen was busy screaming and frothing, as she went through detox before her young daughters' eyes. Now she is clearheaded enough to ask if she can give him anything. He hesitates, as if having to make a decision, then allows himself to ask for a glass of water.

When he drinks, you can feel the liquid slide down his tongue.

Such is the veracity of the world built up in *Ulee's Gold*, a film that is properly being released amid summer blockbusters, since it can outdo them in kinesthesis. You get to the point of registering its events physically—as you don't in *Con Air, Speed 2* or *Batman & Robin*—because *Ulee's Gold* is a film you can inhabit. Touch it anywhere, and it's solid.

The house, for example: Ulee Jackson and his granddaughters live in a small, low, wood-frame building set on a shady side street in a Florida Panhandle town. Bit by bit, you see the yard on the driveway side, the kitchen door, the front door, the living room, the dining room and main bedroom, until you could find your way around the place on your own. You also get to see the interior of the garage, which is filled with the tools and machinery of Ulee's trade of bee-keeping. You get a notion of the money he makes (the opening scene shows him negotiating for delivery of the tupelo honey harvest), and you believe he'd be able to buy and furnish this house—nothing better, but nothing worse. He owns a few good, old pieces (the bed with its mahogany headboard) and a few worn-out junkers (the living-room couch), but they're all kept perfectly tidy.

As the house, so the man. When Ulee drives to the grammar school to pick up his younger granddaughter, Penny (Vanessa Zima), he sits upright behind the wheel of his old pickup truck, radiating all the joy of a man flossing his teeth. When his elder granddaughter, Casey (Jessica Biel), dressed like an invitation to a prison sentence, insists on stepping out with her boyfriend till hours unannounced, Ulee protests but will not raise his voice. Real men are supposed to be laconic, as somebody observes, but Ulee carries it too far.

What lies behind his silences? A tour in Vietnam; the death of a wife he loved; a period of inattention, let's call it, that permitted his son, Jimmy (Tom Wood), to land in jail and his daughter-in-law to become a druggie. These catastrophes, so devastating and so normal, make themselves known to you as the rooms of the house do, bit by bit, while Ulee is engaged with more pressing matters. Helen needs to be rescued from her husband's criminal partners (the wonderfully sleazy Steven Flynn and Dewey Weber), who reside in parts of Orlando that Disney doesn't want you to know about. Within the same two weeks, the tupelo has to be harvested, hives shifted, granddaughters soothed and a new set of criminal threats defused. You decide: Is stiff, silent Ulee redeemed by his sense of honor in wanting to march through these trials unassisted, or by his willingness, after each moment of failure, to accept as much help as fits in a glass of water?

As the man, so the actor. At the same time as you're learning to recognize the deliberation behind Ulee's every word and gesture, you appreciate how Peter Fonda has thought through every moment of his performance. Like Ulee, he seems too methodical at first; you're aware of how Fonda has worked out the careful habit of putting on his eyeglasses one earpiece at a time, or the way he's developed a gait that will hint at an old back injury. There's nothing surprising about this; though Fonda always holds the camera well, he's never been an effortless performer. But in *Ulee's Gold*, you don't just see through his outward, actorly tricks. You gradually see *into* them. The care they reveal—pride in craft built upon an awareness of fallibility—radiates through the film as one of its deepest satisfactions.

Of course, films are supposed to be radiant. They're nothing but the rebound of light. *Ulee's Gold* is one of those rare movies that live up to their own physics.

Victor Nunez not only wrote, directed and edited the film but also served as camera operator (the director of photography was Virgil Marcus Mirano), and he's filled *Ulee's Gold* with beautiful, infinitely variable light: the wide-awake whiteness of noon on a small town's main drag, the fruity colors of Orlando's neon signs at twilight, the taillights of a truck burning through the blackness of a swamp at night, a soft glow that suffuses the room when a little girl shows a drawing to her mother. There's nothing showy about these effects, any more than Nunez would think to show off with his framing or camera movement. At his wildest, he'll place a figure surprisingly close to the camera, so there's a jump in space; or he'll casually pan, just a little, so that characters who are coming together emotionally also share the frame. I can think of only a few other contemporary filmmakers—such as Charles Burnett, Abbas Kiarostami, Hou Hsiao-hsien—who have a comparable talent for letting their images live from within.

Ulee's Gold is crammed with incidents, some of them life-threatening; but there's a great calm at the heart of the film. You get such a calm only when all of the characters in a film turn out to be interesting, when the house can be inhabited, when the glass of water turns out to be full. A gauge of completeness: Ulee turns out to be short for Ulysses, his wife was named Penelope, the rescued woman is Helen, the helpful neighbor across the street (played by Patricia Richardson) is named Constance Hope—and the picture is so good, thank God, that you don't even notice.

Bill & Ted's Bogus Journey
Terminator 2

A rich man's son, acting on impulse, invites a talkative old codger to dinner. Once there, the guest carries on so whimsically that another member of the company bets money he can't give a straight answer to a simple question. Sure enough, the old rogue continues to tease his listeners, make up stories and put forth all manner of ridiculous ideas, among them a proposal that we should model our behavior on that of dogs.

Perhaps the most amazing facet of this little drama—which you may find in Books I–III of Plato's *Republic*—is that so many people have taken it seriously, including its suggestions for editing the works of Homer. Such revisions are necessary, Plato has Socrates claim, if poetry is to carry out its mission: educating us all to be good doggies.

That the obedience-school theory of the arts survives to this day is a tribute to its versatility. It serves everyone from Jesse Helms to the editors of *The New York Times*, who couldn't put together a single Arts & Leisure section without it. Someone is always worried over the effect of the latest role models on a populace in need of guidance. Useless to ask, in the words of another satirical rogue, "Who will educate the educators?" Useless to hint that Socrates, far from endorsing this theory of art, might have been poking fun at it.

Fortunately, we have in our midst two young men who have spoken with Socrates directly and can tell us what he really meant. I refer to Bill and Ted, who burst upon an unsuspecting public in *Bill & Ted's Excellent Adventure*

(1989) and now have returned in the more elaborate but no less ebullient *Bill & Ted's Bogus Journey.* Time-traveling high school students from San Dimas, California, Bill (Alex Winter) and Ted (Keanu Reeves) are more innocent, and have strayed farther abroad, than any fictional characters in recent memory. Though useless as role models for anybody—which is a large part of their merit—they nevertheless have been chosen by fate to save the world, and to my mind are doing a very fine job of it.

Bill is the one who wears a baseball cap backward on his curly blond head. He has a tendency to scrunch up his face, and he says "Whoa!" slightly more often than does his partner. In terms of body language and overall goofiness, he might remind older viewers of Ed Norton. But this is Norton without Ralph Kramden as a foil. Instead of playing off of an opposite type, Bill enters into a frictionless *folie à deux* with Ted, a character who is even more Norton-like than he. With stringy dark hair perpetually falling over his eyes, Ted seems a bit more inward than Bill, perhaps because he can't see much. Apart from the minor differences, though, the two friends are indistinguishable. Enclosed in a mutually validating fantasy, they copy each other's vocabulary (which is limited but high-falutin), mimic each other's air-guitar technique, insist to each other (since the world will not yet pay heed) that "Together, we are Wyld Stallyn!" Yes, Bill and Ted are so dumb, they even screw up the misspelling of their own not-quite-existent band.

Are they capable of being educated? Their new movie offers a partial, last-minute answer, with implications so satisfying that I wouldn't dream of giving you their benefit in a review. Let's just say that Bill and Ted seldom feel the need for self-improvement. This optimism, about themselves and the benevolence of the universe, was the explicit theme of their first film, in which Authority demanded that the boys pass an exam in history. Rather than study, they took advantage of a time machine built into a telephone booth, delivered to them by a futuristic guru named Rufus (George Carlin). The device enabled Bill and Ted to consult some of the greatest figures in Western Civ, from Plato's codger (whom the boys kept calling So-Crates) to Joan of Arc (who was, they supposed, the wife of Noah). In other words, Bill and Ted learned nothing. Rather, it was the giants of the past who were enlightened by their encounter with Bill and Ted. That's how good it is to be an American teenager.

Authority, as embodied in various film critics, shook its mature head and muttered. Never mind that the Bible itself tells us the last shall be first—a creature so despicable as the underachieving adolescent was simply too far back in last place to be accorded any respect. The characters being portrayed were stupid; and so, following a line of reasoning that might have given So-Crates himself the giggles, most commentators concluded that the film must be stupid, too. It made the insult all the more keen, then, that the movie recapitulated its characters' prophesied success. Budgeted on the Hollywood equivalent of spare change and dumped onto the market in February, *Bill & Ted's Excellent Adventure* annoyed everybody who was halfway serious by jumping to the top of the box-office charts and staying there, week after week. It finished the year on *Variety*'s list of top-grossing films, went on to glory in the video-rental market and now has spawned a sequel with the identical attitude. Deference to authority? This time, the boys come clunking in their oversized sneakers right up to the throne of God. "Congratulations on a most excellent planet," Ted says to the Almighty, by way of greeting. "Bill and I enjoy it on a daily basis."

Bill & Ted's Bogus Journey also takes the audience on a tour of Hell, dramatizes the conquest of death and concludes with a vision of universal redemption. In terms of theme, it's nothing less than a dudespeak translation of *Paradise Regained*. Clearly, *Bogus Journey* is the most ambitious work of the imagination that America has produced in recent years, with the possible exception of James Merrill's later poems—and you'll note that Merrill, too, speaks through a medium that can't be taken seriously. He uses a Ouija board, whereas the creators of Bill and Ted—Chris Matheson and Ed Solomon—use teenagers. Either way, pomposity dissolves on contact.

To judge the advantage of this method, you might compare *Bogus Journey* with the biggest of the summer sequels, which also has an explicitly redemptive theme: *Terminator 2: Judgment Day*. The subtitle isn't kidding. More than just another shoot-'em-up, *Terminator 2* shows us that the apocalypse is at hand, conceived in mundane terms as nuclear war. Salvation lies through a young man named John Connor and his almost-virginal mother, Sarah (Linda Hamilton), a Madonna with deep-cleft deltoids and much experience with automatic weapons. And who gets to play Our Father? It's Schwarzenegger, redeemed from his bad-guy role in the first *Terminator*. This Second Coming has Arnold turning into the Protector—a robot from the future who will guard John Connor with absolute devotion and superhuman strength. As Sarah comes to realize, in one of the film's frequent moments of hilarity, only the Protector can meet her standards for paternity.

But *Terminator 2* is above all else an action movie, which means that sacred conversation can sneak in only as a pause for breath, between the car chases and firefights. These are unfailingly spectacular, showing off the very latest in Hollywood pyrotechnics and special effects, including a new-model Terminator that can change shape at will. (Like Schwarzenegger, this creation is something of a revenant. It's based on special effects developed for *The Abyss*, the previous film by writer-director James Cameron.) My only reservation about all this machinery is that I sense it has reached a point of diminishing returns.

At a cost of undisclosed millions—it's reportedly the most expensive movie ever produced—*Terminator 2* has made all previous special-effects extravaganzas look cheesy. But audiences are getting harder and harder to amaze, as their expectations rise in parallel with the price of illusion-making. The average 14-year-old today probably sneers at *2001: A Space Odyssey.* It looks phony. How soon will the effects in *Terminator 2* become laughable? How much will have to be spent the next time to get beyond the gee-whiz barrier?

Faced with such questions, I like to recall that the history of the special-effects film is essentially that of a mistake. While shooting on the streets of Paris one day in 1896, Georges Méliès jammed the feeding mechanism of his camera for a few seconds. When he later projected the film, he was amazed to see people vanish abruptly, then reappear in another spot. He'd invented the trick film, by accident. We might think of the fantasists who have come along since as belonging to two groups. The first, which includes Méliès himself, leave a few traces of the accident visible in their movies. That is, they allow you to see that the magic trick is only that. Their characteristic effect is charm, achieved through a deliberate staginess; the film's frame might almost be a proscenium arch, separating you from the make-believe space you're watching. The other tradition, which has reached its temporary apex in *Terminator 2*, strives to shut out even the thought of error. Its characteristic effect is that dumbfounded submission to power that we call astonishment. So long as the illusion remains state-of-the-art, such a film wows the crowd. When its accidents start showing, though, the movie in this category doesn't become charming—merely dated.

Terminator 2 shows the danger signs, chief among them a zeal to educate the audience. In defense of the film, I should note that Cameron adopts an Aristotelian theory, not the bogus-Platonic one. He offers an education of the emotions. First, Cameron cranks up the audience's desire for bloodshed; then, he tries to purge that desire, in the act of satisfying it. Early in the film, for example, John Connor orders the Protector to stop killing people. The Protector's initial response is to kneecap his victims instead. This lack of all sense of proportion was also a feature of the original Terminator, lending a comic exuberance to the violence he perpetrated. But in *Terminator 2*, Cameron makes an effort to transform this bloodlust. By the end of the picture, he has the audience cheering when the Protector *doesn't* kill anybody. Schwarzenegger blows up a lot of property, but the casualty count is zero. Good enough—and yet I can't help regretting the attendant note of self-importance that has crept into the production. A movie this expensive had *better* seem important. To make sure it does, Cameron seems willing to provide at least two of everything—including characters who die so that others may live.

Bill and Ted would never load themselves down so heavily. Granted, they too encounter a pair of robots from the future; but the Bill and Ted cyborgs are hopeless, low-budget doofuses compared with Schwarzenegger, which is the whole point. Like everything else in *Bogus Journey*, the robots seem to have sprung from the characters' own limited store of knowledge. The movie plays as if it had been scripted by Bill and Ted themselves; the direction, by Pete Hewitt, consistently adopts a simple, straighforward, dude's-eye point of view. The performances are equally seamless. Unlike Hope and Crosby in the *Road* movies, or Billy Crystal in the current, dismal *City Slickers*, Alex Winter and Keanu Reeves never break character, never tip off the audience that they're smarter than the movie they inhabit. Bill and Ted don't make jokes; they *are* a joke, and so is their entire universe, right down to its Hell (a truly original one, designed by David L. Snyder) and its Grim Reaper (gleefully portrayed by William Sadler, with a tip of the scythe to Bergman's *The Seventh Seal*).

As for the problem of education: At the end of *Bogus Journey*—or the beginning, it's hard to say which—Bill and Ted do take on the role of instructors. They are the founders of Bill and Ted University, where everybody tramps around in a Frankenstein's monster gait, wearing those oversized shoes, and headphones are required equipment for students attempting to do homework. Do not be dismayed. The entire curriculum of the university, along with all of the law and the prophets, may be summarized in Bill and Ted's dictum, "Be excellent to one another." The wonderful thing about Bill and Ted is that they have nothing more than that to teach. All they really want is to make you happy, and they don't even expect to be thanked for it.

Ed Wood

There's something lacquered about the black-and-white cinematography of Tim Burton's new film, *Ed Wood,* something hard and shiny. You see it in the gleam of Johnny Depp's teeth as he grins in the title role, his incisors glistening too brightly against the void where his front teeth should be. The whites in this film have the unyielding sheen of coffin linings, entertainers' starched shirts, giant arc lights and rolling eyeballs. The blacks are the black of night on a studio soundstage—inky, impenetrable, as profound as the hero's lack of talent.

Known best, if he is known at all, as the perpetrator of *Glen or Glenda?* and *Plan 9 From Outer Space,* Edward D. Wood Jr. dwelt among us from 1922 to 1978, inhabiting a world where good and bad could seem as distinct as black and white—a world that judged him pitilessly for the ineptitudes he piled up on the screen, and never asked about the feelings that might have prompted him. Now, in Tim Burton's film—a sad, touching, hilarious tribute to a big-hearted loser; an improbable masterpiece, spun with magic around a figure for whom mere competence was too high a goal—we at last see the link between the out-ward, awkward forms of Ed Wood's visions and their inner glory, which other-wise would have remained trapped behind his forehead, glowing like a little cloud. On screen, that all-forgiving mental fuzziness seems to spread outward from Johnny Depp, resolving itself into the emblematic form of an angora sweater, whose fluff provides a relieving softness amid all those sharp black-and-white edges, a mediation between cross-dressing Ed and the all-too-harsh world of Hollywood in the fifties.

When first seen, Ed is in the wings of a little theater, rapturously mouthing his own dialogue for a play about men at war, based in part, it would seem, on his own experiences as a paratrooper and in part on his miasmatic recollections of ghost stories, B movies and uplifting radio sermons. He does not appear to distinguish among these sources; he finds them so compelling, so thoroughly his own (no matter their origin) that he does not even notice how they play onstage, or care that his cast of three considerably outnumbers the audience. No, it's enough for his ideas to take physical form—any physical form will do—for Ed to believe in himself, thus satisfying, according to Hollywood in the fifties, the most important condition in life. Just look at Johnny Depp, his eyes brimming over like two bowls of melted ice cream, while a cool perspiration bespangles his brow. How could you blame such a man for believing in himself? How could you hurt him by admitting that you *don't* believe?

His girlfriend and leading lady, Dolores Fuller (Sarah Jessica Parker), swallows hard and goes on believing in Ed, even after he lands his first assignment as a film director and (purely on his own initiative) transforms the project into a confessional drama about his deep need for women's clothes. But even characters who are more hardened than Dolores have a way of falling for Ed. Such is the case with Bela Lugosi—a has-been, impoverished and morphine-addicted, who rallies at the end of his life when caught up in Ed's enthusiasm. A study in contrasts: Johnny Depp, using his teen-idol charm to convey Ed's slightly rancid, over-30 boyishness; and Martin Landau, apparently stooped over by the weight of his eyebrows, bringing a virtuoso's skills to the impersonation of Lugosi, while simultaneously calling to mind the majestic pathos of a Yiddish trouper playing his last *Der Koenig Lear.*

Should you laugh or weep when you see Lugosi, weary and shivering, fling himself into a puddle and pretend to wrestle with a rubber octopus, giving his all, despite the circumstances, to the honor of his profession, and (more important) to Ed? Should you mock Ed's entourage of weirdos, misfits and dope fiends (as Dolores calls them), or rejoice that they care for one another, however imperfectly, when nobody else will? The wonder of *Ed Wood* is that it does not cheat you out of either the grotesquerie or the warmth of this strange community. In its narrative structure, the movie is a satiric reversal of standard biopics, with their singular heroes struggling through adversity toward triumph; but in the working out of its emotions, *Ed Wood* bypasses the great man (or, in this case, the not-great man) to dwell on a group of people. The theme of the film is friendship; if you want irony to leaven it, you'll have to bring your own.

The unembarrassed warmth of *Ed Wood* emanates first of all from the director, Tim Burton, who has always sided with the misfits and weirdos. Here, in his generosity, he even realizes a few of Ed Wood's dreams for him, supplying, for example, a rubber octopus that *works*. This openness of spirit and that of the screenwriters, Scott Alexander and Larry Karaszewski, is particularly welcome given the origin of the Ed Wood cult in a sneering book by Michael Medved and Harry Medved, *The Golden Turkey Awards*. The book, which named *Plan 9 From Outer Space* as the worst film of all time, helped to launch innumerable festivals of bad movies, attended mostly by white, male, middle-class college students. I note that the period was the early 1980s, when people of that description were no longer being allowed to feel superior in and of themselves. The lazier ones found solace in Ed Wood: For a few hours, they could recapture the joys of insolence by deriding his movies.

Now, thanks to Tim Burton, only a hypocrite viewer will be able to look down on Ed Wood or deny a brotherly semblance. My thanks to Stefan Czapsky, whose cinematography has summoned up these visions; to the production designer, Tom Duffield, who gave form to the delirium; and to Howard Shore for his music, appropriately scored for the sci-fi swoops of a theremin, plus savage, pulsating bongos.

September 20, 1999

The Muse

To suffer humiliation can be tragic. To bear humiliation for much longer than necessary, yet with loud impatience, is the comic gift of Albert Brooks. For some twenty years, beginning with *Real Life*, Brooks has presented himself in his movies as someone too openly intelligent to be Everyman, yet too middling to escape the indignities that are Everyman's lot—someone for whom the old shtick of the slow burn may appropriately be refined into the just plain slow. In Brooks's performances, the mirth-releasing eruption is not merely delayed but indefinitely postponed, so that it seems to get sucked back into his body, as if he were practicing a form of tantric humor. Those fidgets and stares and embittered wisecracks, which ripple through him for whole scenes at a time, are the hiccups of outrageous interruptus.

Here he is in *The Muse* as screenwriter Steven Phillips, enduring (to take just one example) a meeting with Hollywood's most powerful man. Failure is announced the moment Steven wheels up to the Universal Pictures lot, only to be told he's received a "walk-on" pass, not a "drive-on." If we, as movie civilians, understand the meaning of this distinction, then surely an industry foot soldier such as Steven must recognize the rank to which he's just been assigned, and the futility of his mission. Yet he begins the trek anyway, laboring toward The Spielberg Building through a series of no fewer than five shots, all of which are funny, though only one offers the comfort of an identifiable gag. If Steven won't spare himself the ordeal, what makes us think we're going to get off easy?

And why, once he's attained the office of Mr. Spielberg, should Steven be in any hurry to leave? No matter that he sees, as soon as he's entered the door, that the interview amounts to a practical joke. The sweat he's worked up on his walk—the outward and visible sign of an inward terror—betrays the urgency of his mission, to revive a moribund career. Steven has a charming family, whom he may no longer be able to support. He has the right kind of car, on which he probably won't keep up the payments, and enough years vested in screenwriting that the car shouldn't be parked miles away, as if already in the repo lot. And so, despite the lack of a welcome, he stays put in the Spielberg office. Steven needs to confirm, to the last detail, that the cruelty to which he's being subjected is as thorough as it seems.

Besides, to leave any sooner would show a want of professional pride.

What is humiliation anyway? In Steven's terms, it's the experience of having someone younger, someone who isn't even Spielberg, call you into his office with a crooked finger, in a gesture that combines "Koochie-koo" with "Here, Fido." It's having the smooth lad tell you that your latest script lacks edge (whatever that means), then jot down your comeback because he thinks it's amusing. It's hearing him explain that people nowadays run through several careers—the smooth lad has read that in the *Wall Street Journal*—so isn't it time to start your next? But all that is mere prelude to the main exasperations of *The Muse*. Bad enough that Steven has failed to cope with producers. Soon enough, he'll be reduced to begging for a meeting with a mythological figure.

She goes by the name of Sarah, wears long scarves and diaphanous, off-the-shoulder lavender outfits and is played by Sharon Stone. Obviously, she's a goddess. At least, it's obvious to everyone who matters in Hollywood. Even children (or at least those who live in Bel Air) know that Sarah, an honest-to-Zeus muse, holds the key to success. Only Steven seems to have been kept in the dark, as usual. But now his buddy Jack (Jeff Bridges) has broken the code of silence and wrangled him an introduction, so that he, too, may benefit from Sarah's inspiration. The only problem is that Steven, being an Albert Brooks character, can't accommodate the demands of a muse with good grace. He's got to fret and negotiate and try to cut corners.

The needs of a muse are of course outsize—much like the needs of Hollywood's big winners, who contribute cameo appearances to the film, in which we see them flock to Sarah for help. How fragile they all turn out to be! At times, *The Muse* seems to suggest that Steven, too, might be a winner, if only he had their extravagance. Even people who don't claim creative genius—people such as his wife, Laura (Andie MacDowell), who is so wholesome that she dreams of launching a cookie-baking business—start to blossom when Sarah encourages them to plunge ahead in life, and purchase only top-of-the-line, brand-name products.

Steven is too guarded, not to mention cheap, to fling himself forward, Sarah-style, yet too desperate to hold back. So he toils through most of the film as the errand boy to greatness—a grousing errand boy at that. His lips, sopping with irony, sometimes squeeze together, as if wringing every bitter drop. His torso, though thick, has a downward pitch, pulled by the stony grievances that amass behind the forehead. Everything about Steven—or rather about Albert Brooks, as he's generally re-created himself in his films—is squared-off, gravity-bound, stubborn and in delicious contrast to Sharon Stone's Sarah, who seems always about to drift away at forty-five degrees to the horizon. Only at the end of *The Muse*—well, three-quarters of the way through—does it become possible to appreciate in retrospect the wonderful consistency of Stone's performance. The giddy tilt of the head; the ingenuous pop of the eyes; the flood of uncomprehending tears when room service at the Four Seasons won't bring her a Waldorf salad at midnight: such signs of Olympian birth, or symptoms of flightiness, would understandably be worshiped in Hollywood by everyone except a reasonable man. And Steven, as we learn, resorts to reason only when demeaned.

You and I, who are always reasonable and never envy others' success, may laugh safely at *The Muse*, knowing that its lunacies are peculiar to Hollywood. And so they are. Nevertheless: If you know a woman of mature years who yearns to start a cookie-baking business, send her to see *The Muse* as a warning. The enthusiasm she'll need to unloose in herself is a form of madness, as the ancient Greeks understood. It can spark high achievements but also low silliness, and you can't tell in advance which you'll get.

If you're Steven Phillips, you won't even know afterward.

Erin Brockovich

S tar vehicle? *Erin Brockovich* begins with Julia Roberts already in close-up, eyes eager as salesmen in matched gabardine suits, lips vibrant and playful as double-dutch jump-ropes, skin glistening in a perfectly even light, which borrows its tint from the wall behind her, as if she were posed in a photographer's studio. Her oodles of hair—magically brown, blond and red all at once—rise majestically in the pile of a working-class heroine. Her wire earrings take the only form they could: little hearts. Speaking straight to the camera, brightly, twangily, Roberts shares a few personal details in the most disarming fashion, as a way of selling herself.

It seems you're watching a job interview, and Roberts, as the title character, isn't doing so well. Thanks to her candor, you quickly learn she's got three young children, no visible means of support and a wardrobe composed solely of handkerchief-size dresses, as if she'd economized by purchasing only so many square inches of clothes. To her interviewer, the effect is doubly disconcerting. Not only does Erin lack qualifications for the job—she's applying to be a nurse in a medical office, on the strength of having cared for her kids—but she's shown up looking like a cocktail waitress, which makes the male, middle-aged doctor act uncomfortably thirsty.

Later, seeking a payday from an auto accident, she chooses to testify in court wearing a neck brace and a little form-fitting polka-dotted number, with a neckline that plunges to Buenos Aires. Such behavior eventually prompts her lawyer, Ed Masry (Albert Finney), to challenge her taste in clothes. "I like how I look," she shoots back—which is the correct answer for the character and the correct answer for Julia Roberts. Many, many moviegoers like her to dress this way; and so she does, in a role that keeps her onscreen for virtually the entire length of the film.

Yes, *Erin Brockovich* is a star vehicle. More than that, it's a perfect match between star and vehicle, with Roberts playing a down-on-her-luck but fiercely determined single mom, who just happens to be a former Miss Wichita. (She still has the tiara and at one point wears it to bed.) While occupying the center of each scene, she gets to be chummy, ingenuous, exasperated, furious, sly, empathetic and at last, following the pattern of *Pretty Woman*, rich.

And yet there's even more, since *Erin Brockovich* is a based-on-a-true-story movie. In the early 1990s, the real Brockovich, though unencumbered with a law degree, managed to organize the citizens of a small town to sue a grossly negligent corporation. The plaintiffs won—and so she gave moral and material aid to hundreds of people, while doing a little something for her own family as well.

So now, at a moment when America's corporate apologists are trying to prevent injured citizens from taking to the law, Julia Roberts has marched her stardom squarely into the path of the tort-reform movement. Granting due respect to the differences, I might almost liken her to the fellow who blocked the tanks going into Tiananmen Square. With those legs, she won't be easy to knock down.

In fact—I use the phrase in its strict meaning—*Erin Brockovich* stands so firmly on Roberts's legs that it can name a corporate bad guy: Pacific Gas & Electric. Let me say that again: Pacific Gas & Electric, Pacific Gas & Electric, Pacific Gas & Electric. The movie is so indelicate as to assert, without fear of incurring legal action against Universal Pictures, that PG&E poisoned the residents of Hinkley, California, knew it had poisoned them and actively lied about the poisoning to the victims, who therefore thought their tumors were the fruit of bad luck and so went on drinking carcinogenic water. You can't make this stuff up, nor do you have to.

While Erin is on her way to the rousing conclusion, in which she and many honest citizens collect millions through the courts, she further demonstrates her feistiness through jokey bickering with her boss, played by Finney as a pudgy, gravy-spotted fellow who tends to trip over the file boxes littering his office, so that he spills the takeout coffee that's forever in his mitt. Erin also enters into an affair with her next-door neighbor, George (Aaron Eckhart), who proves to be the nurturing type, despite his bandanna headcloth, Harley-Davidson and broad expanse of chest hair.

It is only one of the film's reversals of expectation when manly George volunteers to care for the kids so that Erin may pursue a profession. A more subtle reversal: Although Erin uses her body as if she'd seen *Pretty Woman* and meant to emulate its heroine, she doesn't spend much of her time in bed. When she needs to get access to a trove of documents, she distracts their guardian by leaning forward and squeezing her elbows to her sides, making her breasts the most animated to be seen since Jessica Rabbit's; when her boss issues one of his gruff reprimands, her reflex is to taunt him sexually; but when she comes home at midnight for the 128th day in a row, she discovers that George has packed his bag, having gone untouched for too many months.

A further reversal: Even though Erin begins the picture by talking about her children, even though she's shown making sacrifices for them (including going hungry), she is capable of neglecting the kids, once she's found paying work and an outlet for a formidable mental energy. Sure, she's warm and caring; that's why the residents of Hinkley trust her. But for all that, the film, with a knowing grin, lets us identify her main sources of pleasure: intellectual stimulation and a whole lot of money.

Though it's overly fond of connecting dots, Susannah Grant's screenplay provides an efficient enough plan of action for the movie. The responsibility for realizing that plan, and for putting life on the screen, falls to Roberts, of course, and to the director, Steven Soderbergh. He's always found exhilaration in scenes where women assert themselves—think of Andie MacDowell grabbing the camera in *sex, lies & videotape*, or of Jennifer Lopez kneecapping a bad guy in *Out of Sight*—and so he seems utterly assured in directing Roberts through her star turn. He's also developed a masterly repertoire of editing tricks, which speed the action through those connected dots. The image of the present scene overlaps with sound from the next, to help you bound over the transition; a scene of courtroom testimony breaks apart into multiple viewpoints, varied and rapid; several days of job hunting turn into a montage of Los Angeles locations. In his sleights of hand, Soderbergh is so deft that he even makes it look as if he'd truly risked Julia Roberts in a staged car wreck.

She's far too valuable to endanger, of course. And I don't for a moment imagine she might suffer for her present stand in endorsing a citizen's right to sue. But let's be as hardheaded as Erin Brockovich herself, or the film that bears her name. This is how some women get things done in America: through the use of whatever they've got. If neither the star nor the character wins a halo at the end, that's just fine, because they didn't ask for one. Money will do—money, and a little justice.

Magnolia

I n his novel *A Flag for Sunrise*, Robert Stone invents this old American saying: "Mickey Mouse will see you dead." I have spent many profitable hours mulling over that coinage; and I've concluded it has something to do with our national aversion to tragedy.

American novelists have written "tragedy" into their book titles; America's playwrights, sending doomed men to center stage, have told us that attention must be paid; but the audience, after a dutiful sigh, always turns back to comedy. I don't mean just the banana-peel stuff (though we've certainly had our share of that). I'm talking about fictions that end with fresh beginnings: couples paired off, society renewed, May buds blooming over pots of gold. The comic mode rules in America, no matter the sufferings that lie in our past or the catastrophes that await, well prepared, in our future.

Perhaps the only form in which tragedy has flourished in America has been film noir—though "flourished" may be the wrong word for a mode that mushroomed at the bottom of cheap double bills and then had to be named in French. In the years when noir was fully alive, a few such films were deemed respectable and given awards, if Billy Wilder had made them; but most, like their protagonists, lived in the shadows. Noir was, among other things, a shade cast by the uneasy conscience of the people who won World War II; the grief and terror that underlay victory played in distorted shapes across the walls of grind houses. Eventually, noir succeeded in emerging into the light; it entered the museums and film societies. And so it became an object of nostalgia, drained of a large measure of its power.

As for those recent productions known as neo-noir: You can't sweat out a movie like a guilty secret when the picture keeps offering to be your guilty pleasure.

The historians who someday will define us by our stories, as we define the Greeks and Elizabethans by theirs, will note this curious gap in our imagination. But they won't be able to judge us by nonexistent tragedies; their only measure will be the comedies we've produced. If we hope to make a good showing, then those comedies had better be something more than funny. They will need at times to be deep and challenging—which is why I return to *Magnolia*.

It is a long, emotionally taxing film, one that elicited from my friend Gerald Peary a groan of, "Cry me a river!" As I noted last month, the characters in the film's intersecting stories include two men dying of cancer, two women who are walking pharmacological experiments, four abused children and one professional misogynist. Did I mention the dead dog?

The writer-director, Paul Thomas Anderson, throws that in, too—and yet the mood at the end is comic. You can place *Magnolia* by the startled laughter that erupts at the climax, during events that are (paradoxically) both cleansing and slimy. There's comedy as well in the final reconciliations, the pardon-granting, the blossoming smile on which the picture ends.

I had hoped a film this strong might win a few critics' awards. (To date, only the Toronto group has cited it.) I also hoped it might inspire analysis and debate. But *Magnolia* is being neither honored nor much discussed; and so, rushing into the near-vacuum, I want to review it in more detail—especially now that it's in wide release, its secrets having been revealed by several critics who should know better. Those of you who haven't seen the picture and want to preserve its surprises intact should stop reading now. All others may join me in pondering how much weight *Magnolia* will bear.

Let's start with a theme that's announced in a prologue: Some coincidences, especially when they're mortal, are so uncanny as to prompt us to imagine a guiding hand. Unsympathetic reviewers have suggested that this theme is a mere ploy, meant to rescue Anderson from the banality of his individual story lines. I suspect many of these same reviewers would tag as sophomoric the whole question of randomness versus design. True enough: This is the sort of riddle posed at college bull sessions. It's also asked, in a different tone, by the middle-aged at 3:00 A.M. By raising this theme, Anderson puts himself in a line that runs from the Greek tragedians—those connoisseurs of implacability—to

D.W. Griffith, the first great filmmaker to cut between scenes on the basis of theme and not story.

What is montage, that basic tool of the movies, if not the construction of a pattern, devised by a godlike hand that goes unseen by the characters? Far from being a superficial ploy, Anderson's prologue goes to the heart of both drama and filmmaking. The only question is whether the film can live up to the question.

The answer begins with a whiplike montage sequence in which Anderson introduces the characters you'll be following for the next three hours. And, in a sense, he keeps on introducing them. It's not just that he gradually reveals their interrelationships: the business tie between the two dying men, for example, or the sexual loneliness that's shared by the cop (John C. Reilly) and the onetime quiz kid (William H. Macy). Anderson also tricks you into judging these characters, then smilingly changes your mind about them.

A small example: When the brilliant Philip Seymour Hoffman, in the role of a private nurse, shyly phones a convenience store for a delivery of white bread, cigarettes and three porn magazines, you will certainly guess what's coming next. But the narrative hint turns out to have been a feint; the man has an altruistic use for stroke books. A larger example: A young black kid (Emmanuel Johnson) comes across an obviously wealthy white woman, who is slumped unconscious in her open car. He rifles through her purse—and, having found her cell phone, calls for help. Finally, two glaring examples: Here are Frank (Tom Cruise), a strutting TV preacher of male supremacy, and Claudia (Melora Walters), the coke-addled, bar-trolling daughter of a quiz-show host. Talk about bad first impressions! The whole burden of *Magnolia* is to show that even these monsters—highly plausible ones at that—may conceal human hearts.

Is this, too, a mere narrative ploy? Not when so many other characters get their chance to be better than expected. A generosity of spirit, which is comic in itself, runs through all of *Magnolia*—which is fortunate, with that rain of frogs on the way.

Yes, it's time to talk about the frogs. Only the laziest movie-watcher could claim they've simply been dropped into the picture. All through *Magnolia*, to prepare you for the plague rain, you're kept informed of the changing weather. The younger of the quiz kids, Stanley (Jeremy Blackman), even asks for meteorological instruments (and has been studying a book by Charles Fort, chronicler of unexplained downpours). Three times, amid normal precipitation, characters say, "It's raining cats and dogs." Three times you see signs that read "Exodus 8:2," giving chapter and verse of the second of Egypt's plagues.

Still, who could believe that Anderson would pull such a stunt? Playing on your expectations, he begins the episode with another feint: While having you follow the cop along a midnight street, Anderson lets you think you've heard gunshots. That's what the cop thinks, too, having been fired upon earlier in the day. Now he slams on the brakes—and sees two frogs sliding down his windshield.

Suddenly, the rain of frogs becomes general. It translates the cop's personal humiliation into widespread, public calamity—something *out there*, which calls for him to do what he likes best, helping others. To Claudia, by contrast, the frogs manifest themselves as the ultimate drug heebie-jeebie. (With classic slapstick timing, they fall only when she looks away.) At the home of the dying TV producer (Jason Robards), the frogs plop down comfortably in and around a spot-lit swimming pool; a sterile Southern California "oasis" suddenly teems with life. To the producer's self-destructive wife (Julianne Moore), lying in the back of a careening ambulance, the frogs are disaster piled on catastrophe. To the quiz-show host (Philip Baker Hall) they're a judgment from on high, prolonging a life he no longer wants. To young Stanley, smiling dreamily in the grammar school library amid their drifting shadows, the frogs seem the fulfillment of a promise.

In brief, there is no single rain of frogs; there are many. And that's what makes this plague—or blessing—seem so miraculous: not the freakishness of the event but its democratic multiplicity. I could say much the same for the miracle of *Magnolia*'s performances—each flamingly intense, yet all blended into an ensemble—or for the wonder of an actor-centered filmmaking that's intricately imagistic. On every level, from its montage technique to the objects of its meditations, *Magnolia* tests to the limit the tendency of life to fall apart; and in pulling against that entropy, to gather (some of) its characters into a (mostly) happy ending, it offers a comic vision that almost does the work of tragedy.

From now on, under the legend "E Pluribus Unum," let the dollar bear the sign of a frog.

A.I. Artificial Intelligence

What fresh hell is this?" might be what I'd ask of *A.I. Artificial Intelligence*, had I not seen so much of the movie before. Let me rephrase the question: What old heaven of Steven Spielberg's is this, reimagined as hell?

Here again are the floating ring of light from *Close Encounters* and the screen-filling moon of *E.T.* Once they were vehicles of hope and wonder. Now they convey us toward slaughters out of *Schindler's List* and *Amistad*. As with the film's imagery, so with its narrative conventions: Whatever was subtly troubled before in Spielberg's suburbia has turned bizarre and menacing. Sibling squabbles, no longer played for laughs, lead to the hospital, or worse; the missing father, once found, is self-involved and manipulative; fairy tales dead-end in cruel fact.

That's not to say that I enjoyed *A.I.*; but having watched most of it in astonishment, I'm more impressed than ever with Spielberg. Who else would have the power to mass-market this thing? Granted, he's trashed his own best efforts, concluding the movie with a twenty-minute "happy ending" whose quotation marks need quotation marks. Yet even this ploy has a crazy integrity. The plot resolution plays like the harsh, mirthless laughter of *A.I.*'s protagonist: It strains to ingratiate but instead sends a chill.

The pretext for all this entertainment, as you may know, is a 1969 science-fiction story by Brian Aldiss. Stanley Kubrick purchased the rights to it and then spent ages mulling over the project, after which it wound up in Spielberg's hands, in circumstances that will generate many happy years of gossip and doctoral theses. All I know is what the Warner Bros. publicity department tells me: that Kubrick discussed *A.I.* with Spielberg and eventually encouraged him to take over the project, including the storyboards that had been worked up by comic-book artist Chris Baker.

Judging from the evidence on screen, I guess there's some truth to this account. The movie is furnished with objects that look as if they'd belong in a Kubrick future: a natty little three-wheeled car, a suburban house that's all cylinders and glowing pods. Shapes are poised on the border between biomorphic and geometric, as if some merger of the organic and inorganic realms had already taken place. Spielberg's use of this design scheme seems Kubrick-like as well. His pacing is deliberate, his camera placement often distant and detached, and the lighting (managed by cinematographer Janusz Kaminski) frequently sends cold washes of white across the screen.

But it's a mug's game, trying to figure out which part of *A.I.* is inspired by Kubrick or means to pay hommage to him. Whatever its sources or stylistic tricks, *A.I* is a Spielberg film, through and through. Only he would have expanded Aldiss's story into a monument of anguish; only he could be so hugely, unassuageably shocked to learn that mommies die and fairy tales don't come true.

Mommy in this case is Monica (dark and pert-featured Frances O'Connor), who lives in the tropical rain forests of New Jersey. (Due to global warming, raging waters have swallowed the coastline, and hundreds of millions have perished. So does Spielberg's pain, unbounded, overflow to compass the world.) Now into Monica's home comes a short blond robot named David (Haley Joel Osment), an electrical appliance that has been made to look and behave like a boy. And more—for this is the world's first electrical appliance with emotions. When Monica recites a magic sequence of seven words, David falls in love with her in a way that humans cannot: purely, selflessly, irreversibly.

A.I. is the story of how David becomes separated from his love object—the one he didn't ask for, the one he can never forget—and suffers endless trials in seeking to rejoin her. Since Monica has been thoughtless enough to read him *Pinocchio*, David chases after another female figure as well: the Blue Fairy, who will, he firmly believes, make him into a real boy, so that Monica will return his love.

Has dramatic irony ever taken a more elaborate form? For two full hours, through the costliest and most spectacular settings that Spielberg can devise, we follow a lost, blundering character who doesn't know as much as we do and wouldn't be helped if he did. There's no question of our lording it over him in imagination, as other works of dramatic irony might invite us to do. The vast disproportion that yawns between David and his gargantuan world helps push pathos to its limit; and to this extreme mismatch of scale Spielberg adds an insoluble dilemma. While you squirm to see David in ignorance, you fear for him should he ever wise up.

The effect would no doubt be more engaging if *A.I.* dramatized any human relationships; but the robots are by far the strongest presences in the movie, while people, even when in close-up, seem to be curiously absent. For all we know about Monica, she might be a robot herself, or somebody's holographic projection of the Pretty Suburban Mother. She's void of detail, idiosyncracy or anything but the most generic version of an inner life; and she's the deepest of the human characters. Yet despite this lack, or perhaps because of it, *A.I.* on the surface level is a memorably disquieting picture. Even the sentimental touches seem creepy. There's a cuddly Teddy bear, for example, that moves and talks and is as lifelike as can be—which is horrible, because this is precisely the condition that David can't escape. As for the non-sentimental touches: Since robots in this future world are manufactured as sex toys, and robo-prostitution is a huge enterprise, some appalling possibilities flash into mind once David is on his own.

That said, if David were no more than a suffering innocent abandoned in a world of corruption, *A.I.* would not have affected me so much. (Prince Myshkin is not necessarily improved by being digitized; nor need he be made as cute as Osment, with his droopy eyes, buck teeth and white pajamas.) What really drew me in was the film's symbolic level. If David serves as a stand-in for Spielberg, as seems likely, then the relationship between ourselves and the character is inverted, piling irony upon irony. The movie's most vulnerable figure is not so secretly its most powerful, controlling everything we see.

It's hard to miss this symbolism, since *A.I.* is explicitly a movie about show business. The point comes across most emphatically in a great set piece that brings out all of Spielberg's virtuosity, in which an impresario who calls himself Lord Johnson-Johnson stages a Flesh Fair: an outdoor spectacle that combines elements of the arena rock concert, wrestling match, demolition derby and Klan rally. Marketed with transparent cynicism as "A Celebration of Life," the Flesh Fair plays to the resentments of a noticeably working-class audience, whose members envy the wealthy for being able to buy robots—"mechas," in the movie's jargon—and hate the mechas for taking their jobs. Show biz at its ugliest offers a catharsis: the sight of mechas being blown up, hacked apart, burned, crushed and doused with acid, while giant video screens flash behind the bandstand and roaring trucks churn up the dirt.

Of course, the meanness of show business gets exposed in *Pinocchio*, too, but not with such violence. You'd think Spielberg was vomiting out his disgust at the worst his trade can do. (Here's another show-biz staple that gets splattered onto the screen: a blackface comic, or a mecha built to behave like one, who can't help wisecracking even as he's stuffed down a cannon's mouth. Boom. A flaming Negro head, still grinning, flies into the chain-link fence.) Who thinks up this stuff? Not the audience. It's Lord Johnson-Johnson who decides to haul little David into the arena, proposing to liquefy him—at which point the ticket-buyers abruptly decide they won't lynch a kid. They're not yet that degraded. They lynch the showman instead.

I won't call this sequence a critique of the entertainment business; critics are supposed to argue, not hallucinate. Even so, the list of topics is pretty complete: from the class division between producers and consumers, to the grotesque nature of the artifacts put on display, to the mortal perils of misjudging the audience. And Spielberg implicates himself in these horrors, if we may deduce anything from the resemblance between Lord Johnson-Johnson's robot-catching gear (a glowing airship with a full-moon balloon) and those celebrated, sentimental images from *Close Encounters* and *E.T.*

No doubt the film's denunciation of show business is most obvious in this sequence; but the theme is present from the start. The mechas, as first introduced, are nothing less than an allegory of the movies.

Let's say that the basic thing the movies have to sell is an alluring face: something youthful, sexy and ostensibly available, yet also aloof. We take this face to represent a person, known as a star; but it's really the outward image of a machine, whose parts include cameras and lighting equipment, microphones and editing decks, photo labs and mixing tables. I can think of no better figure to summarize all this than Sheila, the sex-toy mecha who is demonstrated at the beginning of *A.I.* First her creator, Professor Hobby (William Hurt), shows us how well she can converse. Then he pulls away her lovely face to expose the wiring behind.

"What is love, Sheila?" the professor later asks, having clicked her features back into place. "Love," replies Sheila, "is when I raise my skin temperature slightly, increase my rate of breathing," and so forth. I wonder what the answers might be if Spielberg were so interrogated.

What is fear, Steven? Fear is when I put some lub-dub music on the soundtrack and poke a shark's fin through the water. What is joy? Joy is when I put twinkly music on the soundtrack and have everybody smile up at the light. What is integrity? Integrity is when I don't put any music on the soundtrack, just gunfire, and use black-and-white.

Spielberg knows the complaint against him, that he's a mechanistic filmmaker. He knows the truth of the allegation, too. So when I hear David in *A.I.* say that he wants to be a real boy, not a robot, I imagine Spielberg crying out that he wants to be a real director. But he, unlike David, understands the Blue

Fairy won't help him; the clockwork filmmaker must humanize himself, and he fears he doesn't know how.

I won't argue, if you say Spielberg has taken the concept of personal film-making and inflated it to absurdity. Ten bucks, to listen to a rehearsal of his self-doubts: this is chutzpah. Then again, Spielberg represents much more than himself. He *is* the system. Symbolically, he's turning into a nightmare the entice-ments of the entire military-entertainment complex; while on the surface level, for all those who thought they were getting the story of a cute little robot boy, he's also providing his equivalent of the *Songs of Experience*, slashing away with cold fury at our myth of true love.

Every frame, by the way, looks gorgeous.

5 FOREIGN AFFAIRS

La Vie de Bohème

When I first ran across Aki Kaurismäki's *La Vie de Bohème*, I thought it one of the funniest movies I'd ever seen. On second viewing, it turned out to be one of the saddest.

Based on the novel by Henri Murger rather than on the later opera by Puccini, *La Vie de Bohème* reawakens the pang of the original, its desperate humor, by the eccentric strategy of denying all sentiment. It's as if Kaurismäki were a physical therapist who heightens your awareness of a limb by amputating it. The bohemian life is over, his movie seems to say. The setting is not the 1850s but present-day Paris—or rather its suburbs, the center of town now being too expensive for misunderstood genius. Besides, the era of being misunderstood has yielded to that of being funded; and yet the characters in *La Vie de Bohème* seem oblivious to the presence nearby of the Pompidou Center and Canal+ television. Absurdly, they carry on a dream that in a sense was always absurd—the great Irish composer Schaunard, the great French poet and dramatist Marcel Marx, the great Albanian painter Rodolfo.

They are so caught up in their visions of artistic glory that they don't even seem to notice they're living in a black-and-white film. Nor do the skewed dimensions of their world seem to faze them. Marcel Marx sees, but seems not to care, that the wine glasses at his favorite bar are no bigger than a thumbnail. Rodolfo thinks it nothing more than a curiosity that the trout he's been served at the local bistro has two heads. Schaunard, when he at last purchases the automobile he has longed for, does not take it amiss that the vehicle has three wheels.

Now, it is one thing to drive a three-wheeled car. It is something else to believe that the ownership of such a car makes you better than other people. But then it is something still more different (why must bourgeois propriety make us stop at *two* things?) if the sincerity of your belief, however ludicrous, really does confirm in you a kind of crazy, unwashed nobility. Kaurismäki's bohemians are achromatic, anachronistic and far more eloquent than anybody needs to be. Isn't there virtue in such stubbornness? Even if their art didn't stink, nobody wants that sort of thing anymore; and yet they go on, supporting one another and ultimately sacrificing their precious few comforts for the sake of Rodolfo's beloved Mimi when she falls ill.

Not that she ever seems exactly well. Evelyne Didi, who plays the role, is not your frail little flower from the provinces—she is, in fact, rather robust—but for that very reason she conveys a sense of doom that would be lacking in the conventional, romantic spasms of tuberculosis. She's made it to Paris only a little before middle age will make it to her, and from the way she carries herself, you can tell she's taken some hard knocks along the way. She behaves very much as if she's been hit over the head and can't quite clear her noggin. Even before she starts coughing, life seems to have lost a strong grip on her—as when, accompanying Musette to the opera on a couple of freebies, she stares straight ahead for the longest time, until a shy, tentative smile lights her face, just a little. (The opera, by the way, is *The Marriage of Figaro*. Aki Kaurismäki has ordained that you will hear *not one tune* by Puccini in his *La Vie de Bohème*.) Perhaps the most touching and desperate moment of Didi's performance, though, comes when Rodolfo returns after a long absence and she wordlessly leaves her new boyfriend to follow him. She's on the border between being in love and being a zombie— which is what it would take to stick with Rodolfo.

In his first major role as an Albanian, the lugubrious Matti Pellonpää brings to Rodolfo all the lankness of hair, droopiness of mustache and general lack of affect that have distinguished him in his many previous roles as a Finn. "I am a hot-blooded man," he warns Mimi on their first encounter, rolling the strange phonemes of French around in his mouth as if some of that two-headed trout were stuck behind his back teeth and he had to cough it out. And yet something must be smoldering in him, because he looks no worse the next morning for having slept outdoors—on top of Henri Murger's grave. He even steals the flowers as a little present for Mimi.

As the poet Marcel Marx, André Wilms naturally gets the most long-winded of the dialogue. He rattles off the lines in the approved Kaurismäki monotone; the effect is improved by Wilms's hulking body and craggy face, which would convince you he was a tough guy if he didn't make such a fuss over a little thing like a bloody nose. To complete the trio, we have Kari Väänänen as Schaunard, a man who devotes himself alternately to the art of music and the craft of balancing a cigarette butt between sneering lips and an overhung nose. The high point of his performance—and certainly one of the most gripping moments of the entire *La Vie de Bohème*—is his rendition of a new composition for piano, voice and police siren, which so moves Mimi and Musette that they resolve to leave the artists. Or maybe they had to get out because of the sausage Schaunard fed them. The point is, we don't really know what's at fault—the art or the food. There is no doubt some causal connection, but which way does it run?

As if made lightheaded by some cinematographic malnutrition of its own, Kaurismäki's camera stares blankly at these scenes, neither forcing you to laugh nor cuing you to weep. (Maybe the darkness of some shots is meant to elicit a corresponding emotional gloom, but I don't think so. Kaurismäki is just underlighting so he can get away with the cheapest possible sets.) How is it possible, then, that the picture's tone suddenly shifts, when nothing else has changed? Eighty minutes into the film, you'll probably be laughing your head off at these stooges. By the ninety-minute mark, your heart will be broken.

At the end, when Rodolfo is once more alone (except for his faithful dog, Baudelaire), a dirge plays on the soundtrack; and though it's a Japanese dirge, it seems right all the same, not just for Mimi's death but for the death of a century and a half's sacred follies. Maybe the bohemian life does not rise again in *La Vie de Bohème,* but it dies once more, and does it beautifully.

Moulin Rouge

A tale of social upheaval and artistic ferment set in the Montmartre of 1899, Baz Luhrmann's *Moulin Rouge* is (in its own words) spectacular! bohemian! wevolutionawy! It is a tribute paid by one turn-of-the-century decadence to another: a lavish, excessive, exuberant, silly, two-hour pile-up of stroboscopic editing and primary colors, musical pastiches and campy poses, pop-up-book settings and sparkly special effects.

Moulin Rouge is also a faithful work of cultural history. It made me dream of the movie Alfred Jarry might have made about his circle, had he been privileged to toy with super-digital equipment.

But first, the can-can!

Luhrmann rushes us out of the frame story and into the mosh pit of the Moulin Rouge, where women clad in parrot hues alternately shriek into the camera and hike their skirts in your face, where black-suited men sweat and bellow like Circe's pigs. A jungle, an inferno, a pop-music battlefield. Disco clashes against grunge rock: "Voulez-vous couchez avec moi?" call the showgirl prostitutes, to the rich johns' response, "Here we are—entertain us!"

Tucked away in one corner of this hoopla sits Ewan McGregor, done up as a poor young English poet named Christian. A thin disguise: It calls for inky hair to flop across his brow, while he mimes a high-strung eagerness to please and pops his blue eyes at Nicole Kidman. She is dressed for the occasion as Satine, queen of the prostitute showgirls; but her true status as a movie star is revealed by the sequence of loving close-ups through which she is introduced. Kidman gets to show off, without delay, the tidily sculpted angles of her face, several versions of her pert little head-tilt and the full glory of her hair, which Luhrmann makes blaze like a fire in a copper foundry. Impressed? So are her suitors on the screen. Kidman dangles like bait over the rich johns' heads, swings in a circle beyond their grasp, dips in and out of their arms and is at last popped upward from their midst (she's the champagne cork, they're the bottle); all this, as she mimics Monroe, Madonna and Rita Hayworth, while warbling "Diamonds Are a Girl's Best Friend."

The scene is flabbergasting, hilarious, wevolutionawy (to quote once more the film's Toulouse-Lautrec, played with oily glee by John Leguizamo). But where *is* the can-can? Grabbing a moment for thought—and a moment is as much as Luhrmann will allow—you notice that for all the frenetic movement, you don't see a dance, just glimpses of dancers. Luhrmann edits choreography into Cubist shards.

Or, to put it another way: He creates no coherent space within the Moulin Rouge. Outside, the city of Paris is spread out in legible dimensions, and beautifully too. (Viewed from above, it looks like a hand-drawn postcard that can magically gain depth of field.) The immediate neighborhood also seems geographically stable. From the roof of Montmartre's celebrated windmill you see Christian's garret, and from his window you see the windmill's sails. Often enough, the camera takes you flying between the two. But inside the Moulin Rouge, Luhrmann has given his characters no shared place in which they might build a dance routine.

I am reminded of the joke about Tolstoy's having a panic attack, the night after he hands in the manuscript of *War and Peace.* "What?" asks his wife, as he sits bolt upright in bed. "My God!" he gasps. "I forgot to put in the regatta!"

I doubt that Luhrmann forgot, either. He is an obsessive-compulsive director; and in *Moulin Rouge,* this man who made *Strictly Ballroom* has preferred song to dance, for reasons that are still to be discovered. However much his characters jig about, in standard patterns that are continually interrupted, the film's emotions and ideas live in the songs, which establish the common ground that is missing for the dancers. By singing to one another, Christian and Satine create a space for themselves.

You see it happening on the gorgeously improbable rooftop where Christian and Satine sing the medley-to-end-all-medleys. (Among everything else, *Moulin Rouge* is a thesaurus of the movie musical, offering a set of variations for each type of production number. The categories include the medley, the backer's audition, the Latin intermezzo, the cross-dresser's novelty act—in which Jim Broadbent, as manager of the Moulin Rouge, performs "Like a Virgin"—and the Bombay extravaganza.) But, to get back to the roof: Christian has gently taken hold of Satine's fingertips. As he sings to her, he drops his head and gazes down, as if in wonder, at the sight of her hands; then, with a rise in the musical phrase, he looks up again. A conventional bit of musical-comedy blocking, which is over and done in a second. As performed here, it's also a truly memorable piece of acting—as good in its way as Humphrey Bogart's casual glance toward a shop sign in *The Big Sleep*, which Manny Farber called the finest moment in 1940s film. With this offhand detail, the screen's space turns into a world that is open to untold possibilities. A radio playlist cliché, such as Elton John's "Your Song," can suddenly sound heartfelt; show-biz shtick can dissolve into unforced emotion.

I'm tempted to go over the top—that is, to follow the film's unswerving direction—and speak of the redemption of musical-comedy conventions. But Luhrmann doesn't seem to believe these gestures need redemption. To understand his faith in them is to realize why *Moulin Rouge* qualifies as cultural history.

The historical perspective opens in one of the film's early scenes, when Christian performs, impromptu, the schmaltziest number in the Rodgers and Hammerstein songbook. To Toulouse-Lautrec and his gang of absinthe-soaked zanies, Christian's song is a revelation: This, *this*, is the art of the future. Well, of course it is. The piece won't be written for another fifty years. And of course it is: because, as Luhrmann cleverly reminds us, pop culture (*The Sound of Music* included) has spent the past century promulgating the bohemian virtues of Truth, Freedom, Beauty and Love.

If this observation seems too broad to mean anything, then think back to the current that flowed between Rimbaud's drunken boat and Picasso's Bateau Lavoir. Within that rivulet of time, a few influential people began paddling away from the grand-scale seriousness that had characterized 19th-century art, preferring to find novelty, and even a sense of defiance, in frivolity and populism. These artists began devoting themselves to pastiche, collage and parody; they got high and stayed out all night, proclaimed freedom for love in all its forms, forged an alliance between low-rent living and dandyism. This way of life was new in the 1890s. It would be revived many times in the future, on a much larger scale, with the encouragement of movies and pop music—which is why nothing is more serious in *Moulin Rouge* than Christian's statement that he came to Montmartre during the Summer of Love.

The analogy between the two legendary time periods becomes even more compelling if you recall that the artists of the 1890s were among the first to promote their aesthetic taste as a program for social transformation. This wasn't at all the same as wedding radical art to radical politics, as the Constructivists would do, or the Berlin Dada group; but during the Summer of Love as at other times, people have tended to lose the distinction, forgetting that "wevolutionawy" is *juste* the *mot* for bohemia's cult of personal freedom. Luhrmann knows that, too. When he mocks the peace-and-love avant-garde for breaking a promise he knows won't be kept, he does so in the appropriate spirit: lightly, lovingly. And yet he also conveys a sense of disillusionment, which cuts through the film's effervescence like a spurt of bile.

At first you spot only hints of this hopelessness. During your search for coherent choreography, you might notice that Lurhmann's hyperkinetic spectacle can seem oddly static. Images and jokes are conspicuously replayed: within only a few minutes, the crotch shot of a can-can dancer is recycled, as is a codger's warning to avoid this "village of sin." Camera movements are repeated, too, as if to signal that the fastest, flashiest journeys wind up taking you nowhere. You're always zooming back and forth across the rooftops of Paris, in a motion that feels exciting until you realize you're stuck on a pendulum. Then, at the film's end, comes the ultimate stasis, the one that was announced at the beginning: death. Despite the triumph of bohemian ideals and a musical-comedy plot, the human body gives out—at which point, the film does not conclude but simply stops, while laughter dies in the audience's throat.

The abruptness of the come-down has brought on complaints. Your feet hit the pavement so flatly—you're sent out of the movie house with so little emotional release—that you wonder who, or what, you're supposed to mourn. Satine doesn't function within realist conventions; she's no Camille. But while you don't sense that an individual has passed out of the world, neither do you feel the force of a collective loss. Satine doesn't work as an allegorical figure for Youthful Illusions, AIDS Victims, Abused Womanhood or even Doomed Starlets of History. She just dies.

On one level, I find that all the more reason to respect the picture. It took nerve for Luhrmann to create the whiz-bang of *Moulin Rouge*. It took more daring still to savage expectations and end with solitude, mortality and a narrative thud.

On another level, as an obsessive-compulsive moviegoer, I find myself cataloguing the other thuds. Despite its unanticipated harshness, the ending of *Moulin Rouge* turns out to be kids' stuff, compared to the glance into the abyss that concludes Mike Leigh's 19th-century musical, *Topsy-Turvy*. The updating of the Parisian avant-garde is clever here, but it is sharply intelligent in Aki Kaurismäki's *La Vie de Bohème*, which achieves its merger of time periods with an economy that puts *Moulin Rouge* to shame. And though Luhrmann delightfully imitates the look of primitive cinema, Guy Maddin did it earlier and better. In his five-minute paean to Soviet silent film, *The Heart of the World*, Maddin even trills the r's of revolutionary fervor.

So, as high as *Moulin Rouge* lifts me, I don't go over the top. From roof level, I watch the movie continue to shoot upward and then, just short of its Méliès moon, plummet back toward the dirt. But how spectacular, as it flies! What a glorious waste of rocket fuel! Like the none-too-clearheaded artists whom it so knowingly sends up, *Moulin Rouge* reminds us that before they fizzle out, some people also dazzle.

Pass the absinthe.

The Lovers on the Bridge

L egend has it that Potemkin, burdened by duties and melancholy, once neglected to order the packing up of one of his stage-set villages. The boards remained standing many versts outside Ivanovo in a field cut through by Catherine's route. Tall stalks of grass—the painted planks' only neighbors—grew heavy with seed, blanched and bent in the autumn chill, and sank beneath months of snow. When the earth softened again, the facades were still upright, though most of them had tipped on their heels. Houses and storefronts reeled away from one another. Outlines of doors and windows dissolved as paint followed the melt-off's track.

Now it happened that religious folk from the east came wandering toward Ivanovo. One minute they were passing through untilled fields; the next, they found themselves walking down a main street of drunken, weeping buildings, where the only sounds were the songs of grasshoppers and the chanting of their own hymns. The procession shuffled to a halt. Two dozen penitents, bearing all their belongings in their hands, stared into the mirror of two dozen wooden structures, whose faces were their sole possession. With that, the wanderers came to rest. They dwelt in the road from that day till the last penitent died, living outside homes they could not enter; and never once did they violate this gift by looking behind the facades.

I tell this story because *The Lovers on the Bridge (Les Amants du Pont-Neuf)* is about to open in the United States. One good legend deserves another.

A famously troubled production, *The Lovers on the Bridge* acquired an aura of extravagance, madness and doom even before its opening, held in Paris in autumn 1991. Some called the film the most expensive ever produced in France—an inaccurate claim, since two other pictures from the same moment, Maurice Pialat's *Van Gogh* and Claude Berri's *Germinal*, cost roughly as much. But Pialat and Berri committed their money to sprawling period dramas with high-art allure. The director of *The Lovers on the Bridge*, Leos Carax, blew 160 million francs (roughly $28 million) on a romance about bums.

In interviews, Carax said some reasonable things about his choice of subject. He noted that realtors had priced working people out of the heart of Paris; the only people who now live with the fabled sights are the rich and the homeless. If you want to make a contemporary movie that shows the Louvre and the *bateaux-mouches* and the Eiffel Tower twinkling in the distance, the honest way to do so is to make your characters bums. Carax also said he wanted to strip a love story to its essentials—to show the people, rather than the telephones and answering machines. So his lovers camped out in the debris of the Pont-Neuf (the bridge was closed for repairs in 1989), living with almost nothing but their feelings for one another.

How did a scheme that was so straightforward, so humble, come to cost a fortune? Carax needed to control his set. To do so, he went to a field outside Montpellier and built his own Pont-Neuf. Roughly full size at its center, the Carax Pont-Neuf tapered off at either end to two-thirds scale, providing forced perspectives toward quais and boulevards lined with Potemkin-style buildings. Now Carax could realize sequences such as the Bastille Day bicentennial, for which he restaged the immense fireworks display as a private show for his lovers. Beneath the bridge, he dug a Seine-like pond, deep enough for the big water-skiing scene.

The first producer died. Filming stopped. Carax broke up with his lover and lead actress, Juliette Binoche. After the release of *The Unbearable Lightness of Being*, she had become an international star, receiving offers of roles that were far better paid and far less grubby. But out of loyalty to Carax's vision, she stayed with the film; another producer, the valiant Christian Fechner, stepped in; and despite further interruptions, *The Lovers on the Bridge* was finally completed, though it took three years to make and ran three times over budget.

Critical response in France was rapturous; audience response, less so. A year after the Paris opening, judged a box-office failure and still without an American distributor, *The Lovers on the Bridge* had its US premiere at the 1992 New York Film Festival. Reactions ranged from irritation to ecstasy, sometimes within the same viewer. In the *New York Times*, Vincent Canby wrote that the gorgeous exuberance of the film's high point was its own excuse for being. He also noted that after this high point, the film still had half its running time to go. Such a notice from the *Times* will not embolden distributors. *The Lovers on the Bridge* went unreleased in the United States.

And so, among filmoids, the picture became a legend. Isolated moments from it seemed to crop up in other movies: a scene of Juliette Binoche being lifted to view an old painting, which recurred in *The English Patient*; a shot of lovers forming themselves into a ship's figurehead, which made its way into *Titanic*. Apparently, filmmakers were watching *The Lovers on the Bridge*. Mere enthusiasts could only wait for special screenings, swap rumors and gossip about the film, and pray for a US release.

Miramax Zoë and Martin Scorsese Presents have answered those prayers, seven years after the film's American premiere. *The Lovers on the Bridge* is opening theatrically in New York and Los Angeles, with further runs to come.

Now, having dutifully brought you up to date, I feel free to abandon the historico-descriptive mode and launch into polemic, as one of the film's partisans. Bear in mind, as you read the following, that I served on the selection committee that brought *The Lovers on the Bridge* to the New York Film Festival. In a book written in praise of the film folly I called *The Lovers on the Bridge* the perfection of the form; and in recent months I've shown up in various cities for one-night screenings where, griotlike, I've sung the film's genealogy and praise. I couldn't back off even if Orson Welles were to descend from heaven and anathematize the picture, with Renoir at his right hand and Ozu at his left.

Nor would I want to back off. *The Lovers on the Bridge* is one of the most splendidly reckless films ever made—the film that might have torn through the mind of Godard's Pierrot le Fou, after love made him paint his face blue and tie sticks of dynamite to his hair.

It is not a film that "tells the story of," even though there is a story of sorts—about Michèle (Binoche), an aspiring artist from a well-to-do family, driven by illness and heartache to live on the street, and Alex (Denis Lavant), the mumbling, skinheaded loner who fixes on her. There is also a third character, an elder-statesman bum called Hans (Klaus-Michael Grüber), who helps move things along—but the linking of events, as I've said, is not the film's main concern. While the fuses sizzle near your head, Carax makes a film about orange flames shooting across a black sky; about a subway passage that turns into an inferno; about the thrumming and skittering of a cello sonata, random gunfire, a snowfall out of an old movie musical. *The Lovers on the Bridge* is about the face of Juliette Binoche, haggard and grimy and intent, with one eye bandaged and the other rolling up into her skull, and the tense, tumbling, doughily muscled body of Denis Lavant, which is always getting shattered or blown apart.

As extreme in its naturalism as it is in fantasy, *The Lovers on the Bridge* begins almost as a documentary, with footage shot in a homeless shelter outside Paris. Nothing pretty here. You see actual human beings in actual misery. To witness them, stumbling and writhing, is to think that existence is a rapidly sinking rock to which we're chained; "freedom," a few millimeters' slack in our restraints. This is reality, as Carax first provides it for Alex. But then, as the film introduces Michèle and transfers its action to the bridge, Carax begins to envision the world as a more malleable place, where fact yields to emotion. Dreams intrude onto the screen; images shake and distort and overlap; the city itself, that Potemkin illusion, begins to shimmer and dematerialize. On Bastille Day, Alex's longing and Michèle's need for abandonment meet in a climax of drunkenness—at which point, in the great fireworks scene, *The Lovers on the Bridge* bursts into glory.

Here, like a wandering penitent before the icons of "home," I must fall silent. Description fails, because the central section of *The Lovers on the Bridge* dwells apart from the realm of language. It's pure essence of movie, the stuff that movies might have been invented to give us. If you tell me that the rest of the film can't live up to these sequences, I'd have to agree. The lovers slide down a long slope from that infatuation—and Carax's eye, which is so unconventional yet unerring in the first part of the film, slides with them, sometimes becoming lax in the second half.

And so what? Have you never burned yourself up for an impossible fling?

"If the fool would persist in his folly he would become wise." *The Lovers on the Bridge* is a film by and for the persistent fool—the one who, full of regret, would do everything a second time. It's a mistake, a wreck, an absurd imposture—a priceless gift. Best to accept it with empty hands, as if you were a character in an old Russian tale that someone just made up.

The Dreamlife of Angels

I t's characteristic of Erick Zonca's extraordinary first feature, *The Dreamlife of Angels*, that we never learn how Isa got that scar across her right eyebrow. It's just there: a fragment of personal history, borne in the flesh by someone who doesn't think much about her past.

Barely into her 20s, Isa clomps onto the screen sporting a brush haircut that was surely self-administered and wearing the motley layers of a wanderer. Her clothes, like her eyebrow, must have a history (or histories—these wrappings may have belonged to three or four different people before Isa put them on), but she carries her outfit comfortably, as if she weren't living in it as a transient.

We soon learn that Isa has traveled to the northeast of France in much the same spirit. She's arrived expecting to stay with a friend. But she can't have kept in touch with him; he's long since moved on from the trailer where he slept. The neighbors have no forwarding address; in fact—no surprise—they scarcely know his name. But Isa doesn't worry, despite this transition from borrowed shelter to none. Having made her way to the provincial capital of Lille, bundled up against the snow, she now simply camps out.

By now, only five minutes have passed in *The Dreamlife of Angels*. Already we know that this dark young woman, with her oval face and ripely assertive mouth, is as rootless as a person can be. And yet, miraculously, she's fully a person. Isa (Elodie Bouchez) comes onto the screen intact—as complete as if the filmmakers had found her, instead of making her up.

The Dreamlife of Angels is the story of one season of Isa's vagabondage and of the lives she inhabits while slowly passing through Lille. Spending time in a city that's not her own, squatting in the apartment of someone she's never met, Isa adds her plenitude to two other characters, who in their different ways give her a void to fill. One of them, a teenager named Sandrine, lies in the hospital in a coma, the victim of a car wreck. Isa not only reads the diary Sandrine has left behind but also inserts herself into it, as if carrying forward the girl's interrupted life. The other character, Marie (Natacha Régnier), can still walk, talk, smoke cigarettes and swill wine; yet in her own way, she turns out to be as present-but-absent as Sandrine.

At first, though, Marie seems to be the assertive and capable one, compared with Isa. The two meet at a small factory, where Isa has found a minimum-wage job sewing the sleeves for blouses—a job she loses as quickly as it was found, since she stitches her whole first batch inside out. But before getting the boot, Isa has experiences that are denied to most characters in movies today. She performs manual labor, receiving an apprenticeship whose rough-ness will be recognized by anyone who's done the same. She falls in with the other women, who share their lunches with her and otherwise offer the brusque yet easy welcome that's common on shop floors, though unknown amid the computerized cubicles you usually see onscreen. Most important, Isa retreats into the refuge of working women, the toilet, where she has her first encounter with Marie.

Bonier than Isa, more conventionally pretty but so pale that she looks translucent, Marie is your basic 20-year-old *enragée*. When she meets a luxury car, her first response is to kick in its taillights. So when the new girl follows Marie "home" from the factory—that is, to the apartment where she's been squatting—Isa temporarily seems like a mouse, and Marie like the skinny lion who *wants* a thorn in its paw. It's Marie who provides shelter and Marie who shows Isa around town. But when the new friends try to get into a concert without paying, you notice that Isa does all the talking. Marie hangs back. Her mane, you see, is limp, and so is her rebellion.

The rest of the film might be described as the playing out of a double obses-sion. Marie, who can be so forceful against a fancy car, goes supine when con-fronted with its owner, a sleek-haired rich boy named Chris (Grégoire Colin). Suddenly, all her ferocity pours into the fantasy that Mr. Money might make her his girlfriend. Isa, meanwhile, sets off on a different avenue of escape. Having learned that the rightful owner of her squat lies in a hospital, unconscious and unvisited, Isa begins spending time at her bedside. On one level, she's caring for

Sandrine, making her recovery slightly more likely. On a second level, she's behaving like Marie: disappearing into the imagined life of someone with property. And then, on yet another level, Isa is circling back to her own reality, as Marie refuses to do. Sandrine's diary shows that her life, despite the property, hasn't been all that great.

What do I like best in this story? The air currents. Zonca films all this with such immediacy—and his two astonishing actresses perform in it with such self-abandonment—that you can smell the cigarettes and unchanged sheets in their apartment, and catch the chill of the breezes that ripple through Lille's streets. There's a sense of space—real, open space—in every scene. Maybe that's why Isa and Marie, though so unalterable in character, never seem predictable as they develop throughout the film. They have room to unfold.

They even have room for silliness. In one inspired sequence, Zonca sends the two friends to search for jobs at a new theme bar called The Hollywood. The waitresses there will impersonate American film stars, so Isa and Marie can't simply apply for work; they have to audition. Of course, the scene is a gift to the actresses: Bouchez and Régnier get to perform as Isa and Marie performing as Madonna and Lauren Bacall. But even within this diversion, fresh revelations come whistling through the picture. Asked to demonstrate how their characters would "act," Bouchez and Régnier push themselves to the point of caricature. They show us an irrepressible, outgoing Isa, who bounces nuttily onstage next to a withdrawn, narcissistic Marie, who can scarcely bring herself to look up and speak. And Zonca, as usual, lets the actresses work. He keeps the camera back just far enough so that he doesn't crowd them; he lets the take continue just long enough so that he doesn't force anything. Moments of pure artifice don't get more natural than this.

There is, toward the end, another moment, brief and unforgettable, when the film's sense of open air becomes awful. Of course: Isa and Marie can't float forever in their fantasies of other lives. But that's a measure of the integrity of *The Dreamlife of Angels*. While the characters are blowing around loose, the ground remains at their feet. Anyone who's been on the scuffle at 19 or 20 will recall that feeling, with a mingled smile and shudder.

And for Erick Zonca, *The Dreamlife of Angels* must be such a recollection. Although the picture seems absolutely contemporary, Zonca is in his early 40s. Surely his own wandering years, or those of people he knew, have figured into the atmosphere. You might even say that his self-projection into Isa and Marie is the film's ultimate case of living through others. In *The Dreamlife of Angels*, a middle-aged man fantasizes himself into two young women. That he does so almost invisibly, with the ease of breathing, is part of what makes his film a revelation.

What's revealed is that impossible thing, the truth. Reviewers ought to tremble when they write the word; filmmakers themselves don't dare mention it. In fact, I have before me an interview with Zonca in which he claims to want to make "tragic, violent, moving stories that have nothing to do with real life." Tragic, violent, moving—all right. But "nothing to do with real life"? That's the one lie he's told so far.

November 22, 1999

Rosetta

Ever since *Rosetta* won the top prize at this year's Cannes festival, American journalists have puzzled over the jury's decision, or written it off as mere insolence. To hear them tell it, the film is so slight as to flirt with nonexistence. There are no stars and no big actorly turns, no amusing settings and no enviable clothes, no songs, no suspense, no excitement, no romance—nothing but an angry and impoverished 18-year-old girl, living in a trailer park outside some Belgian town that looks as if it were all poured from the same cement mixer.

This description is accurate in fact; but it is not truthful. It doesn't tell you that *Rosetta* is both subtle and stunningly direct; that its narrow focus is more like a stare, at once penetrating and compassionate; that suspense, excitement, romance and even music animate the picture—though an audience habituated to American movies might not notice these qualities without first purging itself. A painless procedure: Simply abandon the things you think you know; stop busying yourself with emotions you think you should feel. Open your eyes, ears and mind to *Rosetta*, and discover how full this movie can be.

At the film's center—and its periphery, too, since she occupies every frame—is the title character, played by Emilie Dequenne, who shared the prize for best actress at Cannes. Before *Rosetta*, she had not appeared in front of a camera; she performed as if she believed, once the filming stopped, she would no longer exist at all. From the opening scene onward, Dequenne seems to hurl herself against the world, which is as much of a strategy as the character herself can manage.

We first see her from behind, without knowing why she's stomping and panting her way down a corridor. The camera, which is handheld throughout the movie, chases after Rosetta, scarcely able to keep up with her fury. Suddenly, in a blur of action, she is in a shouting match. She has completed a training program at a factory, only to be told there are no jobs—and now, in desperation, she not only refuses to leave the premises but assaults the personnel manager.

So much for introductions. It's only when she's been peeled off her opponent and is outside again, riding the bus toward home, that we get a clear view of Rosetta. She has the sort of broad, flat face that runs down in straight lines from hairline to jaw, then slants in abruptly to a square little chin—features that are left harshly unframed, since her dark hair is sheared no more carefully than a dog's. Her costume—a zippered sweatshirt, a jacket with red and black stripes, a short skirt that looks too flimsy for the weather—leaves her looking short and chunky. You can believe this young woman subsists on waffles and French toast.

In the washed-out light that predominates in *Rosetta*, these brute facts strike the eye bluntly. And yet half the action is invisible. You observe the minute details of Rosetta's routine—the way she hides her town shoes in an out-of-use drainpipe, the way she sneaks into the trailer park from the rear, through the woods—but the reasons for these actions never rise to the surface. That's the subtlety of *Rosetta*: The film is as reticent as its protagonist, who refuses to let people see her enter the trailer park and won't expose her precious shoes in that place.

The shoes are her tokens of "a normal life," the name she puts on the seemingly unattainable ideal of a job, a fixed home, a friend. Without them, Rosetta lives between shame and rage: shame that she strenuously conceals in the face of "normal" people, rage that explodes when anyone penetrates her mask. Watch what happens when Riquet (Fabrizio Rongione), a very casual acquaintance from town, follows her to the trailer park on his motorbike. Rosetta launches herself at him and has to be wrestled into submission in the mud—and all the poor guy wanted was to direct her toward a job, and maybe ask for a date.

Dates are a delicate issue for Rosetta. She suffers from chronic cramps, which she treats by warming her belly with a hair dryer. Maybe the problem is all that rage and shame; or maybe it's her mother, who likes to get drunk and screw. No matter that those are among the favorite pastimes of normal people. Sex and booze are dangerous luxuries to Rosetta, who eats her own gut trying to keep Mom in line. Still, when Riquet sets her up with a job, she consents to visit his apartment.

The film, which has been moving headlong, slows down for the first time, as

Rosetta allows herself to sit at Riquet's table. She eats the starchy meal he serves. She listens to his music. Abruptly, unexpectedly, she accepts a beer and downs it in one gulp. Romance, song, suspense: Have they ever been felt more intensely in a movie than they are here, in this narrow, smoky room, with people who are so awkward, inarticulate and touching?

"Your name is Rosetta," she says to herself later, lying in darkness, and answers, "My name is Rosetta. You have a job. I have a job. You have a normal life. I have a normal life." As the camera hangs above her, you watch this young woman trying to become the self she hopes for; and though the actress is still and the image still, something trembles in the scene. It's the movement of your thoughts and feelings.

People say *Rosetta* is a slice-of-life drama; and that description, too, is accurate in fact. But it says nothing about the whirl of three or four extended scenes—set pieces, in effect—which rise to such a pitch of irony that realism falls away. By the end, the buzz of Riquet's motorbike sounds like the wings of the Furies; the weight of a propane tank in Rosetta's arms becomes as inescapable as the rock of Sisyphus. Big dramas are enacted by these little people in the trailer park, even while their physical presence remains hard and irreducible.

Rosetta was written and directed by Luc and Jean-Pierre Dardenne. Their previous film, *La Promesse*, also took the outward form of a social-problem picture, about undocumented workers from Africa and the people who smuggle them into Belgium. It was a good piece of work; but I thought it was a little too flattering to the audience. Whenever the main character faced a moral choice, he did exactly what you thought he should.

Rosetta is not so convenient. Its protagonist does what she thinks she must. Her choices will probably sit uncomfortably with you; but there's an almost fanatical integrity to them, which is matched by the integrity of the film-making. For the Dardennes, good direction is not just a question of maintaining an honest viewpoint, or telling a story with all due economy. If they found even one frame in *Rosetta* that struck them as a lie, you feel, they would go to the projection booth, tear it from the reel and burn it.

Would Rosetta herself watch *Rosetta*? I don't think she'd want to. She'd probably believe that movies, like sex and booze, are dangerous luxuries; if she dared to indulge, she would choose one that "normal" people were going to see. But if she found herself in the dark with these images, I think she would recognize herself. Maybe then she'd say, "Your name is Rosetta. You are worthy of attention," and quietly answer, against all odds, "My name is Rosetta. I am worthy of attention."

After Life

T hanks to the genius of millions, who over the generations have created
our language, we may speak of the most uncanny experience in terms
that suit the most common. We call a place haunted to say that it feels
the touch of the other world—and also to describe it as a hangout of
the day-in, day-out kind. Whether this overlay of meanings holds in Japanese, I
do not know. But thanks to the genius of Hirokazu Kore-eda, I have just visited
an unforgettably day-in, day-out place: an old high school or municipal
building where coat hooks are fixed in the ocher walls, potted plants perch on
the ledges of casement windows, gooseneck lamps sit on wooden desks and the
residents are hard-working ghosts.

As brisk as a snow flurry, as straightforward as a photo-booth portrait, as sly and
heartbreaking as memory, Kore-eda's *After Life* is the story of a half-dozen ghosts
who staff a kind of social service agency for the newly dead. We witness one full
cycle of the weekly routine: receiving the caseload on Monday, officially informing
the clients of their demise, helping them prepare for the beyond and then seeing
them off on Saturday. We learn something about the lives of most of the week's
twenty-two cases, who range from a teenage girl with a plaid scarf and singsong
voice to a perfectly round old woman with round eyeglasses who smiles perpetually
but seldom speaks. In addition, we learn something about ourselves as viewers of
these characters—because *After Life* is also a story about watching movies.

For each of the dead, the caseworkers diligently reproduce on film a single moment from his or her life. It will be the one memory to sustain that person throughout eternity; all else will vanish. So the haunted municipal building does double duty as a haunted movie studio. The main business during the first half of the week is to interview the cases and help them choose their moments; during the second half, to make a series of one-scene movies, each crafted for a singular audience, using production methods from roughly the same era as the building. The world to come has not yet converted to digital. Sets still require carpentry; sound effects are played on cassette recorders.

The setting and methods may be humble, but then so are the people. A 50ish man with a broad, chewed-up face wants to recall the breeze he felt as a boy, as he rode home on a steamy bus the day before summer vacation would begin. A tiny woman in her 70s, with short gray hair and a blue knit suit, chooses a memory of dancing for her older brother in a red dress he'd bought her. Though many of the week's cases lived through earthquake and war, their lasting memories seem to have happened to one side of these great events. The dead hold on to a privileged moment with their parents, an unanticipated act of kindness from American soldiers, a change in the light.

One essential function of movies is surely to show us other people and satisfy our curiosity about them. In *After Life*, Kore-eda meets this requirement again and again, and in the most direct way possible, presenting these characters in a series of interviews shot head-on. The people seem to speak to us directly; and since they've been asked to address their favorite subject—themselves—they give us everything.

But, of course, we want more than they give. Movies don't just tell us stories; they also provide plots. Kore-eda meets this requirement, too, but in a more oblique manner. He eases us into a delicate constellation of hopes, conflicts and disappointments, beginning with the interviews of two people who can't, or won't, choose their moments.

One of these hard cases is a 21-year-old with geometric clothes and electrified hair. This is Iseya (Yusuke Iseya), who figures "your whole setup needs rethinking." Scrunching up in the chair with his boots on the seat, he proposes filming one of his dreams, which would be cool, or maybe realizing an event from the future. But select something from the past? That's *old*.

The other hard case, who proves to be even more troublesome, is Watanabe (Taketoshi Naito), age 71: a gravel-voiced gentleman with a professorial look—eyeglasses, goatee, turtleneck and sport coat—and an expression of pained befuddlement. After a lifetime of doing everything right—a college education, a proper marriage, an executive position with a steel-making company—Watanabe realizes he can't think of a single memory he'd want to keep. The caseworkers, ever helpful, call in his videotapes. (It seems there's a cassette for each year of our lives.) But when Watanabe reviews the tapes, he only feels worse. His life plays back like a travesty of an Ozu film: long takes of ordinary moments, which don't fill with emotion but instead dribble it out pathetically as the seconds pass.

If Watanabe is to salvage anything, the caseworkers will have to help—which is where the plot takes hold. On Wednesday, Mochizuki (Arata) asks to be removed from the case. A fresh-faced man with a fashionable black suit and floppy hair, he has become uncharacteristically rattled by Watanabe. This uneasiness draws the attention of his partner Shiori (Erika Oda), who observes Mochizuki with sharp, sidelong glances. She's the birdlike apprentice among the caseworkers: a very young woman who dresses for invisibility in a nondescript cardigan and bowl-cut hair. But as Mochizuki drifts away from her, into thoughts of his own, Shiori begins to resist, showing she's of the same stubborn generation as the week's other hard case.

Who would have thought the dead have such complicated relationships? It's as surprising as the news that they drink Earl Grey tea and cheat at go. So many little things to give up before they can finish dying—not least those changes of light. And what if they refuse to give up? What if they insist on staying in a world of asymmetrical shots and hand-held camera movements, instead of yielding to the simple finality of a head-on view?

After Life is too full of what-ifs for me to give a complete list. But I can at least mention a few more questions that press forward. What if lived experience is like documentary video—just point and shoot—but memory has to be constructed, like a scene in the movies? What if a movie had one scene made just for you? What if our lives—good, bad or indifferent—all took their place in a collective creation: an infinitely long film, which would turn the humblest detail into magic? What if there were a place—not in this world, obviously—where films were made solely for love?

Going on my mundane round, I don't expect to encounter magic, or to feel the rapture of falling into the screen. All I ask is that filmmakers show respect for the instruments in their hands, while proceeding as if my life, and yours, might be taken seriously. How often I'm disappointed. But then comes Kore-eda with *After Life*. It's a film that treats the impostures of moviemaking as a high vocation, though a comic one—a fiction that wants to make room for everyone who sees it. I fell into *After Life*, and I intend to fall in again and again, at whichever movie house will show it. I'm haunted.

Dr. Akagi

Has no one informed Dr. Akagi that he's living in a complex and serious drama, about the morale of Japanese citizens toward the end of World War II? Apparently not, to judge by the way he behaves like one of the Marx Brothers. Here he is, hurrying through his seaside village—

But I've committed a redundancy. Dr. Akagi (Akira Emoto) knows no form of motion other than the headlong. Despite his middle-aged heft, despite the white in his mustache, he goes everywhere at a trot, huffing and sweating and pumping his arms as if God had called, "On the double!" So, to start again: Here he is in his seaside village—

But in what sense is Dr. Akagi "in" the village? His jog carries him over bridges by fishermen's shacks, across fields planted with vegetables, up the hill near an old factory (which now serves as a work camp for prisoners of war). En route, he pauses to examine people in their homes, in his office, in the brothel that's been turned into an officers' club. But do any of these spaces contain him? How much less is he held in by their aggregate? Whereas another film might patiently assemble its settings into the mental image of "village," *Dr. Akagi* lets them bounce past one another, like rainbow-colored balls in the drum of some cosmic lottery game. So, again: Dr. Akagi—

But that's not what people call him. They prefer to use a half-affectionate, half-mocking nickname, bestowed in honor of his single diagnosis. No matter which patient he sees, no matter for which ailment, he invariably declares, "Hepatitis!" So he's now known as Kanzo Sensei: Dr. Liver.

I'll try once more:

Past vegetables, prostitutes and prisoners of war trots an out-of-breath man, crying "Hepatitis!" By acting this way, he claims, he does his bit to serve the Emperor, and help "liberate Asia from the white race." So long as Dr. Liver pursues his private, all-out war against hepatitis (which he wants to make known as epidemic), he need not think too much about his son, who is stationed somewhere in Manchuria; or about Germany, which now presents a woeful example of a nation in defeat; or about the less meritorious habits of Japan's soldiers, which may be observed even in the village.

Singlemindedness may insulate Dr. Akagi from these troubles, but it cannot forever keep him from falling apart. Like the Marx Brothers toward the end of *Duck Soup*—another important war movie—the doctor is already in pieces, unable to stay in the same costume from one shot to the next. First you see him puffing along in a straw boater, bow tie and ice-cream suit; then, after the cut, he's running in the same direction but in a different outfit.

Is this merely a mistake in continuity? Not likely. *Dr. Akagi* is the work of Shohei Imamura, who in his 70s has tapped into a new vein of his prodigious talent. Last year saw the belated release in the United States of his fantasia on redemption, night fishing and UFOs, *The Eel*. I struggled in these pages to convey something of its brilliance. Now I have to chase behind *Dr. Akagi*, hoping again to catch a few of the bright fragments Imamura scatters in his wake.

Speaking of fragments and mistakes: When Dr. Akagi receives bad news in a letter, he rips up the paper and flings its pieces into the air. Of course, they tumble back down—but then they keep tumbling, as if his grief, so endless and impossible, had turned into a snowfall. In *Dr. Akagi*, apparent ruptures in the natural order can be decorative (like that shower of paper); or stupefying (like the finale, which cannot be anticipated and should not be described); or mordant, grotesque and generative all at once, like the momentary resurrection of a fisherman.

While you try to think of another film that treats resurrection as just a passing incident, I will explain that the fisherman died (though not completely) while administering a disciplinary beating to his daughter Sonoko, a tall, lithe, bronzed young woman who has been working as a prostitute. With his dying breath—the real one—the fisherman commends Sonoko to Akagi's care, thereby bringing into the doctor's house a character who is in every way his equal. I suppose the film might just as well have been titled *Sonoko*. We meet her before we see Akagi, and her dreams and memories inform the film as much as his.

It seems she loves the father who beat her; she believes he could have killed a whale, singlehanded. "One day *I'll* kill a whale for *you*," she promises Akagi, when (to his alarm) she falls in love with him. Love is not simple, especially in the summer of 1945. Akagi will not allow himself to accept this bundle of needs and vitality that wants to dump herself in his lap; watch his eyes, and you can see him add her to the list of subjects to be avoided through diligent medical research. Sonoko nevertheless clings to him all the more firmly—perhaps because everyone else wants her to abandon the straight life she took up so recently.

Tomiko (Keiko Matsuzaka), the matronly brothel owner, presses Sonoko to fill in—just for one night!—to entertain the prison-camp commander. It's hard to say no to Tomiko, or to the woman who begs Sonoko to initiate her son. The lad has been called up for the army, and mom thinks he'll be less likely to attract bullets if he's no longer a virgin. Even Sonoko's younger sisters want her to resume the trade. "We're starving," they plead. "Go back to whoring."

Kumiko Aso, who plays Sonoko, reacts to these pleas with the disdain of a born whalehunter. Rangy and thin, she projects a whiplike energy held in check for great things, though in the meantime she's got enough exasperation to make her twitch. It's a wonderful, half-mimed comic performance, which also manages to be touching, without for a moment resorting to waiflike appeal. (Movie waifs are generally in need of light dusting; Sonoko seems filthy, even after she's cleaned up.) I think she's fully a match for Akira Emoto's Akagi, who reminded me of Groucho in his moments of high, or even middling, dudgeon. He, too, moves low to the ground and is perpetually busy in an obsessed, irascible way. The difference: Emoto clings to the dignity that for Groucho was only a toy.

Perhaps it was another of those miraculous mistakes for him to have retained this sense of gravity and purpose while living through *Dr. Akagi*. The dramatic-irony meter is on its highest setting, all the way through the film. We know how soon the characters' doings will be made futile; in case we forget, we have a soundtrack full of Americanized music to remind us. Beyond that, we can see how patched-together is the little family that forms around Dr. Akagi. This stalwart of the Emperor keeps company not only with Sonoko but with a drunken Buddhist priest (Juro Kara), a cynical dope-fiend surgeon (Masanori Sera) and even a Dutch soldier (Jacques Gamblin) who has escaped from the prisoner-of-war camp. Which illusions, exactly, can he expect to hold when he casts his eyes upon the people in his own home?

Not the illusions that obsess the commander of the prison camp. That man fantasizes about discovering why Japan is not doing so well in the war. His answer, of course, is of the one-size-fits-all variety and can be easily remedied. There must be a spy in the work camp; find the spy, kill him, and Japan will win. For Akagi and Sonoko this kind of thinking does not simplify life; it complicates matters, in unhappy ways. They prefer to pursue other kinds of dreams: ill-matched, improbable, at once grand and funny.

Shohei Imamura honors them greatly for chasing after their illusions, and he honors the audience by offering us this tragic, home-front *Night at the Opera*. On the program this evening: the Marx Brothers in *Götterdämmerung*—and the surprisingly young and lovely Margaret Dumont isn't wearing any underpants.

The Sweet Hereafter

A s Mitchell Stephens, a lawyer prowling for someone to sue, Ian Holm presents himself to five households in *The Sweet Hereafter*, insisting to each set of characters, "It's important that we talk." *How* he talks varies from one listener to the next. All are residents of a community tucked into the snowy mountains of British Columbia; all have been devastated by a catastrophe—the crash of a school bus—that has killed nearly every child in town. What might the survivors need, or want? Mitchell Stephens, a gray-haired Mephistopheles with a cell phone and a rented sedan, continually alters the themes of his speech, his tone of voice—even his posture—as he goes to and fro, converting mourners into litigants.

Upon entering the Bide-a-Wile Motel, Stephens sniffs the musk of envy and shame coming off its thick-bodied proprietor, Wendell (Maury Chaykin). Soon Wendell is devouring the bowl of chips he's ostensibly brought out for his guest, all the while drinking in Stephens's description of him as a "good, upstanding" citizen, one of those "who will help us with our cause." Then it's down the road to Wanda and Hartley (Arsinée Khanjian and Earl Pastko): fuzzy arts-and-crafts types who live in an A-frame house of their own construction. Stephens discovers them clinging to each other, clutching their grief like a blanket. Within five minutes of getting in the door, he's literally stalking them on hands and knees, moving in until he gets Wanda to strike back with a cry of animal rage.

Dolores (Gabrielle Rose), who drove the fatal school bus, has not abandoned her habit of good cheer, even though she's now in a neck brace, sitting amid photographs of dead children whom she thinks of as her own and still speaks of in the present tense. Perhaps her need for moral exoneration is so great, she'll settle for the legal clearance that Stephens can offer. During her strangely chipper monologues, he lets his mind wander, as if he feels he could take her for granted—something he'd never do when visiting Sam (Tom McCamus), the local carpenter, whom he's made into his closest buddy. Sam requires such special attention because his daughter was the only child to live through the crash. Her name is Nicole (Sarah Polley), and she has the advantages of being pretty, talented and smart. Better still, from Stephens's point of view, she's now in a wheelchair. He can't wait to get her into court.

But then there's the hard case: Billy (Bruce Greenwood), an amateur guitarist with an Allman Brothers mustache who runs the local garage. Only recently, Billy lost his wife to cancer. Now his children are dead, too. Left with nothing but a clear mind—and the occasional stolen hour with Wendell's wife, Risa (Alberta Watson)—Billy holds out fiercely against the notion that there must be a reason for the crash, and someone to blame. In his mounting rage, he even threatens Stephens; and so Mephistopheles is driven to speak of his own damnation. His daughter, too, is gone, lost to drugs in a city a thousand miles away. For ten years she's been no more than a voice to Stephens, alternately wheedling and accusing, calling collect on his cell phone.

If I feel at liberty to explain so much, it's because summaries can't spoil *The Sweet Hereafter*, a film in which everything has already happened. A faithful account would not lay out the characters in order, as above, but would start like this: Stephens remembers sleeping with his young family, twenty-five years ago. Stephens remembers entering town two years ago, all the while arguing by cell phone with his daughter. Nicole remembers singing for her father at a fair, a few months before Stephens came to town. And in the middle of the memories, tugging everything toward itself: a void.

In a way, this is familiar territory for Atom Egoyan, who directed *The Sweet Hereafter* from his own screenplay, based on the novel by Russell Banks. All of Egoyan's films have dwelled on the theme of life after a loss: the way your mind keeps circling back until time becomes spongy; the way the present moment seems to pass at a slight remove, just beyond the dead space that surrounds your body. From early on, Egoyan has been especially sharp about film-watching itself as a memorial practice, which easily becomes obsessive: a motif of *Family Viewing* and *Speaking Parts*, which reached its climax in the droll, fake-autobiographical *Calendar*.

The absences in these films have been sexual, familial, even national. (By background, Egoyan is Armenian—reason enough to know about black holes.) But despite their power to fascinate, his rituals of re-enactment have always seemed somewhat unworldly. Characters have replayed their losses on video monitors; in the model home of a spookily unpopulated suburban development (*The Adjuster*); within the aquarium-lit fakery of a striptease club (*Exotica*). Now, thanks to Banks, Egoyan has abandoned (if only for the moment) his fascination with stage sets and mechanical reproduction. He has grounded his characters as never before: in a settled community, and in a sense of class distinctions.

One result is that his actors, led by Holm, inhabit their characters more fully than ever before. I'd love to offer praise, but there's nothing to say, really; there are no performances in *The Sweet Hereafter*, only characters. And yet the film provides a curious sort of grounding, one that doesn't prevent it from continually floating away.

Egoyan's camera drifts down from the sky, hovers its way across the scene, takes off again into the blue. Sometimes it flies away in a helicopter; sometimes it lingers in an airplane at 30,000 feet. While the characters sleep, the camera will even look straight down at them, passing overhead like a watchful ghost. Since Egoyan is still Egoyan, there's nothing showy about any of this. (He's a thinker, not a swooper.) He just wants to do justice to the power of memory, which has a way of overriding the law of gravity—a strange circumstance, when you feel you could run your fingertips across every object on the screen. *The Sweet Hereafter* is full of polished wood floorboards, rumpled sheets, car windshields rippled by water, sweaters and lap robes, bales of hay, blankets of snow, crusts of ice. You feel an entire world is gathered behind these surfaces; yet you're suspended among them.

As the flacks might say, you'll laugh, you'll cry, you'll find yourself on the edge of your seat. The flacks wouldn't be lying. But here's a far better promise: You'll go away with a flutter in the pit of your stomach. I don't know how to describe the tremor—but it's there, and it tells you you're alive.

eXistenZ

Hark! The squeal of the two-headed amphibian. Mating season must have begun. Now women loll in motels, dreamily fondling umbilical cords, while men pay midnight visits to gas stations, to have their spines punctured. Into the raw apertures they poke opalescent tissue—synthetic, amphibian-born stuff, capable of causing infection, swelling, short circuit or rapturous fugue. Heavy tongue-kissing follows.

Which is to say that a new David Cronenberg film has materialized, and critics offering the barest description must sound like W.C. Fields. Contemplating *eXistenZ*, I suddenly recall that Fields was a great inspiration to William S. Burroughs, who in turn spurred Cronenberg to make *Naked Lunch*. Perhaps there's a lineage to be traced. It might even be a tradition: grandiloquence wed to disgust for the flesh.

Delirium presides over the union, assisted by gin, heroin or one of the more advanced neuromechanical agents. I suddenly understand that film screenings are advanced neuromechanical agents. I see that Fields's self-reflexive masterpiece, *Never Give a Sucker an Even Break*, may be a model for Cronenberg's *eXistenZ*.

Let us begin at the beginning. *Never Give a Sucker an Even Break* opens on a Los Angeles street, where Fields stands before a billboard advertising himself in *The Bank Dick*. Lonely despite his fame, Fields cannot entice even the idlest

LEFT IN THE DARK

passerby to join him in a cup of mocha java, or attend to his new screenplay. No one is interested—including Franklin Pangborn, the movie producer who subsequently is shown in full fluster in his office, trying to get Fields to stop reading aloud the script for *Never Give a Sucker an Even Break.* Yet the author persists. Despite Pangborn's protests, Fields narrates his story to us, the audience:

The screen fills with a highly fragmentary series of adventures, set in highly unconvincing locales. Intrigues and rivalries abound, to no intelligible purpose. Woo is pitched, with no likelihood of action. Characters and situations seep across the barrier between script and life, but with questionable effect, since both exist within a movie.

The above paragraph may also serve to summarize *eXistenZ.* For "script," simply substitute "virtual reality role-playing game." In place of "W.C. Fields," imagine "Allegra Geller," a game designer portrayed by Jennifer Jason Leigh.

As *eXistenZ* begins, a market research group is preparing to test Allegra's new game, "eXistenZ by Antenna Research." (You can all but see the trademark symbol floating in the air, each time the chief researcher unfurls the name.) The atmosphere feels disturbingly cultlike, even before the trial run begins—perhaps because the setting is a deconsecrated church, perhaps because the marketing people combine forced cheer with tight control. Volunteers for focus groups typically undergo something like indoctrination; but in this case, the brainwashing turns out to be direct.

Allegra's software resides in a fleshlike, pulsating "pod," whose control buttons look like nipples. She downloads her game from pod to players (or "slaves") through cables made in the form of umbilical cords, which plug directly into the base of the spine. At a touch of the switch, the players all slump forward, as if hypnotized.

From here on, things get a little strange. Before the game can begin, a young man jumps up from a front pew, cries "Death to the demon Allegra Geller!" and starts firing a gun, which seems to have been assembled out of bone and gristle. Chaos erupts. "Trust no one," warns the focus group's organizer with his dying breath, wheezing to an Antenna Research trainee named Ted Pikul (Jude Law). "Trust no one." At this, Ted scoops up the wounded Allegra and drives her into the night, into a back country that's crawling (so she claims) with designers for neural role-playing games.

So much for exposition. The rest of the film is a fragmentary chase, which runs through patently unconvincing locales populated by actors with hilariously improbable accents. Transitions from one scene to the next are abrupt, since they're motivated by calamity: gunfire, explosion, heavy tongue-kissing. But the main cause for the jerkiness is the role-playing itself.

To test whether her beloved pod has been damaged, Allegra demands that Ted join her in a round of "eXistenZ." By now the couple has holed up for the night in a ski chalet—the sort of place where movie characters ordinarily proceed from flirtatious bickering to romance. But in the Fields-Burroughs-Cronenberg tradition, arousal takes unusual routes. Allegra and Ted join physically, but only so they can morph into the three-dimensional game world of "eXistenZ"—and then, at the first opportunity, they morph further, into a game within the game.

Disorientation, both creepy and comedic, becomes the norm, as Allegra and Ted trip from one level of hallucination to another. It certainly makes for "a wild ride," as Allegra promises at the start. What's more, the ride comes with its own criticism—a great labor-saving convenience for people like me. "Not a well-drawn character, and his dialogue was just so-so," Allegra says at one point about a figure she encounters within "eXistenZ." A few moments later, she abruptly feels the need to glue her crotch to Ted's. (I hasten to add—Cronenberg being Cronenberg—that I use "glue" metaphorically.) Passion, Allegra claims, has nothing to do with the frottage. The "game architecture" is urging her on, making her do whatever's needed to advance the story—and in this case, she pants, the plot device is "a pathetically mechanical attempt to heighten the excitement of the next game sequence."

While the sound of that line echoes in memory, I should pause to call Jennifer Jason Leigh indispensable. She's also crafty, feral, insinuating, spontaneous and every other quality Allegra Geller might need in her multiple lives. Leigh is capable of underplaying a moment to the point of moving nothing but her eyelids, or overplaying to the point of mimicking a gargoyle. She's the kind of performer who believes (in Martha Graham's words) that center stage is wherever she happens to be; but she's also so alert that she makes other actors look good, too. Jude Law, as Ted Pikul, has the unenviable assignment of impersonating a "total PR nerd" (as Allegra says)—a 21-year-old virgin who still combs his hair just as Mother did. With Leigh to play against, Law makes mere dewiness overflow into a lake of bafflement, exasperation and rising excitement.

Yes, we've circled back (as Cronenberg tends to do) to that rising excitement. Is it the only point of the exercise? Is that what *eXistenZ* is all about?

I will remind you that people have asked the same question of existence. Close your Burroughs, open your Schopenhauer, and you will find page after page on the subject. From a certain point of view, accessible through delirium, the concepts we call "nature" and "reality" are mere illusions; the flow of excitement, the only absolute. I'm not sure whether Cronenberg would speak in those terms. But like Fields and Burroughs before him, he portrays ordinary social relations as a laughable sham; biology as the sickening substratum, absurd and unavoidable; and fantasy as the sole vehicle of escape—a broken-down vehicle, with unwanted passengers popping clownlike through the cushions.

Did you notice, speaking of clowns, that Allegra is the ostensible author of the character and plot device she so coldly dismissed? Take time, on your wild ride, to question a few such anomalies as they whiz past. They won't necessarily point the way toward any ground of existence—but they ought to help convince you that *eXistenZ* is the first North American release of 1999 that can make you tingle while you're watching it, then think three days later while you replay it at home.

Topsy-Turvy

He looks like a pear that's going bad. Tall, corpulent and much the worse for gravity, W.S. Gilbert (Jim Broadbent) sags his way through *Topsy-Turvy*, scarcely stirring except to drawl a sarcasm. His opinion of his mother? "A vicious woman who bore me into this ridiculous world." His contribution to lunchtime conversation? "Oh, horror, horror, hooooorror." His outlook, as one of his brightest operettas debuts at the Savoy Theatre? "As good as any condemned man can expect."

Though born to rhyme "scowl" with "jowl," this man has been wed in his career to someone thoroughly airy and cordial, with a Frenchified smoothness: Arthur Sullivan (Allan Corduner). To attend a Savoy premiere, Sullivan may have to rouse himself from a sickbed; after the performance, he may collapse. But while he's conducting the orchestra, white gloves flashing, he's all smiles, commanding others to take pleasure by exuding it himself.

In 1884, these two men undergo a professional break to match their personal rupture. The story of that near divorce provides the crisis for Mike Leigh's charming, brilliant, seemingly effortless *Topsy-Turvy*. The resolution, dreamed up by Gilbert and Sullivan themselves, is *The Mikado*, the creation of whose charmed brilliance, at the expense of much effort, is the subject of the film's second half.

Topsy-Turvy explores a relationship between antithetical collaborators, whose art (as the title suggests) turned Victorian England upside down, making it into a fantastic Japan. But the film is big enough to contain other dialectical relationships as well: authors and producers; star performers and chorus members; the imperial center and the outlying regions of the world. Ultimately, most touchingly, *Topsy-Turvy* is about barrenness and fecundity, which is to say men and women—men who cloak their spirits in the busy work of art, women who smother their natures and try to keep smiling.

But this is starting to sound serious. I'd better tell you quickly about the candy and oysters.

If you've followed Leigh's career, you know he takes care to feed his characters. (*Life Is Sweet*, which also starred Broadbent, would be the best example.) In *Topsy-Turvy*, he has decided that Sullivan, upon first meeting onscreen with Gilbert, should offer his partner a piece of candy. All through the subsequent conversation, which is tense with disagreement, the two men suck and slurp. Similarly, when the actor George Grossmith (Martin Savage) has to renegotiate his salary with the Savoy's impresario, Richard D'Oyly Carte (Ron Cook), he makes the mistake, just before, of gorging on oysters.

Instances abound of degustation and frailty. To give only one further example, Sullivan romps in a Paris bordello with a Mademoiselle Fromage. All right, a few more: I could also mention the "little problem" of alcoholism that plagues Leonora Braham (Shirley Henderson), the Savoy's ingénue; the festering leg on which Jessie Bond (Dorothy Atkinson) gamely supports herself while playing the gay young flirt offstage and on; the interrupted work session, with rejected snack, that puts Gilbert into a towering rage against his wife, Kitty (Lesley Manville), then sends him hurrying to the dentist. Working for the first time in the mode of period drama, Leigh builds *Topsy-Turvy* out of a hundred such observations of character. They are the past on a human scale—which means the film's people don't knock around loose amid the costumes and sets.

The latter, by Lindy Hemming and Eve Stewart, are as sumptuous and faithful as you could desire, whether they show the "reality" of a Victorian interior or the "fantasy" of *The Mikado* in performance. (When staged scenes burst from the narrative, shining with the light of cinematographer Dick Pope, you might think the gold-leaf heaven of religious painters had been proved to exist, and was much goofier than promised.) Gilbert's home, like the man himself, is dark and heavy. A few sparks can be found in the place, in the form of new-fangled gadgets—a telephone, an electric doorbell—but even these function as instruments of gloom, since they help Gilbert keep his distance from people. Sullivan, as you'd expect, has more aestheticized tastes. Whistler seems to have visited his bedroom recently, to paint a peacock on the door.

The Sullivan of *Topsy-Turvy* is the most pleasant of men—and perhaps the most unfeeling. Early in the film, in perfect self-satisfaction, he speaks of the great music he owes the nation. At the end, more pleased with himself than ever, he sweetly pats his lover (Eleanor David) and dispatches her to end a pregnancy he would find inconvenient. The film's Gilbert, of course, is impossible. But Leigh gives him this much credit: When Kitty, at the end, delivers to him a stunning bedside monologue that sums up her sense of futility, Gilbert's face seems to crumple from within.

But I'm sounding too serious again—a mistake that Kitty wouldn't make. So, in the spirit of topsy-turvydom, I will close with the middle of the film.

At the moment when Gilbert, alone in his study, hits upon the idea for *The Mikado*, he does something remarkable, which he does at no other time in the picture: He moves. Picking up a Japanese sword, he mimes his version of a Kabuki battle. Suddenly, Jim Broadbent's body escapes the pull of gravity. It can pose on one leg; it can swivel and dance. The glummest of Victorians has abruptly become the Lord High Executioner. He's set free—and so, for the moment, are you.

An Angel at My Table

Jane Campion makes films about uncomfortable heroines, women whose imaginations pop the buttons off the mindset they've been given to wear. These characters aren't out-and-out crazy, like the sister in *Sweetie*. They're just slightly off: the woman who guides her life by random signs, who's willfully mute, who yearns to be a tragic expatriate, who demands union with the godhead right this minute. By far the most popular of them has been Ada in *The Piano*, the artist who tamed the wilderness of New Zealand, and brought the tidiness of allegory into a Gothic romance. I prefer a Campion protagonist who's more unruly: Janet Frame, in *An Angel at My Table*.

Her unruliness comes from the best of all sources: the accidents of fact. Frame is real, and three volumes of her autobiography—*To the Is-Land, An Angel at My Table, The Envoy from Mirror City*—provide the groundwork for Campion's picture. It's a richly colored ground, but discontinuous. You have to hopscotch your way across this life, long stretches of which have vanished in the gloom of psychiatric wards, or were zapped into smoke by brain-frying machines. These horrors ought to make you feel outraged for Frame, and they do; and yet the film keeps skipping along, from one oddly vivid moment to the next.

As the brief scenes touch down, they fasten upon details that are too awkward to be anything but true—the leg brace worn by a high-school literature

teacher, or the steam that comes off a metal casket as it's unloaded from a refrigerator car, or (toward the end) the gait of the journalists who clamber straight
up a hill, on hands and knees, to interview Frame. Despite all her sufferings, for
all her vulnerability, Frame at last becomes famous, not as a victim but as a
writer. It's her writer's eye for detail that informs Campion's eye; her honesty that
keeps the movie honest.

Or, to look at it the other way, you could say that Campion's honesty and
keen eye allow her to be truthful to Frame.

Truth in this case is admittedly subjective. The movie begins with a point-of-
view shot—an image, seen by the infant Frame, of a clear sky almost blotted out
by the silhouette of a collapsing woman—and it will show us many more such
treats. But even when Campion centers her main character in an establishing
shot, as if to locate her in a world that values reason and symmetry, the surroundings seem to take shape directly from Frame's feelings.

I suppose that's why all the other women in the film are pretty and can walk
like models—because, in her own mind, Frame is the sole ungainly person to be
found outside the madhouse. She alone waddles; only she breathes through her
mouth, giving herself a semi-snarled lip and double chin. Worst of all, she's been
singled out to live beneath an absurdity of bright red hair. From the time you
first see her, as a pot-bellied, grimy little girl stuffed into a threadbare pullover,
you understand that Frame's destiny is this nine-inch heap of scarlet yarn piled
on top of her head, this flaming massive fungus. Some people ask to touch it,
more or less as they'd pat a hunchback; others, meaning to be helpful, ask if she
can't do something about it. No, she can't. The hair, to Frame, is the outward
and visible sign of everything she's stuck with. The only question is whether the
hair has been dropped onto her, like a weight, or is rising skyward in an excla-
mation of surprise.

The hair does Campion a favor: it unifies her three lead actresses. The child
(Karen Fergusson), adolescent (Alexia Keogh) and adult (Kerry Fox) who successively play Frame look much more alike because of their wigs; and that's a
favor to the viewer, too, given the teasing gaps that open not only in the narrative but also in the character's behavior.

Frame starts out as a spherical child who's a bit too eager to please. Almost
the first thing we see her do is to buy chewing gum for all her schoolmates, using
coins filched from her father's trousers. (This distribution of goodies has a later
echo. As if having to curry favor with her own family, she passes out books to all
of them. She's just received her first library card.) But despite this neediness,
little Janet (or Jean, as she's known at first) has a quiet talent for resistance. She
holds up well against her teachers' bullying; and when her adored older sister
demands that she change one of her poems, she obediently erases the offending

word and then, on the sly, writes it down again. There's something durable about this tyke; but as soon as Janet takes the form of Kerry Fox, you start to worry about her.

She's gone to the city to attend a teachers' college and is rooming with her aunt and uncle, in as dismal a wooden shack as ever squatted in a New Zealand alley. It's not a place where Janet needs to put on airs; besides, she's a paying boarder. But she pretends to be a vegetarian, as if fearing she'll be accused of costing too much to keep, and then furtively, desperately, scarfs the leftover meat from her aunt's dinner plate. More troubling still, Janet hides her sexuality. Her used sanitary napkins get stuffed into a drawer. When the drawer fills, she buries the lot in the cemetery, which also seems to be her favorite place for writing. Things that other people would discard get incorporated, or hoarded. Frame treats her own body as an unquiet grave.

Of course, young people often crack a little when they first go away from home, even a home that, like Frame's, has known too much illness and death. To show us how the fissures have opened, Kerry Fox pulls down the corners of her mouth, as if she's always bracing for a shock. She holds her torso stiff and lets the nervous energy pour out of her only from her fingers; she exposes rotting teeth, so that her eyes mist with shame, while she smiles her dumb, canine trust at the people who will shut her away.

It's a self-denying performance; most actresses wouldn't agree to become such a lumpy sack of insecurity. And yet, at the same time, Fox is so alert that you'd think a layer of her skin was missing. Everything registers; and the eyes, which Campion loves to show in close-up, are as clear as the light itself. That's the marvel of *An Angel at My Table*: the creation of a sensitive, much-abused woman who is consistently stronger than the other people on the screen; stronger, too, than the viewer.

I think of the section late in the film where Frame, to her own amazement, takes a lover. She's in Spain on a writer's grant, working hard (as usual) and enjoying her freedom, though she does feel intimidated by the other foreigners she runs across: 1950s-style bohemians, who condescend to her without having a tenth of her accomplishments. Then one of these characters—a lean, strong-featured American—starts showing a lively interest in her breasts. With what patience she listens to his terrible poetry, while she's stripped to the waist and waiting to get on with it! How she glows when she goes skinny-dipping, and he praises her grace under water! Suddenly she isn't working hard at all. Then the romance evaporates, and she's left to deal with the aftermath, which includes rain in London and worse. Yes, she comes close to disaster. Of course, it's pure luck that she finds a sympathetic doctor. Still, she's the one who pulls herself together, and knocks out a well-regarded novel while doing it.

Later, at a time that isn't covered by this movie, Janet Frame would write a book titled *Scented Gardens for the Blind*, which has to do, in part, with a young woman who ought to be able to speak but does not. You will recognize the germ of Ada, in *The Piano*; and though I don't know whether Campion drew on this source when she invented Ada, I'm sure that Frame makes the better movie character. She talks. She does so haltingly at times, and often in the face of misunderstanding, but still she brings the words out, into a world where she's determined to make sense.

"Oh, Jean," sighs her high-school teacher, pitying and alarmed, when she finds Frame sprawled Ophelia-like on her sister's grave, sobbing and dropping little white pills into water. "That won't bring her back."

"They're aspirin, for the flowers," replies the not-crazy, not-patient Frame through her snuffles. "It makes them last longer."

The Portrait of a Lady

L ate last year, Twentieth Century Fox released a lavish music video called *William Shakespeare's Romeo & Juliet*. I thoroughly enjoyed it, though the first half of the title did puzzle me. The text—what few lines of it crept in—seemed an unwelcome distraction from the gunfire, explosions, watery gurgles and songs by The Artist Formerly Known as Prince, all of which were splashed across the screen with great verve and ingenuity by the movie's one true author, Baz Luhrmann. If Shakespeare had anything to do with this, I thought, he shouldn't have.

With *The Portrait of a Lady*, the relationship between text and film is far more slippery, which is why I've hesitated till now to venture an opinion. Jane Campion's film (script by Laura Jones) clearly aspires to be a freestanding work of art; from its first sounds and images, which are of present-day women in New Zealand, the picture openly declares that it is *not* a novel by Henry James. At the same time, you can see that the literary source has been mined for more than the characters' names. The characters' geometry is roughly congruent between film and novel; people's motives, in both, are tougher to pin down than their actions, and are more important. The furnishings, costumes and social forms all look nicely lived-in, thanks to Campion and production designer Janet Patterson, who follow their contemporary lead-in with a near-hypnotic re-creation of the Jamesian era. Even the syntax of the two works seems to match. During my first viewing of *The Portrait of a Lady*, I often felt as if I were nodding off somewhere amid subordinate clauses, only to come awake toward the end of the sentence with an impression that something significant had occurred.

In short, the picture simultaneously is and is not a version of the novel, a situation that might take quantum mechanics to explain. Like the position of an electron, the status of the film cannot be determined with the exactness we might like, or that common sense would require. Any unease I experience would therefore derive from my condition as a spectator, and not from a flaw in the film. I am learning to enjoy letting *The Portrait of a Lady* flicker in my mind.

Even so, the question remains: What the hell did Campion think she was doing?

One clue crops up early, when the American writer Henrietta Stackpole strides into London and begins pressing a suit on her reluctant friend, Isabel Archer. Their first exchange, concerning Isabel's rejection of the lovelorn Mr. Goodwood, takes place over the husband-and-wife sarcophagi in Westminster Abbey, where a guard repeatedly orders Isabel not to touch the dead things. He does so by blowing a whistle smack into the camera—a sure way to interrupt both the characters' conversation and the viewer's absorption in the scene. So, too, does Mary-Louise Parker irritate, distract and interrupt by playing Henrietta with a nasal whine and vowels as flat as Chicago. In her second interview with Isabel—again on the subject of Goodwood—she warns that her hubristic friend is drifting toward catastrophe. She's right, of course. Having refused to marry till she's had some experience of the world, Isabel will soon fall for exactly the wrong man, putting herself into the very trap she'd wanted to avoid. You can sense it coming, even if you haven't read the book; so you ought to agree with Henrietta. But how can you even listen to her? All the grace, charm, sunlight and sex appeal are on the side of Nicole Kidman as Isabel. Were you to warn her from her course, you'd feel as unsympathetic as Parker's Henrietta, or a guard blasting a whistle.

It seems to me that here, as in the opening sequence with the young New Zealanders, Campion is acknowledging the gap between characters and audience—between what people could do in the 1870s and what we can feel for those people today. It's a slight dissonance, which swells into a Charles Ives symphony as soon as John Malkovich comes on the screen. In the role of Gilbert Osmond, the Florence-based dilettante who adds Isabel to his collection, Malkovich seems very much like Malkovich. You know his repertoire—head-cocking, eyebrow-smoothing, staring, sighing, pausing, slouching, crooning, hissing, with each movement brought forth from a posture of utter stillness, as if the man were a Swiss Army knife and his gestures so many blades. It's not just a matter of a mannered actor playing a mannered character. You're forced into an awareness of the actor's detachment, and his absolute modernity.

Nobody else in *The Portrait of a Lady* sticks out in quite this way. Martin Donovan, for example, seems thoroughly at ease in the role of Isabel's consumptive, semi-bohemian cousin Ralph; he also looks as thoroughly in-period as a photograph of Robert Louis Stevenson. As Madame Merle, the American-born adventuress whose sadness and glamour so attract Isabel, Barbara Hershey gives off a kind of dark radiance, emanating fierceness and intelligence as naturally as her black silks reflect the light. She, too, seems entirely credible—and if Nicole Kidman is any less so, it's only because Isabel herself has been conceived as wavering compared with the others. Kidman's best moments in the film are reactive; her Isabel is perpetually looking into other people as if they were mirrors, perpetually stopping to consider whether their readings of her might be true. Also, her "no" comes out much stronger than her "yes." Charged with playing someone who doesn't quite know what she wants or who she might be, Kidman understandably seems a bit unstuck in time—but unlike Malkovich, she's never out of place.

So why did Campion cast him? Basically, I think, because he works. An Osmond who blended in better with the costumes and furniture might not have represented such a threat to Isabel. The two characters would have existed in a more consistent narrative world—a world of one-point perspective, let's say, whose lines could conceivably extend beyond the picture's frame. Viewers might wonder, then, why Isabel doesn't just divorce the jerk. It's what *I'd* do. But by throwing Isabel into the hands of a modern-day weirdo like Malkovich, Campion heads off any such speculation. She makes Isabel deal with something we recognize as an intractable problem, something that is clearly beyond her ken.

Which brings me to the loudest dissonance of all: the black-and-white "silent movie" that takes over the screen at a crucial point. Titled "My Journey 1873," it's not so much a home movie as a pastiche of popular and avant-garde films of the 1920s. The era is unmistakable. Some of the images recall Surrealism; others, *The Sheik*. Unless the audience has gone comatose, it's going to wonder about the meaning of this artifact, which (however old-fashioned it seems to us) would be impossibly futuristic to Isabel Archer. I believe I've answered the question. What's old to us *is* advanced to Isabel. Or, to put it another way: By the 1920s, a woman like Isabel would have had a way to articulate her dilemma. Fifty years earlier, without such means of expression lying ready to hand, an Isabel could only have blundered ahead.

And now, having dropped that parcel into your lap, I want to return at once to everything in *The Portrait of a Lady* that is *not* neatly wrapped, allegorized and paraphrasable, everything that's blundering and confused, like the flood of images that overwhelms Isabel at the novel's end, in an experience that she (rather than James, I think) compares too conventionally to drowning.

Jane Campion wants to stand back and study that flood—I've nattered on about how she does it—but she also wants to plunge in. So she sends hundreds of intensely colored details eddying across the screen, usually off-kilter. Campion loves details: the train of a dress sweeping across the floor, cigarette smoke billowing from the nostrils, stockings and hems, the backs of people's heads, breakfast rolls, lap dogs, the fringes of drapery, scraps of writing. It's risky to compile a narrative from close-ups of such odds and ends, risky and maybe a little crazy. At times, I wasn't so much following the story as sniffing its armpits. And yet, at around the point where I got used to Malkovich, I began to feel the details had gained cumulative force. I was more into the film than out of it, more drawn toward Campion's emotional engagement than to her critical distance.

The Portrait of a Lady is a force field, in which viewer and character alike oscillate between the poles of rapture and curiosity. I don't think Campion wants to resolve that tension—witness how she ends with a view of Isabel caught in suspense. (In the novel, it's Goodwood.) But she's finally willing to pull Isabel, and the viewer, just a bit off center, till we're closer to the side of rapture. A humane decision; a good movie.

Chronicle of a Disappearance

Afresh definition of the term "terribly funny": while you're eating breakfast, two policemen wearing visored helmets and black body armor show up at the front door, crash their way through the house and disappear out the back, never saying a word. You, of course, are Elia Suleiman, a 30ish Palestinian filmmaker who resides for the moment in East Jerusalem. Dressed in pajamas and bedroom slippers, you deal with the invasion by preceding the cops wordlessly from room to room, as if trying to act the good host.

It's the sort of accommodation Chaplin's Tramp might have improvised—and given the way your dark, curly hair mats itself upon your head, the way your eyes express curiosity more than alarm, you might as well take on the role. But then, the Tramp had a way of wandering onto center stage (especially when he wasn't wanted), whereas you seem to be strangely negligible. After the cops leave, you happen to overhear their report to the Israeli security base: a list of everything they've seen during their fifteen-second trip through your house. It's amazingly complete, detailing the furniture, electrical equipment, pictures on the walls, books on the shelves. At the end, the least significant item in the catalogue: "a guy in pajamas."

That, quite simply, is the import of Suleiman's thoroughly extraordinary *Chronicle of a Disappearance*. It's a film about being last on the list. With cold-

176

blooded intelligence, Suleiman investigates this condition as if performing an exercise in spiritual slapstick. He wrings jokes out of an expatriate's return to a homeland that doesn't exist; he makes sad comedy out of a "peace" that changes nothing.

But first, the facts. Born in Nazareth in 1960, Suleiman removed himself to New York for a dozen years, made a couple of short films and in the early nineties went back to his family in Nazareth. In 1994, he moved to Jerusalem and took a post as visiting scholar at Bir Zeit University. He completed his first feature, *Chronicle of a Disappearance*, in 1996, taking advantage of this time frame to reflect on Palestinian life both before and after the Oslo accords.

He divides the film into three sections: a "Personal Diary" set in Nazareth, a "Political Diary" set in Jerusalem and a brief final section, "The Promised Land," set in newly autonomous Jericho and Nazareth. In the manner appropriate to a serious fellow, he also has taken pains to explain his narrative method within the film itself. About midpoint comes a sequence in which the filmmaker appears at a conference to discuss his work in progress. Unfortunately, the microphone feeds back, a baby starts crying, somebody in the front row decides to walk out and somebody else, taking a call on his cell phone, begins to make dinner plans. We never hear a word from Suleiman.

But of course, that *is* his method. *Chronicle of a Disappearance* is composed of disruptions, most of them minor: light fixtures that turn on and off at will, Holy Land souvenirs that keep falling down on the shelf, scenic water fountains that won't spray when Suleiman is present but start up again when he leaves. His response to this landscape of entropy and exasperation? As writer-director, he relies on one-setup, one-shot scenes: the cinema of the blank stare. As protagonist-performer, he matches himself to the deadpan style: observing much, doing little, saying virtually nothing.

In the latter point, Suleiman differs from the other people we meet in "Personal Diary." His citizens of Nazareth always have something to say—preferably bad, preferably long-winded and most often directed at a close relative or neighbor. On Suleiman's very first morning back, an aunt trudges into the frame as if entering his field of vision, settles herself on the sofa and launches into a hair-raising tirade, addressed straight at the baffled camera. The alternative to such outbursts is torpor. When not roused to vituperation, the citizens of Nazareth either sit around smoking cigarettes or else nod off. As punctuation to these episodes, Suleiman shows us extreme close-ups of the screen of his laptop, on which he types "The day after." But the day after is always like the day before.

Variety enters the film only with the move to Jerusalem and the opening of the "Political Diary." Once in the city, Suleiman catches a glimpse of his opposite number: a young woman named Adan (Ula Tabari). When first seen, she is in the office of a Palestinian real-estate agent, who seems to think that denying her an apartment is a good pickup technique. Girls—and she's such a pretty girl—should stay with their parents, even if they do want to study, because they're only going to get married. (We recognize the echo of a radio program overheard in "Personal Diary"—poetic sentiments, oozed out in the baritone register, on love as Woman's whole life.) For the moment, though, Adan is not set on love. She is set on getting an apartment. Under Suleiman's watchful gaze—maybe he's the one who needs love—Adan proceeds to a pay phone and starts bulling her way in fluent Hebrew through the listings for the Jewish side of town. "Your name's Adan? Really? You don't sound Arab," says one of her interlocutors (evidently meaning it as a compliment) before the phone slams down.

She's really pissed. But is she a guerrilla? The more Suleiman confronts his own inactivity—the status and stasis of an intellectual—the more he envisions Adan as part of an underground resistance. Call it romanticism, gallantry or a shifting of responsibility, but he leaves the fighting to her. And she doesn't disappoint—though her resistance turns out to employ the same weapons Suleiman might have used: imagination and insolent humor.

At the climax, Adan not only breaks with the culture of bad-mouthing and passivity but even redeems Suleiman's artistic vocation, as she cleverly transforms Israel's security police into Keystone Kops. It's a pretty large symbolic agenda for one woman to carry, which may be why the result is among the least uproarious car chases I've seen. Then again, a gangbusters catharsis would be false to *Chronicle of a Disappearance* and false to the lives it evokes. The real purgation comes through a quiet, simple statement: "Jerusalem is nothing special."

That idea is sufficiently dangerous to carry Suleiman all the way out of Jerusalem into the ironies of "The Promised Land." I can imagine the criticisms he will receive. Yes, he's unmasked the absurdity of Jewish nationalism, but without affirming Palestinian nationalism. Such loftiness is possible only for intellectuals, artists and those who have never missed a meal; a day-laborer under curfew in Gaza might prefer a political response that fits in the hand.

These are certainly strong arguments; they must be, because we've been hearing them since James Joyce wrote the Cyclops chapter of *Ulysses*. I hope Suleiman will eventually get as fair a hearing as did that other colonized ironist, who (if memory serves) was also an admirer of Chaplin. And I hope that where stones fail, Suleiman's preferred weapons will succeed: silence, exile, cunning and a dignified recovery from pratfalls.

Three Colors: Red

L ike Prospero drowning his book, our modern-day wizard has gone out with a splash. A muted splash: Although Krzysztof Kieslowski's *Red* works up to a full-scale tempest at sea, the heart of its story lies in an old man's act of abnegation. It's something that can be managed quietly, both for the character in the film and for Kieslowski himself, who claims that *Red*—the final part of his magisterial Three Colors trilogy—is his last film, period.

The old man in the movie, a onetime judge in Geneva (Jean-Louis Trintignant), lives in isolation (if not full Prosperian exile) because of a sexual betrayal long ago. Now he spends his days eavesdropping electronically on his neighbors' phone conversations. He knows all their sins and troubles but does not act on his knowledge, either to lend a hand or to prevent others from being hurt. He does not act *because* he knows; with the network of life spread before him, he sees he cannot touch even one string without setting the whole to jangling, perhaps disastrously. I think of the grieving angel who keeps popping up in Kieslowski's Decalogue series, witnessing the characters' downfalls with mute, helpless understanding. I think, for that matter, of Kieslowski himself, who throughout his career has used sophisticated electronic equipment (not unlike the judge's) to track the intersections of people's lives. Ever since his early feature films such as *Camera Buff* (1979) and *Blind Chance* (1982), Kieslowski has been a connoisseur of fateful coincidences, of missed connections and unforeseen consequences. Now, upon his retirement, his screen double appears before us in the form of a judge, who at last shuts off the eavesdropping machinery and allows life to proceed without his surveillance. When does he relinquish control? Like Prospero, he does so at the moment of sending a young woman into the world.

Her name is Valentine, and she is embodied, more than played, by Irène Jacob. Her lush-lipped features are as mutable as a dream, as free of sharp edges; yet her physical presence is so strong that you can feel her tendons strain when she's at a ballet class, or sense her breath's force afterward when she guzzles a bottle of water. By profession, Valentine is a model; made insubstantial by the camera or a fashion show's runway, she is good for selling chewing gum or evening gowns. In her flesh, though, she is something else: a moral being, whose sense of right and wrong is as direct as her gait. I don't mean to say that Valentine is free of doubt. Worried over her teenage brother (a junkie) and harried by a boyfriend who is never home but always jealous, Valentine does not seem to know what to do about her situation, other than to hold on. But when, by Kieslowskian chance, she injures a stray dog, she does not hesitate. She scoops it up in her arms, lays it in her car and drives off to find the owner. When he turns out to be the judge—a man who no longer wants to take part in the world—Valentine doesn't hesitate about him, either. She muscles her way into his life.

Pared down to its essence, *Red* consists of three complex, extended dialogues between Valentine and the judge. During the first, she discovers his eavesdropping, remonstrates with him and eventually lays bare her own woes, thereby bringing a moral dilemma into his study not as electronic voices but as flesh and blood. The second dialogue takes place after the judge yields to Valentine and gives up his spying; during the third (which as a farewell scene is prelude to the tempest), Valentine finally elicits a confession on the judge's part. The construction is elegantly symmetrical—a characteristic of the screenplays Kieslowski has written with his longtime collaborator Krzysztof Piesiewicz. And yet this skill at pattern-making, though it gives an overall integrity to *Red* (and to the entire trilogy), counts for little compared to the real thrill the film provides, which is simply the sight of the passing moment. Each action, each image, has an uncanny integrity of its own.

Valentine turns down an offer of tea; and so the judge, his eyes fixed on hers, spills the water he'd boiled for her out of the kettle and onto the floor. What a flaunting of desire, with what an avowal of impotence! What haughtiness, combined with what ramshackle despair! Another supercharged moment: The judge halts his conversation with Valentine so she can watch as the room briefly fills with light, then goes dim again as the sun moves on. How thoroughly must he know this lonely house, to be able to time that event? How keenly must Valentine, too, feel her days ticking away? And another moment, the last: The judge sees Valentine's face on television. Unlike the phone conversations he'd tapped into, this broadcast image is public property; yet it's the one communication in *Red* that bears him a personal message. Only he knows the full meaning of that close-up of Valentine, that profile set against a red background, which in one context might express a longing for chewing gum and in another might reveal terror and exhaustion. In a context the judge alone knows—the judge, and of course the audience, which is seeing the finale of *Three Colors*—that same image can suggest the reawakening of love.

I insist that the picture of Valentine is the culmination of the trilogy and not just of *Red* because I believe the trilogy is really one big movie—a point that ought to be obvious, though relatively few people have mentioned it (an exception being Dave Kehr in *Film Comment*). The facts of the production should be enough to make the case. According to Kieslowski's account, he and Piesiewicz finished all three screenplays before *Blue* went before the camera. (Zbigniew Preisner, the composer for the trilogy, contributed to the scenarios by deciding which film should be scored to a tango, which to a bolero; the musical structures worked their way into the elaboration of the plot.) Kieslowski shot *Blue* in Paris from September to November 1992. He began shooting *White* on the same day that he wrapped *Blue*, moved on to Poland (where he completed the trilogy's second section), took ten days' rest, then went to Geneva and shot *Red*, finishing in May 1993. So the parts of *Three Colors* were conceived together and shot continuously; and they were edited together, too, beginning within the first week of production in Paris.

Maybe people have overlooked the unity of this effort (and its magnitude) because the finished product has been so neatly labeled. Kieslowski, a sardonic man with a facile tongue, announced early on that the three sections of the trilogy corresponded to the colors of the French flag, which he took to signify liberty, equality and fraternity. Is there a Polish word for blarney? Kieslowski has now admitted that he had more in mind than slogans, however venerable; so perhaps we may dispense with the labels and look at what's actually on the screen.

What we see most vividly—no surprise—is color. Part one, photographed by Slawomir Idziak, floods the screen with blue light, which filters through water, through cut glass, sometimes through the air itself. The camera is thoroughly subjective here; as Julie (Juliette Binoche) passes through mourning for her husband and child, space seems to warp with her every mood, as if her emotions had the power to fog the air around her. *White*, shot by Edward Klosinski, is correspondingly objective. At the start, its color literally falls out of the sky onto the protagonist, Karol Karol (Zbigniew Zamachowski), in the form of a pigeon dropping; and from there on, Karol keeps getting whited out in emphatically material fashion, whether on the snowy streets of Warsaw or between the sheets with his estranged wife. *Red*, shot by Piotr Sobocinski, is of course the warmest in color but also the most dense. Its reds can be localized in objects (curtains, for example, or items of clothing), giving them a physical insistence that's lacking in the vaporous blues of *Blue*; they're also pervasive, framing the characters at every turn, unlike the isolatable incidents of white in *White*.

Three Colors invites the viewer to play at giving denotations to blue, white, red—a worthwhile game, as far as it goes. Surely blue is appropriate for its meditative heroine, suffering in well-moneyed Parisian gloom. White goes well with the clownish circumstances of its Warsaw-born hero, scuffling his way up from barber to post-Communist tycoon. So blue might be defined as a color of thought; white, as a color of hard facts; and red would be the color of the heart, as suits a film with both a hero and a heroine, who live at a geographic and economic midpoint between Paris and Warsaw. But again, this is to freeze the flow of experience into a pattern, which is fascinating and lovely but inert. Why not take color seriously—Kieslowski seems to—as a mode of perception beyond fixed meanings?

We live in a time of impatience, when people demand a paraphrasable art. In the galleries and museums—especially those that traffic in political engagement—the objects you encounter generally read to the viewer. They make a statement, as if each work were already its own translation. In bookstores and book reviews, direct address is similarly prized. John Ashbery, though eminent, is out; poetry slams are in. As for pop music, I recall an interview of a few years ago with Chuck D. of Public Enemy, who dismissed jazz as that "abstract" stuff his father listened to. It was no good because it had no words—no message.

Into this market steps Krzysztof Kieslowski, an artist who has the bad habit of meaning more than he says. His messages (as in *No End*) used to be blatant enough to get him in trouble with the Communist authorities, though not bracing enough for many of the regime's opponents. His key figure of this period, perhaps, was the title character of *Camera Buff*, who blunders into a career as a filmmaker and dissident when all he really wants is to take some shots of his daughter's birth. A provocative film; but nothing you could rally around.

Since then, the old regime has broken up, and Kieslowski has made his way West, into co-productions that must seem cushy by his former standards. Certainly he's indulged himself in a new sensuousness, beginning with *The Double Life of Véronique*; but his attitude, thank heaven, is still offensive to common sense. First he plots his movies as rationally as a diagram; then he lets the irrational pour in, trusting that blue, white and red will convey more than anything that can be said.

"To me the meanest flower that blows can give/Thoughts that do often lie too deep for tears." The age of revolution was born at the same time as Wordsworth wrote those lines, which the age of reason would have derided. (Is thought a kind of root vegetable, watered by tears?) They're nonsense; but then, the great achievement of the age of reason was to discover reason's limits. Ever since, some of the bravest thinkers and artists have mounted expeditions into the territory beyond, where, the crazy beating of Wordsworth's "human heart" sometimes urges us toward resignation and sometimes toward liberation. Kieslowski's great merit as a political artist has lain precisely in his ability to remain clearheaded while venturing into the elusive, the contingent, the unresolvable. For that, all of us camera buffs owe him thanks.

Films of Alexander Sokurov

R ainer Maria Rilke picked up so many signals from outer space that we shouldn't be surprised to find among his poems the occasional film review, jotted down during some extremely advanced interstellar screening. Recently, for example, I discovered that "Washing the Corpse," written in Paris in 1908, records his impressions of Alexander Sokurov's picture *The Second Circle*, filmed in Siberia in 1989. I yield to a superior critic (translated by Stephen Mitchell):

> They had, for a while, grown used to him.
> But after they lit the kitchen lamp and in the dark
> it began to burn, restlessly, the stranger
> was altogether strange. They washed his neck,
>
> and since they knew nothing about his life
> they lied till they produced another one,
> as they kept washing. . . .

See how quickly Rilke caught the signs of a kindred sensibility: the crossing back and forth between the familiar and the strange; the exaggerated play of light and shadow; the paring away of background and context so that the essential thing—the direct, physical engagement with death—would stand out, stark and inescapable, despite any chitchat evasions. Only a poet—and of a rare character at that—could have intuited *The Second Circle* so clearly and completely. The rest of us must be grateful to the International Film Circuit for enabling us to see a series of the films of Alexander Sokurov. In a moment, I'll give the dates and venues. First, though, another look at *The Second Circle*, this time through prosaic eyes.

Imagine a blizzard howling across a frozen plain. The flat, empty ground is white; the sky, above a high horizon line, is white. Within this landscape, so stretched out and bleak that it seems unreal, only two features stick up: a tower (perhaps an antenna) in the background, toward the left of the frame, and a young man who kneels in the foreground at the right. Who is he? Sokurov never tells us. Where is he? Apparently, in a forbidding region of the Soviet Union—though details of the location and regime matter little. Looking back through my notes, I found the words "fucking South Chicago" scrawled in reaction to an establishing shot. Each of us, in his or her way, recognizes the Last Place on Earth. This is it; and now that the young man has got here, he finds his father has died and is lying in a squalid, dusty room where an untuned radio yammers into the void. Who was the father? What was his relationship with his son? We never learn about that, either. No matter. The son, like it or not, has to bury the old man, and for the next ninety minutes we watch him stumble through the whole procedure: washing the corpse, obtaining the death certificate, negotiating over the price of the funeral, helping to angle the coffined body out the door and down the stairs.

The Second Circle is a clothesline film: One discrete event follows another, and another. So, too, do characters enter the story and leave again. For each encounter, Sokurov uses a subtly different style. In the episode of getting the death certificate, for example, he shows us a static, head-on view of the doctor. She is an old woman, disillusioned but kindly. Sharing the frame with her is a child, who sweetly repeats some of her phrases: "Everything's going to be all right" and "Cancer." Later in the film, during the embalming scene, Sokurov shows us the two morticians at an awkward angle, through a doorway, while the son knocks around nearer the camera.

With the most vivid of the characters, the funeral director, Sokurov at first chooses a conventional strategy: He crosscuts between her and the son as they dicker over costly details, such as whether the corpse needs stockings. By far the best-dressed character in the film, with well-applied makeup and carefully groomed hair, the funeral director is both brusquely offensive and gratuitously kind. One moment, bullying the son, she announces that she has five more funerals to arrange, so he'd better hurry up. The next moment, she's decided to front some of the costs out of her own pocket—and barks at the helpless young man that he'd better pay her back. When she later returns, to put the corpse into a coffin and remove it from the apartment, we witness the most complex sequence in the film. As the funeral director, in exasperation, issues orders and the son crawls around the room trying to comply, the camera gradually rises from near the floor toward the ceiling, then moves forward while sinking again, returning to the floor as the coffin descends the stairs. I can't think of any other shot quite like it—and yet the camera's movement is so slow and smooth, and the events taking place before it are so clumsy, that the viewer might well be oblivious to Sokurov's technique.

The Second Circle is the first of Sokurov's films of which I could make such a statement. A protégé of Andrei Tarkovsky—who got the thoroughly out-of-favor young director his first job, at Lenfilm Studio—Sokurov was both maximalist in technique and gratingly avant-garde, from his earliest feature film, *The Lonely Voice of Man* (1978/87), through the 1988 *Days of Eclipse*. His soundtracks were multilayered and harshly discordant; his use of color, unnatural. He was forever juxtaposing footage from different sources, shot at various speeds and aspect ratios, some tinted yellow or red, some involving the use of blatantly phony models for sets. Such methods did not endear him to the Lenfilm authorities. When Sokurov made *Mournful Indifference* (1983), a fantasy loosely based on Shaw's *Heartbreak House*, Lenfilm stopped the shooting, pulled down the set, confiscated the footage (except for some bits and pieces that the editor refused to hand over) and circulated the rumor that Sokurov was about to issue a political protest. Such is the genius of the censorious mind. *Mournful Indifference* is a heavy work (especially for a film that wants to be antic) and no doubt would have sunk from view all on its own. By their interference, the censors seem merely to have stiffened Sokurov's resolve.

By the time Sokurov made *Days of Eclipse*, his work not only reflected his frustration but also conveyed a sense that the regime holding him back was moribund. Based on a novel by the Strugatsky brothers, the film tells the story of a Russian doctor in a desolate region of central Asia. Unknown forces keep interfering with his research, much as alien powers had interfered with Sokurov's filmmaking. At least, that seems to be what's happening, or part of it. Although the film is eerily compelling, with its quasi-ethnographic footage, uncanny incidents and characters from Beyond, *Days of Eclipse* makes as much sense as the last twenty minutes of *2001: A Space Odyssey*. Still, you can find in it a sequence that in retrospect seems like a trial run for *The Second Circle*.

Days of Eclipse includes a long, extraordinary episode in which police and media deal with a suicide's corpse. Sokurov shot the scene from a single camera setup; though he condensed the action with lap dissolves, the effect remains very close to that of real time. Understated and solemn, the episode feels unlike any other sequence in *Days of Eclipse*. It pulls you in, instead of shoving you back. Though as transparently made-up as anything else in the film, the sequence gives you the leisure and quiet you need to work your own way into the frame.

The Second Circle plays as if that sequence had been expanded to feature length. For the first time, I think, Sokurov concentrated unblinkingly on a subject, as if he'd figured out a purpose for all that avant-garde trickery. His stylistic traits suddenly snapped into place; he became a soft-spoken maximalist. Whether he'll remain one is anybody's guess, just as it's impossible to predict the future of a film industry that kept him pure and feisty by trying to crush him, and that now is itself in ruins. (Perhaps the Russian studios, which are already providing cheap production facilities for the West, will become a Cinecittà for the nineties. Look for a new Hercules cycle out of Lenfilm.) All I can say for sure is that out of the death of the Soviet system, out of a confrontation with death itself, Alexander Sokurov has made a stunning film.

July 3, 2000

Time Regained

Everyone knows you can't film *Remembrance of Things Past*, so Raul Ruiz did it. With hindsight—the only kind worth having, as far as Proust is concerned—I now understand this act of effrontery and genius as the culmination of Ruiz's career.

As if to prepare for this moment, he has given himself many years' practice poking holes in the conventions of storytelling, trying to glimpse what might lie beyond those walls. (In a 1982 work, *On Top of the Whale*, he even allowed a first-person narrator to get into a canoe and paddle out of the film, so that the other characters, and the audience, had to muddle on without guidance.) Ruiz has also cultivated an appropriate obsession with the mysteries of language and identity; in the 1996 *Three Lives and Only One Death*, for example, different persons take up residence in the body of Marcello Mastroianni, moving in and out of his flesh in response to a seemingly random whispering of words. If the gnosticism of such films was un-Proustian, the hermeticism was right in the spirit. So, too, was the sense of loss and longing, which Ruiz carried with him into exile from Allende's Chile, and which he has since poured into many different forms of melancholy laughter.

All this was common knowledge to anyone who had followed Ruiz's career. Even so, I could not believe what I was seeing in *Time Regained*, his version of the final and encapsulating novel of Proust's masterwork. This structure built of memory and meditative intelligence simply could not keep rising into the air, growing more and more complete; and still, as the minutes went by, as I held my breath, the miracle didn't collapse.

First, to my astonishment, I saw that Ruiz had made physical reality as variable as it should be in *Time Regained.* It's only through habit, another name for inattention, that we come to think of objects as inanimate, reflects Proust (or the narrator) at the beginning of the novels; perhaps we come close to the truth when we awake in the middle of the night and think the furniture has shifted on its own. And so, in the film, the writer's bedchamber, with its striped wallpaper, resembles a magical gift box as seen from the inside, expanding or contracting according to the mnemonic presents it contains. The camera moves through this space like a slow but firm pen stroke; and as it does so, congregations of hand-size statuary seem to group and regroup, pieces of furniture crowd together or disperse, and an all-seeing cheval glass, standing watch in one corner, reflects back an author who can occupy three or four bodies at once. First subtly, so that the movement of objects looks like the ordinary displacement caused by a tracking shot, then more and more blatantly, Ruiz makes good on Proust's intuitions of mutability.

Then, one after the other, the principal characters come onto the screen, looking exactly as they should. Marie-France Pisier, all twittering smiles and fluttering black feathers, flounces through a reception room as the tireless partygiver Madame Verdurin. She preens—then squawks, "What's *she* doing here?" as a second figure approaches down the hall. How does the too-much-married Odette dare to show her face in this salon, especially now that she's gone to ruin? But you're wrong, says Madame Verdurin's companion; Odette is *superbe.* And so she is, as we see when she walks through the door, because she turns out to be Catherine Deneuve: her face and body plumper than in youth, and her expression all the more confident for it. She enters like one of the warmer aquatic goddesses, afloat in serenity and blond-radiance.

Odette's daughter, the unhappily married Gilberte, is played by apple-cheeked, pillow-lipped Emmanuelle Béart, who might easily be Deneuve's offspring. (Deneuve's real daughter, Chiara Mastroianni, also appears in the picture, as Albertine, the other person who broke our narrator's heart.) In the role of Gilberte's husband, the ideal aristocrat Robert de Saint-Loup, we have Pascal Greggory: light eyes, carved cheeks, lanky body held perfectly upright. When he comes back to Paris during World War I, on leave from the trenches, he talks with his mouth full and slurps his wine, in a rush to get food into his body and the corpses out of his head. Then there's Vincent Pérez as Morel, the lazily talented, omnisexual flirt who makes the most of all the other characters. A foxlike figure, Pérez squirms his way deep into Morel at all phases of his career, from cloth-capped punk to has-been blowhard in a boiled shirt.

Throughout these scenes, the adult but not-yet-bedridden Marcel is played by Marcelo Mazzarello, who might have been cast out of the photo insert of a biography of Proust. The features, even the tilt of the head, belong to the author; but the slightly stoop-shouldered, flat-footed gait is the actor's invention, and a brilliant one, making Marcel into a silent-movie clown in dandy's attire: Max Linder as literary genius. Watch him at the male brothel he's "just happened" to stumble into; see how he walks off camera for a moment, then returns with perfect aplomb carrying a chair he can stand on, the better to peep through a transom.

This brings us to one of the brothel's clients, the Baron de Charlus, and the masterstroke of Ruiz's casting. Aesthete, moralist, hypocrite, soft touch, conversational terror and all-around instructive figure, Charlus is played by John Malkovich. Supplied with a thatch of frizzed-out hair and a tuft of beard beneath his lower lip, Malkovich looks uncannily like Montesquiou (Proust's model for Charlus), with Whistler thrown in for good measure. Does Malkovich sound like a native speaker of French? Not at all. But he's a sly actor and knows the baron's epigrams might rise languidly to the lips, as if half sung. The care Malkovich must take with his pronunciation turns into a feature of the character. As for the giggle, the imperiousness, the X-ray vision, the vain attempts to hide the bad teeth and, finally, near death, the shambling pathos, these all come directly from the book and from some unknown source within Malkovich. This is easily his best performance.

In sum, *Time Regained* is faultlessly cast, as well as faultlessly realized in production design. The sense of decorum is exact. (To choose one moment out of many: Marcel not only waits for a servant to pour his tea but also observes the nicety of being asked each detail of how he'd like it served.) Most impressive of all, concepts that are elaborated in the book through exhaustive analysis spring into bold and utterly natural visual forms in the film, thanks to Ruiz's inventiveness.

But these are all virtues of imitation. Although they will take you a long way through the screening, if you love Proust enough, they don't guarantee *Time Regained* a life of its own.

It has a life—though you might not sense it fully at first, because Ruiz and his co-screenwriter, Gilles Taurand, have taken extraordinary risks in the picture's long first movement. After a prologue, in which they introduce and intermingle no fewer than three time periods (the 1920s for the narrator, the early months of World War I for the adult Marcel, the 1880s for Marcel as a boy), the filmmakers lead us through a fairly complete circuit of the characters' broken loves. Maybe this part of the film is too tricky to be written off as expository, but it bears a heavy load of information, all the same. Patience. As the first movement draws toward a close, you will find yourself at the rounding off of one narrative loop, and then another. The teacup that Marcel broke in his agitation, any number of scenes earlier, emerges from a drawer in Gilberte's house; the afternoon party with which the narrator's memories began somehow circles back and starts again.

Loops within loops: *Time Regained* continues to build musically (the only way to build, as far as Proust is concerned) throughout two more large movements. The first broods over the decay, or hollowing out, of the characters during World War I; the second, which begins with Marcel's utter disillusionment at the war's end, leads to his discovery of the world that awaits him in memory, intact and redeemed. In my own memory, I will forever treasure the climax of this third movement: the scene in the Guermantes salon where Marcel hears again a piece of music he associates with heartbreak. The music plays; the guests shift crazily in their seats, as if the salon were on a boat tossed at sea; and the camera, which is similarly set adrift, travels past the face of Marcel, who first listens with eyes closed, then seems to smile, then weeps.

How many times has a filmmaker shown you a close-up of a weeping character and asked you, too, to shed a tear? How often have you wanted to respond to the invitation by throwing your box of popcorn at the screen? In *Time Regained*, for once, I too felt the urge to smile and cry, because the moment was fully in motion, and the moment was full.

After such an experience, there is nothing left to do but express one's gratitude. And that's what Raul Ruiz does—Ruiz the insolent joker, the parodic surrealist—in a heartfelt coda to *Time Regained*. He ends with an implied tribute to his source, the novels that contain within them one man's life and everyone's life. It's as if he'd completed the film and seen that it, too, must be absorbed into *Remembrance of Things Past*; as if, having remade this world, he'd stepped back to let it live beyond his grasp.

A tact so exquisite might impress even Charlus.

REALITIES

Public Housing

T he South Side of Chicago is full of places where Fred Wiseman might make a film. Michael Reese Hospital, Comiskey Park and the Illinois Institute of Technology lie so close to one another that he could scout them all for locations and still drive to McCormick Place before half an hour had passed. Were he to commit these places to film, Wiseman would no doubt maintain his usual truth in labeling; he'd call the movies *Convention Hall, College, Ball Park* and *Medical Center*. (He's already made a *Hospital.*) Each picture would function as a species of time-lapse photography; instead of watching a bud open into a flower, you would see an institution unfold.

However startling, troubling or affecting in their details, these imaginary films would take place in settings that most viewers know firsthand. That's not the case with the documentary Wiseman actually made in the neighborhood. *Public Housing* opens up layer within layer of life within the Chicago Housing Authority's Ida B. Wells Homes—the sort of place that's fulminated against on the radio and the Senate floor, that's sketched in as a scary background for every cop show and big-city thriller, but remains unvisited and profoundly unknown by mainstream society. Or, as Wiseman would perhaps label it, white society.

How often do white people see an entire supermarket closed off behind bulletproof barriers? Across the street from the Wells Homes, people wait in line to order their groceries from clerks, who trudge up and down aisles to gather the items and then shove them through an acrylic merry-go-round. Let Wiseman show you the faces on both sides of this divide; the memory will complicate your next use of the term "self-esteem."

Or how's this for uplifting: a screening interview for a drug-treatment program, shown at full length? Here is that stock figure from TV, the black crackhead with a criminal record, somewhat older and thinner than we'd been led to believe and far more chastened in spirit. During the interview, to which he's submitted rather than go straight to jail, this man lays bare for the counselor (and so for the camera) all the errors of a lifetime. He does so patiently, candidly, despite the slight speech impediment left behind from a one-time encounter between his skull and a hostile baseball bat. Has he lost all sense of his right to keep a secret? Apparently. His complaisance is terrifying—though no more so than the outburst that escapes the counselor. The man on the other side of the desk also happens to be black and middle-aged. He, too, spends his life in the projects, where it's his job to listen to these miseries over and over. How long before his blood pressure gets him?

Speaking of the helping professions: Have you ever felt compassion for a Chicago cop? Wiseman will teach you to do it, by showing how a pair of them evict an old man. They know he has to vacate his apartment; he may well need the nursing home to which he's being sent. But you can see the strain on their faces—it feels like forever before the old man will get up and pack a few belongings. The cops politely remind him to bring his medicine; they listen to his mutterings, under the light classical goop that pours from his radio. They have plenty of time, as we do, to inventory every grimy, worn-out thing the man has to show for his life; and one of the cops, I swear it, wipes away a tear.

That's something else Wiseman reveals, which you won't see in the TV shows: Wherever he looks in this cruel place, he sees people trying to help one another. Sometimes the aid is immediate: An exterminator with a courtly Southern demeanor prolongs his visit to an apartment so he can explain how to use boric acid. More often, though, the desire to help outruns the ability. Young women who are facing cuts in welfare join in group counseling, trying to talk themselves into optimism about finding jobs. Everyone agrees on the need to form a plan, though nobody seems to have one. A men's volunteer organization holds a meeting; most of it is devoted to sincere self-criticism for not yet having done anything. In a meeting at the community college, an official preaches economic self-reliance: The residents of the Wells Homes should form their own companies, which would contract to provide services to the housing authority. Some members of the audience nod eagerly. But others seem to have been watching *Public Housing*; they stare impassively at the orator, as if remembering how he offered the same feeble example of entrepreneurship earlier in this film.

As always, Wiseman presents this material through a direct transcription of the present moment; he uses no voiceovers, no archival images and no interviews. "Direct" is, of course, a relative term. To greater and lesser degrees, Wiseman's subjects all play to the camera, which in the past has spurred some critics to complain of manipulation, exploitation, voyeurism, fictionalizing. I see no reason to be so delicate—the achievements of *Public Housing* vastly outweigh the sins of its making. But I do note that Wiseman's method, though magnificent at revealing the how and what of this place, falls short when it comes to why. He allows himself no access to a thirty-five-year history of decline on the South Side: the closing of the stockyards and steel mills, the wasting away of once-active ghetto strips like 47th Street, the flight from the neighborhood of every black citizen who had the money to go elsewhere.

But the real test of Wiseman's method isn't what he leaves out. It's what he manages to convey, precisely because of the limitations he's imposed on himself. Look at the scene he chose to open *Public Housing:* An advocate for project residents talks on the phone to an official, trying to get an apartment for a pregnant teen. What do we get from this scene, apart from a sense that the advocate, Helen Finner, is not a woman to trifle with? We learn that *Public Housing* of some sort is needed. As desolate as they are, the Wells Homes have a waiting list.

And so, since Wiseman provided that much of a context, I will complain of only one fault in *Public Housing*—that the film runs approximately three and a half hours. Wiseman needs that time; he has to get across the feeling of living in this place. He should have gone for twelve.

Public Housing was recently shown at the New York Film Festival and will soon begin making the rounds of the usual small theaters and media centers. It is scheduled for broadcast over PBS in December. I'd recommend that you call your local PBS affiliate now. If you don't ask to visit the Wells Homes, the programmers might assume that you, too, prefer not to know.

February 14, 2000

Belfast, Maine

rederick Wiseman's latest film, *Belfast, Maine*, is having its New York premiere in the best possible setting, as the opening feature in a full retrospective of his work. The picture will also be broadcast on PBS on February 4, which is good news for those who can't get to Lincoln Center's Walter Reade Theater. But if you are able to attend at least part of the retrospective—or are willing to run one of your own, in your mind's screening room—you will find that *Belfast, Maine* is extraordinary in two ways. First, it is an immensely rich and immeasurably valuable microcosm of American life at the end of the twentieth century. Second, and most unexpected, it is a microcosm of Wiseman's art.

He is a student of institutions—the hospital, the welfare office, the housing project, the high school—and sometime during the past thirty years he became one himself. No other documentarian since Robert Flaherty has enjoyed such widespread, superlative-laced praise; few have been so prolific. Yet strangely enough, though critical opinion and public television have elevated him to the status of an official artist (or as close to such a thing as we have in America), Wiseman is an extremist.

He is extreme in the limits he sets on his filmmaking, banishing from the screen all interpretive or explanatory devices such as interviews, voiceovers, texts or archival footage, so that viewers must confront the present moment. In doing so, they may also confront themselves, taking notice of how they read the evidence of their senses. (What store of information do they draw upon? What stock of prejudices?) Wiseman is similarly extreme in his claim on your patience (at four hours, *Belfast, Maine* is not the longest of his films) and in his determination to make you wade neck-deep into realities that don't rate even a splash from most other filmmakers.

These realities, at their harshest, have sometimes been the muck to Wiseman's rake. The stuff he dragged to the surface in his first film, *Titicut Follies* (1967), so displeased the shamed parties—authorities of the State of Massachusetts—that they secured a court order preventing any public screenings. The legal reasoning: By recording the brutalities meted out in a state prison for the criminally insane, Wiseman had violated the inmates' right to privacy. Needless to say, this ruling made *Titicut Follies* a prized item on the film-society circuit and guaranteed Wiseman's fame; and though the ban is no longer in force, Wiseman is still known as the man who documented, in gruesome detail and at excruciating length, such episodes as the force-feeding of a crazy old man.

There has been much in his subsequent films—from *High School* and *Welfare* through *Public Housing*—to maintain Wiseman's reputation as a maker of exposés. And yet: Who would have thought you could appeal to conscience by means of phenomenological contemplation? A protest film by Wiseman is like *The Jungle* as written by Robbe-Grillet.

Wiseman has, by the way, made a picture titled *Meat*, which delivers nothing less than advertised. But other films have taken him far from Upton Sinclair territory. He has looked at dance (*Ballet*), theater (*La Comédie-Française*), religious life (*Essene*), green space (*Central Park*), commerce (*The Store*), life with disabilities (*Adjustment and Work*), life toward its end (*Near Death*), human-animal relations (*Zoo*), police work (*Law and Order*) and the military (*Basic Training*). With the exception of that last subject, all these areas of life—plus welfare, plus high school, plus the criminal justice system and more—find a place in the grand synthesis of *Belfast, Maine*.

In the opening eighty minutes (nearly the length of a normal feature), Wiseman takes you through a day in Belfast, from dawn to dawn. First, in deference to expectations, the film offers the scene that all tourists want to watch: Lobstermen sail out of the harbor at daybreak to collect their catch and rebait the pots. At the conclusion of the day-in-Belfast segment, you see these men again, but in a nontouristic setting. Before going to their boats, they drink coffee in a little pastry shop, where Wiseman shows you how the doughnuts are made.

But well before you reach that doughnut shop, *Belfast, Maine* has gone beyond the postcard view of a "waterfront community" (as a sign boasts at the entrance to town). Wiseman's version of the daily cycle includes an early shift at the dry cleaner's; a class in flower arranging; a tour of a factory, where potatoes come in at one end and packages of stuffed potato skins come out at the other; a conversation about logging and forest management, held at a roadside grocery-tavern; two encounters with deer hunters; a ballet class; a City Council meeting; a choir rehearsal of Handel's *The Messiah*; and the living-room caucus of a circle of activists, who are talking tonight about gay and lesbian marriage.

While you're visiting these scenes, you may deduce the season from the Halloween decorations that appear everywhere, and the year—1996—from the presence in the movie theater of *Thinner*, a Stephen King thriller. Of course: At this time of year, any self-respecting Maine cinema needs a lobby display featuring a life-size cutout of the state's spookiest author. By this point, though, you've understood that every day in Belfast has its scary side.

Among the events recorded in the picture's first segment is a talk given at the Waldo County General Hospital on the subject of managed healthcare—or, as the lecturer pointedly says, sick care. The hospital must change the way it operates, she explains; and so, since we know which medical problems are most common in the county, let's review the causes: smoking, obesity and poor nutrition, alcoholism, early pregnancy, inadequate parenting, dysfunctional family behavior.

Some of these traits have already been documented in *Belfast, Maine*, thanks to the way Wiseman threads together the episodes. He uses three connective devices: shots of the heartbreakingly beautiful landscape, views of the roads in and around town, and scenes of home visits by social service workers. In one such scene, for example, the welfare visitor combs through the hair of a young and semi-toothless woman, looking for lice. While at it, she also asks, in a gentle tone, whether the woman has yet offered any advice about sex to her fast-growing daughter. Oh, sure. Sure.

As *Belfast, Maine* moves from the opening segment into the third and fourth hours, these visits to the poor and ailing seem to multiply. They also stretch in time and deepen in intensity, as in a sequence set in the emergency room at the General Hospital. Who are these middle-of-the-night patients? How did they come to be here? The film, in answer, takes us next to a rehearsal by a local drama club, which is putting on *Death of a Salesman*. As if in a dream, we then move from Willie Loman's desperation to an image of cornered wildlife. A wolf, caught in a trap, gets shot between the eyes and dumped into the back of a pickup truck.

The film by now has shifted in its view of industrial labor, from the deadly boring but relatively clean work at the potato-skins factory to bloodier doings at a fish-packing plant. (As the workers, performing in a mechanical blur, shear off the heads of sardines, Wiseman shows you close-ups of bandaged hands and blank faces.) What happens to the people who can't stomach such a job, can't live on the wages it pays, perhaps can't even get hired on? We witness part of a session at the District Court, where a judge quickly deals with the crimes of semirural poverty: possession of marijuana, possession of psilocybin, driving under the influence, driving a defective auto, speeding, theft of a cord of wood (estimated value, $100).

For the better-off residents of Belfast (those who take classes in flower arranging and live in beautiful old houses) or for the tourists who pass through town, these damaged, self-injuring workers and not-quite-workers are all but invisible. They give evidence of their existence mostly through products, such as the amply priced packages of sliced salmon in the Shop 'n' Save. But Wiseman sees the workers; he takes us to the fish farm and shows us how the salmon was processed. He also sees the young people who will soon be looking for jobs at the fish farm, or at Belfast's one outpost of the so-called New Economy: the office park where workers sit in cubicles, dunning people who haven't paid their credit-card bills.

The fish-packers and dunners of tomorrow are today avoiding the eyes of a dedicated and intelligent teacher at the high school, who is talking about Melville. The students probably register his notion that *Moby-Dick* confers dignity on the common man by raising a commercial fisher to the level of tragic hero; but what good does that do them? As for the teacher's closing remarks, on *The Confidence Man* as a bleak satire about the hoax of American democracy: The kids already seem to have got the point, without having to crack the book.

Obviously, I'm reading into the kids' faces, just as I've read into every other scene I've described. So let me bring to the surface my prejudices, as I said would be necessary. I think *Belfast, Maine* dwells on the persistence of the Old Economy—the one that's now considered to be terminally unsexy by Internet-besotted Op-Ed writers. I think the film quietly but devastatingly reveals the wounds inflicted by this economy. It also reminds us, movingly, of the persistent strength and beauty of the natural world, which is made to serve the economy; and it pays tribute to the courage and good will of people who go out, day after day, to ease what suffering they can.

A fitting summary of Fred Wiseman's work, and of his life as well.

4 Little Girls

N ow in her 40s, the woman can still recall the interrupted ball game. She and her friends were in the yard, starting to mark out a playing field, when one of the kids saw a dead bird in the grass. Kick it aside, the others said. No, said the little girl—we have to bury it. (The storyteller, acting all the parts, rolls her eyes like a 10-year-old: *Whatever.*) Calling in some adult help, the scrupulous one organized an impromptu funeral, complete with eulogy and choral singing, while the others stood around and humored her. "Rest in peace, dead bird, amen. So can we, like, *play* now?"

How full of life the woman seems—laughing, mugging for the camera, miming the way she'd bounced with impatience. It's almost too much for the storyteller herself to bear. She's a survivor, and by idiot mischance her playmate was not. Not long after the bird's funeral, that solemn child was blown up in the Sixteenth Street Baptist Church in Birmingham, Alabama.

Everyone knows the subject of Spike Lee's new film. The picture, his first feature-length documentary, is called *4 Little Girls*—and if you're above a certain age, that's all you need to be told. Or rather, that's all you might think you need.

Over time, the bombing of the church in September 1963 has been reduced to the small change of our political transactions: news photos, popular songs, monuments in parks, well-worn phrases. We walk around with these things jingling in our pockets, as if we didn't know the least penny is a condensed, hardened world of human activity. So it's an act of liberation, no less political than artistic, that energizes this extraordinary film. First Spike Lee acknowledges our subservience to easy coinages, such as *4 Little Girls*. (How cunningly he chose the title.) Then he sets free the laughter and grief of that survivor of the bombing, along with ten thousand other experiences that still live among us, if only we would pay attention.

Few filmmakers other than Spike Lee would have had access to these things. Although he has not made himself a part of the documentary, you can't overlook the trust that's been placed in him, especially by the four girls' families and friends. At one point, Lee's voice comes from offscreen, asking Mrs. Alpha Robertson, the mother of 14-year-old Carole, to lay bare her emotions. Apologetically, he adds, "I don't want to play Mike Wallace on you." With a wry smile, she shoots back, "You mean Ed Bradley," then tells him what he wants to know. At another point, Christopher McNair, father of 11-year-old Carol Denise, recalls the experience that tore into the guts of every black parent in the South: having to explain to a child, for the first time, the limitations of being Colored. For McNair, that moment came when he had to deny his daughter a sandwich from the lunch counter of a department store. He is a big man, a graduate of Tuskegee, who carries himself with considerable dignity and almost glows with pleasure when leafing through the family album. For Lee, this proud man is willing to expose a memory of shame and powerlessness he continues to live with.

The trust was well placed. With the self-confidence of a born filmmaker, Lee has freely merged such personal recollections with archival footage and commentaries from many other sources, creating a picture that's intimate in detail, comprehensive in scope and as full of piss and vinegar as his best narrative features.

Consider the testimony of pink and cheerful Arthur Hanes Jr.—then the defense counsel to the church bomber, Robert Chambliss, and now a circuit court judge. Hanes recalls the speed with which Birmingham grew, so that it called itself The Miracle City: "A wonderful place to live, a wonderful place to raise a family." (Here Lee intercuts a few images of the Klan parading downtown, and of the aftermath of a lynching. "This Nigger Voted" reads the sign hung on the victim.) For a different perspective, we have Howell Raines, who reported on the civil rights movement for *The New York Times*. Birmingham had all the violence of a boom town, he explains, with labor clashes at steel mills and boxcar factories spilling over into racial bloodshed.

As early as 1949, the more prosperous black neighborhood in Birmingham was known as Dynamite Hill, because that's what white people used for removing any house they felt was too grand. I want to write "some white people"; but the distinction is harder to make than it should be, since many of the policemen who investigated the bombings were themselves Klan members, and the Chamber of Commerce types who ran the town didn't care. When Birmingham's most prominent civil rights leader of the fifties, the Rev. Fred Shuttlesworth, was blown up one night while asleep in bed—amazingly, he walked away from the blast—a cop muttered in his presence that he hadn't expected "them" to go so far. Then the cop pulled Shuttlesworth aside and advised him, in the nicest way possible, to leave town. Shuttlesworth—"brave to the point of insanity," as one witness recalls—merely stepped up his activities.

The struggle reached a new political level with the emergence of George Wallace, described by one of Lee's more eloquent interview subjects as "a dynamic expression of the mental derangement of white people." (Lee has some nasty fun—and who can blame him?—showing Wallace in a recent interview, nattering on about his best friend being black.) As the situation worsened, the black leadership in Birmingham appealed to Martin Luther King for reinforcements. "Young people today ask me how we got it together in the sixties," says Andrew Young. "We didn't have it together when we started. We had just fifty-five people at first." Enthusiasm and participation were relatively low in the period after Dr. King came to town. His negotiations with the city were dangerously close to failure. Then came a crucial decision: to recruit children. Classrooms emptied as the kids went off to march and suffer arrest; and the adults, shamed, began to join in.

When Robert Chambliss (known to his friends as Dynamite Bob) resorted to the usual methods to shut down the movement's headquarters—the Sixteenth Street church—the victims might just as easily have been adults. Yet the Birmingham campaign had become a children's crusade, and its martyrs turned out to be children. *4 Little Girls* takes us through the most painful moments of the aftermath—the identification of the bodies, the arrangements for the funerals—but also the most hopeful. Two responses seemed possible at the time, the Rev. James Bevel recalls: Commit murder, or campaign for the right to vote. We might think we know the rest of the story, but we don't. We're still living it.

When Mother Comes Home for Christmas

would rather not tell you about Josephine Perera. Her story being known to me only through the work of a gifted documentarian, Nilita Vachani, I would prefer that you get your information directly from the film, as soon as pigs learn to fly. The sad truth is, *When Mother Comes Home for Christmas* failed to win the affections of *The New York Times* when it was shown just twice, in the recent New Directors/New Films series at the Museum of Modern Art. Never mind that the picture, made by a sometime associate of Mira Nair, is the product of extraordinary persistence, empathy and intelligence; never mind that it opens up the emotional lives of an entire family and reveals, in heartbreakingly direct fashion, the true meaning of the phrase "global economy." Without a favorable *Times* review in her pocket, Vachani is unlikely to attract a U.S. distributor for the film. That's why, with apologies, I now describe something you might never see.

When Mother Comes Home for Christmas opens with a pilgrimage, as round-faced, middle-aged Josephine Perera sails by ferry to a Catholic shrine set amid mountains and deep blue waters. There, after lighting a candle, she consigns her children to the care of a heavenly mother. We soon discover why. While her younger son, still a boy, is growing up in the dank confines of an orphanage in her native Sri Lanka, Josephine works as a domestic servant in Greece, cleaning a splendid modern house and caring for someone else's daughter.

A title card explains that female domestic labor is now Sri Lanka's number one export commodity, having overtaken tea. We get a quick, almost nostalgic, view of Sri Lankan women breaking their backs picking leaves. Then, in a sequence of brief scenes, we visit a government center, where Sri Lankan women learn to play their new economic role. Here is an electric machine that cleans floors and carpets; you push it like this. Here is a machine called a microwave, which heats food very quickly; you enter the cooking time with these buttons, then press "start." Here is a condom; you must use a fresh one every time you have sex and remove it promptly, or else the purpose is lost. We are left to imagine why this last course of instruction should be an official part of the job training. It's enough to know that Josephine, unlike the great majority of Sri Lankan servants, has secured a visa and work permit for the country where she resides. She's got that much of a grip on her rights—enough that she can even risk allowing Nilita Vachani to film her.

"Show your employers that you are working hard, and they will be very happy," advises the government training center. We see Josephine vigorously scrubbing mirrors and floors in Athens. We also see her employer, an itinerant Frenchwoman, hopping about at an aerobics class, with her exertions and Josephine's crosscut so blatantly that Eisenstein himself might blush. "I need a long rest," Josephine confesses in a voice-over, in a text from one of her letters home. A rest is more than she can hope for. But as we come to learn, the cross-cutting implies more than a dialectic of master and servant. It also invites us to consider in what sense Josephine might be like her employer. She, too, can claim a measure of autonomy as a working woman—as we see when Josephine returns to Sri Lanka and her family for the first time in eight years.

The airport in Colombo: Sri Lankan women are returning from their overseas labors, loaded down with goods. One woman carts in a refrigerator with her luggage; Josephine wheels along a washing machine. The sight of it makes sense, somehow. She'd need a box that big to bring eight years' worth of feelings back to her children—a cardboard box, since nothing in their lives is going to be too fancy. Out of Colombo she goes, to her sister's place (a pop song on the soundtrack, government-produced, lauds the joys of working abroad as a servant); and there Josephine proves to be the boss. She has bought a bus for her older son, so he can run his own business. She is going to buy a house. Her daughter wants to marry, having chosen a young man with a perpetual grin and no prospects; Josephine is the one to negotiate the dowry and living arrangements. Her younger son, the one who ordinarily lives in the orphanage, needs straightening out; only Josephine can do it.

What must it be like, to cram your whole domestic life into just one month? And what if the need for cramming should demonstrate, in a perverse way, your success? As one of the lucky few who made money abroad and kept her dignity, Josephine gets to distribute the goods, make the decisions and preside over the emotional wreckage. The most remarkable thing about her is that in doing so, she so thoroughly transcends the categories of "victim" and "victor."

The most remarkable thing about *When Mother Comes Home for Christmas* is perhaps the way Nilita Vachani's camera stays with Josephine for the entire month in Sri Lanka, as if it were a fifth member of the family. I can think of few recent films that have offered such an intimate human drama while at the same time connecting the dots between rich and poor, First World and Third. *Hoop Dreams* comes to mind; but that was about a subject more glamorous than floor-scrubbing. No crowds will ever pump their arms for Josephine Perera. Still, she's every inch a champion. Watch for screenings at museums and film festivals—and keep an eye out for flying pigs.

Licensed to Kill

L et us consider the economics of damnation. In his documentary *Licensed to Kill*, Arthur Dong shows us interviews he conducted with six convicted murderers for whom gay men were the victims of choice. (A seventh killer appears on a police videotape, confessing in detail to his crime.) No matter where they're in prison, from Texas to New York, these murderers all rat out God as their accomplice.

I suppose that's one meaning of omnipresence. But the author of Leviticus 20:13 seems to exert only a fitful command over these killers. Having mentioned the divine crosser of state lines, they pass immediately to discussions of another boss, the almighty dollar. Most of Dong's interview subjects found themselves well situated to kill a gay man because they were already busy robbing him. And why were they doing that? Because faggots are easy to rob, they say; because faggots, unlike most other crime victims, hesitate to go to the cops. You hear it over and over, blurted almost in a single breath: The Bible says it's wrong, and we could take their money and get away with it.

I suppose the only surprise is the lack of a transition. Evangelists are expected to skip from scriptural quotation to an appeal for funds; but once the God-fearing have been locked up, you'd think they'd learn to articulate their ideas. It's shocking, how they haven't grown thoughtful despite all that time on their hands. But then, you don't watch a documentary on this subject for surprises;

you watch it as if you were a scientist verifying a hypothesis. Before you are seven experiments. Their results confirm something you had reason to suspect but did not truly know until now. In that sense, *Licensed to Kill* may be said to offer satisfaction rather than pleasure—although, given the properly dispassionate mood, you can be fascinated by the minute workings out of even the most malodorous experiment.

Now finishing a limited run at New York's Film Forum, with bookings set for other theaters around the country, *Licensed to Kill* won awards at the 1997 Sundance Film Festival. I feel I'm taking nothing away from Arthur Dong by saying the awards were for his choice of subject matter. Actually, if you're perverse enough to care about form, you will discover that *Licensed to Kill* is a pretty complex piece of montage. Not only does it move back and forth among the seven criminals, but it intercuts Dong's interviews with a variety of found footage, some of it conventional (such as newscasts), some of it from unorthodox sources (notably the police). Dong assembles these materials smoothly and in some ways cleverly. For every obvious, preachy shot he provides ten more that build on each other effectively. Despite his occasional presence during the interviews as an off-camera voice, and despite the addition of a brief, personal story—he, too, has been bashed—Dong removes himself from the film, preferring for you to respond as if to information given directly.

Perhaps the most terrifying information comes from the killers who have attained some understanding of themselves, like Jay Johnson. The son of an administrator at a Protestant seminary, Johnson says of himself, "I believe I was a very confused person. . . . I have gay preferences, but I don't really embrace the gay community—I'm religiously hostile to them." He also feared that his homosexuality, if revealed, would rule out the political career he saw for himself. So he attempted to put temptation out of reach. He committed murders in a Minneapolis park frequented by gay men—including himself—in order to scare away the cruisers. I don't know which is more pathetic: the irony of Johnson's having murdered a gay man who really was a politician, or the misery of his having been a flop even in the bushes. It's awful, Johnson says at last, to be unsuccessful at something you hate.

The other killer who seems to have learned about himself is Corey Burley, who killed a man he'd just robbed in a park in Dallas. Burley at first seems unrepentant. But when Dong, off camera, puts a name to the victim and mentions that he was an immigrant from Vietnam who'd come to the United States to escape the war, Burley grows quiet, almost tearful. So why did he pull the trigger? "I had a heart that pumped nitro. When I was growing up," Burley says, recalling a childhood in a public housing project, "I wanted to be bad. I didn't want to be no cowards and stuff like that. So I built myself up, pumped myself up to be bad. . . . Well, look where it's got me. I'm bad, but I'm locked up. I'm doing time, a lot of time. Where that badness come in? Ain't nobody bad up in here."

This is a lot better than what you get from Raymond Childs, who went to a motel with a near-stranger—a wonderfully friendly married man—and then was shocked to receive a sexual overture. "You gotta defend yourself," Childs explains, defense in this case taking the form of twenty-seven stab wounds. His safety having been secured, Childs then put to good use the dead man's credit cards. At least he can identify the sneakers he bought. Jeffrey Swinford, by contrast, claims he can hardly recall the man he robbed and killed: "By the time we got arrested for it, tell you the truth, I'd really almost forgot about it. . . . I don't want to sound like it wasn't a big deal, you know, but just one less problem the world had to mess with." A citizen of Arkansas who wears his hair like a coonskin cap, Swinford is one of the more profoundly religious of Dong's interview subjects. "Life's just one big opinion and what you make of your opinion," he observes. "I don't have any opinion whatsoever for homosexuals, except they oughta all be taken care of."

Then we have Kenneth French, formerly a sergeant in the 18th Airborne Corps, who so objected to serving with gays that he walked into a North Carolina restaurant and sprayed the place with gunfire. Four dead, seven wounded. "I just needed to voice my opinion," he tells Dong. But for sheer congeniality, no one can outdo Donald Aldrich, currently on death row in Huntsville, Texas. We see a section of his videotaped confession to the police, which he began by stating, "I do not like homosexuals." Then, in a later interview, we hear tones of amazement and self-disgust as Aldrich complains he hadn't known a hate-crime statute had been enacted. The business about hating gays was supposed to make the cops go easier on him, he says, no doubt speaking from experience. And here, because of this stupid new law, he'd only made things worse.

That's what I like about *Licensed to Kill*. It's a film about progress.

The Target Shoots First

f you're looking for invigoration beyond film, allow me to mention a new, hour-long video by Christopher Wilcha, a young provocateur whose diary of corporate life, *The Target Shoots First*, restores the honor of amateurism.

In 1993, fresh out of college with that ever-useful degree in philosophy, Wilcha took a job in New York as a marketing assistant at a record club, Columbia House. The band Nirvana had just startled the music business by selling a gazillion units out of nowhere; now the executives at Columbia House were staring at a new market niche, and they didn't know what it was. Maybe this Wilcha could explain it to them. So, to his amazement, he was given an ID card, an office with a nameplate and access to the employee cafeterias at both Sony and Time Warner. (Columbia House, he explains in voiceover, combines the clout of two media conglomerates.) The only equipment he brought to his job, apart from a knowledge of college-radio rock, was a Hi8 video camera, given to him by his parents as a graduation present. For the next couple of years, Wilcha brought the camera to work every day, videotaping his entire stay at Columbia House.

"Get Alice in Chains and *Beavis and Butt-head* for one low price." If you don't quite understand this proposal, you are in the same situation as Wilcha, whose task, initially, was to figure out why anybody would want the things Columbia House had decided to sell. Having done so, he was expected to descend from the nineteenth floor to the seventeenth, where the company's casually embittered writers and layout artists would translate his message into a sales catalogue. *The Target Shoots First* presents the wondrous gallery of sardonic grins, blank stares, forced smiles, exasperated grimaces and open-mouthed horse laughs that Wilcha encountered—and generated—on his trips from floor to floor. Here, too, are the social rituals of today's office: lunches, parties, visits with babies, the unveiling of new braces for carpal tunnel syndrome. Wilcha kept at it until he succeeded, and Kurt Cobain committed suicide—which seemed like a signal that it was time to quit.

As Marx once wrote, there will be no video artists in communist society. There will be no need for a separate category of "artist," because all people will get to make videos as part of their full range of activity. (I may have paraphrased a bit.) Anyway, the usual American capitalist response is: No problem. Technology has already saved us. The portable video camera puts moving-picture apparatus into everybody's hands; the Internet makes everybody a publisher or music distributor. In *The Target Shoots First,* Wilcha hilariously illustrates both the potential of techno-democracy and its limits. Yes, he was free to make this video (and, along the way, to create his own alternative-rock sales catalogue, which mocked the other Columbia House mailings). But in doing so, he converted the rebellious music he loved into one more revenue stream for Sony and Time Warner—corporations that also wound up owning the right to reproduce Wilcha's face. It seems he signed away his image to Columbia House, for future use in its catalogues. Talk about alienated labor.

THEY WERE NEVER WRONG, THE OLD MASTERS

Grand Illusion

L ike a kid at an ice-cream counter, urging his friends to try the chocolate—like a writer of travel guides, warning tourists not to miss the
Eiffel Tower—I come before you to praise *Grand Illusion*. My excuse for
this superfluity: A fresh print of Jean Renoir's masterpiece is now
making its way into theaters.

Although the story behind this re-release is remarkable, it involves no redis-
coveries of footage, no reconstructions of scenes that were cut. The distributor,
Rialto Pictures, merely offers you a crisper print than any that's been available
for sixty-two years. Under these circumstances, I can't invite you to "See *Grand
Illusion* as it's never been seen before." I say only, "See *Grand Illusion*."

See it and rediscover why footage exists. See it and reconstruct yourself.

Because it's based on the best source possible—the original camera negative—
the new print allows you to peer into nighttime shadows; to gaze all the way from
a mountain meadow to a river; to feel your eyesight rub against the plastered wall
that was Jean Gabin's mug. In short, *Grand Illusion* is no longer just a great story
(as it's been on video and in the old, worn prints). It is also once more what it
was at the beginning: an overwhelming presence. And here the film teaches a
lesson about how masterpieces behave. Now that its images are clear again, so too
is the force of the story.

You know, of course, that *Grand Illusion* concerns French prisoners of World

War I. At the very start of the picture, the aristocratic Captain de Boeldieu (Pierre Fresnay) and the working-class Lieutenant Maréchal (Gabin) fall into German hands—specifically those of one Captain von Rauffenstein (Erich von Stroheim), who pursues war in much the same spirit as he might ride to hounds. He greets his captives with a formal lunch, extending the respect he believes is due to officers—though only to de Boeldieu does he offer the friendship of a gentleman.

With these few quick strokes, Renoir makes you understand you're witnessing a vanished Europe, a Europe that vanished precisely because of this war. Think of how this realization must have struck the film's first audiences. Separated from this period by only twenty years, they must have watched *Grand Illusion* and marveled at the change in their world. On one side of the Rhine, people now had a Popular Front government; on the other, they were ruled (most of them willingly) by Nazis. Yet the Europe evoked by *Grand Illusion*, so soon after its demise, is one of perfect symmetry. Even the set drives home the message. The German field club, where von Rauffenstein plays host to his captives, is laid out as the mirror image of the French officers' club.

I might describe the rest of the film as the introduction of asymmetry—the breaking of the mirror. A cold description, you might say, especially when you consider Renoir's reputation as cinema's great humanist. Surely audiences love *Grand Illusion* not for its formal structure but for the characters, not one of whom considers himself to be incidental. The Russian prisoner who whiles away his time giving grammar lessons; the British officer who fumbles with the tennis racket he's lugged into the trenches; the detention-cell guard who soothes Gabin with the gift of a harmonica (as much to buy some peace for himself, perhaps, as to comfort his fellow man); even the German soldier who comes close to discovering French escapees in their hiding place, and who turns out to be a most genial and boyish threat to life—each of the dozens of characters, no matter how brief his appearance, seems to lead a life of his own. To speak the platitude that only such a film can redeem, *Grand Illusion* overflows with life.

But what is it, exactly, that gets overflowed? Apparently, I do need to describe the structure.

This, too, becomes magically clear with the restoration. Renoir and his co-screenwriter, Charles Spaak, made *Grand Illusion* in three acts. The first introduces Maréchal and de Boeldieu to von Rauffenstein, then takes the two Frenchmen to their initial prison camp. There they meet another major character, the wealthy, generous and emphatically Jewish Rosenthal (Marcel Dalio); they also participate in their first escape attempt, which fails at the act's end through an ironic reversal.

215

A montage of landscapes and prison-camp gates, seen from a train, introduces the second act, set in a Gothic fortress high in the mountains. Here, Maréchal and de Boeldieu are reunited with Rosenthal, and also with von Rauffenstein, who has been forced by injury to retire from the front lines. This act, too, ends with an escape, and a successful one. Maréchal and Rosenthal slip down the mountain to the accompaniment of busy orchestral music, while de Boeldieu, in a bit of ostentatiously symmetrical self-sacrifice, clambers up the mountain amid silence, buying time for his comrades and forcing von Rauffenstein to shoot him.

In act three, Maréchal and Rosenthal trudge through the mountains, quarreling and reconciling, until they find refuge with a German farm wife named Elsa (Dita Parlo), who has been left widowed by the war. Romance blooms between Maréchal and Elsa; but duty also calls. At the end, the two soldiers leave, hoping to cross the border into Switzerland and (presumably) resume fighting the war.

A strange conclusion for an antiwar film. But then, in what sense may *Grand Illusion* be considered antiwar? Certainly Renoir portrays the people on both sides of the conflict as fully human. With the relationships between von Rauffenstein and de Boeldieu, between Maréchal and Elsa, he also dramatizes the human bonds that can cross enemy lines. But this isn't to say that the lines must not be put up. In fact, the kind of sentimental pacifism that might satisfy itself with the bland phrase "antiwar film" is precisely the satirical object of the title. Does Maréchal think that another war won't come? Then he's fooling himself, says Rosenthal the Jew, who first made that judgment not on the Swiss border in 1917 but in a Parisian movie house in 1937.

Let's remember that the author of *Grand Illusion* was an enthusiastic participant in Popular Front culture and a regular contributor to a Communist paper. (This being France, he was subjected to a less-than-iron discipline. Renoir filled his column with whatever happened to amuse him.) Though far from bellicose, neither was he softheaded about the conflicts in the world. He was not likely to ignore the possibility that Hitler might have to be met with force, whatever the Party might say at the moment. And so, having established a moral and political symmetry at the start of *Grand Illusion*—a symmetry reinforced by the three-act structure—he proceeded to upset the balance, showing that choices had to be made. Maréchal loves Elsa—she's the woman he's been hoping to meet since the beginning of the picture, when a planned trip into town was interrupted—but he leaves her anyway. And von Rauffenstein (surely the butch partner in his relationship) shoots de Boeldieu, who in effect betrayed his love.

If you think back to that beautiful three-act structure, the betrayal takes on a physical weight, since each act has its characteristic setting. Act one takes place amid shedlike barracks, guard towers and metal fences: a semi-industrial architecture, which was unknown until the modern era. Act two, in effect, takes the characters backward in time, into a setting that is at once baronial and ecclesiastic. This is the world of feudal virtues and privileges—the world von Rauffenstein cherishes and de Boeldieu tosses away, playfully giving up his life for the sake of a working man and a Jew. It's plain that in doing so, he's not just following his patriotic duty. He's also letting the modern world take precedence over a fellow aristocrat.

And does Maréchal, too, yield to the modern world? That's the meaning of act three. He and Rosenthal escape from feudalism into a pastoral setting, which in turn must be escaped. It's lovely—but for them, it's a fantasy. They have to go back toward the world of barracks and barbed wire, as surely as Elsa, her heart broken, must calmly clear the table and set out food for her little daughter.

An "antiwar film" would try to remain within the pastoral. Or, more sardonically, it might go full circle, returning Maréchal to his original setting. Instead, *Grand Illusion* leaves Maréchal in a field of snow, where he's seen in long-shot with a friend he'd never dreamed of having. Each finely balanced element of the film has shifted, subtly but decisively, yielding an ending that's wide open.

Needless to say, I understood none of this the first eight or ten times I saw *Grand Illusion*. The film was too full of incident and detail, and the performances were too enthralling. (No matter which tricks I could isolate—Fresnay's reluctance, as de Boeldieu, to look directly at any subordinate, or von Stroheim's catalogue of physical rigidities as von Rauffenstein, or Dalio's almost dancelike miming of Rosenthal's sensitivity—*Grand Illusion* taught me that great acting is a mystery. All I could say was that somehow, the leads all gave the finest performances of their screen careers—with the possible exception of Dalio, who was as good in *The Rules of the Game*.) But there was another reason for my getting lost in the picture. The various prints I watched gave no sense of immediacy. They belonged, too visibly, to a past era.

The current print makes *Grand Illusion* look like a new film. (I mean physically, of course, not artistically.) It overcomes one's sense of distance from the screen, so that the mind and the pulse can both quicken. This miracle comes complete with its own war story; and so I will tell it now.

As is well-known, Goebbels declared *Grand Illusion* to be "Cinematic Public Enemy Number One," and the Nazis confiscated prints of the film wherever they could be seized. It is less well-known that a Nazi officer in occupied Paris—Dr. Frank Hensel, a co-founder of the International Federation of Film Archives—safeguarded many films by shipping them back to the Reichsfilmarchiv. For years, it's been assumed that the original camera negative of *Grand Illusion* was destroyed in 1942 by an Allied air raid on Paris; but in fact, thanks to Hensel, the primary materials of Cinematic Public Enemy Number One were by then in a vault in Berlin.

That vault happened to be in the sector that became the Russian Zone. In 1945, the camera negative of *Grand Illusion* rode to Moscow on a Red Army truck, along with a multitude of other films, to build the Gosfilmofond. But the Soviet archivists apparently did not realize what they were holding—and neither did the French archivists at the Cinémathèque de Toulouse, who received the camera negative in the mid-sixties as part of an exchange program. *Grand Illusion* was not considered to be a lost or mutilated film; and so nobody took a close look at the cans until the early nineties, when they were shipped from Toulouse to the main French archive at Bois d'Arcy for cataloguing and preservation.

The result is now available to you. I can say nothing more than, "See it."

And again. And again.

How the First World War Changed the Movies

I was face to face with the awful reality," the French filmmaker Marcel L'Herbier used to say of World War I, despite his never having come near the trenches. Posted to the Army Cinematographic Service, the young L'Herbier spent his war in Paris. Yet each day at work he found his life "turned upside down," just as surely as if he had been in battle.

"Everything that was filmed at the front passed through our hands," he recalled. "We cut, we spliced, we chose what could be shown. I watched scenes of horror; I saw soldiers who had been eviscerated, cut in two, decapitated. That shock revealed to me that I had to become a filmmaker."

As these memories remind us, the Great War was the first to be fought before the motion picture camera. In the field, reconnaisance became airborne and cinematic; at home, propaganda leapt from the page to the screen. The effects were so far-reaching, argues Paul Virilio in his often-cited book *War and Cinema,* that the war zone itself may be thought of as a kind of film. On the front, perceptions became accelerated, discontinuous, mechanized, as if the soldiers' eyes had turned into cameras. From this condition, there was to be no release; after 1918, cinema's shock techniques continued wartime perception by other means.

I summarize this theory with caution, since Mr. Virilio develops it through that mixture of hyperbole and non sequitur which is French scholarship at its zaniest. But grant him this much: If a thoroughgoing aesthete like L'Herbier could be so altered by the movie war, then whose life wasn't turned upside down? World War I, which changed everything, had film as one of its main tools of transformation.

The war also changed the conditions of filmmaking, in France, Germany, Russia and the United States. To a remarkable degree, today's film industry retains the shape it was given by the war—which means that every picture we see is in some sense a World War I movie.

For French cinema, the war was a debacle. Before 1914, the Pathé and Gaumont companies had enjoyed commanding positions throughout the world. After the war, these two giants all but ceased production, and French cinema became (by and large) the work of small, quasi-artisanal companies, perpetually struggling to reach markets outside their borders.

Yet French film could still attempt great things, as a World War I epic soon proved. Abel Gance solidified his reputation and revived the industry's hopes with *J'Accuse* (1919), the story of a frail poet who goes off to the front and comes home, shellshocked, to a village of widows and grieving mothers. For the last of the several accusations he hurls, the poet calls up the specters of the dead, who troop back from their graves by the thousands.

Gance first released this picture in a version that was as long as three normal features; in 1922, he brought out a shortened version, which ran only three hours and was altered in meaning. The original was generally understood as an outcry against the war. In the 1922 version, nationalist fervor resurfaced: Gance trimmed his battle sequences and added a victory parade.

If he was now leveling his accusation exclusively against German militarism, perhaps one reason was the rise of the German film industry. In cinema, at least, the war's losers had come out far ahead of the winners.

The preparation for this triumph was made in 1917, when the German supreme command initiated the consolidation of the film industry, so that cinema might be "put to work with the highest priority." The result was UFA, a company that did little for the war effort (despite such productions as *Anna Makes Artillery Shells*) but that after the war grew to be the biggest and most technically advanced studio in the world.

Comedies, romances, fantasies, historical spectacles and chamber dramas poured out of UFA in the 1920s. But for the most part, World War I went unaddressed until 1927, when the studio fell into the hands of Alfred Hugenberg, an industrialist, publisher and early supporter of Hitler. Suddenly, UFA was bringing out Leo Lasko's two-part *The World War*, a film that was deemed suitable for showing to a paramilitary organization.

It's not surprising, then, that the great German film about World War I, G.W. Pabst's *Westfront 1918*, was made not for UFA but for the smaller, independent Nero-Film. The story of the lives and deaths of four representative German soldiers, *Westfront 1918* came out in 1930, the same year that Universal released Lewis Milestone's *All Quiet on the Western Front*, and was favorably compared to its American competitor. Pabst had made a far tougher film—so tough, in fact, that the most gruesome sequences are now missing from all prints.

On the Eastern Front, the war's effect on cinema was decisive, since there could have been no Soviet film without a Soviet Union, and no Soviet Union without the war. This interrelationship is plain to see in *The End of St. Petersburg* (1927), a film commissioned for the 10th anniversary of the Bolshevik revolution, in which Vsevolod Pudovkin makes his Great War scenes flash across the screen like blasts from a flamethrower.

The experience of disorientation that's key to Mr. Virilio's theory—the soldier's sense of being hurtled through abrupt changes in landscape, as seen from strange and shifting viewpoints—finds stunning formal expression here and in the works of the other great innovators of Soviet film. This visual violence is meant to stimulate the mind as much as the eye. To suggest the causes of the war—a subject that filmmakers in other nations generally avoided—Pudovkin contrasts his soldiers' doomed charge across no man's land with the frenzied rush of stock traders on the home front, as they shove their way toward war profits.

The great victor of World War I in cinema, as in all else, was, of course, the United States. Alone among the combatants, America emerged with its society and economy intact. One immediate consequence was Hollywood's domination of screens around the world. It took over the markets from which France had withdrawn; it hired away (or provided refuge to) the best talent that UFA developed. When you hear studio executives today claim that Hollywood succeeds simply by giving people what they want, maybe you'll want to think of these names: Ypres, Verdun, Passchendaele.

American filmmakers ventured into this territory even before the fighting was done. In 1917, D. W. Griffith went to the front, having received the encouragement of Lloyd George to make a picture for the war effort. (It says a lot about the state of the British film industry that this request should have gone to an American.) But the director of indelible Civil War battle scenes found that trench warfare wasn't what he'd expected. He retired to encampments in the English countryside, to make *Hearts of the World*. It was not his best work. Charles Chaplin did better with his classic *Shoulder Arms* (1918), a picture about the victories that the Little Tramp dreams up for himself while slogging about in the trenches.

The full potential of World War I as a Hollywood subject did not become apparent until 1925, with the making of *The Big Parade*, produced by Irving

Thalberg and directed by King Vidor. The story of a bland young fool who is caught up in patriotic fervor, only to return home maimed and disillusioned but also deepened in spirit, the picture established John Gilbert as a star and gave the newly formed MGM studio its first big hit. With the coming of sound, however, the picture's fame was eclipsed by that of *All Quiet on the Western Front*, which isn't a bad movie if you accept the conventions of a previous era's acting style and stick your fingers in your ears during Maxwell Anderson's speeches. But *The Big Parade* needs no apologies. Both exhilarating and sobering in the best Hollywood manner, it conveys meaning through the sheer scale that's possible in moviemaking. Panoramic spectacles evoke the awesome power of the war; the attractive but loosely drawn protagonist comes to represent the entire World War I generation.

Among the notable movies that followed was the winner of the first Academy Award for best motion picture: the 1927 Air Service drama *Wings*, directed by William Wellman, a much-decorated flier in the war. Special mention should also be made of *The Dawn Patrol* (1930), the first of several World War I pictures by another flying director, Howard Hawks. Although he was later nominated for an Oscar for *Sergeant York* (1941), Hawks took particular pride in this earlier aviation feature because of its terse dialogue and restrained acting—qualities that hadn't been much in evidence in the early talkies, and were surely appropriate to this subject.

But it was a French veteran of the air war who made what is surely the greatest World War I movie—and he did it without filming a single battle scene. In *Grand Illusion* (1937), Jean Renoir brought out the meanings of World War I as no one else had, by dramatizing the journey of French soldiers through prisoner-of-war camps and out into the German countryside. In traversing a series of credible yet symbolic places (industrial barracks, a feudal castle, an idyllic farmhouse), the wonderfully individualized yet highly representative soldiers leave behind the class-bound Europe that the war had destroyed. They end their journey, by implication, on the verge of the next stage in destruction: World War II.

Grand Illusion proved to be a career high point for all of its actors, including Jean Gabin (who wore Renoir's own uniform as his costume). But for Erich von Stroheim, the film was an apotheosis. He had made his name in D. W. Griffith's Hollywood by impersonating the cold, brutal Hun, both on screen and off. Reprising that character in *Grand Illusion*, he received from Renoir what he had never been able to give himself: nobility.

From here, the World War I movie underwent a steep falling off. World War II supplanted the First World War as a subject, and the few filmmakers who went back to the earlier period seemed to have lost touch with its meaning.

(Witness the Technicolor flapdoodle that John Ford made out of *What Price Glory?* in 1952.) I think there's been only one first-rate film made about the First World War since *Grand Illusion:* Stanley Kubrick's *Paths of Glory* in 1957.

Here you do see battle, as no soldier ever experienced it: smoothly, continuously, from above. This clarity of vision may be the film's most terrifying irony—irony, of course, being the mode most appropriate to artworks about World War I, as Paul Fussell wrote in his study *The Great War and Modern Memory.* For Kubrick, the war provided an opportunity to explore the gap between the way people plan (including the justifications they give for their decisions) and the way they behave, as planning meets circumstance. Only one area of life could be held immune from the tricks of happenstance: his own work. In *Paths of Glory,* he gave us human disaster, impeccably realized.

Since then, a mere handful of films have returned to the war as their primary setting. Some have been grand (David Lean's *Lawrence of Arabia,* 1962), some good (Bertrand Tavernier's *Life and Nothing But,* 1989) and others neither (Peter Weir's 1981 *Gallipoli*). Maybe this drop-off in numbers and quality is to be expected. Sentimentalities about "the greatest generation" now seem to mark the horizon of our historical imagination.

But then, out of nowhere, comes *Time Regained* (1999), Raul Ruiz's meditation on Proust's *Remembrance of Things Past,* and we once more feel the shock that L'Herbier experienced. Early in the film, at a moment set in the Belle Époque, young Marcel watches a magic lantern show about chivalric adventures. Then, without transition, he encounters a soldier of World War I—Robert de Saint-Loup—who is gazing through an eyepiece. We see what Saint-Loup sees: black-and-white footage of a wounded horse, struggling in a trench.

These images are not suitable for you, says Saint-Loup. Too late. From chivalry and magic lantern shows to trench warfare and cinema: we've made the transition, and we live with it.

Jean-Luc Godard:
Son + Image

He barely makes it onto the screen. While most of the frame is taken up with an office setting—a desk, a lamp, some chairs and shelves—the world-famous filmmaker intrudes only so far as the screen's left edge, and provisionally at that. A hand darts in and out of view, flicking a cigarette toward the ashtray on the desk. On the soundtrack, you hear the familiar baritone, pebbly in texture, speaking in monotone bursts. The year is 1976; the place is Grenoble. Jean-Luc Godard is sneaking into view.

During his New Wave period, Godard had preferred to let the likes of Jean-Paul Belmondo stand in for him on screen. During the Maoist period of the Dziga Vertov Group (roughly 1968-72), he'd allowed himself to address the audience more directly; but still he hadn't *shown* himself. At most he'd spoken through a persona, as someone who assumed the authority to lecture other people.

Then came the return to order in France and the demise of the Vertov group (really just Godard and Jean-Pierre Gorin). The revolution went splat; so did Godard, in a motorcycle accident that nearly killed him.

Fortunately, he found a new collaborator (and sometime lover) to help with his recoveries, physical, political and spiritual alike—Anne-Marie Miéville. After a couple years of her influence, a new figure became visible in his work. Gone was the Godard who'd imagined himself as Belmondo imagining himself as Bogart. Gone was the Godard who'd hid behind a badge, as chief image-inspector of the revolutionary thought-police. In their place stood a small, middle-aged man, perpetually blue-chinned and rumpled, who answered to the name Jean-Luc. He wasn't necessarily a nice man—at times, he showed himself to be overbearing, lecherous, even sadistic—but he was out in the open as never before, searching, questioning, revising. This is the Jean-Luc Godard who keeps disturbing the edge of the frame in the first part of *Six fois deux,* his 1976 collaboration with Miéville for French television. It's the Godard to whom the Museum of Modern Art has dedicated an invaluable retrospective, "Jean-Luc Godard: Son + Image" on view through November 30.

The MoMA series performs the great service of integrating Godard's post-1972 films with his videos from the same period. In some cases, that allows for indirect comparison. You can see the film *Hail Mary* (1985), then watch Godard play with some of the same images and themes in an elliptical, non-narrative fashion in the videotape *Puissance de la parole* (1988). But there are direct match-ups as well. For example, the 1982 film *Passion* comes accompanied by a videotape from the same year, *Scénario du film Passion,* which is a bit more intellectually engaging than the movie (because it's coherent) and also more entertaining (but I repeat myself).

Sitting at an editing table before a blank screen, Godard calls up images from *Passion,* all the while talking about the choices involved in making the film and about everything else as well: the genesis of writing, the history of film, the relationship between love and labor, the falsity of TV newscasts. What ties this material together, apart from Godard himself? A desire to see; a conviction that seeing might yet be possible; an impatience with everything that dissuades us from seeing.

"I didn't want to write a script," Godard says of *Passion,* "but to *see* it." Cinema, he insists, came from an encounter with life—as when Mack Sennett took his crew into streets and parks and shot whatever passed before his eyes. Writing, on the other hand, came from merchants' lists: "Bookkeeping gave rise to the script." What would happen if film were to recover the primacy of the visible? Godard shows us a detail of hands from a painting by Tintoretto; he shows us documentary footage of a factory worker's hands. The motions are similar. "So there's proof," he concludes. "Tintoretto's gesture of love is linked with the laborer's gesture. It's not just one of Jean-Luc's fantasies." And if we fail to see? Then we get TV newscasts. "They always put the image *behind* the announcer," Godard complains. "The announcer can't see what he's talking about. We need to have the image in *front* of us."

Cogito ergo video: The motto, one of many that Godard tosses out, fits especially well with "Nobody's There," the episode I've already mentioned from *Six fois deux,* his collaboration with Miéville "on and under communication." Think of this videotape not as a commodity—something that comes with its expected mode of use already built in—but rather as research data. The evidence is suggestive, but you have to figure out on your own how to apply it. To people who are accustomed to the prepackaged meanings of television (or of present-day entertainment films—there's no longer much difference), such long-term staring can be an excruciating bore. But it takes time to see; it takes patience. That's one of the possible lessons of "Nobody's There."

In the videotape, Godard sits in the studio he and Miéville set up in Grenoble, conducting a series of interviews with job seekers. (He'd advertised for workers, without specifying what they'd do.) Hopeful applicants pass before the lens, answering questions that at first elicit information rather than emotion: What would you consider a good salary? What were you doing before you became unemployed? Gradually, the tape settles down to longer interviews with two applicants: a woman in early middle age who does cleaning work, and a young man, apparently of North African background, who works as a welder, when he can find a job.

"Settles down" might be the wrong expression. Though the camera remains motionless, the two would-be employees become more and more stirred up, as Godard, almost off-screen, keeps prodding them. What would they *really* like to do? Just what they usually do, they insist—clean all day, weld all day. What if the woman were hired to go out and talk to people, about anything she liked? She couldn't do that, she explains. She's afraid of seeming a fool. Anyway, she says, she's become used to middle-class manners by virtue of her housecleaning jobs; she no longer feels comfortable talking to people who lack a basic civility. And what about the welder? What would he do if Godard hired him but didn't give him any tasks? Would he take a walk, for example? But that wouldn't be allowed, the welder says. Godard disagrees—here, it would be allowed. The welder becomes visibly embarrassed; he can't imagine the situation. At last, shyly, he says, "I'd ask for more work."

The cleaning woman rocks back and forth in her chair; the welder squirms. And I felt uncomfortable, too, watching "Nobody's There." I couldn't ignore the cruelty of the project. Neither could I deny that Godard and Miéville, through their somewhat brutal method of research, had made me see two urban workers more clearly than ever before.

The revelation happened as if by itself. For once, Godard and Miéville had seemed to use no art—which is the main reason, apart from the political, that I've dwelled on this episode. It marks a minimum. (So does the accompanying episode, "Louison," which shows a farmer.) And yet the crucial feature of Godard's thought is present in "Nobody's There," in the cutting back and forth between the two workers. Godard doesn't believe he's truly seen anything unless he's seen two things as one.

"You could take a box of matches and a pencil and make a film out of them," Miéville tells Godard, in a tone midway between awe and exasperation, in *Soft and Hard,* a 1986 videotape consisting mostly of a conversation between the two friends and collaborators. Notice that she does not say he could make a film out of the matches alone. He needs at least two things. Otherwise, he couldn't cut from one to the other. There would be no montage.

Here's the theory Godard spun out for Serge Daney in a 1988 interview in *Libération:* The early filmmakers were looking for montage but never truly found it. Griffith got as far as inventing the closeup, a comparison between something nearby and something farther away. Eisenstein learned how to cut between different angles on the same subject (as in the three shots of the stone lion in *Potemkin*). But cinema fell victim to commerce before anyone developed a montage that was fully critical and revelatory, uniting things that had seemed distinct. Today, when we see early films, we recognize the hints of that failed project: "There was a sign that something was possible if we took the trouble to call things by their name. That [film] was a new way—that no one had ever seen before—of calling things by their name and that was also broad and popular." But "something disappeared when the talkies came in and language, words, took over." Instead of growing up, cinema became a perpetual child.

At this point some critics might object, should they be sufficiently narrow-minded. Maybe montage really is the unachieved Snark of world cinema, but it's been hunted well enough for Pudovkin to have identified five species. (Timoshenko found fifteen; Arnheim, thirty-three.) So when he speaks of cinema in the past tense, calling it a failure, is Godard merely exalting his own present status as montage-hunter? Or has age brought pessimism with it? The man who once declared that "everything remains to be done" now enjoys making catalogues of dead cinema masters, with Fassbinder's corpse punctuating the list like a fat final period.

Call it despondency if you will, or bitterness or inflated self-regard. Judging from what I see on the screen, I prefer to say that Godard is continuing to act as a provocateur. He knows that we need one, now more than ever. When he speaks of montage, he's not talking about a mere technique—much less about a technology—but about the whole political economy in which cinema functions. When he mourns the old masters, he's acknowledging the passing of an era in which cinema promised to be both mind-opening and popular.

All this becomes clear in two videotapes that are among the high points of the MoMA series: *Histoire(s) du cinéma* (1989). Depending on the context—

which varies at mind-boggling speed—the title might be translated as "history of film," "histories of film" or "film stories." There's even a Nazi-era version of the title, in which Godard spells *histoires* with an SS—but I'm getting ahead of the story.

Most people who retell the history of film start with technology. So does Godard, in a way. He begins with a close-up of his editing table. He also shows you himself, sitting at an electronic typewriter and consulting books. So he makes you aware of the equipment he's using right now. What he *doesn't* do is trace the development of cinematic machinery, or turn the history of film into a story about technical improvements. In fact, as an unstated joke on technological progress, Godard relies heavily throughout *Histoire(s) du cinéma* on an editing trick that's simultaneously sophisticated and primitive.

There's a proto-cinematic toy in which you have a picture of a horse, say, on one side of a paddle, and on the other a picture of a rider. Spin the paddle fast enough, and you'll see the rider on horseback. Right there, you've got the essentials of motion pictures, including montage. In *Histoire(s) du cinéma*, Godard frequently recalls the effect of that toy, as he flips back and forth between different images until they seem to overlap. The only difference is that he's using the latest video technology, which lets him cross-cut at the touch of a button. What really counts, Godard implies, is what you make out of the cross-cutting—whether you're working with a 50-cent toy or with a million-dollar editing board.

But something else matters as well: the social relations of production. In Chapter One of *Histoire(s) du cinéma*, in which he promises to relate all the histories of film (including those of the films that never got made), Godard passes over the Lumière brothers and Méliès, over Griffith and Chaplin, and starts his discussion with Irving Thalberg. It's a brilliant gesture—locating the power of the movies not in technology, not in the creativity of any director but in the organizational ability of a producer, the man who perfected the studio system. The second brilliant gesture is to flicker between Thalberg and early Soviet cinema. "The power of Babylon," Godard intones on the soundtrack. Is he talking about MGM or the U.S.S.R.? You see a view of Lenin's tomb. The words MAKE ME A STAR appear on the screen.

For all its splendor, this imperial road of the movies "leads nowhere," Godard rasps. Why? Because both movies and the reality for which they were a wishful substitute reached a dead end in the concentration camps. In the face of that horror, only the newsreel photographers did not disgrace themselves. "You don't see close-ups in newsreels," Godard observes on the soundtrack. "Death is not a movie star. Anguish is not a movie star."

When the camps were opened, the truth about cinema also came out: "The movies were not part of the communications industry or the entertainment industry, but the cosmetics industry." That's the harsh judgment Godard passes in Chapter Two of *Histoire(s) du cinéma,* in which he claims to recount just a single history: the one that answers the question, "Where do I come into it?"

He recalls encountering the movies for the first time at age 20—his high-bourgeois, high-culture background had shielded him till then—when he started attending Henri Langlois's screenings at the Cinémathèque Française. To his amazement, young Godard discovered a world in the movies—"a world with hardly any history, but full of stories." Like practically everybody else, Godard yielded to the fascination of this world. Like not so many others, he also recognized its insufficiency: "Instead of ambiguity, engendering thought and feeling—stories of sex and death."

Consider it to be another flicker of montage: Godard invites you to see him standing both inside and outside the movie world. Similarly, in *Histoire(s) du cinéma,* Godard makes the viewer flicker, since it's impossible to remain either wholly absorbed in the videotapes or wholly detached from them. Godard's energy and wit pull you in, as does the allure of the subject matter. But too much is happening at once. There are always at least two images competing for your attention, along with fragments of movie soundtracks and musical compositions, along with Godard's narration, along with the titles that flash on the screen. Here is the Godardian maximum, in contrast to the minimum of "Nobody's There." With your hands on the videocassette of the programs and a remote control, you could examine all the material bit by bit to see how it's put together; you can think. But, more likely, you'll have to watch *Histoire(s) du cinéma* as if it were a film, letting it wash over you, leaving you frustrated and rapt, dazzled and impatient.

If those last words seem in any way to disparage *Histoire(s) du cinéma,* don't blame me. Godard is right: The movie era is over, and the TV era is here. Two thumbs up—way up—for Jean-Luc Godard's *Histoire(s) du cinéma!* That's as much ambiguity as today's culture allows.

We watch movies with our thumbs instead of our eyes. We get news from people who have willingly blinded themselves. (An example from outside Godard's work: the reports of the Persian Gulf War.) And every once in a while, we marvel when we come across a filmmaker who still knows how to hold on to two ideas at once, as Clint Eastwood does in *Unforgiven.* Is it any wonder that Eastwood is so alone in *Unforgiven?* His good old days are gone, and they were bad, anyway. Godard's good old days are gone, too, having failed to revolutionize either the real world or the movie world. Now he's alone in Rolle, a little town in Switzerland. But Eastwood goes on. Godard goes on. And everything still remains to be done.

September 21, 1998

Touch of Evil
Nights of Cabiria

S ince few figures in world culture are comparable to Orson Welles—
none, in fact—we ought to get straight the details of the last film he
made in Hollywood, *Touch of Evil*. A new print is now going into circulation, attended by the monthlong hoopla that accompanies such re-
editings and re-issues. Well should we hoop; the film is stunning. Compared
with *Touch of Evil*, all other items currently on the screen look as daring as
paint-by-numbers pictures, and as dynamic, too—except (of course) for the
recently re-edited version of Federico Fellini's *Nights of Cabiria*. I'll get to that.
But for now, let us pass by Fellini, as well as the question of whether you should
rush to see *Touch of Evil* (the answer being obvious), and ask to what degree this
fresh print may be considered new.

The story begins in December 1956, when Universal asked Welles to play
the villain in a thriller then titled *Badge of Evil*. At the time, he received no offer
to direct; in Los Angeles, Welles had last worked behind the camera in 1947,
when he shot *Macbeth* with financing from Republic Pictures, an arrangement
that barely fit the definition of "working for a studio." Now, having only
recently returned from nine years in Europe, he weighed the merits of acting
in a script that was "very bad. . . . I said, 'Maybe'" (as he later recalled to Peter
Bogdanovich), "and I was still wondering whether I could afford *not* to make
it when they called up Chuck Heston" to play the lead.

230

Accounts vary on what happened next. Either Heston pressed the studio to hire Welles as director (see Barbara Learning, *Orson Welles*) or Heston mistakenly assumed Welles would direct and his enthusiasm forced Universal's hand (see Welles and Bogdanovich, *This Is Orson Welles*). Either way, Heston laid the groundwork for one of the rare expressions of gratitude to come to him from *The Nation*; and Welles received permission to rewrite the script and direct it, for no more money than if he'd merely learned his lines and walked through the part.

Aided by several typists, Welles threw himself into scriptwriting. He had been given a story about a tough old cop who fabricates evidence in a murder case. A few weeks later, he emerged with film history's most grotesque border-town phantasmagoria, about a Latino-Anglo coitus indefinitely interrupted by dynamite—and by a comic-relief mobster, a pair of homoerotic cops and a gang of reefer-blowing, jitterbugging juvenile delinquents. The core of the script was still the conflict between a low-rent, unscrupulous American detective (Welles) and his aristocratic, upright opposite number (Heston), who in this new version turned into a Mexican. In Welles's treatment, the characters' divergence became shapely: Their conflict breaks into the open halfway through the film, at which point each man literally goes his own way, accompanied by a new ally. But viewers could easily overlook such subtleties of construction amid the film's distractions, which Welles seems to have ticked off from a list of the nightmares of right-thinking Americans, circa 1956: miscegenation, drugs, leather-jacketed lesbians, cheap hotels. All this, and he had yet to add two roles that were largely improvised: Dennis Weaver as a near-psycho motel clerk, and Marlene Dietrich as a fortune-telling brothel keeper.

Filming began in February 1957 and proceeded quickly, ending on April 2. Welles then spent two months cutting *Touch of Evil*, working mostly with Universal editor Virgil Vogel. Barbara Leaming's biography quotes Vogel: "I could immediately see the kind of *startling* film he was shooting for . . . and that it needed *that* kind of editing." According to this account, Welles cared above all about the rhythm of the cuts; he edited for visual effect, then (when necessary) wrote dialogue and looped it in. While shooting one sequence, Leaming reports, Welles told an actor to recite the Declaration of Independence; so long as his lips were moving, the words could be added in post-production.

All went well through June 1957, when Welles took a couple of breaks and Universal assigned a new editor, Aaron Stell, to work on *Touch of Evil* in his absence. Just leave everything in his hands, the executives told Welles. All this time, he had been striving to seem cooperative; so he left everything in Stell's hands. Upon his return in August, he discovered the picture had been recut on orders from Universal's head of production, Ed Muhl, and head of post-production, Ernest Nims. To Welles's distress, they ignored his requests to complete the 108-minute version he'd been working on; instead, they cut even more, releasing a ninety-three-minute *Touch of Evil* in February 1958.

What was changed? First, Universal smoothed out discontinuities in Welles's storytelling. The studio version eliminated abrupt juxtapositions and incongruities and added a few transitional shots. After that, as Welles told Bogdanovich, the studio cut out whatever did not seem to advance the plot, such as background information about the characters or statements of theme: "A policeman's job is only easy in a police state." "They got a lot of moral stuff out," Welles said. "Jokes and morals went. . . . But they didn't absolutely murder it. I was very sorry about the things they did, but the story was still *roughly* intact when they were finished."

What's more, the studio retained its own 108-minute version of *Touch of Evil*, which was shown at a preview. In 1975 Bob Epstein of the UCLA film archive discovered this cut, which has since been put into circulation, and which also serves as the partial basis for a videocassette release. Welles scholar Jonathan Rosenbaum, who edited *This Is Orson Welles* and served as consultant for the new print of *Touch of Evil*, has said of the preview print that it "does not correspond precisely to Welles's original cut, and even contains additional material shot by Harry Keller after Welles was removed from the project." I would observe, however, that it does incorporate the "jokes and morals" that Universal found so unnecessary. In fact, it's virtually complete.

So what do we gain by the version now being offered to us, expertly re-edited and re-recorded by Walter Murch and Bill Varney? The publicity materials make much of their efforts to bring *Touch of Evil* into conformity with a "recently rediscovered" fifty-eight-page memorandum that Welles sent Universal in the late summer or early autumn of 1957. "Recent" in this case means within the past twenty years; on the evidence of *This Is Orson Welles*, Bogdanovich discussed the memo with Welles in the mid-seventies. And even if the memo had turned up only yesterday, I would not be impressed by its length. Although the document is fascinating for the insights it offers into Welles's artistic choices, only its pleading is exhaustive. The changes Welles demanded were not. He called for perhaps fifty alterations. Most of them had to do with removing a close-up here, taking away a bit of the soundtrack music there.

And yet, when I saw the new cut, I felt I understood for the first time what was happening in *Touch of Evil*—an admission I would hesitate to make, if a very distinguished colleague had not made the same confession to me. Mood becomes substance; small adjustments in rhythm and sound translate into big changes in the way you follow the film. The effect is most evident in the opening sequence: the celebrated tracking shot that follows a car, a bomb and four characters from one side of the border to the other. For this shot, the picture has now been wiped clean of credits (which Welles wanted to run at the end), while the soundtrack has been muddied with a raucous mix of overlapping, multidirectional dialogue and music. No great change, you might think; and yet the resulting tension between image and sound might almost summarize the conflict between the story's antagonists: one man making his eyes cut clear to the goal, the other man wallowing in the world's confusions.

A similar revelation awaits viewers of the new print of Fellini's *Nights of Cabiria* (1957), now being circulated by Rialto Pictures.

This vehicle for Fellini's wife, Giulietta Masina, cast as a pugnacious but waiflike streetwalker in Rome, used to be a sure crowd-pleaser at revival houses (back when revival houses existed) even when it was shown in 16 millimeter, and it has remained readily available on video; so the release of a clear, fresh 35-millimeter print, though welcome, might seem to be no more than a refinement for connoisseurs. The provision of new subtitles, written in a more direct, American idiom, is also an improvement—though again, skeptics might question whether the film has truly become "new."

In this case, the claim of novelty rests on the reinsertion of one sequence, which was censored in 1957. While tramping homeward after a trick with a truck driver, Cabiria encounters a character known as The Man with the Sack: someone who visits the poorest of the poor, offering humble comforts and a few kind words to people who live in holes in the ground. According to accounts by Fellini and his biographers, authorities in the Catholic Church objected to this dramatization of a layman's good works, feeling it was put into the film to belittle religious charity; and so, after *Nights of Cabiria* was shown at the Cannes festival, The Man with the Sack disappeared.

Nights of Cabiria has survived all these years without the sequence; and at least one writer on Fellini, Peter Bondanella, has claimed the picture is better without The Man with the Sack: The sequence "adds nothing significant to the themes Fellini had already developed elsewhere." Yet surely it's significant that Cabiria recognizes one of the cave-dwellers visited in the sequence: La Bomba, who used to be famous among the other streetwalkers for the wealth she'd amassed. The immediate pleasure of discovery allows Cabiria to put off any thoughts about the transit of worldly glory. But the audience has already noted Cabiria's standard boast, that she owns her own house (miserable cement block though it may be). The full import of that boast, and the shadow cast upon it by La Bomba, becomes evident in the following sequence, when Cabiria visits a shrine to the Virgin and almost wills herself into believing she can change her life.

Here too, as in *Touch of Evil*, a chunk of the character was cut away, with the excuse that the plot wasn't affected. The result? For forty years we've called the picture a masterpiece, without fully understanding what was happening in it.

We deal with similar problems in other art forms. Students of literature are always wrestling with corrupt texts; art historians do their best with fragments, and with centuries' worth of dubious reconstructions; musicologists have developed a minor industry in removing one another's improvements to Schumann's orchestral works. The ensuing "authentic" and "original" versions then become marketable—rather briefly, in the case of alternative editions of *Ulysses*. So even if we grant that *Touch of Evil* and *Nights of Cabiria* now seem new, what's new about re-releases?

I think we can find an answer if we look back to the early eighties and the re-release of Abel Gance's *Napoleon*. Kevin Brownlow's reconstruction of the film had been conducted more or less in scholarly obscurity until Francis Coppola came in, trailing clouds of hoopla. In his hands, *Napoleon* became the first "rediscovery" to play as an event film—an innovation that happened just as revival houses were beginning to falter and die, as videocassettes were becoming popular and "independent" filmmakers (such as Coppola) were claiming to challenge the studios.

Since then, independence has been institutionalized as part of a new studio system. In the old days, the majors used to diversify their releases, offering so many extravaganzas, so many midlevel pictures, so many cheap programmers. Now, after about two decades of confusion, the studios have once more learned to diversify; expensive pictures go out under the Universal or Columbia or Disney label, while midlevel or cheap pictures (the so-called independents) go out from the majors' subsidiaries, as October or Sony Classics or Miramax films. The system having been rationalized, just enough screens are left open so these little pictures may play amid the *Godzillas*, *Armageddons* and *Avengers*.

Foreign-language pictures are now to a large extent a part of this two-tier system of distribution and exhibition; and so, too, are re-releases. *Nights of Cabiria* is the exception, having been undertaken by small operators; *Touch of Evil* is more typical, having been launched by Universal. The initial theatrical run recoups the cost of the new print, after which the videocassette release makes the profit. I simplify, of course, for the sake of irony—though not too much simplicity is required, if we are to smile at the irony of Welles being cooperative with the Universal executives, even in death.

We have a slightly corrupt text by Gogol that comments on such uses of the past. But, if you prefer the low-culture reference, here's Marlene Dietrich in *Touch of Evil*, shrugging about the pianola in her brothel: "The customers go for it. It's so old, it's new."

Film Comment, January/February, 1995

Francesco Rosi

Exterior: day. A young man lies facedown in a Sicilian courtyard, bloodstains visible on his shirt, a handgun and a rifle by his side. Around him are gathered perhaps a dozen living men—cops and town officials. One, circling the corpse, is busy dictating an inventory; item by item, he translates the enigmatic physical reality of this scene into bureaucratic language, which will soon prove to be no less enigmatic, and no less disturbing, than the body itself.

Such is the opening of *Salvatore Giuliano*, the film that established Francesco Rosi's reputation. Using a gambit he would frequently play again, Rosi hooks the audience with the mystery of a violent death, then spends the next 107 minutes refusing to solve it. Why should he? In that opening sequence, Rosi already has laid bare what he conceives to be the real mystery: the process by which potentially disruptive events yield to official control. Bureaucratic language turns out to be the most dangerous weapon used in *Salvatore Giuliano*—so dangerous that the town official, in describing the corpse, might be said to murder the title character right before our eyes.

Critical reputations can be dangerous, too. Rosi's jelled between 1962, when *Salvatore Giuliano* came out, and 1976, when he released *Illustrious Corpses*. During those years, a significant number of filmgoers came to see Rosi as a figure of probity, both political and artistic. A man of the left, he used film as an investigative tool, exposing the convergence of power among business interests, political parties, and organized crime in his native Naples, in Sicily, and throughout Italy. And yet, as he told David Overbey of *Sight and Sound* in 1976, "I don't make documentaries . . . I make documented films on a certain reality of life." Like the neorealists, he favored shooting on location, often with casts full of nonprofessionals, but he rejected the neorealists' use of sympathetic characters embedded in well-rounded plots, preferring instead to tease and provoke the audience in the name of a critical cinema. Rosi's storytelling was disjunctive, characterized by brusque editing and jarring chronological jumps. His principal characters were often strangely distant, or even absent from the scene.

"In the general economy of the stories," Rosi told Overbey, "personal lives have no real importance." Some of the protagonists bore the names and manners of well-known figures; others were entirely made up. But during these key years, Rosi's view of character was consistently long-distance, so audiences would understand that his films were not so much "based on a true story" as "based on a true social force." Watching *Salvatore Giuliano*, we rarely see the Sicilian bandit leader, who comes into closeup only when laid out for burial. Nottola, the politician and real estate developer who is at the center of *Hands Over the City* (1963), goes through the entire film with his son in hiding from the police; yet we don't hear him voice any concern, nor do we get a single glimpse of his family life. The title character of *Lucky Luciano* (1973) does come before the camera; every few minutes he even speaks occasionally but he never does much of anything, except to smile knowingly and eat his dinner. As for Rogas, the detective who provides the point of view for *Illustrious Corpses*, Rosi grants him one scene at home, which is just enough to establish that he is divorced and lonely—and, more important, that he realizes his phone is tapped.

Perhaps Rosi, too, became like one of the protagonists from this period. Considered as an auteur, he was an exemplary figure, more of a locus than a person, on which different critical interests converged. But I would suggest that this image, like that of his characters, was tricky, too—as filmgoers discovered when *Christ Stopped at Eboli* was released in 1979.

On its surface, the film's subject seemed fitting for Rosi, since it dealt with both politics and the South. The story—even some of the language—came from a memoir of the same name published in 1945 by Carlo Levi, a Jewish physician and painter from Turin, who spent several years of the Fascist era in internal exile in a village in Lucania. But Rosi turned this material into something that was sensuous, meditative, thoroughly enveloped in the presence of its point-of-view character—something that invited viewers to dream, rather than to debate. "Francesco Rosi" never would have made this picture.

The films that followed—*Three Brothers* (1981), *Carmen* (1984), *Chronicle of a Death Foretold* (1987)—made it obvious that *Christ Stopped at Eboli* was no fluke; audiences were going to have to revise their notion of Rosi. Now, with the completion of his *Neapolitan Diary* (1992), the most personal film he's yet made—and with the screening in October 1994 of a complete retrospective at Lincoln Center's Walter Reade Theater—we have a good occasion to rethink Rosi, to see what the connections might be between the jumped-up, critical modernist of the earlier films and the warm, suave director of *Eboli*.

Salvatore Giuliano "was the first film in which I felt I had mastered the delicate balance between reality itself and an interpretation of reality," Rosi has said. It was his third feature, and still commands critical attention as the starting point for everything that is distinctive about his work. But when Rosi released his first feature, *La sfida* (The Challenge), in 1958, he was already 36 years old and had ten years' experience in the movies behind him, plus another four years on the stage and in radio. By any standards, he was mature, and the film shows it.

Perhaps the most striking aspect of *La sfida*, for those who know only the later work, is the fluidity of Rosi's direction. He choreographs the movement of the actors and the camera, so that action runs continuously from the beginning of a scene through its end. He also builds up a sense of space through cross-cutting, as when the film's Neapolitan slum-goddess Assunta (Rosanna Schiaffino) spies across a tenement courtyard at Vito (José Suarez), the pampered tough guy who wants to muscle his way into the Camorra. It's too easy to dismiss these directorial conventions with the word "Hollywood." For one thing, relatively few people in Hollywood have ever handled the conventions so adeptly as Rosi did his first time out. For another thing, this sort of seamless storytelling has been practiced outside of Hollywood—in Luchino Visconti's *Bellissima* and *Senso*, for example, films on which Rosi had worked as assistant director.

You can see how much Rosi learned from those experiences in big set pieces, such as the wedding sequence of *La sfida*; he's absolutely confident in handling dozens of extras. And, of course, you can also see the influence of his very first job in film, as an assistant on Visconti's *La terra trema*. Like so many neorealist films, *La sfida* is a blend of real, down-and-dirty people and places with an artfully un-real story. Not only does Vito publicly announce his intention of marrying Assunta, but he does so immediately after their first sexual encounter and immediately before the film's intermission. Not only does Vito come to a bad end, but he does it in front of Assunta's eyes, on their wedding day. Sentimentality, you could say, echoing one of the standard complaints against neorealism; but again, this is too easy a response. I think Rosi's screenplay, written with Suso

Cecchi d'Amico and Enzo Provenzale, may give us an important key to the later films.

Again and again—in the stories of *Salvatore Giuliano*, of Nottola in *Hands Over the City*, of Enrico Mattei in *The Mattei Affair* (1972), of Inspector Rogas in *Illustrious Corpses*, even of the bullfighter Miguel in *The Moment of Truth* (1965)—Rosi repeats a pattern he established in *La sfida* with Vito's rise and fall. A tough man, whose energy and singlemindedness make him admirable even when his motives do not, dares to imagine that he is bigger and stronger than the existing power structure, with consequences that usually are fatal. From a political perspective—the one Rosi has most often taken in his interviews—these stories are about how people break with authority, and how authority seals the rupture. From a literary perspective—which Rosi does not often discuss—the stories are of course tragedies (or near-tragedies, since Nottola wins his bet). But from a personal perspective—which Rosi almost never takes—Vito and his successors are figures out of a family romance.

In a series of conversations edited and published by Michel Ciment—Rosi's most consistent and eloquent champion—the filmmaker spoke revealingly about how he remembers his childhood, and about the different worlds he intuited through his father's family and his mother's. Talking about the father's side, he suggested the origins of the Francesco Rosi who is morally rigorous and intellectually tough. His paternal grandfather, of Calabrian peasant stock, came to Naples alone at age 9 to look for work. He became a tailor, and while at work managed to put himself through school, meanwhile saving enough money to bring his mother to Naples. Though Rosi's father had to work for a while in the new family business, he soon broke away, selling sketches (especially caricatures) to the newspapers, taking up photography, and eventually settling into a job with a shipping company. As Rosi narrated this story to Ciment, his father's family emerged as disciplined, dignified, politically serious, tied to both the world of ideas and the world of the Neapolitan working class. On the one hand, Rosi first visited Pompeii and Herculaneum with his paternal grandfather, who had an interest in archaeology. On the other hand, Rosi got to know the Neapolitan docks by hanging around his father's office.

With Rosi's account of his mother's side, though, we get hints of another aspect of the filmmaker. Here we have the man who is fascinated by "imagination and liberty"—the one who can't stop making films about swaggering, self-destructive gamblers.

His maternal grandfather, from a rich merchant family in Naples, fell passionately in love with a cousin when he was 16 and declared he would commit suicide unless he was allowed to marry her. His parents, suitably impressed by the gun he was waving, decided to grant his wish, at the expense of getting a special dispensation from the Vatican. Such theatrics were evidently not uncommon in the family. One of Rosi's great-aunts was a soprano who indulged in the usual love affairs and scandals. An uncle was the head of the claque in Naples and spent as much time as possible at vaudeville shows, operettas, and circuses. (He took young Francesco to see Josephine Baker.) On the New Year, some of the other uncles (who were secretly socialists and Freemasons) took advantage of the hubbub to go out on the balcony and shoot their pistols. Reading the account Rosi gives of this "tribe," you get the image of a mansion (complete with a private chapel) ringing night and day with madcap antics.

But then, the grandfather's antics were not so funny. When not engaged in propagating the family—nine children survived—he was off gambling in San Remo and Monte Carlo. He lost everything, and in losing it "he let the family taste the joy of the fall." Eventually, Rosi claims, he became a croupier in the Naples casino where he'd gone bust, just so he could remain close to the game.

The veracity of this wonderfully colorful story is both questionable and beside the point. Rosi clearly believes in the tale (even though he might not believe it), which is enough to account for his fascination with figures such as Vito, Giuliano, and Mattei. He could easily have chosen some other type on which to base his cinematic investigations; but perhaps a more sober character (like the teacher played by Vittorio Mezzogiorno in *Three Brothers*) would not have sparked in him the exuberance of those earlier films.

Understandably, the possibility of Rosi's personal engagement in those pictures has not much been discussed. His attention, and that of the audience, was always directed straight toward the subject matter, which not only was impersonal in nature but often alarmingly prescient, too. (Rosi managed to bring out *The Mattei Affair*, about intrigues in the international oil business, just before OPEC became a household acronym. He portrayed the political situation of *Illustrious Corpses*—what we might call rigidly controlled anarchy—just before the 1978 kidnapping and murder of Aldo Moro.) And yet Rosi's overextended gamblers keep cropping up, to emotionally complex effect. It's true, for example, that the title character is largely absent from *Salvatore Giuliano*, but Rosi fills that void with Giuliano's lieutenant Pisciotta (played by the American actor Frank Wolff), who gradually takes on the air of a tragic hero. By the time Pisciotta becomes central to the film, he is already a prisoner, standing trial with the remnant of Giuliano's bandits for having massacred a Communist Party rally. Clearly he's a villain—a smirking, bullying villain at that. But as Pisciotta begins to understand how many different ways he's been betrayed—by the police, by the government, by the Mafia—his wiseguy manner gives way to defiance, and he seems to grow. There is nothing "honorable" about this man (any more than there's honor in throwing your money away at the roulette table); but now that he's gone too far, now that he's accepted the dare and exposed himself to ruin, he plays out his fate magnificently.

Through Pisciotta, Rosi gives the viewer (and himself) a chance to become emotionally engaged in *Salvatore Giuliano*. And there's another hook as well: Rosi's bursts of stylistic flamboyance. When the bandits stage their first night attack, for example, Rosi shows us how the band silently takes up positions around a police station. The station stands in the distance; poking into the foreground, at the left of the frame, is the barrel of a machine gun. There's a pause; then the screen abruptly goes black, except for a roaring stream of white light from the gun.

Such stylized, expressionistic surprises recur throughout the first phase of Rosi's career. In *Hands Over the City*, Rosi dramatizes Nottola's deepest crisis by showing him pacing through his office alone at night, while the camera patiently tracks him—for close to three minutes! (As if to underscore how unnatural a moment we're watching, Rosi fades out the ambient noise—sounds of traffic on the street below—and brings up a full-length rendition of Piero Piccioni's jazzy theme music.) Or, to take an example from *The Mattei Affair:* A journalist who is preparing a report on the sudden death of the industrialist Enrico Mattei holds up an old photograph of him, taken in 1945. The camera moves in until the screen's frame matches the photograph's; then the still image comes to life, and the story continues in flashback. It's essentially the same trick that Orson Welles used when he brought to life a photograph of Charles Foster Kane's newspaper staff. Is it pure coincidence that Rosi should have duplicated Welles—another hubristic figure who thought he was bigger than the establishment, and suffered for it? Is it just coincidence that the journalistic investigation of Mattei's death recapitulates the inquiry into Kane's? I also note that *The Mattei Affair* begins with a mystery about a private airplane. So, too, does *Mr. Arkadin,* the alternate title of which—*Confidential Report*—would go very nicely with half a dozen of Rosi's films.

I would suggest that in both his style and his choice of central characters, Rosi was indeed acting out a personal drama—something that did not contradict the critical and political agendas of his films but helped to animate them. With *Illustrious Corpses*, though, both of these aspects of Rosi's filmmaking seemed to reach their limit.

In this utterly paranoid story about political assassination—Rosi based the screenplay on the novel *Il contesto* by Leonardo Sciascia—a cop named Rogas (Lino Ventura) investigates the murder of a judge, and then another murder, and then another. Death swallows death, suspect swallows suspect, until it seems as if virtually every institution of Italian society is implicated in a grand conspiracy, reaching from the Mafia and the banks to the Communist Party and the terrorist left. In style, the film is ponderous and baroque, its figures dominated by the grandiose architecture that forever looms over them; in a word, it's Wellesian. But by this point, Rosi's ideology was one of despair. Power is absolute in *Illustrious Corpses*, and absolutely violent. Though Rogas tries to forge ahead, he's dogged rather than defiant; there's no thrill to his gamble, and no chance at all that he might win.

It was at this point in his career, when he had envisioned complete stasis, that Rosi took up a different character and a different kind of story. He turned to Carlo Levi and *Christ Stopped at Eboli*.

Here at last we do not have the sympathetic tough guy who must see his gamble through to the end. Instead, we have an artist, a thinker, a quiet observer, played with great wit and depth of feeling by Gian Maria Volonté. Exiled from Turin to the village of Gagliano in Lucania, Levi has no one to whom he can speak freely, no scope of action; and so, for all his otherness, he is oddly in tune with the villagers around him. As Jean-Philippe Domecq wrote in *Positif,* "Rarely as in this film has the art of the image been so skilled at translating that which resists image-making: silence. Because exile is the weight of silence, especially in this village, where the peasants communicate by gestures or daily rituals more than by words."

It's as if Rosi had now imaginatively accepted the condition dramatized in *Illustrious Corpses*, that of the futility of all action, and in accepting it had discovered a new range of possibilities, both emotional and sensuous. Or, to put it another way: It's as if Rosi had forced himself to rediscover another part of his personal history, coming from his own experience of the Fascist era. In 1942, he was drafted into the army and sent to officers candidate school. By the time he finished his training, apparently, Mussolini had fallen; yet Rosi was sent to the north to fight. Once there, he discarded his uniform and, in the company of a few friends, spent a year hiding out in Tuscany, where he made contact with the Resistance. Silence, exile, cunning: Although he had traveled in the opposite direction from Levi—south to north—Rosi wound up in a place that was existentially similar.

If *Salvatore Giuliano* is the masterpiece that set the tone for the films of Rosi's first period, then *Christ Stopped at Eboli* is the masterpiece that established the second. There, and in *Three Brothers* and *Carmen*, Rosi seems to sink into the landscape in a way that's new for him. Before, his actual locations and nonprofessional casts had been at the service of a dramatic outrageousness. (Think, for example, of the Neapolitan town councillors in *Hands Over the City*, who play the role of the Naples Town Council. Did Rosi use them because they were the real thing, or because no other actors could have gone so far over the top, waving their hands in the air while screaming "Our hands are clean"?) Starting with *Eboli*, though, flamboyance gives way to sustained observation. The films are less exciting, perhaps, and less provocative, but they're infinitely more absorbing.

There has been a throwback to the older style, of course—a film that might have been called a revisitation, had it been successful, but which may more accurately be described as a relapse. Although *To Forget Palermo* (1990), an examination of the politics of drug-dealing, attempts to revive the investigative thriller, it's ultimately unwatchable. How could it be otherwise, with James Belushi and Mimi Rogers in the leads? But the script (by Rosi and his longtime collaborator Tonino Guerra, with an assist from Gore Vidal) is even worse than the performances. It's touristic—the last thing you'd expect of a Rosi film set in Sicily—and its slide-show method of documenting the drug traffic betrays Rosi's entire career of *interpreting* reality. Watching the film's illustrated lectures, you cannot doubt that the people on screen are explaining what you should know, and you—poor, dumb media-prole—had better take notes.

It would have been heartbreaking for Rosi to have ended his career with that mess. Fortunately, the old trickster has had at least one more surprise in him. With *Neapolitan Diary*, he at last put himself on the screen—not as part of the investigation (as he'd briefly done in *The Mattei Affair*) but as a subject. Not only does he interpret the reality of Naples, but he is implicitly interpreted by it.

The frame of the story has Rosi coming back to Naples to attend a 30th anniversary screening of *Hands Over the City* at the School of Architecture. Rosi holds forth for the students; so do various professors. Then Rosi wanders off in one direction, his two young assistants wander off in another, and the film becomes a peripatetic meditation on change, in both the city and the generations. The sense of futility that has hung over Rosi's work since *Illustrious Corpses* is still present—all the authority figures seem to agree that Naples has gone from bad to worse, with no good in sight. But there's humor as well (as when Rosi is mistaken for Vittorio De Sica), mingled with a retrospective mood that almost gives nostalgia a good name.

By the end of *Neapolitan Diary* you feel as if the hemmed-in, neglected core of Naples, its historic heart, was absorbing Rosi. He, too, is going to be part of the city's past; he takes pride in knowing he deserves to be remembered and worries a bit that the conservation effort might be shoddy. That much you can guess on your own. The part that Rosi tells you, explicitly, is that he still dreams and is not at all resigned. The final sequence of Neapolitan Diary? It happens in Rosi's head while he dozes on the train back to Rome. He sees the celebrated scene from *Hands Over the City* in which the tenement collapses—only this time, the rubble slowly rises from the street and reassembles itself into a part of the old, filthy, impoverished, dangerous Naples that he loves.

The New York Times, September 26, 1999

Pietro Germi

I n the sweet repose that settles upon us after drubbing an Adam Sandler movie, we film critics sometimes become wistful. If only readers could look into our hearts! How we long to enjoy the same films as everyone else. How we yearn for the companionship of a public that would like our films.

These wishes and sighs are audible at this year's New York Film Festival, which is presenting a retrospective of the work of Pietro Germi.

Rare among those film authors of the past half-century who have spoken on behalf of the people, Germi also succeeded in speaking to them. As evidence, we have the dozen films on view at the Walter Reade Theater—pictures that show us once more what film as a popular art can look like, when it's fully popular and fully an art.

Americans know Germi primarily as the director of two great comedies set in Sicily: *Divorce, Italian Style* (1961) and *Seduced and Abandoned* (1963).

For people who have seen only the fuzzy videos of these films, the retrospective's prints should be a revelation. These ferocious, cold-blooded, intricate and hilarious pictures also turn out to be unexpectedly gorgeous. No less an authority than Martin Scorsese has described the black-and-white cinematography of *Divorce, Italian Style* as some of the richest and most beautiful ever put on film.

The retrospective will also offer a second, more general revelation. It will introduce Americans to the earlier films of Germi, whose sudden emergence as a master of comedy thoroughly surprised his Italian audience.

First known at home as one of the neorealists, Germi gradually won a large following as the director and star of tearjerkers about working-class life in Rome, like *The Railroad Man* (1956), and of a hard-boiled police procedural, *The Facts of Murder* (1959). Follow the retrospective, and you discover that *Divorce, Italian Style*, too, was part of this lineage. Only after the script was well along did Germi turn it into a comedy. The film was to have been a conscience-stirring drama, set in the rural areas of Sicily where he'd begun his career.

Born in Genoa and educated in Rome, Germi first went to Sicily professionally in the 1940's, following a southward path already taken by his more celebrated colleagues Roberto Rossellini and Luchino Visconti.

For these founders of neorealism, Sicily had the allure of being part of modern Italy yet raw and primitive—a foreign landscape within the national borders. In the film that brought him to prominence, *In the Name of the Law* (1948), Germi was unusually honest about viewing Sicily as an outsider.

"This land, this boundless, sun-flattened solitude, is Sicily," intones a deep-voiced narrator, travelogue-style, over the opening shots. Very soon, those images of rock-strewn vistas and magnificently harsh skies seem to merge into a second landscape, one that was also foreign and yet familiar to its audience. *In the Name of the Law* makes Sicily look like John Ford's Monument Valley.

In the first of his many gestures toward popular cinema, Germi adapted to local circumstances not only the look of the Western but also many of its stock characters: for example, the lone lawman, come to tame the frontier.

In this case, the Wyatt Earp figure becomes a magistrate from Palermo (Massimo Girotti), determined to bring order to a town ruled by horse-riding, rifle-toting vigilantes—in other words, the Mafia.

The film's ingredients don't always mix well. *In the Name of the Law* contains a grindingly formulaic romance between the magistrate and the equivalent of the local schoolmarm. Worse still, the inspirational finale sinks from the model of John Ford to that of Frank Capra. Nevertheless, the film is remarkably adept at fusing realistic observations and social commentary with the conventions of an easily understood genre. Germi's landscape imagery, notes the film historian Mira Liehm, "has since become a commonplace in Italian cinema—part of a code of signs along with the sinuous streets and dusty roads, the houses with closed shutters, and the villagers with inscrutable faces. In 1948, all this was new, and to capture it on the screen was an act of courage."

Still, though *In the Name of the Law* came out at the same time as some of the founding works of neorealism—*Paisan, Bicycle Thief, La Terra Trema*—Germi was labeled a latecomer and imitator. Speaking ex cathedra for neorealism, Rossellini described Germi as one of the movement's "popularizers"—someone who was probably harmless, and may even have done some good.

We who live in the Adam Sandler era may look back in puzzlement at this judgment. We have grown accustomed to seeing the films of festival heroes draw blank stares from the public—think of *A Taste of Cherry*, or even *Rushmore*—while movies that only a producer could love set new box office records each week (and lose 40 percent of their audience the following Friday). What's wrong with a little popularization?

But in the late 1940s and early 50s, the split between an author's cinema and the people's movies had not yet been institutionalized. Partisans of the new cinema could still hope to appeal to a broad public (however badly Vittorio De Sica's *Umberto D.* flopped at the box office). Meanwhile, conscious of their high vocation, even the most audience-friendly cinéastes could belittle Germi for being a bit too skilled at giving the people what they wanted.

Federico Fellini, who collaborated on the screenplay for *In the Name of the Law*, later spoke of Germi as "the great carpenter." François Truffaut, echoing this faint praise, said Germi's films were "as solid as stone posts." In the eyes of many colleagues and critics, Pietro Germi was always the craftsman, never the artist.

Some also called Germi a "director of compromise," a tag given in response to his politics. Neorealism was, by and large, a film culture of the left—and Germi (in the words of his most ardent champion, the critic Mario Sesti) was not just an anti-Communist but "an angry and hysterical anti-Communist." For those whom he systematically offended, it was all too easy to interpret his use of genre conventions as a selling out of neorealist principles.

In this regard, *The Railroad Man*, which became one of Germi's best-loved films, may be seen as a deliberate provocation. Among other things, it is a quasi-sympathetic portrait of a strike-breaker: a train engineer who fiercely maintains his sense of integrity but who does so while driving away his family and alienating his fellow workers. In a risky move, Germi chose to play the role himself, inhabiting it in classic big-lug style. His most expressive moments come when he turns his back to the camera, letting his shoulders do the acting. His most enigmatic moments, strangely enough, are the close-ups.

What makes *The Railroad Man* so compelling (apart from the overstuffed story and that impeccable craftsmanship) is the impossibility of deciding whether it's a film of self-pity, self-glorification or self-loathing. All three can be read at once in the chronic discomfort of Germi's face, a structure that might have been piled up, like a wall, by day-laborers. The rocks that are his cheekbones jut painfully through the flesh. His upper jaw is an outsize ridge, jammed uneasily into place; his chin, a boulder that's started to slide down into his neck.

You sense the workers had been given too simple a diagram. A square, slashed down the middle with a curved line for the nose, was all they'd had to go on in making the face of Pietro Germi. Or maybe that face, "as solid as a stone post," was built up as a fortification against the world.

Like the title character of *The Railroad Man,* Germi was adored by people and wanted nothing to do with them. He refused to answer the telephone, broke his doorbell so he wouldn't have to answer it, shut out even his lovers from any knowledge of his past and kept both actors and crew at a distance by periodically exploding in rage. *Difficult* is a word that frequently figures in the testimonies of those who knew him, along with "tormented."

Perhaps those traits reach their crisis point in another of his fictional self-portraits, as Inspector Ingravallo in *The Facts of Murder.* Like all such police stories, this one provides an occasion to explore the multiple subcultures of a city—Rome, in this case. But the hustlers, hookers and schemers have seldom been so pathetically unequal to their crimes, the police so inept or the chief detective so clumsy in his vulnerability. Growling, hulking and ranting his way through the film, Ingravallo discovers (of course) that everybody's guilty of something—but the big scoundrels get away, while the little ones take the rap. Faced with such corruption, he can only sink deeper into a furious but clear-sighted isolation.

Or he can make comedies.

Divorce, Italian Style and *Seduced and Abandoned* both resemble *The Facts of Murder* in concluding with the restoration of social order. It's a brutal order, of course. In one film, a marriage is ended at the expense of a woman's life; in the other, a marriage is arranged at similar cost. But what can you do? The community is satisfied; and Ingravallo (or Germi) has by now removed himself from the picture, to stand back at a safe distance and laugh.

Instead of the voiceover tour guide of *In the Name of the Law,* whose baritone throbs with fervor, you now hear the wised-up voice of Marcello Mastroianni—sublime as the impecunious, lounge-lizard aristocrat of *Divorce, Italian Style*—giving his self-satisfied account of Sicilian sociology.

Instead of the father in *The Railroad Man,* who gut-wrenchingly forces his pregnant daughter into a marriage she doesn't want, you now have the father in *Seduced and Abandoned*—equally overbearing, but now ludicrous, and played not by Germi but by his long-time acting sidekick, chubby little Saro Urzi.

And instead of the suffering daughter of *The Railroad Man,* you have (in both films) Stefania Sandrelli—amazingly young, amazingly beautiful, amazingly defiant.

We might well be astonished to see Germi remake, in a new mode, the world of his earlier movies. But if the film festival's retrospective teaches us anything, it's that Germi had been a remaker from the start. That was his way of documenting some of the most troubling realities of his own time, and his own spirit, in great depth and complexity: by fashioning them successively into Westerns, melodramas, police stories, comedies.

As a craftsman, he did this carpentry well. As an artist, he never did it for its own sake, but to observe, investigate, argue, explore and awaken his audience to itself.

The New York Times, March 11, 2001

Ousmane Sembene

When the interview is over and the tape recorder is shut off at last, a grateful Father of African Cinema declares himself free to smoke. Ousmane Sembene of Senegal, loosely draped in a striped cotton shirt and trousers, starts to becloud his Park Avenue hotel room with the aid of a gnarled, bent-stem pipe. He's warming up a reply, it seems, to the question he has evaded for an hour: What price has he paid for his career in films?

Now a vigorous 78, Mr. Sembene has spent decades creating his own remarkable films and, simultaneously, the cinematic infrastructure of sub-Saharan Africa. He has trained technicians, established a distribution network, made ordinary citizens into actors, mentored other filmmakers. When an interviewer asks him to look back, he politely refuses to discuss his headaches: the run-ins with two governments (of Senegal and France), the necessities of self-financing and shipping film overseas for processing, the long gaps between productions. But, with a heavy fragrance hovering in the hotel room, he chuckles at the memory of a physical threat.

The danger, encountered during the shooting of his 1992 film, *Guelwaar,* could easily have come from a religious group. He had made light of the friction between Senegal's Muslim majority and the country's Roman Catholics, yet no harm arose from those quarters. Nor was Mr. Sembene bullied by the Francophone elite (a frequent butt of his satire) or by the particular target of *Guelwaar*, the profiteers who fatten themselves on Western handouts to Africa. The attackers, who surrounded him in a rural village, were bees. While on location, Mr. Sembene recalls, he lit his pipe under just the wrong tree and brought down a swarm on his head.

So he finally owns up, with a laugh, to a bruising share of "everyday heroism"—the sort of valor practiced by the title character of his new film, *Faat-Kine*.

Faat-Kine glows with the high spirits of a woman who has overcome half a lifetime of abuse. Born in 1960, the year of Senegal's independence from France, Faat-Kine (Venus Seye) is seduced and abandoned on two separate occasions, barred from school, and disinherited. Her father tries to set her on fire; her mother prays for her death; and after she nevertheless lives to see 40, Faat-Kine suffers fresh wounds from her grown daughter, who belittles the way she earns her living.

Having risen from a job as a gasoline pump jockey, Faat-Kine now manages a Dakar service station. It's a place that "symbolizes the energy of life," Mr. Sembene says, while also suggesting "a man's world, where the language is very crude." By working there—and not just working, but ruling from behind a spotless desk—"Faat-Kine subverts the society of the past."

"She establishes her own independence," Mr. Sembene adds, and does it so well that the film ends with a close-up of her feet in bed, toes wiggling with pleasure.

In each scene leading to that happy ending, Faat-Kine demonstrates yet another aspect of Mr. Sembene's conviction that "Africa's society and economy are held together today by women."

"But how can women have these responsibilities and yet be denied the same privileges as men?" he says. "That's the problem."

It's a problem that has evidently touched Mr. Sembene's audience. When *Faat-Kine* opened in Dakar, Senegal's capital, last May, he says, "All the women came."

"Whether in Senegal or Gabon, Cameroon, Chad, Côte d'Ivoire, it was women who patronized the film. They told me that my depiction didn't begin to reach the level of suffering of African women. And for a month, women came flooding to see me. Some of them even brought along their husbands!"

Can the continent's most celebrated filmmaker be so accessible?

"Why should I hide, after I've made my films? Everybody knows where I live. I don't have a housekeeper in Dakar. My house doesn't have a gate.

"You see, every one of my projects begins with research—because how can I know anything, unless people tell me? *Faat-Kine* required a lot of this research, since there are three generations in the film: the mother, who symbolizes traditional society, the daughter, who is modernity, and Faat-Kine herself at the confluence. To understand the experience of women in African society, the contradictions in their lives between past and present, I had to talk with people—because, after all, I'm not a woman."

For similar reasons, Mr. Sembene personally takes his films to cities and villages throughout Senegal, "because it's very important to talk with the public wherever the film goes," he said.

"It's what I call the traveling cinema. You don't make a lot of money out of it, but at least you get ideas. I have to be with the public—because, if I claim to speak on behalf of the people, then I have to be accountable to them."

Out of this desire for conversation grew Mr. Sembene's career in film—and with it a large part of the cinema of sub-Saharan Africa.

Born in 1923 in the Casamance region, Mr. Sembene left school at 15, supported himself in Dakar as a plumber and bricklayer and at 19 enlisted in De Gaulle's forces, with which he fought in France and Germany. It was not the last combat he was to see. After the war, he spent a decade as a union activist and Communist militant in Senegal and France.

With the publication of his books *The Black Docker* (1956) and *God's Bits of Wood* (1960), Mr. Sembene left behind manual labor and claimed his place as an important African novelist. But he was a novelist working in French, in a new nation where the most popular tongue, Wolof, was only starting to take written form and where most of the population could not read at all. Calculating that a book could speak to 10,000 people at most, whereas a movie might reach 1 million, Mr. Sembene left for Moscow and a year's training at the state film school. By 1963, he was back in Senegal, 40 years old and ready to start the major part of his career.

Since then, Mr. Sembene has made a handful of shorts and eight features, counting *Faat-Kine*. These include delicious urban satires, overflowing with incidental characters and local color (*Mandabi* and *Xala*); a modern-day political murder mystery, set in a shady village (*Guelwaar*); rural period pieces, done in quasi-folkloric style, about the early and late colonial eras (*Ceddo* and *Emitai*); and even a based-on-a-true-story epic of David Lean dimensions, *The Camp at Thiaroye*, about a French massacre of African troops at the end of World War II.

If these films seem astonishingly varied in style, period and setting, they also share certain strategies that date from silent movies, or for that matter the era of hieroglyphics. Wanting to convey legible ideas about his society and needing to communicate them across language barriers, Mr. Sembene constructed a cinema in which gestures, props and settings are all made to speak.

His first feature, *Black Girl* (1966), told its story not only through the protagonist's voiceover narration but also, and more emphatically, through elements like her choice of clothes. (In defiance of her white, French employers, the title character insists on wearing a fancy outfit while doing housework, to show she's more than a maid.) *Faat-Kine* finds Mr. Sembene still deploying these strategies—for example, by showing women in traditional dress parading through concrete high-rises, bearing brightly colored plastic buckets on their heads.

Used by a lesser artist, such hieroglyphs would be just that: inanimate stick figures. But Mr. Sembene's cinema of conversation brings irrepressible life to his characters; and in retrospect, the loving attention he's devoted to the women among them is fully evident. The modern, educated daughter of Faat-Kine has her counterpart in the outspoken young daughter of a bureaucrat in *Xala,* and in the princess who solves her village's problems more directly than any man would dare in *Ceddo.*

The "everyday heroism" of Faat-Kine herself can be traced back to the widow in *Guelwaar,* addressing a bitter monologue to her husband's empty clothes; to the scuffling wives in *Mandabi,* working around their improvident husband as best they can; to the rebellious village women of *Emitai,* standing up (as the men will not) to murderous French authority; and even to the wife in a short film, *Borom Sarret,* who tartly assures her husband that he'll eat tonight—exactly how, he'd rather not know.

What's new in *Faat-Kine* is a wholehearted endorsement of its heroine's entrepreneurship. Isn't she a bit like a filmmaker—at least, the kind of filmmaker who raises money on his own and tours the countryside with his movies?

Mr. Sembene turns aside the suggestion, as he does all other hints about his own brave persistence. But before the interview ends, he willingly goes on the record about political change:

"Forty years ago, we had nothing—no doctors, no engineers, no writers. We had no university. We thought a flag and a national anthem were enough for independence; and we thought we could count on the government. That is now a thing of the past. One has to count on the people. And despite all the problems, success for us is a certainty. Every day we're working hard, because we're dreaming of a better quality of life. And that is Faat-Kine—someone who wins out through a daily struggle."

The proof? During the presidential run-off election last March, when Abdoulaye Wade of the Senegalese Democratic Party, an opposition party leader for 26 years, unseated Abdou Diouf of the Socialist Party of Senegal, "It was the women who changed the entire order of things," Mr. Sembene says. "When they held a protest march in the streets, everything was frozen. It's a new power for women in our society."

I Am Cuba

T he strangest film to be released this year, and perhaps the most exciting as well, turns out to be a thirty-year-old tribute to the Cuban revolution. Recently sprung from the archives of the former Soviet bloc by Martin Scorsese, Francis Ford Coppola and Milestone Film, *I Am Cuba* is a work of cinematic delirium and great political ambition, of political delirium and great cinematic ambition—a fabulous beast of a movie, part white elephant and part fire-breathing dragon. Useless to say that such a film could not be made today. The point is, it shouldn't have been possible to make back then.

Co-produced by Mosfilm and the Cuban Film Institute (ICAIC), *I Am Cuba* went into pre-production in the latter part of 1961. Whether the planning began a few weeks or a few months after the Bay of Pigs remains a subject for research; all we know is that officials in Moscow and Havana must have been newly keen on investing in a big feature film in support of the revolution.

ICAIC, which was founded in March 1959, until then had devoted its resources mainly to making newsreels and documentaries and to expanding the exhibition circuit. (Among its initiatives was the "mobile cinema"—a projector loaded onto the back of a Soviet truck, sent to roam the villages.) Feature film production would not take hold decisively until 1966, with Tomás Gutiérrez Alea's *Death of a Bureaucrat*; so for ICAIC in 1961, the project of making a 140-

minute fiction was extraordinary. The subsequent evolution of the project into an art film would be flat-out inexplicable, were it not for two factors: the context of Havana itself, and the personality of Fidel Castro.

Havana had for years been a movie-mad city. Under Batista, Hollywood product had crowded out most other fare; but for the curious, there were opportunities to see all sorts of films, opportunities that expanded in the years right after the revolution. This rich film culture had its effect on those Cubans who longed to make films themselves. By mid-1961, when the proposal for *I Am Cuba* would have been floating about, there had been just enough production beyond the aesthetic limits of the newsreel to elicit a landmark speech from Fidel Castro, "Words to the Intellectuals." This was the occasion when he put forth the formula "Within the revolution, everything; against the revolution, nothing." Given its timing—two months after the Bay of Pigs—this doctrine was not so much a threat as a daring promise. Despite the all-too-credible prospect of destruction by a vastly superior force, Castro pledged that non-revolutionary (as distinguished from anti-revolutionary) artists would find in Cuba "a place to work and create, a place where their creative spirit . . . has the opportunity and freedom to be expressed."

It was this proposed wonderland of personal expression (newly established on an island where northerners had long been accustomed to letting go) that greeted Mosfilm's production team, headed by director Mikhail Kalatozov. A few years earlier, Kalatozov had scored an international hit with *The Cranes Are Flying*; he also had enjoyed a successful bureaucratic career, having served, at various times, as a studio head, Soviet consul in Los Angeles and Deputy Minister of Cinematography. On the face of it, he would not have seemed a man to run wild in the tropics. But Kalatozov's tastes had been formed during the Soviet Union's era of heroic experimentation, under the influence of Dziga Vertov and Esther Shub, and his career since then had been marked by frequent gaps, the result of official disfavor over his chronic "formalism." Even while he was readying *I Am Cuba* for the camera, in October 1962, Kalatozov came under attack from Mosfilm's Art Council on the grounds that he had irresponsibly subordinated the subject matter and characters of his latest film, *The Letter Never Sent*, to the pleasures of direction and cinematography. By the time of this attack, of course, the screenplay for *I Am Cuba* had been finished (written by Yevgeny Yevtushenko and Enrique Pineda Barnet) and the casting was set; everything was in place to make a rhapsody, rather than a manifesto. Still, we may guess that the Art Council contributed something of its own to *I Am Cuba*, inadvertently digging a spur into Kalatozov just as the starting gate clanged open.

He began shooting in late November 1962—immediately after the missile crisis—assisted by cinematographer Sergei Urusevsky and camera operator Alexander Calzatti. At once, Kalatozov plunged into the sort of death-, convention- and gravity-defying camera excursion that characterizes *I Am Cuba*. To show the corruption of the bad old days in Havana, he had his camera wander among the participants in a bikini contest, staged on the rooftop of a fifties Moderne hotel; then descend as if by elevator to poolside level; then snake through the tables of well-moneyed cocktail-sippers; then take a side trip onto a terrace overlooking the beach, and then (this is all happening in one continuous take, by the way) become fascinated by a woman in a leopard-skin bikini, tracking her as she gets up from her chaise longue and following her into the pool, to dive at last beneath the surface. Seal-like capitalists swim by, accompanied by bubble-breathing pimps and bimbos, while the soundtrack modulates into a glub-glub version of the hotel band's jumpin' jive.

This is damn near a normal sequence in *I Am Cuba*. The film's different sections may vary somewhat in style, incorporating a gauzy flashback here, a bit of suspense-building cross-cutting there. (The four main episodes, which are linked by theme rather than character or plot, concern the people's misery in the city and in the country, the students' revolt in Havana and the peasants' uprising in the mountains.) But whatever the episode, you're constantly being hit by a sense of hallucinatory rapture, conveyed by the black-and-white cinematography (which transforms palm trees into giant white feathers and sea into molten lead); a willful dizziness, implied by the framing (with its nonstop tilts); and above all a breakneck daring, boasted of by the long, hand-held takes. Again and again, Kalatozov incites you to marvel at a never-before-seen shot; he even gives you onscreen cues, in case you're slow to react. When the camera descends to poolside during the hotel sequence, for example, some of the extras stand and applaud. Ostensibly, they're clapping for the participants in the bikini contest; but they might as well be congratulating Kalatozov. Immediately after, as his camera glides past the poolside tables, you see a Batista-era tourist making his own movie with a little Bolex. Miserable capitalist! Can he hope to achieve a socialist camera movement like *this?*

Here's where I begin to wonder if the Mosfilm Art Council had a point. Had I been hauled before the Council in 1964, when *I Am Cuba* was released, I hope I would have defended Kalatozov's direction, perhaps by invoking Shklovsky and his principle of alienation: By making the world seem strange, the artist shows that reality is mutable, thereby encouraging viewers to understand that they, too, have the power to change their lives. I might also have appealed to Malevich's Suprematism as a precedent; like the painting *White on White*, Kalatozov's look-Ma-no-hands camera movements demonstrate the triumph of human will over brute fact. But then, Kalatozov is an equal-opportunity alienator. He makes *everything* look strange and wondrous, so that you feel as thrilled by the decadence of a Batista-era nightclub as you do by the exuberance of an anti-Batista street demonstration.

Considering the fortunes of the Cuban revolution since 1964, this all-purpose thaumaturgy now can have the effect of underscoring the film's dramatic clumsiness, while at other times it allows viewers to forget the subject matter altogether. Surely most audiences will chortle over the film's nightclub sequence, in which a chinless, bow-tied American geek (played none too steadily by French actor Jean Bouise) takes sexual advantage of Downtrodden Cuban Womanhood (Luz María Collazo). Less funny, though no less kitschy and stiff, is the episode about an old, illiterate sugarcane farmer (José Gallardo) who loses his land to the United Fruit Company. In these sections of *I Am Cuba*, the too-muchness of Kalatozov's style works against any attempt to exercise one's historical imagination, to think oneself back into the core of lived experience that might once have animated what is now a lump of propaganda. But in a more dramatically vivid section of *I Am Cuba*—the episode about a student activist named Enrique (Raúl García)—the style winds up being equally inimical to meaning. You often ignore the subject—for example, the outpouring of popular emotion that results from Enrique's self-sacrifice—because you're busy screaming in astonishment at a crane shot you *know* was impossible.

Why not go all the way, then, and try looking at the film from the Castro-has-failed point of view? Let's say for the sake of argument that nothing was ever worthwhile about *I Am Cuba*, *except* for its flamboyance. By effecting that divorce between style and subject matter, we would be treating Kalatozov more or less as certain critics treat Leni Riefenstahl. Are the two in fact equivalent? Would we have any valid reason—other than a belief in the good intentions of one and the bad of the other—for justifying Kalatozov's propaganda but not Riefenstahl's?

Actually, I think there's something to be said for good intentions. Put the worst possible construction on Kalatozov's film. Claim that it promoted a dictatorial regime that betrayed and bankrupted the Cuban people; you will still have to admit that *I Am Cuba* was meant to defend the Cubans' right to govern themselves, in conditions that would allow the poor to become a little less wretched. Judged in that way, Kalatozov's faults are essentially aesthetic misdemeanors—sentimentality, overstatement, tone-deafness. (He did not commit the graver crime of hero worship; Castro is mentioned a couple of times in *I Am Cuba*, and that's it.) Now put the best possible construction on *Triumph of the Will*. Claim that Riefenstahl was improbably naive and failed to foresee the ends of Nazism; you will still have to admit that *Triumph of the Will* was meant to praise the force of arms, the glories of regimentation and the inherent goodness of the Aryan race, all embodied in the figure of the Great Leader. Unlike Kalatozov, Riefenstahl was so deft that she committed almost no aesthetic missteps; but politically, her masterpiece is one giant felony.

It's all the more telling, then, that *Triumph of the Will* was useful to its producers, in a way that *I Am Cuba* was not. Upon the film's release in Havana in 1964, audiences reportedly had a good laugh, then unofficially changed the title to *I Am Not Cuba*. I would guess they cringed at the "poetic" voiceover narration, murmured in alternating lines of Russian and Spanish, and at the Soviet crew's tireless interest in floor shows and hot babes. Besides, it must have rankled that the job of telling about the revolution had fallen to a bunch of Soviets. Meanwhile, on the Moscow end, there was even less enthusiasm for the film. Mosfilm struck only a few prints, and the picture seems to have quickly dropped out of sight—helped into oblivion, no doubt, by the contemporaneous disappearance of Khrushchev. It was not a moment for eccentricity.

Now the film re-emerges, into a world that is likely to feel no ardor for its politics, nor even much nostalgia. How strange, strange and sad, that *I Am Cuba* will at last be appreciated, but probably for its technical trickery. Or is that strange? In our post-everything era, people pretend to talk politics by discussing Clinton's weight problem versus Newt's; they rave over the special effects in *Forrest Gump* or the editing in *Natural Born Killers* and ignore the rancid content. This seems to me an ideal situation for the restoration of Leni Riefenstahl's reputation. Perhaps it's not so good for Kalatozov's.

I Am Cuba is a film that still has not found its historical moment. We can enthuse over its multitudinous wonders; we can, and should, give thanks to all the people who have fetched back the cinematic hippogriff. But I suspect audiences today will fail the film, and do so in a way that oddly parallels its own worst failure.

At the very end, as the guerrillas in the Sierra Maestra advance toward victory, the soundtrack soffers a final poem—by Yevtushenko, I would guess, rather than Pineda Barnet, judging by the characteristic note of tin-plated bombast. "Now a rifle is in your hands," the voiceover says, apostrophizing Cuba. "You are not shooting to kill. You are firing at the past." As if real people don't get killed in a revolution; as if the murder of the past would somehow be guilt-free.

And in our era? We don't poeticize bloodshed; we just laugh it off, with the same arrogance we use to mock the past. Maybe today's audiences will surprise themselves and discover through *I Am Cuba* that the past is more than a playground of irony. Then again, maybe they won't; in which case, *I Am Cuba* is destined to be this year's artiest roller-coaster ride.

Warner Bros. Before the Code

As of this writing, seven bills are pending in Congress to regulate violence on television. On the streets of Harlem, activists protest against the outlaw manners flaunted in rap videos. In a banquet room in Beverly Hills, our First Film Fan implores movie executives to clean up their products and save their souls. Once again, it's time to ask how (and why) America polices the moving image.

Actually, America's first film censors were cops. Beginning in 1907, under the leadership of Deputy Superintendent Major Metellus Lucullus Cicero Funkhouser, the Chicago police banned some films outright but more often chopped and rearrranged them to suit their own tastes, if not those of nickelodeon patrons. It's instructive to see what kind of material particularly offended Major Funkhouser. In his 1990 study *Behind the Mask of Innocence*, film historian Kevin Brownlow cites a list of one month's excisions: "the application of the third degree by police; the bribing of a policeman; brutal handling of prisoners by police; prison guards failing to preserve order; bribing of a detective; theft of a police uniform; love scene between a married woman and an army officer."

What a useful figure he makes, the self-important cop with the comic-opera name! How unfortunate for civil libertarians that the world's censors do not all live down to Major Funkhouser. On Christmas Eve 1908, a less risible figure,

New York Mayor George Brinton McClellan, wrote the next chapter in film censorship. He shut down all the nickelodeons, ostensibly to insure public safety. (By operating in filthy, malodorous buildings, nickelodeons endangered the working-class immigrants who crowded the shows.) McClellan's more likely motive, though, was to safeguard public morals, broadly construed. (By crowding into nickelodeons, working-class immigrants endangered a prime chunk of New York real estate, making it filthy and malodorous.)

What to do? A committee of Progressive Era reformers associated with the People's Institute quickly convened to protest the Mayor's ban. Clearly, there was no need to deprive poor people of their entertainment. The proper course was to *improve* the entertainment and through it the poor themselves. So, in March 1909, the People's Institute formed a Board of Censorship. It was a private initiative, without governmental authority or police powers; and yet the dominant organization of American movie producers, the Motion Picture Patents Company, readily volunteered to submit all new releases to the board.

The movie producers chose this form of self-censorship mostly to avoid a multiplicity of imposed censorships, with all their trouble and expense. Every state, every locality, had its own Major Funkhouser waiting to happen. Better, then, to seek the approval of a reasonably sympathetic and intelligent board, which (with luck) would function on a national level.

But the producers had more than one reason for their decision. The Motion Picture Patents Company, better known to film history as the Edison Trust, was a monopoly, which in 1909 was attempting to throttle all competition, domestic and foreign alike. The Trust's policy of self-censorship may therefore be compared to the policies of many other industrial monopolies during Theodore Roosevelt's presidency; they came to accept some degree of friendly regulation rather than risk a breakup. Beyond that, the trusts, and the Trust, wanted to seem public-spirited. Soon, edifying views of world landmarks became common in the Trust's productions, along with advice on hygiene and informative tours of factories and farms. Good, hair-raising murders and hot-blooded love affairs became correspondingly more difficult to find. The Trust's producers were going upmarket in search of middle-class dollars—which happened to be the very strategy of some would-be competitors who just then were starting to take on the Trust, certain sleazy operators with names like Zukor, Mayer, Fox and Laemmle.

So a pattern took shape in 1909, one that has held ever since for all major attempts to control the moving image—in 1922, 1933–34, 1947 and now. Each time, the censorship (self-censorship, in fact) has coincided with a consolidation of power within the industry. Each time, at this moment of consolidation, the industry's bosses have sought in part to protect themselves from interference, in part to create a more respectable product and in part to disso-ciate themselves from a segment of the audience that is deemed to be not respectable enough. Reformers always seem to feel that moving images, with their magical power, have inspired bad behavior among one group or another—working-class immigrants, or single women with bobbed hair and access to motorcars, or black male teenagers with their caps stuck on backward. Note that in each of these cases—by a strange coincidence—the misbehaving group is *already* seen as dangerous and in need of control. The desire to improve (that is, restrict) the moving image thus merges with a desire to improve the members of the savage group, or at least to limit their damage.

In 1921–22, for example, a series of Hollywood scandals, most of them involving free-living women, led to the creation of a new trade-regulating organ-ization, the Motion Picture Producers and Distributors of America, with its own in-house censor, Will Hays. Women such as Virginia Rappe, the would-be starlet who died in the vicinity of Fatty Arbuckle, would henceforth be protected from their own infatuation with the movies. Meanwhile, Hollywood's bosses were free to institute the studio system (as Irving Thalberg was doing just then at Universal), to create vertically integrated trusts and to colonize Europe with their products.

With all that accomplished, Hollywood settled down to a period of relaxed self-censorship through the Hays Office—a practice that needed no revision until the next consolidation of power, the next threat of subversion. First came a shake-up from within (caused in large measure by Warner Bros.' introduction of sound); then came the industrial regrouping, which was complete by 1934. Jack and Harry Warner, the newest partners in the oligopoly, signed a deal that year with William Randolph Hearst giving them access to story material from his magazines, as well as favorable treatment in the Hearst newspapers. At the same time, Upton Sinclair was scaring the bosses with his End Poverty in Cali-fornia campaign, and trade unionism was taking hold in the studios.

Trying to maintain a grip on the market with one hand while beating back insurgents with the other, the studio bosses proved to be sympathetic when they next heard calls for censorship. In April 1934, for all the usual reasons, the Catholic Church founded the Legion of Decency; a boycott of Pennsylvania movie theaters soon followed. In July 1934, studio bosses allayed the protests by establishing the Production Code Administration, an office within the Motion Picture Producers and Distributors of America. It would rule American film-making for the next thirty-four years.

Of course, none of this matters very much if you think of film merely as "a business pure and simple, organized and conducted for profit." (I take that lan-guage from Justice McKenna's opinion in *Mutual Film Corporation v. Ohio*

Industrial Commission, the 1915 case in which the Supreme Court laid down a justification for the censorship of films.) But if movies are sometimes more than commodities, if they're also worth thinking about as a medium of expression, then no issue could be more vital than that of censorship, nor could any exhibition be more illuminating than "Warner Bros. Before the Code," a series at New York's Film Forum. Here's a chance to replace abstract issues of law with the particulars of the films themselves, so you can feel what was lost when the Production Code went into force.

I feel as if the whole world was lost. The pre-Code Warner Bros. movies are renowned for their tabloid-journalism plots and hard-edged visual style, their breakneck pace and air of raffishness; but their most remarkable quality is the sense they project of being engaged with the life of their time. You feel these movies *are* the early 1930s in urban America, much as Dickens's novels are the England of the Industrial Revolution. Of course, you can watch these movies just for the mindless pleasure of cataloguing taboos. (How many times do you glimpse Joan Blondell's peekaboo nipples? How far will Cagney go *this* time?) But the great merit of Film Forum's series is that it allows you to escape this account-ledger way of looking at pictures, which jibes all too well with a censor's mentality. The real question is, What *else* disappeared from the movies, once Joan Blondell's nipples were removed?

Among the tarnished treasures to be shown at Film Forum (nicely shined up, I might add, in new prints provided by Turner Entertainment) you can find at least two no-holds-barred portraits of Depression-era capitalists—amoral workaholics who spend their days cutting the throats of competitors and their nights boffing the employees. in *Employees' Entrance,* the alluring monster runs a department store; in *Female,* the business is automobiles. The directors of these pictures (Roy Del Ruth and Michael Curtiz) probably didn't know much about department stores or Detroit; neither did the writers. But they undoubtedly had seen Jack Warner in action, which explains the films' irresistible combination of flamboyance *and* verisimilitude. On top of that, it's interesting to see how the boss in *Employees' Entrance* is played by Warren William (a missing link between John Barrymore and Liam Neeson), whereas the sharklike, sexually predatory star of *Female* is—Ruth Chatterton. Yes, the protagonist's gender makes a difference to the working-out of the plot; but no, the difference is not that big. At the end of *Female,* Chatterton retains control of her company and still gets her man. Maybe *he* believes her last-minute speech about retiring and having nine babies, but nobody in the audience will fall for it.

The lesson, for men and women both, is that it's a tough world out there. The Warner Bros. world allows for some slight indulgence in sentiment, and there's always room for humor, but the rewards in this not-entirely-fictional

America go to whoever has the most energy, just as the audience's hearts go to the actor who most thoroughly burns up the screen. That spirit died when the Production Code went into force, not only at Warner Bros. but throughout Hollywood. Before the Code, at Columbia, Frank Capra was making pictures such as *The Miracle Woman,* in which Barbara Stanwyck, as a revival-meeting huckster, winds up going toe-to-toe with a lion. After the Code—nothing but blowhard populism and Jean Arthur acting winsome.

And today? Once again, we are witnessing a consolidation of power in the moving-picture business, this time in television (which has long been the dominant medium). Huge conglomerates are behaving like Ruth Chatterton and Warren William, trying to push one another out of an electronic oligopoly that doesn't quite exist.

At the same time—no surprise—we hear a renewed sympathy for self-policing expressed by bosses such as Rupert Murdoch (proprietor of Twentieth Century-Fox and Fox Broadcasting and proud sponsor of media whiner Michael Medved). The old pattern holds—right down to its program of moral uplift and social control, redolent of the Progressive Era. This time, the most talked-about targets of the censors are black musicians. Their videos, my colleague Armond White has shown, come as close as anything you'll see today to the edgy, alert, free spirit of the old Warner Bros. movies.

When the picture business started censoring itself in 1909, there were gains as well as losses. Filmmakers started tackling classy material such as *Romeo and Juliet* and *Hiawatha.* They made hash out of the stories—and so the filmmakers also dreamed up more sophisticated narrative methods. We got the works of D.W. Griffith. The institution of the Code in 1934 had its upside, too—it spurred the ingenuity of Ernst Lubitsch and Preston Sturges.

When the moving-picture bosses give in to censorship this time, as they almost certainly will, we can expect a few comparable benefits—including, perhaps, rap videos with polyrhythms and polysyllables. Anything can happen. But I won't expect to see an art that's truly of my time—not until the next industry shake-up and the next longed-for rising of the rabble.

NOTHING
BETTER THAN
THEY DESERVE

Gladiator

According to Gibbon, the emperor Commodus spent the early years of his reign "in a seraglio of three hundred beautiful women and as many boys, of every rank and of every province." Later, adding bloodshed to his round of pleasures, he launched a career in murder, beginning with the dispatch of the usual senators, ministers and family members and continuing with the slaughter of beasts. Styling himself the Roman Hercules, he went as a performer into the amphitheater, where he cut down before the public a number of ostriches, a panther, a hundred lions, an elephant, a rhinoceros and a giraffe. He then entered the lists as a gladiator. Commodus fought 735 times and paid himself such a high fee for each appearance that a new tax had to be levied. No harm came to him in the arena, if only because he furnished his opponents with weapons of lead; so it was left to Marcia, his favorite concubine, to rid Rome of Commodus. One night, aided by a chamberlain and the Praetorian prefect, she admitted a professional wrestler to his bedchamber to strangle him as he lay in a drunken stupor.

I say there's a movie here. Unfortunately, DreamWorks and Universal disagree with me, and so the public is stuck with *Gladiator*, one of those productions that betray their disarray by crediting three screenwriters, none of whom is Gibbon. *Gladiator* is the tale not of Commodus (Joaquin Phoenix) but of a disagreeably virtuous general, Maximus (Russell Crowe), who from the height of military honor is sold into slavery, made a gladiator and then elevated to the status of demagogue, all without relaxing his expression from a glower.

For its first half hour, *Gladiator* consists of gloomy, sidelit close-ups of Crowe and a handful of other players, who by means of a relentless shot-countershot scheme are prevented from acting with one another. Worse still: While sitting for their portraits, they are made to worry at length about the future of Rome. Will it become a republic again? Will Commodus succeed white-maned Marcus Aurelius to the throne? And who the hell lugged all those statues into "Germania," just to decorate Marcus's field tent? The Germanians, if that's what they're called, interrupt the heavy sighs of Roman conversation by dying in battle. Orange flames from the imperial lines fly across the gloomy, blue-gray twilight into Germanian territory, giving the signal for slo-mo, strobe-mo and jitter-mo to ensue, until such time as expository dialogue may resume:

"In this hand, Caesar, I hold a shiny new quarter."

"Strength and honor! Will you exchange it for a nickel and two dimes?"

"Where, in all the province of Zucchabar, does a parking meter accept— *dimes*?"

You heard me right: Zucchabar. After valiant, glowering Maximus has been stripped of his command, informed of the sure demise of his family and left for dead, he awakens into the Hollywood version of the Middle East: a place of mud-brick architecture and ululation, where stoop-shouldered, burnoose-clad merchants pass the days in sibilant larceny. Here, as it happens, *Gladiator* temporarily springs to life.

Having severed its few feeble ties to reality, the movie is free to become a backstage comedy. What is a gladiatorial contest, if not showbiz? What is the amphitheater in dusty Zucchabar, if not a stop on the bus-and-truck circuit? And who is Maximus's new owner, Proximo (stately, plump Oliver Reed, done up in a turban and several tins' worth of bronzing makeup), if not a two-bit producer trying to claw his way back to the big time? I do not interpret; I report the surface features of the movie, which include an instructive speech by Proximo about getting the audience onto your side.

Meanwhile, back in Rome, Commodus toys with a model of the Colosseum. Why should an emperor suffer the risks of real warfare, he asks, when he can mount a play war instead? The image shifts from Commodus's toy to a different kind of model: a computer-generated picture of the Colosseum, into which we descend to view the first of the emperor's games. It will be the re-enactment of a battle from the Second Punic War—in other words, a show about history, which stands in relation to the characters in *Gladiator* as *Gladiator* stands to us.

At this point, noting how the movie has collapsed into itself, cinephiles under the influence of too much caffeine might hallucinate a political vision. Doesn't *Gladiator* lay bare the purpose of today's media wars?

Well, no. In the first place, the movie is far too concerned with turning Maximus into a man on a white horse—again, I merely report surface details—who will restore Rome to democracy by becoming a dictator. (Of course, the minute he's seized power, he will abdicate in favor of the Senate and retire to his country home—good little Cincinnatus, covered with blood and scars.) In the second place, the film's satirical impulse twitches fitfully at best. *Gladiator* is no *Wag the Dog*. In lighter moments, it's more like Sternberg's 1928 *The Last Command*, in which an exiled Russian general winds up playing himself on a Hollywood lot.

I wish that Russell Crowe, as the Roman general remade into a showbiz soldier, had been granted the opportunities for sentiment and irony that Sternberg once offered his star, Emil Jannings. Most people assume that films of the silent era were crude and naive compared with today's movies; and yet for all the money and technology that were dumped into *Gladiator*, and for all the logistical skill of its director, Ridley Scott, this picture is a kazoo compared with the symphony orchestra that Sternberg conducted. Crowe is a wonderful actor, as you can see from *The Insider*, or even *L.A. Confidential*. Yet no one in charge of this film thought to allow him an emotion, other than a single-minded desire for revenge and an equally dull rectitude. Crowe gamely wears whatever costume he is given; he tromps around with his arms held out from his sides, like a tough soldier whose muscles ache. And that's about all he can do under the circumstances, other than work his basso into ever more alarming registers. Some might say it's a voice produced midway between diaphragm and testicles; others, that it sounds like a cement mixer that's just stripped its gears. But neither organic nor mechanical similes will do. I must turn to geology: In *Gladiator*, having no other use for his energies, Crowe has made his voice sound like the grinding of tectonic plates.

Or maybe it's just the grinding of teeth. What else could Crowe do, when asked to stand by impassively during "love scenes" with the film's lone female figure, Connie Nielsen? It is the filmmakers' conceit that Nielsen, as the emperor's sister Lucilla, had a premarital fling with old Maximus. Now she is once more tantalizingly close to him and yet out of reach, in a ponderous subplot that turns her into a surrogate for the general's dead wife, with her son completing the imaginary family. It's a role that's as thankless as it is forgettable; and Nielsen fades with it so thoroughly that you'd think she'd been born in a vat, from whatever stem cells they use to grow starlets.

Of course, if you go by Gibbon, members of the imperial household did not let such a small thing as marriage impede their sex lives. Lucilla's mother had inspected most of Rome's manhood for hernias; and who knows what Lucilla herself might have done, in a less duty-bound movie? But just as *Gladiator* denies you the bloodlust it advertises—scenes of carnage, in both field and amphitheater, are programmatically chopped into blurry fragments—so too does it withhold the elements of hotcha that were always a chief pleasure of the sword-and-sandal picture. Like its hero, the film is solemnly pious; and though Christianity this time is noticeably missing from Hollywood's Rome, the sense of morality oppresses as never before.

It needn't have been this way. Even within *Gladiator*, lurid entertainments are present, though concealed. I have it on good authority that the late Oliver Reed bore on the head of his penis a tattoo in the form of a dragon's claw. I mention this adornment only to point out that the tide of life, though doubtless lower now than in the days of Commodus, has not ebbed entirely. Why couldn't Reed have given more of himself to this movie? (He died during the making of *Gladiator*, perhaps from the strain of being changed into a virtuous character.) Why couldn't Russell Crowe have been freed to act? And when will a producer haul a bag of money to Winnipeg, so that Guy Maddin can have his shot at reviving the sword-and-sandal epic? So far as I know, Maddin hasn't brought out a picture since *Twilight of the Ice Nymphs*, whose title alone should tell you how well he could adapt Gibbon.

Let's decline and fall again real soon.

The Accidental Tourist

Here are five reasons you might prefer watching a *Star Trek* episode for the seventeenth time to seeing *The Accidental Tourist*:

1. *Star Trek* is shorter. Only "The Menagerie," which is a double episode, lasts as long as *The Accidental Tourist*, and even with that one, you can get up periodically for a beer. There are no commercial breaks in *The Accidental Tourist*, which drags on for two hours and seems longer than any film I've seen since *The Dawn*, an epic tribute to Indonesian military prowess shot in CinemaScope and bad color.

2. The acting is better in *Star Trek*. Yes, it's hard to believe that William Shatner could out-act anybody. But then, *The Accidental Tourist* stars William Hurt at his most deeply committed. He sighs; he speaks his lines as if talking to himself; in rare moments of animation, he lifts his head. Cast him in *Batman* and he'd probably underplay.

Hurt's character in this film is a man addicted to routine. He systematizes his emotions out of existence—but there's no sense of the underlying panic such a man must feel as the world presses on him. For that, he would have to show the possibility of losing control, and control is to Hurt as broken crockery is to Julian Schnabel, the sign and substance of his intention to be regarded as serious. In *The Accidental Tourist*, Hurt is like Mr. Spock trapped in the body of Captain Kirk, trying halfheartedly to mimic those strange emotions of the humans.

In the role of Hurt's estranged wife, Kathleen Turner goes about her task with grim determination. What has become of the brilliant comic actress who went toe to toe with Steve Martin in *The Man With Two Brains*? All we have left of her is the voice of Jessica Rabbit. Geena Davis, as the dog trainer who saves Hurt's soul, provides just the gawky charm that's required of her. But then, the requirement is all too easy to read, which leads us to the next point.

3. Lawrence Kasdan did not write or direct any episodes of *Star Trek*. You may therefore watch them all without fear of the Kasdan Touch. Too smart to revel in the more vulgar tricks of filmmaking, too constricted to invent anything better, Kasdan typically provides physical detail in place of character but then forbids his actors (and his audience) from having fun with the shtick. Think of the parade of suitcases in *The Big Chill*. You are what you pack is the message of that scene (and of *The Accidental Tourist*). First Kasdan defines his characters as so many brands of hair dryer, then he urges the audience to care about these walking, talking appliances.

A comparison between the film and the Anne Tyler novel it is based upon is instructive. I assume people read her books for the same reason they eat Quaker Instant Oatmeal—it requires no effort and seems to be good for you. Though the product may be bland, it is nevertheless warm and comforting. Little did I suspect that film, the barbarians' medium, would make Tyler's perfectly inoffensive novel read like Rimbaud. But that's the Kasdan Touch. He prunes the main character of bizarre habits—his system of keeping the dishes stacked in a solution of chlorine bleach, his method of doing the laundry while showering by means of trampling the clothes underfoot—leaving Hurt with a single, emblematic bit of business in the laundry room to show that he's quirky. It's as if Kasdan wanted to make a film about an eccentric but was afraid to make him seem odd.

4. The morals you derive from *Star Trek* are more impressive. *The Accidental Tourist* presents Hurt as a guidebook writer who specializes in advice for business travelers—that is, for people who want to feel as if they've never left home. At the beginning of the film, Hurt encounters a satisfied reader who assures him that the guidebooks let him travel as if in a cocoon. At the end of the film, Hurt announces, "It's wrong to think we can plan everything, as if it's a business trip." I assume most people knew that from the start. Is there supposed to be some pleasure in watching the character spend two hours catching up with the audience? I prefer *Star Trek*, which tells you things you need to know—for example, that you should respect the other life forms in the galaxy and live with them in peace. That's a potentially useful lesson; and, given the disparity on our planet between the rates of moral and technical evolution, it's probably none too soon to start driving it home.

5. In one of my favorite *Star Trek* episodes, Captain Kirk travels back in time

and falls in love with Joan Collins, who is goofily cast as a manager of a Depression-era rescue mission. It's a magnificently silly bit of drama, which nevertheless ends with a cleverly understated plot twist and a moment of pathos. *The Accidental Tourist* ends just as you would expect, on a long and overstated close-up of the star. He has chosen a new life with Geena Davis. But does he love her? Is he full of joy and desire? No. He merely accepts her, as if life went around handing out Geena Davises on every corner. Don't expect to want other people; just make do with them. That's the real moral of *The Accidental Tourist,* a film that uses mature resignation as a mask for self-satisfaction. And that's why I prefer *Star Trek*—because Captain Kirk really loved poor, saintly Joan Collins.

Austin Powers:
The Spy Who Shagged Me

n the movie that has been assigned to us to write about, *Austin Powers: The Spy Who Shagged Me*, Mike Myers from *Saturday Night Live* plays a secret agent named Austin Powers. He did this before, in the first Austin Powers movie, though not on *Saturday Night Live*, where he doesn't actually make appearances anymore, except when he's a guest. I didn't used to watch *Saturday Night Live* back when Mike Myers was on, because in high school my friends didn't really watch that program, or if we did we didn't admit it, because of its being on on Saturday night. But we knew about Mike Myers, especially from the second *Wayne's World*, and that's part of what's interesting about this new movie, in that it's mostly about time travel, and old things like the sixties.

In this paper, I will show that *The Spy Who Shagged Me* completely summarizes Western Civilization as Mr. Klawans has explained it to us, making it an appropriate movie to be assigned for this final paper.

First, Western Civilization was built to be Phall-o-Centric. That was why in the Greek theater, which proceeded movies, they trademarked the original special effect, which got strapped on for comedies. After that, it was proved many times that nothing is funnier or delivers a bigger box office than this Phallus effect. There are two reasons. First, everybody in the locker room or wherever wants to look at a really big one, but nobody wants to stare. So when they strap on a special effect, you get to look at it right there in public, even though you're not supposed to, and you laugh out of appreciation.

The second reason it's funny is that when they strap on a Phallus, you see they could take it off again. I think this is what Mr. Klawans meant when he talked about the sense of detachment they had in certain parts of Greek culture.

Now, as a movie about time travel and the sixties, *The Spy Who Shagged Me* tells about detachment, and how Austin Powers's Phallus comes loose. Only they call it his "mojo," and here's how it happens.

In the first Austin Powers movie, Austin Powers was an English secret agent and fashion photographer from London in the sixties who got frozen. By the time they thawed him out, in the nineties, he didn't know about AIDS or MTV. As a result, Austin Powers had to learn a lot about history and how people have changed, which I didn't completely know about myself, though the movie made it funny so I didn't mind. However, the idea for the new Austin Powers movie is this:

Dr. Evil, who opposes Austin Powers, uses a "time machine" to go back to 1969, where he steals Austin Powers's sex drive. To recapture it, Austin Powers himself has to go back to 1969, where he's more comfortable anyway. But even back in the sixties, because his mojo has been stolen, he can't make a commitment to his new spy partner and girlfriend, Felicity Shagwell. The actress who plays her is named Heather Graham, who according to Mr. Klawans was in some good movies like *Drugstore Cowboy* and *Boogie Nights*, which I didn't see.

Now comes the second trademark of Western Civilization: the Timeline. This doesn't just mean useful things like flow charts but also intellectual ideas such as they put in our non-major course requirements. By this, I mean history going in only one direction and having a meaning and coming to an end. Generally I don't see how this applies to my career, but it seems to work out in this course, because of the way Mike Myers is middle-aged. The whole idea of *The Spy Who Shagged Me* is that if Mike Myers or Mr. Klawans could go back to the sixties, the way Austin Powers does, they would be young guys again, so they'd be able to go to bed with Heather Graham, assuming she would do that, considering she's so much better looking. But secretly, people from their generation know they can't go back from being middle-aged, even though they want to. So in the movie Austin Powers has no mojo, even in the sixties.

This is where the detachment comes in. If time only goes one way, to The End, you're going to think history is like one big filing cabinet, where everything has its place and nothing ever gets lost. Mr. Klawans says that's how it is in this important book by Don T., the Italian comedy writer. I didn't see what was so funny about this idea. But then, I realized it means that when Mike Myers turns middle-aged and his Phallus gets detached, the mojo can't just disappear. It has to go somewhere, like it was filed wrong. So in the movie, it goes to Dr. Evil.

It makes sense that the mojo thief would be Dr. Evil (who is also Mike Myers), because he's got this totally globular bald head with a long scar that looks like a vein. It's like, he *is* Austin Powers's mojo, or what happens to somebody's mojo when it gets to be middle-aged and creepy. Dr. Evil's son, Scott Evil, more or less points that out to him, whenever he tells Dr. Evil what an old dick he is. Then, for a second thing, Dr. Evil now has a dwarf clone called Mini-Me. Dr. Evil really loves Mini-Me and sings songs to him, until I got the feeling Mini-Me was like this other Phallus that had got loose, and Dr. Evil was kind of playing with himself.

But the funniest part of the whole movie, no question, is Dr. Evil's rocket, which looks exactly like a Phallus. Everybody says so—airplane pilots, Little League umpires, teachers in China, Woody Harrelson. Only the joke is, they *don't* say it. Every time they come close, the movie cuts to somebody else, over and over again, so it looks like people all over the world are sort of saying this thing you're not supposed to say in public, and the rocket Phallus floats around, not attached to anything.

I can't describe it. You'd have to see the movie, which I guess you have, in order to grade the papers.

To complete what I'm doing in this paper in summarizing *The Spy Who Shagged Me* and Western Civilization, I will now point out the third and final trademark that Mr. Klawans mentioned, which he called cultural hedge money. Being the teacher of a non-major requirement course who doesn't really know about business, I think he was pronouncing this a little wrong. Also, we usually say "hedge fund." But, if you make allowances, Mr. Klawans probably had the right idea when he talked about winners and losers, and how you're not supposed to let on about how they get that way.

In my career, once I'm managing a hedge fund or whatever, I know I will be a winner. That's because if you can conceive it, you can achieve it, unlike people who become losers. However, even if you point out to people how it's their own fault if they're not winners, like I will be, you still feel sorry for them a little. So the main thing is to not let that get out of hand, where it would interfere with your success, even though you want to be a nice guy. This is an example of cultural hedge money.

For example, the third person Mike Myers plays in this movie is a really disgusting, ugly Scotch guy called Fat Bastard. They make a lot of fun of Fat Bastard, and I noticed that one or two of the people in this class who are pretty big themselves were laughing really loud at these parts of the movie, but not like they thought it was funny. Then, at the end, Felicity Shagwell asks Fat Bastard if he's happy, and he makes this sensitive speech, and for a minute you actually feel sorry for him. At that point I had to think about the one or two people in the class. But then the movie made another joke against Fat Bastard, and I understood being sensitive was also funny. This shows it's OK to laugh at these people, as long as you put in a little sensitive speech as a hedge.

Another example of cultural hedge money is when you get to look a whole lot at Heather Graham's great body, without having to worry that you're going to hear about it from the women in class. The hedge is, Mike Myers right away does something goofy, like put himself in a bikini, too, which lets you get away with it. Or it's a good use of a hedge when Dr. Evil does a rap number, so they don't need to put any black people in the movie.

In conclusion, I thought *The Spy Who Shagged Me* was really funny, and I would watch it again, though probably on video the second time. The movie also made me appreciate how for some people of the older generation, like Mr. Klawans, the sixties are kind of like their Phallus, which got detached.

Speaking as someone who is looking ahead and building an agenda to win, I want to say in public in this paper that I would give this course a high grade, sincerely, no hedge. The course was very interesting and well taught, and youthful in the way it showed me how *The Spy Who Shagged Me* represents everything that makes Western Civilization great.

Star Wars: Episode I— The Phantom Menace

Not only now but every week, I am reminded at two-minute intervals of the influence of *Star Wars*. It's enough for me to pause in my writing; the computer goes black, and dots of light begin streaking toward me from the machine's illusory depths. If you were to seek the origin of this common screensaver, you'd probably go back to *2001: A Space Odyssey*, where the plunge through deep space made its appearance as a novelty. It took the popularity of *Star Wars* nine years later to transform such imagery into a visual cliché, so that the star-field animation is today the unconscious of my writing machine.

In 1977 *Star Wars* was all about that crossover between novelty and cliché. I joined in one of the many opening-day audiences and can testify to the viewers' reaction when the long-winded opening text finished scrolling into the distance and the shining underbelly of a spaceship slid onto the screen. For the first few seconds the crowd remained quiet, having seen this sort of thing before. But when the ship kept coming, stretching beyond all expectation, a murmur grew with it, and kept growing until more spaceships—fighters—zoomed into view, at which point the rumble opened out to a full-throated cheer. This was a picture we felt we'd carried in our minds, even though we'd never seen it before. Now George Lucas had realized it more fully than we could have hoped, joining familiarity with surprise.

At that moment, some of us were also giddy enough to feel we'd triumphed over the past. Lucas was young. He lived in Northern California, not Hollywood. He'd previously made only small, personal films (*THX 1138* and *American Graffiti*) and was allied with Francis Coppola, who seemed at the time to be a rebel shaking the film industry from within. If Lucas's rebellion in *Star Wars* involved the summing up to perfection of a century's worth of sci-fi illustrations, that merely proved the vitality of his project. Too many older directors had abandoned the virtues of visual storytelling—so said the conventional wisdom. But Lucas, like others from the film school generation, had returned to earlier and better models. In *Star Wars* he carried you along for minutes on end with sequences that were virtually wordless.

The feeling that the past had been redeemed was made visible in *Star Wars*. Its most conspicuous sign was the use of the old-fashioned scene-changing device of the wipe: An image would roll up like a window shade or a fan to reveal another, as in a serial from the thirties or forties. There was no sense of nostalgia about these throwbacks. They hinted instead at an awakening to innocence, as if the "simpler time" that Americans see in the past could now be achieved, thanks to the vigor of the young.

In 1977 it was easy for Americans to think in such terms. Only two years before, ill-equipped rebels in a faraway place had in fact defeated the empire, whose citizens, never comfortable with seeing themselves at the controls of the Death Star, now wanted to join the winning side, if only in fantasy, if only for a laugh. And laughter was easy, now that Richard Nixon had relieved us of his burden. That stiff, cold-eyed figure with the booming voice, our national Darth Vader, had fled the world's stage—permanently, we thought—taking with him a load of schemes and slaughters. *Star Wars* played upon this recent history, sometimes with insouciance, sometimes with a sap-headed religiosity—which was pretty much how Americans in 1977 mythologized their country, lauding what they saw as its fundamental goodness, mocking the lone madman who had betrayed it to the dark side.

Now the President we mock is of the same generation as Lucas. "Star Wars" has become the tag for our empire's space-based missile defense system. Images of deep space, unrenewed by wit, gape from every desktop. After twenty-two years, as we contemplate the "beginning" of the *Star Wars* series with *Episode I—The Phantom Menace*, perhaps the least interesting question we could ask would be, "Is this a good movie?"

If "good" denotes a combination of technical polish and narrative drive, then I suppose the trivial answer would be yes. The settings are impressive and beautiful: an underwater city made of glowing bubbles; a palace complex that might have been built by Shah Jahan after a visit to St. Peter's; a Metropolis the size of a planet, where you never see the subterranean levels but only the sections that float in the sky. You go from the core of a world to the clouds, from lush forest to desert to the chill of space; and just as Lucas takes care to vary his terrain, so too does he skillfully change pace and mood. Big, noisy set pieces, such as a race in *Ben-Hur* style, make way for intimate moments such as a boy's leave-taking from his mother. Even the climax is varied: In a sequence of extended virtuosity, Lucas cuts among battles in four different locations, involving as many sets of characters. Whatever you may think of the substance of *Episode I—The Phantom Menace*, you can't deny that Lucas has repeated his feat from the opening shot of the original *Star Wars*. He gives the audience more than they'd expected of exactly what they'd expect.

But if we ask "Is this a good movie?" in a nontrivial sense, the nature of the expectation must come into question. Here we run up against the curious fact that *Episode I* is really number four. The beginning of the story is its continuation; instead of calling up the wonder of someone else's old-time movies, Lucas now recapitulates his own.

You watch *The Phantom Menace* ticking off the *Star Wars* tropes and note how they've been amplified—the robes and hairdo of the young queen made more outlandish than in the past, the demeanor of the villain more explicitly diabolical. Everything seems to have been doubled. The plot follows not one but two Jedi knights (Liam Neeson and Ewan McGregor), drawn into an ambush in the galaxy's far reaches. The queen who comes under their protection—Natalie Portman, with a beauty mark dabbed onto each cheek—has a clever trick of replicating herself. (She's also good at quick costume changes. When alien forces storm her palace, she makes time, before being arrested, to put on something black, with feathers.) The Evil One who shadows these characters—Ray Park, as a spook with horns and a red-and-black jack-o'-lantern face—wields a late-model, two-beam light saber. Even the galaxy's black population has increased by a factor of two. It now consists of Samuel L. Jackson and another guy.

Then there are the doublings of events from other films. Once again you see the massing of goofy, "primitive" creatures for war; a light-saber duel conducted over a mechanical precipice; an attack by a small, outgunned fleet on an orbiting warship; the introduction of a young, towheaded Skywalker to the Force. But Lucas no longer makes this "more" seem like "new." Never once does the too-muchness of *The Phantom Menace* foster an illusion, however false, of innocence awakened. In keeping with the spirit of 1999, the story funnels itself toward a foregone conclusion, with each exploit of the Skywalker boy—the future Darth Vader—reminding you that his talents will yield misery.

If the Skywalker of twenty-two years ago was a self-portrait of Lucas as self-styled young rebel, bringing hope to the world of film, then perhaps this new

Skywalker shows us a sadder Lucas, who now sees that his misused gifts led only toward the exhaustion of Clintonism. Assuming that reading to be correct, you might expect to sense some moral unease in *The Phantom Menace*, and yet the atmosphere seems guilt-free, despite the weight of an unredeemed past.

Can a believer in the Force even admit the possibility of guilt? A brief spiritual digression, courtesy of the late Rabbi Abraham Joshua Heschel: Commenting to an interviewer on the definition of God as "the ground of being," Heschel said, "Why not? Ground of being causes me no harm. Let there be a ground of being. Doesn't cause me any harm and I'm ready to accept it. It's meaningless. Isn't there a God who is above the ground? Maybe God is the source of qualms and of disturbing my conscience. Maybe God is a God of demands." Only not in *Star Wars*.

If you, unlike Lucas, are the qualms-feeling, disturbed type, you will feel the pull of an unredeemed past every time you encounter the comic-relief creatures: double-dealing, fish-faced traders who conform to Fu Manchu models; a guttural-voiced Middle Eastern merchant in the form of a huge bluebottle fly; an endlessly irritating sidekick for the heroes, who looks like a gangly reptile and acts like Mr. Bones. This is racism without the races—a characteristic dodge of Americans, starting with the President, in the era of the Dim Nineties.

Once upon a time, George Lucas proposed that renewal might be achieved without a struggle for the new. Today, he gives us more of the same and collects the money. His insouciance gone, he now blows hard about myth and evil and the Force, to the encouragement of Bill Moyers in *Time*; while you, the moviegoer, search for a reason to cheer but see only hairstyles. Liam Neeson wears his loose and long; Ewan McGregor has a little ponytail and a long braid. And Lucas is magnificently blow-dried—just like the more-of-the-same President who won't slink away.

The Matrix

L ike a guest at a potlatch, laughing to see his host's worldly goods go up in flames, I roared at *The Matrix*—roared and at the same time was humbled, knowing Warner Bros. had such magnificence to burn. What I witnessed was not a movie but a ceremony of power, a celebration of waste, a demonstration that my daily cares loom over me only because I am like unto a beetle, and they are my dung.

So I was told, in plain words, by the gods and heroes who reign over *The Matrix*. But first, what is "the Matrix" (to quote the Web site: www.whatisthe-matrix.com)? Here, words are meant to fail. According to a line in the screenplay—which by a curious coincidence also figures in the trailer—"No one can be told what *The Matrix* is. *You have to see it.*" Maybe you do. But in case your mother warned you not to jump off a bridge just because someone told you to, here is an explanation:

The world as we know it is merely a computer simulation, wired into our neurons by evil beings. All the world's an Oakland; there's no there anywhere. The motive for this deception, and the nature of the reality beyond the simulation known as the Matrix, need not concern us here. It is enough to know that the weavers of cyber-Maya are inhuman, and only half a dozen people have penetrated their secret. The other 6 or 8 billion of us are just dozing in the void. At best, we're idiots; at worst, threats to the well-being of the half-dozen gods and heroes, who scarcely feel regret when they twist off our heads, kick our spleens into our throats or riddle our "illusory" bodies with "virtual" bullets.

Maybe I'm being too harsh. As one of the cyberheroes says, speaking to a virtual nonentity like me, "We know you live alone and stay up all night at your computer." This remark hints at sympathy, or at least pity, coming as it does from a woman in dark glasses and a slick black bodysuit that fits like a paint job. She calls herself Trinity (Carrie-Anne Moss) and wears her hair short and wet, and you can tell that she'd feel superior to a guy who spends his days typing in a cubicle and his nights as she's described. "You have no life" would be the readiest translation of her comment. In other circumstances—say, a Jonathan Demme movie—she would appear for the sake of rescuing her guy from white-collar servitude and sexless anomie. But Trinity does not drop in to redeem a drone from his daily round; for 6 or 8 billion of us, no redemption is possible. Her mission is to contact the one drone who is exceptional—who is, in fact, The One. He is destined to become the cyber-Jesus—and though you may once have known him as Keanu Reeves, he will henceforth be called Neo.

Whoosh! Bang! Off zooms Neo to meet his John the Baptist, otherwise known as Morpheus, though you might call him Laurence Fishburne. He, too, wears really cool shades—pince-nez!—and does something extreme with his hair (like, shave it all off), and his leather coat trails to the floor. Morpheus has dedicated his entire life to searching for Neo and proclaiming his coming reign. This entitles him to say things like "Free your mind," and "The body cannot live without the mind," and "There is a difference between knowing the path and walking the path," and (at the climax, to the singing of a heavenly choir) "He *is* The One." But I'm getting ahead of myself. First Neo must get his own dark glasses and leather coat and train in kung fu.

If *The Matrix* did not originate as the tag line for a trailer, then it surely got its start as a video-game scenario. For half the film, Neo and Morpheus are not so much characters as figures in a computer graphic, who are made to rise from the floor, hang in space and rotate with a slight telltale jerkiness. Watch them, and you can already see millions of kids furiously pressing buttons in front of their monitors, while millions of parents pay credit-card bills. If *The Nation* kept a video-game reviewer on its masthead (some drone who would live alone and sit up all night at the computer, in exchange for Navaskyan wages), then we might dispense with the advertisement and go straight to the product. But since this magazine, like the entertainment industry, goes on pretending that films are primary and licensed merchandise merely the spinoff, I will continue. Besides, you ought to know about the guns.

"What do you need?" asks one of the lesser heroes, when Neo and Trinity prepare to re-enter the Matrix for a daring rescue attempt. "Guns," replies Neo.

"Lots of guns." And there they are, appearing out of nowhere with the magic of computer graphics: racks and racks of automatic weapons. Cyber-Jesus packs; cyber-Buddha has compassion for all sentient beings and the firepower to *back it up*. Of course, since this world is an illusion, Neo should be able to rise above such methods. Even kung fu would ultimately be too crude. On the other hand, what's a leather-coated god without his piece? *The Matrix* may ask us to think beyond the limits of our ordinary world, but it doesn't venture *that* far into the unknown.

In fact, *The Matrix* hardly ventures at all. It's one part techno-Brahmanism, one part holodeck from the Starship Enterprise, a little *Alice in Wonderland*, a bit of *Twenty Thousand Leagues Under the Sea* and a whole lot of spaghetti western. (Note the jumps in space, between a face shown in close-up in the foreground and the action happening in back. It's the one directorial trick known to the auteurs of *The Matrix*, Andy and Larry Wachowski, who ought to have called Neo "The Computer Nerd with No Name.") But if the sources are familiar, the effect of mixing them is not.

Here is the moment we've been hearing so much about: the end of humanism. Forget the poststructuralist pronouncements, the postmodernist blather, the double-talk statements handed out at 10,000 contemporary art installations. While intellectuals have labored in vain, trying to will out of existence the human subject, the Wachowski brothers and producer Joel Silver have gone out and done the job. They have seen that you and I are mere blips in a system: binary switches, for which "on" means "buy" and "off" means "not buying yet." They have now told us as much—explicitly, loudly. You might even say that our belief in our inherent worth as humans is the biggest item to burn at their potlatch—which might be why I laughed out loud.

It's not just that *The Matrix* is to overblown silliness as Mount Rushmore is to big stone heads. To demonstrate their power, the makers of this trailer/video game/theatrical come-on have taken something precious to me, something that felt (dare I say it) essential, and tossed it onto the fire. No one could stop them. No one wanted to. And so I watched the flames dance and shook with glee, liberated to insignificance.

That Void in Cyberspace Looks a Lot Like Kansas

Young men in the movies have been turning into God at a rate that should alarm monotheists. Last year, in *Dark City*, Rufus Sewell discovered he had the power to recreate the world just by turning his thoughts to it. This year, it's Keanu Reeves's turn. In *The Matrix*, he learns he is The One: someone born to flex his brain like Schwarzeneggerian biceps, making the walls bulge with his bulky intellection.

But these actors may have attained no more than a con artist's divinity, since the worlds over which they reign are frauds. In *Dark City* and *The Matrix*, alien beings substitute a three-dimensional simulation for reality. Humankind dwells numbly within the illusion; only the hero can pierce the veil. *The Thirteenth Floor* (from the makers of *Independence Day* and *Godzilla*) offers yet another variation on the theme.

A computer expert finds that he doesn't just program cyberspace; he lives in it, too. The news comes as a terrible shock, but after much agitation he (and he alone) transcends the simulation's limits.

Much could be said at this point, and usually is, about the Internet.

Perhaps these films do reflect a society that spends its time staring at computer screens, or passing through a generic sprawl on the way from one data port to the next. That said, we still need to ask whether cyber-anomie and its accompanying disorder, cyber-megalomania, are wholly new conditions or the aggravation of an older one.

To judge from film history, these fantasies are less novel than they may seem. Americans were playing now-you-see-it, now-you-don't in virtual space long before the digital era. Witness *The Wizard of Oz*.

When people today say, "It's all smoke and mirrors," they may have in mind a scene from the best-known of the story's retellings. In the 1939 film starring Judy Garland, jets of flame shoot ceilingward in the Throne Room of Oz, clouds churn, and a huge head floats into view—all because that little man behind the curtain is busy at the controls. In reality, the Throne Room is empty, except for the projections of a humbug.

Consult the source of this scene, and you encounter an even greater void that waits to be filled with fantasy. The staging ground for Dorothy's adventure, the background against which the foreground can take shape, is Kansas—a state that functions as a peculiar placeholder in the American mind, a kind of psycho-topographical zero. "When Dorothy stood in the doorway and looked around, she could see nothing but the great gray prairie on every side," wrote L. Frank Baum in *The Wonderful Wizard of Oz*. "Not a tree nor a house broke the broad sweep of flat country that reached the edge of the sky in all directions."

By the time these words were published, in 1900, the supposed emptiness of Kansas had long since filled the imagination of Americans.

What's more, this zero had proved to be useful, time and again.

"The Great American Desert": such was the tag stuck on Kansas by Stephen Long, one of its earlier explorers. Throughout the 1800s, this midcontinental vacuum served as a dumping ground (into which Congress dropped Native Americans, expecting them to be forgotten); an empty stage (on which Free Soil and Slave State forces rehearsed the Civil War); a blank check (to be cashed by homesteaders, who came to claim the land but not necessarily to settle).

What many sodbusters did on a small scale—taking title to some acreage, then trying to resell it and move on—was later done in a big way by railroads and organized speculators. During the 1880s, Kansas went through a building boom, in which a settlement of thousands might sprout within weeks along a railroad right-of-way. If the new town failed to develop an economic base, it would vanish almost as quickly as it had sprung up, with residents sometimes picking up the buildings and moving them to the next place that promised fortune.

The notion that the Great Plains might be a real landscape populated by real people, did not enter American literature until the 1890s, when Hamlin Garland began to write of characters like Mr. Haskins from Kansas, who was "eat up 'n' drove out by grasshoppers." This tradition reached an early peak in the work of Willa Cather. It also contributed to the movies—most notably through Victor Sjöström's *The Wind* (1928), in which the isolation of prairie life drove Lillian Gish to the brink of madness.

But compared with the Oz books—and the Oz stage shows, and the Oz films that were launched in the nickelodeon era—the realist tradition scarcely touched the American imagination. When the region has figured in more-or-less plausible fictions, usually Westerns, the plains have appeared mainly as something to be crossed. (We have modernized this idea only to the extent that we now speak of Kansas as a flyover.) More often, the Great American Desert does not appear at all. Fantasies appear.

In the recent virtual-reality movies, the blank that underlies fantasy becomes visible: as a rain of numbers streaming down a computer screen (in *The Matrix*), as a desert that trails off into a three-dimensional grid (in *The Thirteenth Floor*), or (at the most literal, in *Dark City*) as a wasteland where buildings are moved around, in 1880s style. The transition from the void to the simulated world is no longer effected by a cyclone, as in *The Wizard of Oz,* but by a plunge through a twisting, crackling tube—that is, an electrified cyclone.

Apart from these innovations, the newer fantasies seem striking only for their substitution of a young man for Dorothy, and for the character's goal of dominating the fantasy world rather than making his way home from it. If this shift into a masculine, heroic mode says anything about the Internet, I suppose, it testifies to the current popularity of another type of story: the one about online entrepreneurs who become wealthy overnight. Perhaps the public's faith in these stock market cybergods might not be grounded—but that merely reminds us that humbuggery plays a role in the history of the real Kansas, and that it was a major theme in the work of L. Frank Baum.

The one recent movie to go beyond this model—and the wittiest simulated-world fantasy by far—is David Cronenberg's *eXistenZ*. Unlike the others, it focuses on a young woman, Jennifer Jason Leigh, who is already a "goddess" of virtual-reality games when the film begins. But divinity does her little good. As Cronenberg knows, a fictional world is only as rich as the imagination that forms it; and in *eXistenZ,* the dreamers prove to be hilariously literal-minded. They create features like a country gas station labeled "Country Gas Station," manned by a pump jockey called Gas.

The simulation has a way of going blank—while underneath it lies not a void but human flesh, raw and insistent. Much as the characters try to live in a mental world, evidence of their organs keep poking clownishly into the picture.

Yes, we're still in Kansas. But in *eXistenZ,* for a change, the conspirators are inept, their leader is Dorothy, and the ground zero of fantasy is the human body.

Shakespeare in Love
She's All That

When a young woman in high school frets about the folks in Mogadishu—when, for that matter, she can spell "Mogadishu"—American moviegoers know she needs a fashion makeover, a boyfriend and an eventful night at the prom. *She's All That* fully meets these expectations for its heroine, and exceeds them in ways that make me fear for the picture's tender viewers.

These are likely to be in the 12-to-20 range. The 12-year-olds look ahead to the dangers and opportunities they will soon taste in high school. The 20-year-olds, if bored at the mall, will consent to glance back at embarrassments only recently escaped. Yes, our children are our future (I think Bill Clinton said that); but the future looks grim indeed if the makers of *She's All That* have guessed right about their audience. Not only does the girl who can spell "Mogadishu" go to the prom—now she even learns to care about being elected prom queen.

I call these matters to your attention because high school is America's great engine of normalization. Children in all their variety get dumped into its hopper, undergo processing and come out at the other end packaged as socioeconomic types. Acting as a safety valve for this machinery is the high school movie, which (among its other functions) vents the steam that can build up in the raw material. All that normalization can make kids feel odd. Pretty soon, they need to spend money at the multiplex, to watch other odd-feeling kids make peace with the social order. That's what worries me. How meager is the pressure that builds up nowadays, if it can be relieved by *She's All That?*

The symbolic oddball here is one Laney Boggs, played by a young actress whose parents certainly couldn't handle "Mogadishu," to judge from what they did to her name. (It's Rachael Leigh Cook.) But, to resume: Our Laney suffers from being the middle-class kid in a rich kids' school. Of course, she's not so deprived as to lack a swimming pool; but since her father cleans pools for a living, we understand that she dwells in relative misery—a state aggravated by the absence of her mother, who died many years ago. Apparently, single-parent households are rare in the more affluent neighborhoods of Southern California, so Laney feels like a freak. She therefore shuns all contact with other students and spends her time painting dark, brooding canvases, in which she merges her own agony with a cry of pain for the victims of planned famines, or the ocean life killed off by waste disposal at sea.

In short, Laney has ideas and ambitions beyond those that are conventional for a young woman of her time and place. These needs, which cannot be understood by others or even expressed to them, compel her to put aside party dresses (though she looks fetching in them) and disguise herself in mannish clothes. But then, while giving a performance at a local theater, she is accosted by Zack Siler, a brilliant and sociable young man with a long face and dark, narrow-set eyes—someone who has "winner" written all over him and yet seems vulnerable, someone who holds forth the prospect of a love she longs for, though she knows to be impossible.

But now that I re-read the last paragraph, it suddenly occurs to me that I've summed up *Shakespeare in Love.*

Can that, too, be a high school movie, slyly marketed to grown-ups? Perhaps that's the source of its high reputation, which I would otherwise find inexplicable. Strip away the aura of prestige that comes with the name of Shakespeare—ignore the period setting, as the droll anachronisms encourage you to do—and Joseph Fiennes in *Shakespeare in Love* begins to look a lot like Freddie Prinze, Jr., in *She's All That.* Why not think of our latest movie Shakespeare as a senior class president and soccer team captain who (recently thwarted in love) now questions the talent that once flowed so amply through him? Only by seizing upon a woman and transforming her does this darling of the gods reassure himself of his right to greatness, and the rightness of the social order.

And so, in one film, Shakespeare converts Viola (Gwyneth Paltrow) into his mistress, stage interpreter and fictional heroine, thereby growing into the writer he was meant to be. In the other, Zack remakes Laney as his prom queen and girlfriend, and so gets up the nerve to accept an invitation to attend Harvard or Yale, rather than his father's alma mater of Dartmouth. Either way, it's a tough business, being history's greatest playwright, or a handsome rich boy who can take his pick of the Ivy League. Either way, it's a necessary business for a young woman to accept her place in the world, as unhappy wife (Viola) or young chick who looks fetching in a party dress and no longer worries about Mogadishu (Laney).

I suppose Laney gets the better deal; 400 years have brought us a *little* improvement. I also suppose that an undisguised high school movie may proceed with a liberty that is denied when the genre goes incognito. Although *Shakespeare in Love* benefits from a delightful screenplay by Marc Norman and Tom Stoppard—and a flattering one, for viewers who can congratulate themselves on recognizing this or that tatter of the Bard—the film's virtues peter out beyond the level of verbal wit. The camera direction seems to have been bought by the yard; the supporting performances (for the most part) purchased off the shelf at some storehouse of British character actors. As for the leads: Although they catch the light beautifully, they may have something to do with my impression that *Shakespeare in Love* delivers everything it promises, except for the last two words.

But with *She's All That*, we see how true garbage may nevertheless teem with a life of its own. The director, Robert Iscove, is a former choreographer who also has tried his hand at Shakespeare, with the televised extravaganza *Romeo and Juliet on Ice*. Although he has not imported from this background all the fluidity you might hope for, his training does seem to have contributed to two or three genuinely cinematic ideas in *She's All That*. These are two or three more than you get with *Shakespeare in Love*: moments when two scenes glide effortlessly together, or when the camera loses itself in the pleasure of watching some outburst of physical energy. Matthew Lillard (known to the children who are America's future as a bad guy from *Scream*) provides the funniest, most raucous of the latter moments in his role as a very minor TV star who hangs out around the high school. And as the leads, you have the lanky Freddie Prinze, Jr. (who is so loose that his mouth sometimes wanders to the left while the rest of his face goes right) and Rachael Leigh Cook, who seems about nine inches too short to look like a star and turns it to her advantage. When Laney is supposed to be infuriated, her little frame quakes with rage. When Laney hopes to be kissed, she spills over with dark intensity.

I liked these people well enough that I left *She's All That* wishing they had something better to do. Why shouldn't Zack become independent from his father in a much bigger way—say, by taking up one of those causes that inspire Laney? (He could begin by protesting against the movie he's in. Surely he noticed that the high school's black kids are like figures in a Venetian painting, dancing attendance upon the whites.) And Laney, instead of dropping her causes (as she now does) could keep up with them, all the while plunging into the social whirl that Zack has revealed—maybe even getting together with more than one boy, for more than a single kiss. Artists do that sort of thing.

But having put up only the mildest revolt, Laney and Zack wind up settling for a mild resolution. Will it settle the 12-to-20-year-olds who go to watch? Maybe they'll file out of the multiplex in full docility—their dissatisfactions, though unassuaged, rankling so slightly as to be unfelt. And someday, when needs left unmet since high school threaten to rise again, our citizens of the future will pass two hours with *Shakespeare in Love*, then comfort themselves by telling each other it was grand.

Run Lola Run

The title character in *Run Lola Run* lives underneath a fibrous growth that in shape resembles a neglected patch of lawn and in color brings to mind a fire engine—or maybe a fire engine crossed with one of those '59 Fairlanes that flirted with pastel. This isn't hair; it's a flickering aura of free associations, which in itself may serve as emblem of Tom Tykwer's much-praised new picture. Even should Lola pause in her running (and the whole point of the movie is to make sure she doesn't), suggestions of wildness, speed, calamity and chic would continue to shoot forth from her head.

When first seen, in pop-off-the-screen close-up, Lola is as much at rest as she's going to be—meaning she's ajolt in her room at home, shouting down a telephone at her boyfriend, Manni. The big lug has just bungled his attempt to step up from petty crime to middling. Now, as we see through crosscuts, he's twisting and sweating in a phone booth across town, like a sausage being squeezed in its skin. He's called to inform Lola that he's got exactly twenty minutes to restore a large sum of money to a gangster—and in his pocket is nothing, except a gun.

What's a movie character to do? That's the big question—because, even though this action takes place in Germany, Lola is most emphatically a creature of Cinemaland. Able to slip back and forth amid formats, Lola can exit a room and immediately reappear in it on TV, or change into a cartoon figure with Fairlane fire-engine hair, or shrink herself to accommodate the demands of a triple-split-screen effect, all while the robo-rock pulse of the soundtrack pounds louder and louder. In these circumstances, a movie character would run.

So off sprints Lola—the blunt-featured actress Franka Potente, in tank top and baggy slacks—pumping her arms, breathing hard, scooting past or bumping into a stock company's worth of passers-by, all of whom dribble out brief streams of consciousness in her wake. Her immediate destination: the office of her bank-president father.

Knowing she has only minutes to prevent disaster, a character from outside Cinemaland might save time by using the telephone. (A receiver was already at hand.) But Lola runs toward the bank, for the same reason that she Truly Loves Manni, for the same reason that her destiny (temporarily) is to be Shot Through the Heart at High Noon. It's cool to live in the movies.

Coolness, rather than love, conquers all in *Run Lola Run*. Coolness precedes love as its precondition and grants Lola power to make the movie turn out as she'd like. I will say no more, since it would be as heartless to reveal the structure of Tykwer's film as the plot of another director's. It's enough to say that Lola dashes through the film like a punked-out Road Runner, pursued not by Wile E. Coyote but by an accident-prone Fate, whose assaults are as reversible as the workings of Acme products.

The popularity of the film—which has been making a triumphal progress through the world's festivals and into its movie houses—reminds me that audiences, too, long to feel cool. Unfortunately, today's films rarely include that pleasure in the price of a ticket. Perhaps the most notable recent picture to do so, whatever you thought of it, was *Pulp Fiction*, which came out five years ago. I believe that gap partly explains the laments of some critics about the demise of movie culture—laments that have been sighed, paradoxically, over the living bodies of any number of vital but less fashionable films. When the movie cult fails to offer vicarious coolness, it no longer recruits young acolytes or renews the dedication of elders who would like to feel young.

That's why I welcome *Run Lola Run*. Its excitement, cheap but harmless, might spur millions to indiscriminate moviegoing, and maybe to the discovery of films that are good but unflashy. Only for the sake of placing *Run Lola Run* in context will I behave as a spoilsport—the true name for "critic"—by pointing out that European directors before Tykwer have made on-the-run films that trafficked in the coolness of movies, the dangers of True Love and the ne'er-do-well winsomeness of a homely-handsome criminal. With full knowledge that I'm being unfair, I must mention *Breathless*.

Well, so much for Tykwer. He draws on the allure of movies; but unlike Godard, he has nothing to say about the way that allure works on people. He keeps his film speeding along, mimicking a pace that is often imputed to American films (though seldom achieved by them); but unlike Godard, he never dares to let time stretch, as in the great, long, rambling conversation at the heart of *Breathless*. Tykwer also kicks around a few pop-philosophical notions, which rise and fall as pleasingly as a soccer ball (to use his own image). But he avoids burdening the audience with any of the substance of German culture—which is why, I suppose, *Run Lola Run* has won the hearts of certain Americans who ordinarily disdain foreign films. The alien has never been so familiar.

Does any of this matter? Confronted with questions about meaning, a figure at the beginning of *Run Lola Run* shrugs and says, "The ball is round. The game lasts ninety minutes." That's a good answer, if your head's filled with the same stuff as the ball. Which is to say: You'll probably get a kick out of *Run Lola Run*. Just don't forget which part of you is getting booted.

The New York Times, March 26, 2000

Political Ethnography of the Academy of Motion Picture Arts and Sciences

To most people, the Oscar is a sleek and gleaming statuette, 13 inches high and weighty enough to be a weapon in *Clue.* To political commentators, though, an Academy Award is something less substantial, on the order of a Rorschach test.

Consider the inky meditations that attended the elevation of *Forrest Gump* to the status of best picture. Some writers saw the award as a token of sweet forgiveness in a once-divided nation. Like Forrest, the American people were good, if a bit simple, and would overcome all adversity just by floating along. Other opinion mongers composed a gloomier allegory: Forrest represented an America that was blind to the consequences of its actions, heedless to the burden of its history. In either interpretation, *Forrest Gump* sounded like the key film of the Reagan presidency, which was strange, since it was voted the best picture award in the early months of 1995. By then, America's most prominent political figure was Newt Gingrich, not exactly a let-it-float kind of guy.

This year's best picture will probably occasion further blot-reading. In fact, I'm sure of it, since I plan to view some butterflies of my own—or are those elephants, dancing back to back? Before I start to squint at them, here are a few words of caution, which I address to myself and all other editorializers.

Those who would find political meaning in the whims of the Oscar voters ought to remember that the Academy of Motion Picture Arts and Sciences is not a nation-state but a tribe. Its members are fewer than 6,000 in number and markedly endogamous in their mating habits. Their deliberations make sense only within the context of the local folkways, an inbred kinship system and the seemingly irrational trade mechanisms of the Hollywood People.

Why do a billion of us, rapt followers of the Oscar broadcast, persist in thinking that the annual meeting of the academy's clans—Actors Branch, Writers Branch, Directors Branch and so forth—has anything to tell us about the wider world? The answer, perhaps, lies in the tribe's own belief in its global importance.

Writing in one of the early issues of the academy's Bulletin, Mary Pickford offered this evidence of the Hollywood People's self-regard: "The Academy is the League of Nations of the Motion Picture Industry." This was in April 1928, one year after the academy's founding, and eight years after the United States Senate decided that America had no need of the real league.

Nor did workaday Americans feel the need to think much about foreign countries so long as they had the movies. By the mid-1920s, Hollywood's back lots were crowded with replicas of the world's architecture; Hollywood's front offices, as active in Europe as the State Department, were busy buying up large chunks of their foreign competition. In the inward-looking company town of Los Angeles, the movie studios' bosses and employees might well think of Metro-Goldwyn-Mayer, Fox, Paramount and Universal as if they were England, France, Germany and the remains of the Austro-Hungarian Empire.

Of course, Mary Pickford knew what she was talking about. The academy—or International Academy, as it was first called—was founded for explicitly political purposes: to "take aggressive action in meeting outside attacks" and to "promote harmony and solidarity among the membership and among the different branches." Translation: The academy would seek to ward off government censorship of the movies. It also would ward off unionization, helping the studios to hold back collective-bargaining efforts by the actors, writers and directors.

By the mid-1930s, the academy had lost both of these primary political functions. The studios, by agreeing to enforce the Production Code, had turned aside the most vigorous threats of censorship; and the talent, by sheer perseverance, had succeeded in forming guilds. America's internal league of nations now had no grander goal than to promote itself, and publicize its members, by handing out awards.

The annual awards ceremony, which at first was a cliquish banquet, grew bigger and gaudier, especially after the members of the writers' and actors' guilds gave up boycotting it. With the addition of radio broadcasts, the rite of self-congratulation became a public ritual; the awards themselves, a kind of ambassadorial message from the Hollywood People to the world at large.

For the next few years, academy voters would repeatedly demonstrate their seriousness by giving awards to uplifting movies, social-problem pictures or, best of all, uplifting social-problem films: *Mrs. Miniver, Going My Way, The Best Years of Our Lives, Gentleman's Agreement.* Of course, for long stretches the voters were just as willing to give the Oscar to a musical: from 1951 to 1971, six of them were named best picture, out of 15 nominated. And yet as anyone knows who has followed the studios' release schedules—or watched the production numbers on Oscar broadcasts—the musical is now moribund in Hollywood, while the big-statement movie lives on. In the last 20 years, best picture awards have gone to at least half a dozen of them, from *Gandhi* and *Platoon* to *Schindler's List.*

What the academy does as a body, its members will surely do one by one when they take the podium. Given a microphone and a huge television audience, the Oscar winners and presenters have spoken out on any number of subjects: their opposition to the Vietnam War; their opposition to people who opposed the Vietnam War; their support for Native Americans' rights, Palestinians' rights, Tibetans' rights. Academy members have ostentatiously stood to applaud for Elia Kazan and ostentatiously sat on their hands for him, and in the case of Steven Spielberg seemed somehow to do both at the same time.

It is as customary for news editors to deride these political outbursts as it is for the broadcast producer to cut them short. But it's the producer who brings the academy's self-importance before a billion viewers, and the news editors who faithfully confirm it, naming the winners on the front page while publishing ink-blot readings in the op-ed columns.

Who is responsible, then, when in the wake of the Oscar ceremony a mere movie character such as Hannibal Lecter is made into an agent of "toxic feminism," a promoter of gay-bashing, a symbol of technocratic hubris in the Gulf War and also the last, best hope for stopping Martha Stewart?

I, as a film critic, am responsible—not ultimately, perhaps, but a little bit, in the short run. And now that the day has arrived, the urge to overinterpret the Oscars is upon me again. Why not? I, too, have been to Los Angeles, four or five times, and I talk a lot on the phone to people who actually live there. On the basis of this extensive field work, I hereby analyze the politics of the 72nd Academy Awards:

Leading the nominations this year is *American Beauty,* in which the middle-aged Kevin Spacey undergoes a second adolescence, complete with recreational drugs, a fast car and a masturbatory infatuation with a teenage girl. Toss a tennis ball into the Shrine Auditorium tonight, and it will bounce off four dozen tuxedos containing men who match that description. Among the Hollywood People, Mr. Spacey's character is more than a sympathetic figure, he's heroic.

As for the weightier political significance of *American Beauty:* Just substitute a brunette in her early 20's for a teenage blonde, and change Mr. Spacey's job description from "magazine staff writer" to "President." When it comes to a well-publicized affair of the heart, most of the public has echoed the movie's sentiments and forgiven Bill Clinton. The success of *American Beauty* might be less promising, though, for Hillary Rodham Clinton. While the husband gets to be flawed but lovable, his wife, Annette Bening, is nothing but a cold, career-driven gargoyle.

The Insider is one of those based-on-a-true-story movies that academy members have always favored. It is a drama about two whistle-blowers: Jeffrey Wigand, who came forward with evidence that a tobacco company had knowingly lied about the addictiveness of cigarettes, and Lowell Bergman, the television producer who tried to put Mr. Wigand on *60 Minutes,* then revealed to the press that corporate executives at CBS had blocked the broadcast of the interview.

What is the meaning of *The Insider* within Hollywood's politics? All I know is that CBS is now controlled by Viacom, which also owns Paramount Pictures, while *The Insider* is distributed by divisions of the Walt Disney Company, whose other properties include ABC. If *The Insider* is named best picture, we may soon see a Paramount release about the underhanded dealings of a wealthy mouse.

The Sixth Sense was Hollywood's successful summer ghost story—unlike *The Haunting*—and a reassuring picture for the filmmakers who got scared to death by *The Blair Witch Project.* I don't mean scared by the movie but by its box office take. Would the clientele at Le Dome and Spago now have to change into hiking boots and go running through the woods with camcorders? No. *The Sixth Sense* proved that Hollywood, too, can make a spooky summer blockbuster without gunfire, explosions or a revolving credit account at Industrial Light and Magic, so long as it has Bruce Willis.

The broader political import may seem elusive; but since I grew up in Chicago, I can explain that the film's ghosts are all registered voters, who won't let a little thing like death hold them back from their civic duty. The boy who learns to talk to them and attend to their needs? He'll have a great career as a Cook County precinct captain. Let us be grateful. The statistics on voter participation would be even more depressing if the dead began to shirk.

The Green Mile, a sort of death-row fairy tale, won a best picture nomination right after Florida got queasy about its electric chair—too many people bursting into flames, as in the movie—and within weeks of the Illinois moratorium on executions. There's been a little problem with sentencing innocent people to die—again, as in the movie. So *The Green Mile* would seem to be a characteristic work of Hollywood liberalism. It's like a Stanley Kramer picture, only twice as long and with special effects.

Notice, though, that the movie's condemned man really wants to die in the electric chair, so he can bear away the sins of the kind prison guards who throw the switch. Whatever this fantasy might mean to the wider public, it has a special allure for academy members. For the most part, they are pale people, who believe they get along well with the darker-skinned. They are also chronically hungry for work, in a business where African-Americans are fighting for screen time and jobs. Self-interest conflicts painfully with a hip self-image. What a pleasure, then, for the Hollywood People to see someone as big and black as Michael Clarke Duncan reciprocate their love, and prove it by going away.

Finally, we have *The Cider House Rules*. The film won no awards from the major critics' groups and was passed over by the Golden Globes. Yet here it is, nominated as best picture. To the members of the academy, whose ideas about the political process are conspiratorial if not downright superstitious, this turn of events proves again that Bob and Harvey Weinstein of Miramax wield dark powers.

To the rest of America, though, *The Cider House Rules* has a different meaning. It is the picture that teaches Tobey Maguire a lesson: women sometimes need access to a properly trained person who is willing to perform an abortion.

I stare in wonder at the preceding paragraph as I realize again that a clear idea from John Irving's novel made it intact into Lasse Hallstrom's film. *The Cider House Rules* takes an unambiguous stand on an issue that is subject to ongoing and furious debate. Whatever you may think of the political position itself, and of the merits of the filmmaking through which it is expressed, it is plain that *The Cider House Rules* has already won a distinction, and one far more rare than an Oscar.

Safe

Margaret, who lives across the hall from my mother, keeps her TV tuned day and night to the Security Channel. It provides each apartment in the building with a live black-and-white image of the lobby, made strange by the optics and camera placement. You see a slantwise, plunging view full of Cézannesque conundrums: The floor tilts sharply upward, the welcome mat looks like a trapezoid and the right side of the doorframe warps into a curve as it drops out of sight. My mother doesn't often watch the Security Channel, but I'm with Margaret. I love it, even during off-hours when no one strolls indifferently across the screen. The picture reminds me of the best of public access cable, crossed with Michael Klier's masterwork *Der Riese (The Giant)*, an eighty-two-minute video assembled from footage mindlessly shot by security cameras in various German cities.

Where in the movie theaters can I find anything half so compelling, now that it's summer? I scan the listings here in Chicago, where I'm visiting Mom, and find my choices run to *Judge Dredd, First Knight* and worse. Nothing lives up to the Security Channel, except possibly Todd Haynes's new movie, *Safe*.

Haynes can be counted on to stir up thought among the filmoids. His previous pictures—*Superstar (The Karen Carpenter Story)*, *Poison* and *Dottie Gets Spanked*—were all wickedly smart; and though he's disappointed me somewhat (by being too quick to let his will do the work of the imagination), no one doubts he deserves his place at the forefront of New Queer Cinema. With *Safe*, Haynes has spun out the most sustained narrative of his career so far, though his adherence to convention is of course deceptive. In both the chilliness of its *mise en scène* and its themes, *Safe* has a lot in common with the Security Channel—though the film's worldview does prove to be more orthogonal than those pictures of the condominium lobby.

The story: Carol White, who lives in spooky, wraparound comfort in the San Fernando Valley, comes down with the heebie-jeebies. First she undergoes fits of coughing and finds herself gasping for breath; then she gets a nosebleed; then, while picking up the dry cleaning, she tumbles into a full-tilt seizure. "The heebie-jeebies," says her doctor (more or less), no doubt suspecting what the audience already knows: Carol's two biggest challenges in recent months have been to arrange for the delivery of a sofa and to keep her eyes focused on the ceiling while Mr. White humps away. No wonder the psychiatrist she consults can't help her. Carol White is as bland as her name; she can't examine her inner life because she hasn't got one. In fact, she's such a dumb bunny that she takes advice from fliers posted at her health club and advertorials on cable TV, which eventually persuade her that she's chemically sensitive—in effect, allergic to the twentieth century. Soon, Carol goes off to live in spooky, wraparound good vibes at a high-priced New Age compound in the desert, where she hopes at last to feel *Safe*.

Yeah, it's a metaphor—but for what? Not the emptiness of modern bourgeois life, one would hope. That would make *Safe* nothing better than a two-hour cliché; besides, Todd Haynes is not the type to say, "Carol White, *c'est moi*." Nor is *Safe* a metaphor for the experience of living with AIDS. More likely the movie is about the straight world's self-absorbed indifference to AIDS; or about the straight world's preference for "good" people with AIDS, those who look enough like a Carol White to be allowed to address national political conventions. All I know for sure is that beneath the antiseptic gleam of its surface, *Safe* rages with undisguised glee against Carol, whatever she stands for.

Often Haynes positions her far to one side of the screen, composing the shot to emphasize a void at the center of the frame. But there's no ache in that void. In *Safe*, the light almost pings as it bounces off porcelain, chrome, glass and Carol herself, who is the shiniest, most brittle object of all. Julianne Moore, the brilliant young actress who plays Carol, realizes the character almost entirely by means of withdrawal—a daring strategy, which is abetted by Haynes's clever shot selection. You're maybe a third of the way through the movie before you get your first close-up of her face—just in time for Carol to have one of those periodic crises when things literally break to her body's surface. Except at such times, the camera keeps its distance, and Moore seems to keep sinking inward from her own skin, reinforcing the impression that Carol is fully alive only when in extremity. Her disease is all she's got to make herself interesting.

Which brings me back to the Security Channel. When you watch such a setup, you seldom feel involved with the people passing through the lobby. In fact, that's the point. But you know there's at least the risk of an encounter, and you have the thrill of spying on people who are actually present. But I can't imagine Carol White passing through any condominium lobby, however bleak and suburban its decor. There's no possibility of engagement with her because she's not a character in any deep sense. She's a sarcasm, directed against the stereotypes on TV's disease-of-the-week movies.

With that understood, I suppose I can excuse Todd Haynes's contempt for Carol White. But I can't get as much pleasure from her as I would from even a truly objectionable human—one of my relatives, perhaps—who buzzes from downstairs. For all of its skill and intelligence, for all of its rightness about the white noise between much of America's ears, *Safe* turns out to be curiously straight. It never imagines that Carol White might be odd *without* her disease, as we're all odd on the Security Channel. Nor does it approach the weirdness of the more expressionistic modes of the demotic moving image, which you can watch once you come upstairs. How about the videotapes of my cousin Sherwyn's knee operation, or cousin Danny's colonoscopy?

Lone Star

My editors disagree completely with the following remarks. Nevertheless: I think John Sayles gave away his game a couple of years ago in *Passion Fish*, his movie about a soap-opera star who is paralyzed in an accident—the sort of event she's been confronting five days a week on TV, and which she now faces in "real life." The suppression of quotation marks, I think, is the game. "You know the boundaries of fiction," Sayles seemed to say. "Now see how I break them down, to let in life itself."

In other films, too, Sayles has announced his triumph over narrative conventions: the self-dramatizing lore of one time radicals in *The Return of the Secaucus Seven*, the myths of sportswriters in *Eight Men Out*, the fables of Irish patriarchs in *The Secret of Roan Inish*. To this list we may add the local legends and received histories of Texas, which Sayles now attempts to overcome in his new film, *Lone Star*.

In the border town of Frontera, in Rio County, everyone can tell a few stories about the late sheriff, tough-but-honest Buddy Deeds. One person in particular has heard all the yarns, at least a thousand times: Buddy's son Sam (Chris Cooper), who has returned to Frontera after a long absence and has been elected sheriff in his turn. One legend above all has come to obsess Sam: the tale of the night in 1957 when a young Buddy ran the previous sheriff out of town.

That man—Charley Wade (Kris Kristofferson)—was an openly corrupt, racist killer. After Buddy faced him down, Wade simply disappeared. But now, as *Lone Star* begins, a couple of officers from the local Army base stumble across a ring, a badge and a set of bones, which no doubt belong to Wade. It falls to Sam ("Sheriff Junior") to decide whether to follow Frontera custom and ignore the evidence, or to investigate and perhaps determine that his father's shining career began with murder.

While Sam busies himself debunking Frontera's rich oral tradition, a teacher named Pilar (Elizabeth Peña) is engaged in a similar struggle, this one against official history. With her support, her high school has instituted a new curriculum, to the distress of that half of the faculty for whom Sam Houston and Davy Crockett are still heroes of the white race, rather than agents of the cotton- and slave-traders. For a brief moment, Pilar's revisionism intersects with Sam's, after the town elders vote to put up a monument to Frontera's Korean War veterans, as exemplified by a sculpture of Buddy Deeds. Pilar's faction at the high school would rather see a sculpture of a Latino soldier—and so, it appears, would Sam.

But Pilar's main intersection with Sam takes place on personal grounds: their memories of having been high school sweethearts; their rancor and bafflement at having been separated back then; their present-day resumption of a relationship, carried out at a pace so glacial that it's more of a slide than a flirtation.

Once again, Sayles has set up narrative convention on one side and real life on the other, with Sam and Pilar carrying in their flesh all the truths that have been excluded from accepted history. That's the theme of *Lone Star*, and the structure, too. Pilar's perfunctory engagement in the debate over curriculum, and Sam's pursuit of the McGuffin-like killer, function almost entirely for the sake of exposition, providing excuses to introduce the information that Sayles feels the audience needs. (Like *Springtime for Hitler*, *Lone Star* is just crammed with historical goodies. Did you know that Texas used to be part of *Mexico*?) As for the climax of the film—the proof that the exposition matters—everything depends on the coming together of Sam and Pilar.

It's a well-conceived scheme, and ambitious, too (so ambitious that I haven't even mentioned a third major strand of the plot). And that, in a way, is the most damning thing I can say about *Lone Star*—because I've been able to get this far in my account without needing to discuss the movie.

How do characters hold themselves when they talk to one another? Are they proud of the clothes they wear, or would they dress differently if they could? When Pilar walks down the street, does Sam follow her with his eyes, or does he make himself look away? What is the camera looking at, while Sam stares at Pilar or his boots? How close does the camera stay to the characters? Does it plunge the audience into their eyes? Or does it hang back, allowing us to see people caught in the web of personal and local and national history? The life of a movie, from second to second, depends on the answers to these and a thousand other questions, none of which, unfortunately, requires comment in a description of *Lone Star*.

I'm not saying that Sayles is indifferent to these concerns, only that his direction is so slack it feels indifferent. Witness the scene in which Sam and Pilar finally find themselves alone. It's late at night in a deserted cafe. Here's Pilar, so lonely she's in danger of drying up; and here's Sam, a lean, handsome, serious man, in a town where such types are as rare as a geyser of lemonade. "You asked why I came back," the geyser says with appropriate steam. "I came back because you were here."

What does Pilar do? Does she bite off his lips? Does she perform an impromptu for percussion, using whatever beer bottles come to hand, to suggest that she won't allow Sam to screw her up again? No—although those responses might perk up the audience, they would be too soap operalike for Sayles. Reasonably, veristically, he prefers to make Pilar hesitate in the face of temptation; he just can't figure out how she would do it. Sayles has her cross the room, walking as if she were balancing a book on her head, till she comes to the jukebox, where she pauses to comment on the antiquity of the selections; then, task accomplished, she drifts into Sam's arms and begins to dance with him. None of this action feels as if it comes from within Pilar—which is to say, it doesn't arise from any emotional exchange between Elizabeth Peña and Chris Cooper, or from any momentum generated by editing, camera placement or camera movement. It's just a bit of business, which Sayles has imposed upon the character.

It would be easy to multiply examples, but pointlessly cruel. Everywhere in *Lone Star*, Sayles's version of "real life"—let us reinstate the quotation marks—turns out to be as factitious as the conventions of soap opera, only blander. And that is often the case in his movies. When his actors are exceptional—Alfre Woodard, David Strathairn and Joe Morton come to mind—the screen comes alive, however fitfully. When the actors can't pull off the trick, we're left with an abstract world, populated by characters who are little more than moral categories: Sayles's notions of how people ought to behave and what they ought to believe.

In past years, Pauline Kael used to amuse herself (and a few million readers) by railing against moral improvement. I would suggest she was slightly off the mark. Moral improvement has been a goal of the arts for millennia; anyone who looks forward to seeing it end had better take her vitamins. The problem, rather, lies with those moralists who are so concerned with their own virtue that they don't feel the need to perform an artist's labor, or don't know what such labor might mean. Do they define virtue in civic and political terms? All the worse; they make politics dull.

Sayles is intelligent and prolific, low in budget and high of mind. For those reasons, I have passed over his films in discreet silence till now, preferring to turn my aggressive tendencies against products such as *Twister*. If I break the silence now, perhaps it's because Bill Clinton and Bob Dole will be broadcasting their own homilies nonstop from now through November. If movies are to provide us with public space during these wan times, then let it be a space where people bite off each other's lips and smash beer bottles, where political debate entertains and romance comes complete with secretions. Better to be of the devil's party, I say, than to stand with Sayles and the angels.

The Cook, the Thief, His Wife and Her Lover

Albert Spica doesn't know much, but he knows there's a connection between sex and food. It's the sort of Freudian tidbit of which a gangster—or any upwardly mobile lout such as Albert—may feel proud. Similarly, he's proud of owning an elegant restaurant, Le Hollandais, and an elegant wife, Georgina, and abuses them both—for their own good, of course. Fat, sputtering, violent, vain, Albert is the bogeyman with whom Peter Greenaway tries to frighten the audience in *The Cook, the Thief, His Wife and Her Lover*. As portrayed by Michael Gambon, Albert is the businessman as Mafioso, the arts patron as self-indulgent boor, the husband as brutal, moralizing proprietor. He's pure evil. He is also the film's only source of vitality.

Throughout such works as *The Draughtsman's Contract, The Falls* and *Vertical Features Remake*, Peter Greenaway has combined a rather literary wit with a studious, almost didactic cinematic style. In *The Cook,* you notice his artifice at once, as two uniformed figures—ushers, perhaps—part a curtain to reveal the opening tableau. The camera moves from a nocturnal blue parking lot to the cavernous green kitchen of Le Hollandais, then to its plush red dining room, then the stark white toilet. As Georgina (Helen Mirren) passes from one color-coded setting to another, her costume miraculously changes to suit the decor.

Time is similarly turned into a pattern. *The Cook* takes place over the course of a week, with each day's passing (save one) marked by a close-up of the restaurant's menu.

Though the framework is elaborate, the events taking place within it are fairly simple. Albert feeds and rants and bullies. Meanwhile, Georgina catches the eye of Michael (Alan Howard), a man who sits quietly at a nearby table. You know he's good because his table is piled with books. Without a word, Georgina and Michael meet in the toilet, grope, get interrupted by Albert (but not discovered, not yet). Soon, with the aid of the Cook (Richard Bohringer), Georgina is having an affair with Michael, using the only area of freedom available to her: a succession of pantries, which she visits on the pretext of going to the toilet.

The film's structure is so impressive, Albert's grossness so transfixing, the photography by Sacha Vierny so expert, that I watched at least four menus' worth of this plot with considerable pleasure. If nothing else, *The Cook* held my attention, which is more than I can say for almost any other movie released in the past few months. And if Greenaway had wanted to do no more than that, I would gladly recommend *The Cook* as a *jeu d'esprit*. But how playful is it, really, and on whom is the wit being exercised? As the story proceeds, taking on the character of a Jacobean revenge play, those questions become troubling.

You can see the problem most clearly when Greenaway has to shoot an apparently simple scene: a conversation between Georgina and the Cook. Suddenly, he has no pattern to fill out, no symbols to insert into the decor, no lurid events to stage, no verbal cues for his camera. His only task is to create a moment of human contact—and he falls on his face. It's painful to see how he cuts meaninglessly among close, medium and long shots, trying desperately to keep the scene going. He simply doesn't know what to do with the camera, any more than he knows how to direct the actors. They're both excellent performers, who might have done well enough if left to their own devices. But you can see all too plainly how Greenaway blocked their gestures, fitting them to the paragraphs of godawful dialogue that have to be mouthed.

At this point, a Greenaway fan might object that what I call "human contact"—no doubt a hopelessly bourgeois concept—has nothing to do with the film. If Greenaway can't put a couple of fine actors into a two-shot and come away with a watchable scene, well, that just proves he's more ideologically advanced than Jean Renoir. Maybe so. But let's turn now to the biggest piece of symbolism in *The Cook,* the backdrop against which Albert plays out his enormities: the principal decoration of Le Hollandais, an enormous reproduction of Frans Hals's *Banquet of the Officers of the Saint George Guard Company.*

It's a very interesting painting. A dozen citizen-soldiers sit around a lavishly appointed table, midway through the sort of self-congratulatory feast that used to last for a week. These burghers were in some sense the prototype of the modern middle class; their gluttony—over a period corresponding to the action in Greenaway's film—reinforces the identification between Albert and the figures in the painting. When first seen, he even wears a sash like the guardsmen's. His face, and those of his gang, resemble the figures' faces.

And yet the men Hals painted were not gangsters. In 1616, when the painting was made, they had indeed grown fat, lazy and middle-aged. But these men had risked their lives to free Holland from the double yoke of the Hapsburg Empire and the Spanish monarchy. They were patriots and sellouts, grasping businessmen and pioneers of civil liberty. As much as being forerunners of the modern bourgeoisie, they were throwbacks to the free guildsmen of medieval republics. They contributed mightily to the development of the slave trade and also of international law. In his group portrait of their militia company, Hals, who most likely had been born in the same year as the Dutch Republic, created something unprecedented. In effect, he caught the guards off-guard, rendering each man's character almost as if in a snapshot, through fleeting, revelatory gestures. Moreover, though the figures were made individually—much as a film is shot out of sequence—Hals had the novel inspiration of grouping them casually around the table, so that it looks and even feels as if they were painted together.

I have carried on at such length about the painting only because I had to. It looms over *The Cook* as an emblem and also an implicit rebuke. Greenaway utterly lacks the traits that were strongest in Frans Hals—an interest in character and a talent for informality. Nor does Greenaway care about the contradictions of the men Hals depicted, their substance as historical actors. All he wants is an image—a high-toned, arty image at that—with which to insult an upwardly mobile villain whose faults include an inability to pronounce the words on a French menu.

By the time Greenaway drags in a few mentions of the French Revolution, just for the sake of mentioning it, those viewers who can watch and think simultaneously might have fallen into some distress. *The Cook* is a film of ideas by a man who hasn't really got any, a tale of passions by someone who apparently has never felt them. You might try it anyway, just for the wretched excess of Michael Gambon's performance and the fun of seeing Helen Mirren's dress change colors; but don't expect a work of art.

SPIRITUAL
GUIDANCE

The Last Temptation of Christ

N o one should go without spiritual guidance to see *The Last Temptation of Christ*—Martin Scorsese's adaptation of the novel by Nikos Kazantzakis—so I went in the company of Rabbi Simcha Feffeferman, leader of Congregation Anshe Tsurres. "Rabbi," I said, as we left the theater, dodging the Bible-laden protesters, "is this film bad for the Jews?"

"And what isn't?" he replied.

"Let me rephrase the question. Here we have a picture directed by a Roman Catholic, based on a novel by a Greek Orthodox writer, with a screenplay by Paul Schrader, who is, I understand, Dutch Reformed. Yet, because the producer, Lew Wasserman, is Jewish—"

"The producer," the Rabbi said, "is Barbara De Fina. This Wasserman is just the studio big-shot. He knows from this movie like Lee Iacocca knows from wiring a dashboard."

"Exactly my point. But there was a demonstration outside Wasserman's home in which a man representing a Jewish producer whipped another man, portraying Jesus, through the streets of Beverly Hills."

"So what's that got to do with anything? Tell me, did you see anything Jewish in this movie? Any hint that Jesus or maybe the apostles were Jewish? Arabs, maybe. Africans or Italians from New York or these theater crazies that want to take off their clothes all the time. But Jews?"

"Well, Scorsese wasn't interested in the historical Jesus. He was trying for pan-Mediterranean atmosphere—something, more universal and also more exotic."

"Exactly *my* point. So Scorsese goes to Morocco. He hires this big rock and roll star who writes music they think sounds Middle Eastern, and he puts tattoos all over the women, and when John the Baptist shows up, it's this big production number with African drummers and naked women, and who's John he Baptist? André Gregory, that's who! My baptism with André!"

"So what are you saying?"

"I'm saying the fundamentalists get in a tumult because the movie isn't just like the Bible. And maybe some other people could get in a tumult because it's not like history. But you know what really is Jewish about this movie? The interpretation."

"You mean, casting David Bowie as Pontius Pilate?"

"He's very good, this Bowie. But no. I mean the interpretation Scorsese got from the book. In Judaism, if you got something in the Bible that don't make sense, you sometimes tell a story to explain it. It's called *aggadah*. That's what this here Kazantzakis did. He adds some stories to help the Gospels make sense. For example: What kind of carpenter was Jesus? He makes crosses for the Romans, that's what kind. It eats him up inside. All he thinks about is crucifixion. And who is Judas Iscariot? He's this friend of Jesus, a rebel, very upset his friend helps the Romans kill Jews. You see? An *aggadah*—and then, when you get into the story that is the Gospels, it already tells you more."

"I agree, Kazantzakis's conceits are fascinating. And, of course, the most audacious of all is his invention of a fourth temptation, which takes place while Jesus is on the cross. If you care about fine distinctions of Christian doctrine—and you'd better, if you intend to enjoy this movie—this additional temptation makes the story slightly more Arian than *Paradise Regained*. When Milton related the three temptations in the desert, he showed Jesus gradually becoming aware of His divinity. *The Last Temptation* extends the process, of course, and also makes explicit Jesus's internal struggle. He even says, 'God tells me only as much as I need to know.' So the progressive revelation—"

"Boychik," the Rabbi said, "let me explain you something. Books are books. A movie is something with scenery and costumes and maybe Eleanor Powell. Now, in this here movie—"

"Look, if you start talking about Eleanor Powell again—"

"Wonderful talents she had. But not an actress like Barbara Hershey, the one who plays Mary Magdalene. And you see places on Barbara Hershey that with Eleanor Powell, you couldn't imagine."

"Rabbi, this is degenerating fast."

"Just the opposite. In this movie, you got no historical Jesus, you got no real

Jews, you don't even see more than a couple soldiers. This Scorsese doesn't stage battle scenes, he makes fistfights. The whole Sermon on the Mount has maybe a dozen people. So what *do* you got? For starters, you got Barbara Hershey's nipples. And blood. Right at the start, Jesus helps the Romans crucify some *shlemiel,* and the blood hits him smack in the eye. They go to the Temple, and the blood from the sacrifices is running down the gutter, and the little dogs are drinking it. They celebrate Passover—I never seen a Passover like this, but all right—and they're cutting the throats of all the sheep and throwing the blood everywhere. When the Romans beat up on poor Jesus, it's worse than Sugar Ray Robinson hitting Jake La Motta in *Raging Bull.* You see my point? Jesus actually *pulls out his own heart* in this movie."

"You're saying that Scorsese, as a Catholic, has emphasized the creatural side of Jesus."

"I'm saying, his very first picture, *Who's That Knocking at My Door?,* it ends with Harvey Keitel kissing the foot of the crucifix and cutting his lip wide open on the nail. I'm saying, in *Mean Streets,* this same Keitel is talking about Saint Francis all the time and holding his hand over fires to purify himself. I'm saying, you go to see *The Last Temptation of Christ,* and who's got even more temptation than Jesus? Judas Iscariot, that's who—Harvey Keitel."

"I assume that's the *aggadah* that most troubles Christians. Judas comes to love Jesus. Then Jesus orders him to lead the soldiers to Gethsemane, and Judas almost rebels. He can't bear the thought of betraying his master. He's so agonized that Jesus tells him, 'God gave me the easier job.'"

"Some easy job. Scorsese already showed us, Jesus knows what's a crucifixion. They *hurt.* But sure, you're right. Jesus saves everybody else, but Judas in a way saves Jesus, and this probably bothers some people, though not as much as the nipples."

"The creatural—"

"Whatever. So, you got actors like Keitel and Barbara Hershey, who already mean something to Scorsese. You got all the blood. You got parts of the crucifixion where you actually see things from Jesus's point of view! You remember, it used to be in movies they didn't show Jesus's face. Him, and Franklin Roosevelt. This here movie, the big moment comes, you're right there on the cross with Him! Tell me, who ever did this before? Cecil B. DeMille? Nicholas Ray? George Stevens?"

"If I understand you, then, you're most impressed by the intimacy of the film, combined with Scorsese's characteristic physicality. And as for the incongruities—the hipness of the casting, or the ethnographic impurity of the *mise en scène,* or even small details, such as the inexplicable presence of Red Delicious apples in the Holy Land—these are winks at the audience, to let us know this isn't supposed to be the Gospels but is rather a personal essay on the battle of the spirit and the flesh."

"You're getting warmer. Tell me, you like this Willem Dafoe, the one who plays Jesus?"

"I think he gives a strong and well nuanced performance in a terribly difficult role."

"Would you maybe like De Niro better?"

"What are you getting at?"

"If you had De Niro, you'd know who Jesus is supposed to be. He'd be Travis Bickle, the King of Comedy. Am I right? But instead you got Dafoe. He's as mixed-up as anybody De Niro ever played for Scorsese, but with Dafoe that's where it stops. Jesus is a hole, right in the middle of the movie. He doesn't know who He really is, and you don't know."

"So *The Last Temptation of Christ* is about the absence of Robert De Niro?"

"*Now* you got it!"

"You've gone too far. Ladies and gentlemen, *The Last Temptation of Christ* has truly miraculous cinematography by Michael Ballhaus and immaculate editing by Thelma Schoonmaker. The screenplay is a little too eager to turn biblical sententiousness into colloquial rambling, but it never falls into inadvertent humor, even in the trickiest scenes between Jesus and Mary Magdalene. As for Scorsese's direction, it exploits the tension between historical fantasy and existential drama in much the same way as the Kazantzakis story pits the spirit against the flesh. I doubt this is Scorsese's best film—to me, that would still be *Raging Bull*—but it is an honorably eccentric effort, which has the virtue of becoming more absorbing as it goes on. Do you care to add anything, Rabbi?"

"*Born to Dance* it ain't. But if you like to see people whipped and tortured, which is the general idea, you should go see. And interpret."

Natural Born Killers

I was on Broadway at the Arcade, amid the cheerful clacks and drings of electronic entertainment, enjoying a round of Street Fighter II with my spiritual adviser, Rabbi Simcha Fefefferman. On the video screen, a plug-ugly named Balrog had just cut loose with a series of side-kicks and elbow blows, against which the old sage was only too helpless. Game over. Onto the screen came a diagnosis: "Your problem is you don't have any rhythm."

"Funny," I said. "You could say the same thing about Oliver Stone." The rabbi resettled his hat and declared, "I want to see this *Killers*, you should forgive the expression. You've got maybe another quarter?"

"Sure—but you've got a better deal pouring money into this machine than you will watching *Natural Born Killers*. To start with, Street Fighter II has lively, well-observed settings, compared to those in Stone's movie. I particularly like this Chinese market background, by the way, with the laughing onlookers and the chicken flapping in its cage. Also, the video-game characters, like Balrog, have a real vivacity, next to Mickey and Mallory Knox."

"You're talking now about Woody," said the rabbi; "and that pretty girl, somehow Jerry Lewis was the father."

"Woody Harrelson and Juliette Lewis, yes, who play the lovers turned mass murderers turned celebrities. Why do you want to see that *dreck*?"

"They say it's good—no?"

"*They.* This is a pseudo-movie, a void, which the Warner Bros. publicists have managed to hype into a pseudo-debate about violence and the media, thanks to the cooperation of a few journalists. *They* are Stephen Schiff in *The New Yorker,* Jack Kroll in *Newsweek,* Richard Corliss in *Time,* Owen Gleiberman in *Entertainment Weekly* and (dutifully reporting what everyone else says) Bernard Weinraub in *The New York Times.* The only thing interesting about *Natural Born Killers* is the way it's hooked these writers, who ought to have known better."

"It's time, I think, for Mortal Kombat II. You'll join me?"

"Yes, and another thing. Look at *why* they're hyping this, this tour through Oliver Stone's empty head. Gleiberman calls it 'revolutionary . . . unlike anything you've ever seen before.' He's referring, of course, to the stylistic barrage—the way Stone goes from 35mm to 16mm to video to black-and-white to animation, with rear projection and special effects thrown in for good measure, all within a single scene, all without motivation. But there's nothing *new* about this sort of crazy-quilt montage. Bruce Conner was doing it in 1958 in *A Movie,* mixing western footage, porn footage, Academy leader, you name it, to create a kind of proto-Pop delirium. 'Unlike anything you've ever seen before'? We've been seeing this since Eisenhower was President!"

"Boychik, you've got maybe another quarter?"

"Sure. And Kenneth Anger—how about *Scorpio Rising*? In 1963, he was splicing together shots of bikers with some tacky Sunday school footage of Jesus while the soundtrack played 'He's a Rebel.' So the point—rabbi, are you listening?—is that *Natural Born Killers* is nothing new, it's just thirty-year-old avant-gardism made *expensive,* which means people like Gleiberman and Schiff will notice it. See, Schiff is too bright to claim that Stone is an innovator. Instead, he says that *Natural Born Killers* is 'the most radical film *any major studio*—my italics—has released' since so-and-so."

"Meaning *Natural Born Killers* is this avant-garde you enjoy so much from when you were a bar-mitzvah boy, plus $34 million."

"Yes! You see so clearly, rabbi (though you've let Mileena cream you again). These methods have gone from being innovations (with Conner and Anger) to novelties (on MTV), and now, with Oliver Stone, they're just another set of sensations. Next stop, the Mickey and Mallory Shootout at Six Flags—certainly the most radical thrill ride that any major theme park has installed since—"

"Mortal Kombat II?"

"Nice try. But then, even if you grant him the style, Stone doesn't come *close* to being a 'virtuoso' (Richard Corliss's word); he does *not* put the movie together as precisely as Picasso put together a cubist picture (as Jack Kroll had the chutzpah to claim). There's all this fetishization of the *size* of the movie—Kroll points out that it has 3,000 images and took a year to edit—as if that meant the conjunction of images would turn out to be meaningful, or fresh or (can you imagine?) deeply felt. But for long stretches, *Natural Born Killers* is just tossed together; one choice of camera placement and film stock and editing rhythm turns out to be as good as another, which is to say they're all equally dumb, though they do make a splash. I mean, if a bum threw up on your shoes, you'd be disgusted. But if *Donald Trump* threw up on your shoes—you, in this case, being Stephen Schiff—then you'd notice all the interesting colors and textures, the dynamic thrust of the *pattern,* the sense of anguish implicit in the upchuck of this man who is so powerful and yet so deeply troubled. Here, listen to—"

"Boychik," the rabbi said, "relax. Come, you be Kitana this time. Now *I'm* Mileena."

"O.K. But look out, rabbi—I'm comin' to *getcha.* Wham! Wham! Wham! Wham! Wham!"

"You're experiencing maybe a little of the violence of our consumerist and media-saturated culture?"

"That's what Oliver Stone would like you to think. But look—game's over—look at how deeply Stone himself believes in the Hollywood clichés. With one exception, all of the people whom Mickey and Mallory kill *deserve* to die, if you judge them by traditional movie values; they're expendable because they're obese, ugly, horny, low-class or work for the police. Within a world defined only in terms of movies—the world of *Natural Born Killers*—Mickey and Mallory do no wrong."

"With one exception."

"Yes—Mickey kills a Native American healer (played by Russell Means, no less). That's the sin leading to Mickey and Mallory's capture, and the endless second half of the movie."

"You've got maybe another quarter?"

"Exactly! You don't see Russell Means cadging quarters for video games, like a *real-life* spiritual leader. You don't see *him* getting creamed every time by Balrog and Mileena. No, he's got so much movie insight, he just looks at Mickey and sees the word 'Demon' written on him in glowing letters. Which is interesting, because Mallory gets off with a joke—*her* glowing letters read 'Too much TV.'"

"A gentleman, this Stone."

"Not really. He just doesn't care about Mallory (who is merely half his movie). Stone has never tried too hard to invent thoughts and feelings for *any* of his female characters. So this time, wanting to do better, he makes up a background for Mallory. Guess what? She's a victim of incest. It's the same cheap ploy that Robert Zemeckis uses with the character of Jenny in *Forrest Gump*—

answering the director's need to appear sympathetic to a woman without his actually having to think about her."

"Then she's not so bad, this Mallory, just *farblondjet*. And Mickey—he's really a demon, you think?"

"Stone seems to think so. I mean, he keeps making Mickey's face distort, like in a science-fiction movie. And then, at the end, Mickey frees Mallory and leads her away from the scummy TV journalist who's been exploiting the murders and making the couple into celebrities. That would imply, I suppose, that Mickey's evil isn't just a shadow of the media after all. His evil must be something absolute, something that escapes the media—which would justify Stone himself for having played to the public's bloodlust in making this movie. If demons are real, then the journalist becomes a remissive figure for Stone himself, someone who comically screws up a job that Stone thinks is worth doing, and worth doing well. You know the journalist I'm talking about, the one who's played by Robert Downey."

"Ah, *Chafed Elbows*. This I liked very much."

"That was his father's movie. We're talking about Robert Downey Jr."

"Him I don't know. But from what you say, this *Killers* still sounds like a very interesting picture."

"All right," I said, pulling out my copies of *Time* and *Newsweek*. "You're a Talmudic scholar."

"I've been called worse."

"Then read."

Bobbing his head, the rabbi began to pore through the columns. A frown came over his normally beatific features. "No," he said. "This Corliss in *Time*, he contradicts. First paragraph, he says he's sick of this crazy violence on TV. Fifth paragraph, he says *Natural Born Killers* is good precisely because movies now are too timid. This one gives him lots of what he says he doesn't want, so he's happy. A mishmash. Also Stone himself, over here. He says 'Even the national news is perverted, because the news has become a profit-oriented enterprise since Tisch took over CBS. It's the old yellow journalism. If old, then not new and therefore *not* perverted, just more of the same. Yes?"

"You're beginning to catch on."

"And this Kroll in *Newsweek*. Paragraph two, he says the movie is good. Why? Because it gives you no rest, no way to 'get your bearings—physical, esthetic, moral.' But in paragraph one, he complains how the media—the movies, for example—have a 'crucial role in a process of dehumanization.' Not having any physical, esthetic or moral bearings—*this* I would call dehumanized."

"Yes."

"So him, too—the answer to what he doesn't like is *more* of what he doesn't like."

"Exactly. That's why, as I said, the noise *sounds* like a debate, but when you listen, all you really hear is self-congratulation. And look—"

But the Broadway Arcade's manager had stepped up to us with a glower. "No reading," he said.

"Excuse me, we were just—"

"I really mean it. No reading here."

"But this man is a spiritual leader—the head of Congregation Anshe Tsurres."

"You're gonna read, you take it outside."

We had no chance to negotiate; the world of Mortal Kombat II (and of *Natural Born Killers*) permits no dialectics. Onto the street we went, exiled from our playground of cheap sensation, having spent $15 in quarters, or a buck less than we'd have blown on two tickets to *Natural Born Killers*.

"But this is a mishmash," the rabbi kept moaning, as he waved the magazines and blinked in the sunlight.

"But there's a *current* avant-garde," I kept yelling, "and it addresses violence of *all* sorts. What about Chantal Akerman's *From the East*? Or Su Friedrich's *Sink or Swim*? Try finding them in the pages of *The New Yorker*. And you want *real* virtuoso montage? You want film-about-film that's meaningful, fresh, deeply felt? What about late Godard? What did *Entertainment Weekly* have to say about *Hélas pour moi*, or even the climax of Wes Craven's *Shocker*?"

But the sidewalk was deserted. Only a few tourists wandered by, staring at the rabbi and me as if we were crazy, or maybe even dangerous.

The Birdcage

I know I'm late in telling you about *The Birdcage*—the Mike Nichols/Elaine May/Robin Williams/Nathan Lane remake of *La Cage aux Folles*—but I was waiting till I could see it with my spiritual adviser, Rabbi Simcha Feffeferman. For the occasion, the rabbi wore black, with accents of fur on his hat. "Rabbi," I cried, as we stepped out of the theater onto Upper Broadway, "what excuse can they possibly have for making this picture?"

"Eighteen million gross, the first weekend?"

An avid gleam in his eyes told me he wasn't kidding. "If you're going to put it on that level," I said—

"And it tells us here in *Variety*, this picture's got legs. Which is more than I can say for Nathan Lane. Eleanor Powell, he's not."

"Well, the choreography—"

"The choreography, you should excuse me, wasn't half what they got in *Priscilla, Queen From the Desert*. The costumes, neither. But a nice hour and a half with Miami Beach, the pretty colors, the disco-disco-disco—"

"The old-fashioned, stock gay characters."

"Boychick," the rabbi said wearily, "you don't know what's a farce? It's the kind of comedy you get in the Torah when Isaac our father gives his blessing to the wrong son. One son is dressed up like the other, which looks ridiculous but somehow it works, and meanwhile outside the tent flap Rebecca our mother is clutching her forehead and doing double takes, because she's the one that cooked up the whole *mishegoss*. That's farce. You think they got any time in it for psychological insight? Sociological analysis? A shopping trip to Bed Bath & Beyond? Of course the characters are stock! They're practically bus-and-truck."

"Well, I admit I liked how they played it up that Armand the drag-club owner is a Jew. Robin Williams even got to wear a little Star of David on a chain around his neck."

"Superfluous *Yiddishkeit*—the only kind worth having."

"But aren't you offended that Hollywood keeps giving gay roles to straight actors?"

"What makes you so sure this here Robin Williams is straight? And what about Al Jolson, *ahava shalom*?"

"What, now you're outing Jolson?"

"I'm saying, who knows who's straight? Or, for that matter, what's straight? How about young Dan Futterman, who plays Robin Williams's son? Could he be a gay actor, maybe, taking a straight role? Not that such a thing has ever happened."

"But rabbi, you're missing the point. *The Birdcage* is so sanitized, so middle-of-the-road. Look at those scenes in the drag club. It seems as if three-quarters of the audience is straight."

"Just like in the movie theater. You think they're gonna spend umpty million dollars making a movie, *boychik*, and then chase thehet breeders away?"

"Aha! So you admit, the project was commercially compromised from the start."

The rabbi rolled his eyes toward heaven; or perhaps it was only toward the wooden sign above the door of Congregation Anshe Tsurres, where we had at last arrived. "You know," he said, "all the time in this magazine of yours, which I stopped getting, maybe the subscription ran out, all the time you're writing about this here New Queer Cinema. It's Su Friedrich this, Rose Troche that, Gregg Araki the other thing, Todd Haynes—"

"What's your point?"

"My point? I can give you 18 million points the first weekend, with legs. The New Queer people know from points like that in their dreams. Now you come in here," he said, tugging at my arm with surprising force, "you put something on your head, and you say a *b'rocho* for *The Birdcage*. Because here we got Pat Buchanan and Ralph Reed and the kind of people like that senator in the movie who comes visiting, the one Gene Hackman plays—he's good, this Hackman, no?"

"He's always good."

"You got those terrible people out there, saying terrible things about us—"

"Whatever that means."

"And here comes this movie where it's the senator who's got to lie all the time about himself, but the big Jew, Robin Williams, is proud of who he is, and he calls Nathan Lane his wife, and it's a hit. *Kusch mir im tuchis*, Buchanan! Not to mention that this Nathan Lane, even though he's no Eleanor Powell, makes a very good Ethel Merman, and some goofball with a big chest named Hank Azaria steals all his scenes playing the Cuban manservant, and Mike Nichols actually stopped being such a stiff of a director for once and had some fun, maybe because Elaine May wrote the script. You say a *b'rocho* for all that, and remember when *faygelehs* in the movies had to suffer like *The Boys in the Band*."

"So that's it. You don't see anything wrong with *The Birdcage*, except that the choreography and costumes aren't flashy enough for you."

"You know what? It's a nice little movie, as good as *La Cage aux Folles*—no better, no worse. But you're right, *boychik*. I give you credit. Better you should see those New Queer movies, provided they don't get lost like my subscription to *The Nation*. Those are the movies that are really about gay people."

"And *The Birdcage*? And all those other cutesy-poo Hollywood drag movies like *Mrs. Doubtfire* and *To Wong Foo*? What are they about?"

With a smile, the rabbi reached out and pinched one of my cheeks. "Those," he said, "are just a way of making sure—even when they got a good part in Hollywood for a woman, they give it to a man."

The Lost World: Jurassic Park 2

M y spiritual adviser, Rabbi Simcha Feffeferman, called in great excitement this morning to say that Steven Spielberg's new film is the greatest motion picture of all time. Drawn by the advertising slogan "Something has survived," the rabbi had discovered *Schindler's List Part 2: Die Farloyrne Velt* to be the exciting story of European Jews who survived the Nazi camps.

You will recall, the rabbi told me, that *Part 1* ended with the German businessman Oskar Schindler repenting of his role in maintaining the camps—nightmarish industrial parks, as Spielberg depicted them, in which Jews were confined for profit. *Part 2* begins several years later, after some of the characters from *Schindler's List* have immigrated to the New World. Schindler—who has taken an Americanized name, John Hammond—is still brooding about his terrible error. So he calls to his mansion the man who used to serve as his conscience—his numbers-cruncher Itzhak Stern, played in the original film by Ben Kingsley and here elongated into Jeff Goldblum. He, too, has taken a none-too-convincing American name, Ian Malcolm—and he doesn't for a moment trust Schindler's change of heart. (The boss looks terrible, by the way. Age and infirmity have shrunk him from a robust Liam Neeson to a wizened Richard Attenborough.) As Stern remarks bitterly, Schindler has gone "from capitalist to naturalist," or humanitarian, or what have you, with unpersuasive celerity. And that's when Schindler reveals the shocking truth: There is a remaining Nazi camp, filled with those relics of history (as they have been called), those dinosaurs, the Jews. Itzhak Stern must bring back from it what the Holocaust deniers always demand: photographic proof.

Rabbi Feffeferman felt it was highly significant that Spielberg had assigned this heroic mission to Stern. *Part 1* of *Schindler's List* was frequently criticized for making a German Christian the main character in a story about the Holocaust. In *Schindler's List Part 2*, we find a proud, self-reliant Jew at the center. But according to the entire breakfast club of Congregation Anshe Tsure (which followed the rabbi into the theater), Spielberg's most moving decision—and perhaps his most controversial—was to turn *Die Farloyrne Velt* into a meditation on the split between present-day American Jews and their European past.

It becomes painfully clear that Stern has rejected the world from which he came. He now views the European Jews as ugly, devious, smelly, dangerous and to be avoided at all costs. All too typically, this Americanized Jew has chosen as his soul mate an emphatically non-Jewish woman, Dr. Sarah Harding, played by Julianne Moore. A wonderful actress, the rabbi told me—did you see her in *Safe* and *Vanya on 42nd Street?*—but not to put too fine a point on it, she's got shiksa written all over her pert red head. Stern, suffering from the classic syndrome of self-hatred and shame, will do anything to keep her away from the European Jews—but to his discomfort, she actually likes them. She wants to pet them. She thinks—get this—that they have an enviable family structure. Just what Stern wants to hear! His people are so warm and nurturing.

Spielberg wrings some drollery from this *Abie's Irish Rose* material; but he has a more serious subject in mind. Suddenly, the Nazis reappear, led by Arliss Howard in a telltale brush cut. They are determined to hunt down the Jews, just as they did in the past. Many of the Jews fight back valiantly—here again, Spielberg has taken into account the criticisms of *Schindler's List Part 1*. He has shot many exciting scenes of partisans battling the Nazis—and the audience screams with pleasure as the Jews take their revenge. But as in the ghettos of Europe, this resistance may be doomed. Stern and Sarah race to stop the Nazis but cannot prevent the next horrifying turn of events. The Nazis import the concentration camp to America!

Spielberg's answer to this threat is an emphatic "Never again." Audiences will not soon forget his vision of the Jewish resistance fighter T. Rex rampaging through the streets. Since this takes place in San Diego, the rabbi suggested there was another group close by, made up of Latinos, who might be shown to be herded behind walls, made to work for pennies and hunted by heavily armed police. A missed opportunity. And the rabbi fretted that T. Rex, like the Golem before him, might be seen as going too far. But perhaps we should not invent problems, the rabbi concluded. People love *Schindler's List Part 2*. It's bigger, louder and bloodier than the original—and more colorful, too.

"Perhaps I misunderstood," I said when he was done. "I thought the dinosaurs were dinosaurs."

For which trouble I got only, "Dummy! If *that* was true, you wouldn't *have* a film—just another *shtick dreck* for making money."

Arguing the World/Spice World

At the urging of my spiritual adviser, Rabbi Simcha Feffeferman, I pass on a recommendation for a film he has seen and I have not: the highly praised documentary *Arguing the Spice World*.

After a black-and-white prologue set in the thirties, in which we learn how Daniel Bell, Nathan Glazer, Irving Howe and Irving Kristol honed their talents in City College's celebrated Trotskyite alcove, we catch up with these controversialists in the nineties after they've moved progressively to the right—*way* right, into transatlantic confrontation with pop music's chart-busting Spice Girls. Come along for the ride, and find out how four old Jewish guys plus five hip and swinging chicks add up to big fun in London!

Nathan Glazer discovers the true meaning of "beyond the melting pot" when he first feasts his eyes on the Girls—each with a distinct, unassimilable identity all her own, yet able to harmonize with the others in the Western tradition of girl groups. Yes, Sporty will always be the sporty one; Posh will remain posh. Yet see what a civil society they make, shaking it for the camera!

Want to witness the end of ideology? Just watch Daniel Bell when he melts before Baby Spice's smile. As she sucks on a lollipop and sticks out her chest, Baby proves to Bell that sixties retro-chic can *and will* yield to superior market force, faster than you can murmur "cultural contradictions of capitalism."

Irving Howe's favorite Spice is Ginger. The group's outspoken militant for

Girl Power raises no dissent from Irving when she says her revolution means fun for everyone—so don't feel threatened, guys!

But there's always one wallflower at the party, and wouldn't you know? It's Irving Kristol. Determined to keep his intellect as crisp as a check from the American Enterprise Institute, he hangs back from the Girls—especially that tawny, leopard-skinned Scary. But he just can't leave Third World Trouble alone—not until she makes him gulp down those Victorian morals with a gurgled "Himmelfarb!"

"But Rabbi," I protested, "how can we believe these tough-minded social critics would fall for the Spice Girls? The New York intellectuals are defenders of independent thought as it's been enabled by our free society, whereas the Spice Girls are nothing but a marketing ploy engineered to separate people from their money."

To which the Rabbi merely lifted a shaggy eyebrow, saying, "And?"

OUT OF THE
BUSINESS

Shined Shoes
(*The Band Wagon*)

must have been nine or ten when it happened—which means that *Brown v. Topeka* had been decided, the Montgomery boycott won. Young militants would just then have been getting yanked off their stools at the Greensboro lunch counter; while in South Chicago, in the barber shop my family frequented, a middle-aged Negro grinned at me and said, "All the girls gone dance with *you*, 'cause *you* got shined shoes."

Until that moment, I'd been admiring his virtuosity: the slip-slap of polish, the pattering brush, the snap of his rag glancing off my shoes. The oddity of this fingertip tap dance—the incongruity of its being performed at my feet—didn't strike me until my mother spoke. She was a Stevenson Democrat; she might hire a grown man to kneel before me, but not without conversation. "He's going to a birthday party," she volunteered for me; at which point, even though it was 1960, we got the full minstrel show.

That was the second time I shrank from a black man's servility—the episode that confirmed what I'd learned months before. During the winter, my uncle Phil had sent down his handyman, Willie, from the store on Maxwell Street—a dim, two-story shack with bare-plank floors, piled high with the warehouse-damaged goods that Sears would not sell—telling him to deliver another slightly dented something. My parents would be gone from the house; so I was given a two-dollar bill and told to hand it over once the job was done. "Sir," Willie called me. "*Thank* you, sir," and he bobbed his head—twice—while shuffling backward, tugging his wrinkles into a smile.

Let's say the bit was overdone—unnecessary to perform before a mere child, and misjudged for a kid who would grow up to be a critic. I could not yet guess at what terrors lay behind the show, but already I cringed at blatant acting: Willie miming his gratitude, the bootblack turning up his grin.

But before long, the shoeshine stand disappeared. The barber shop's sole black employee—its only black presence—once again became the nonsyncopated man who swept up the clippings. The patrons preferred to shine their own shoes; ours was not a neighborhood for pizzazz.

Our stretch of Ninety-fifth Street ran parallel to the Illinois Central's weedy embankment; our shopping center (as we then called a strip mall) faced the tracks on which boxcars ran all night. We'd learned to sleep through the rattling of wheels and blaring of horns, as we'd grown used to the orange skies, lit up till dawn by the steel mills' burn-off towers. Smells were complex: a single sniff of autumn air brought you sulfur and raw gasoline, mulch, oil, ammonia, car exhaust, and a hint of freshness blown off the lake. But the visible world was simple and unadorned. You saw a duplex house behind its lawn. Then you saw another; and both were probably painted dark green.

A few black women worked by day in those houses. A black man worked in the shopping center's garage. At the grammar school, I saw no black people at all. Two years after my remarkable shoeshine, I memorized Vachel Lindsay's "The Congo" as a class assignment and recited it to an accompaniment by my friend Ron Klein, whose parents had bought him a trap drum set. How pleased I was with the Negro rhythms we made: "Boomlay boomlay boomlay BOOM!" We still hadn't heard the fifes and the whistles of the warriors. When we graduated from grammar school, two months before the march on Washington, our wittier classmates turned to the black endpapers in their autograph books and wrote, in shiny lead pencil, "Best wishes for the future. Malcolm X."

That's what I knew about black people, ten years after *The Band Wagon* came out.

Forty-one years after *The Band Wagon* came out, I moved into a new apartment on Manhattan's Upper West Side. Here, too, the smells were complex. I had leased a third-floor walk-up in a tenement, where the garbage was kept on the second floor and the first belonged to a sushi restaurant. A steep stairway, scarcely wide enough for a single climber, channeled the odors upward to my one and a half rooms. Unofficially, this new home could qualify as a doorman building: a succession of street people, all of them black, took turns opening the door for the sushi bar's patrons, accompanying themselves with the rattle of a paper cup.

I felt lucky to have the place. In September, my previous apartment had become uninhabitable, as apartments do when an ostensibly stable relationship goes radioactive. By January I was still hot enough to alarm a Geiger counter; but at least I had no one to burn in my living quarters, and no one to burn me. I was forty-four and single again and paying my bills as a freelance scribbler. Perhaps you will understand why the first song in *The Band Wagon* had begun to sound in my thoughts: "I'll go my way by myself . . . I'm by myself, alone." If you know the film, you'll also understand why this memory cheered me.

Fred Astaire, too, had been single and middle-aged in New York, with no steady means of support. That, at least, was the situation of his *Band Wagon* alter ego, Tony Hunter. Again and again I heard his tenor bobbing along behind the beat, and into my mind's eye came the sight of him in his blue-gray summer suit, strolling along the platform at Grand Central: "I'll face the unknown—I'll build a world of my own." Back in Manhattan after his career in movies has ended, forgotten by his fans and ignored by the press, Tony Hunter is still no less than himself, a great song-and-dance man—even if the song floats out just for himself and the dance is a matter of putting one foot in front of the other.

I couldn't amble like that; I couldn't sing. Nor was I truly alone. Every day brought me another reason to thank the friends who had seen me through autumn and into the new year. How could I thank my friends? I'd invite some of them to my apartment and play *The Band Wagon* on video.

Of course, I wasn't just showing a movie; I was putting myself on display. My friends were to see that I could live up to Tony Hunter's example, if not his style. That settled, let them enjoy the film. One of them, a choreographer, could be expected to bore her eyes into Michael Kidd's dances. Another, author of endlessly self-reflexive plays, would smile at the reversals between backstage and center stage in Comden and Green's script. The third was an amateur of Tin Pan Alley. He would love the Schwartz and Dietz songs; and (like my other guests) he somehow had never seen *The Band Wagon*.

Up they trudged, having first paid their respects to the doorman, and squeezed into my apartment, single file. With the lights dimmed and the radiator faintly hissing, we huddled before the tube and began watching Minnelli's scenes of a New York summer.

Soon would come one of the film's biggest treats, "A Shine on Your Shoes": the scene of Tony Hunter's true homecoming, when he first makes good on his promise in "By Myself." Feeling out of sorts and out of fashion, Fred walks into the Penny Arcade on Forty-second Street—"Wasn't this the Eltinge Theatre?"—and wills himself into good spirits. In the decision to get his shoes shined, he discovers an occasion for song and dance; in his exultation, he discovers an audience among the nickel-and-dime public. Over the past weeks, "By Myself" had become my consolation, easing my bachelor walks. But "A Shine on My Shoes" was my drug; and I was going to get high with my friends.

And yet it didn't happen. Never mind whether my friends understood I was secretly Tony Hunter. For the first time in my experience of *The Band Wagon,* when the genius atop the shoeshine stand cried "Wonderful!" I didn't feel like calling it out with him. I couldn't rejoice with Fred. I was staring at the bootblack, thinking, "All the girls gone dance with *you.*"

How had I managed to watch this scene so many times and never really see him? An old shame suddenly sent the blood pulsing to my forehead— boomlay!—as I realized I was watching the second great pas de deux in *The Band Wagon* but was for the first time acknowledging Fred's partner in it. Would I have ignored Cyd Charisse in "Dancing in the Dark"? Yet the bootblack was clearly *dancing* with Fred—dancing at his feet, dancing before him on his knees. If this scene were to lift me up, how could I *not* ignore the bootblack?

It had been late when we pushed the PLAY button. When the movie ended, my guests were not so much huddled as slumped. I was wide awake, futilely hoping the closing credits might answer my questions. As I sent the friends off, a new obsession nagged at me. Who played the bootblack? Where did he come from?

Watch closely, and you'll see he emerges from the backside of a question mark. The camera tracks to the left, a sight line opens, and the bootblack slides into view, looking like part of the decor. Within *The Band Wagon*'s Penny Arcade set, this chunk of Forty-second Street reimagined on the MGM lot, he at first appears as a mere patch of chocolate and orange added to the polychromy: a figure so distant from the camera that he lacks a face, so far removed from society's favor that life in the background might be his fate.

Foregrounds belong to Fred. Here he is, hopping off a tall contraption that looks like a gymnasium's scale. "Electricity Is Life" reads its sign: a proposition that Fred finds unpersuasive, having unwittingly traded money for a shock. He smooths himself and moves to the left, where he bumps into a still more puzzling object: a metal box, fitted with cranks and handles. Its purpose is obscure; its only sign, the huge red-and-white question mark that now dominates our scene. Soon this coin-catcher, too, has thwarted Fred. He won't even glance at the next machine: a test-your-strength game. Of what use to him is brute force?

By the time Fred abandons these shrines, built to the gods of the arcade— Material Progress, Mystery, Manly Power—the camera has brought the bootblack into the middle distance. Now, perhaps, you'll notice how he's bent over a customer's shoes, which he buffs in dispirited boredom. Look quickly, and you'll also make out his processed hair, his smooth, deep-toned skin and chubby cheeks. He can't be more than thirty. Shoeshine men don't lead pampered lives; yet this one has the head of a young sensualist. His shirt is a raging Hawaiian sunset; the khaki slacks are cut full, as if the wearer remembered nights of zoot-suit pleasures; the socks that peek out at the ankles are pink. Were you to pause and think about this figure, a new question mark might form around him. But Fred doesn't pause. He passes by, taking the camera with him.

And so, for the next half a minute, *The Band Wagon* pretends to forget the bootblack, as I used to forget him.

Let me cut short the looping path by which Fred returns to this star of obscurity. By consulting books, I finally learned who played the shoeshine man: LeRoy Daniels, a name given by Stephen Harvey in *Directed by Vincente Minnelli*. Then, having discovered that much, I could find nothing more. I sifted through reference works on African-American performers, scanned the cast lists of musicals, meditated upon the collected obituaries of *Variety*. Except for earning a credit in *The Band Wagon*, LeRoy Daniels had vanished from show biz without a trace.

For a researcher facing such a gap, it's helpful to know a choreographer. I phoned my friend, who put me onto someone who told me to call someone else, who promised to pass on a message to Michael Kidd; which is how I came to be jamming the telephone to my left ear one afternoon, straining to take in every word of a brusque but friendly voice from California:

"I'm reading your fax and thinking, 'Who the hell is he talking about? LeRoy Daniels?' Then I read some more and say, 'Oh! The shoeshine man.'"

"I wouldn't have bothered you," I said, "except, before I go to the archive at the Schomburg Center—"

"You're looking at archives? Let me save you the trouble. You won't find anything. LeRoy Daniels was a bootblack."

Backstage becomes center stage. In *The Band Wagon*, Fred plays a character who is essentially Fred. Nanette Fabrayand and Oscar Levant, as the on-screen husband-and-wife writing team, essentially play the off-screen writing team of Comden and Green. Of course the bootblack was a real bootblack.

"He had a stand downtown in Los Angeles. A report came back from someone, 'Take a look at this guy. He snaps the cloth, he hits the brushes together, he does it all on the beat.' This was his act, to attract customers. We brought him in, and he was perfect! He had a great sense of rhythm and style."

"Had he danced before?"

"He wasn't a trained dancer. He was what I'd call a street dancer—but he picked things up. I never even knew his last name. We just called him LeRoy."

"What happened to him?"

"After we shot the picture, I never saw him again. He went back downtown. Probably he hung the clippings around his stand. I bet they helped business."

Did that answer my question? It did, as much as a set of facts could. Once more I offered Michael Kidd my thanks, knowing that despite his generosity, the real answers would have to come from LeRoy Daniels himself, or from those few moments of his life that had been made visible to me.

As Fred circles back in the arcade, so did my thoughts come around to LeRoy.

He's abandoned himself to idleness and the dust when Fred comes into his life, stumbling over the legs of a recumbent LeRoy. Were the star to right himself at this point and keep going, there would be no LeRoy Daniels story; but Fred, having craned to see what he tripped over, takes it into his head to return.

LeRoy tries not to notice. The white guy has started to sing him an uplift number—standard stuff, which might be summarized as "Pull yourself up by your own bootstraps." Very soon after the release of *The Band Wagon*, Dr. King would retort that such pulling-up can't be done when you have no boots. Maybe that's why LeRoy so clearly has to force himself to glance up toward Fred, only to look away again, scowling. Who is this natty customer, that he preaches self-reliance to a black workingman?

Yet there's something unconvincing about the scowl; it looks more like a pout. Maybe the flimsiness of the disdain proves that LeRoy is an inexperienced actor, who responds mechanically to his cue and then waits for the next. Then again, maybe we're seeing evidence of the real LeRoy. The sharp clothes and sensualist's head can't be complete inventions. The man is an entrepreneur; he runs his own business; if this were downtown L.A. and not the MGM lot, he wouldn't be caught dead moping like that on his stand. And just so, when Fred at the end of the verse crows, "Give your shoes a shine," LeRoy answers with a smile that's far more convincing than his show of disgust.

He gets to his feet and begins flipping a pair of brushes on the beat—left hand, right hand—as Fred starts singing the chorus. LeRoy isn't smiling now; he stands open-mouthed, gazing down at his hands, absorbed in a little routine that shouldn't require this much concentration, since he must perform it dozens of times a day. But he doesn't ordinarily perform it before Minnelli's camera. Only when he's made it through the first eight bars, when he's allowed to turn away from the camera and start slapping down polish, does he begin to loosen up.

He moves. He pokes out his ass and bobs his head, and though the camera frames him from the thighs up, you can see his feet are tapping. This is LeRoy's art; he's now eased into the motions that draw him customers, down at Union Terminal. You might even think he's begun to enjoy himself. His hands patter at Fred's shoes; he keeps his eyes up. And when the camera pulls back, allowing room for the gestures that grow more expansive as the mood rises, LeRoy does something astonishing between one phase of the shine and the next: he executes a spin.

With that, LeRoy Daniels has gone beyond his art. For sixty-four bars he synchronizes his every movement with Fred, playing flawlessly before a camera that runs nonstop, until he's no longer giving a dancelike performance at a shoeshine stand, but dancing. Even when Minnelli finally cuts to another setup—when Fred's vocal ends, and the band cranks up for an interlude—the interruption doesn't hamper LeRoy. Effortlessly carrying on the high spirits, he prances around the shoeshine stand, strutting and shaking with his hands empty of tools, as if he had nothing to do in this world but have a good time. Fred, on top of the stand, is jolting from one angular pose to another, in a preview of the jazz stylizations Michael Kidd will give him in the "Girl Hunt" ballet. LeRoy, by contrast, is round and undulating and as vernacular as they come. Yet the two men move together; once they even do a little step together, just before LeRoy spins again and drops to his knees. Maybe *The Band Wagon* hasn't elevated him to the level of Fred Astaire—the film's too realistic for that—but it has substituted a singular partner for his run of customers; and LeRoy can't contain his delight.

Watch as he completes the circuit and momentarily turns his back to the stand, gazing toward the left of the frame. You can see him look off-camera at someone—Michael Kidd, maybe, or a family member, or a buddy he was allowed to bring on to the set—while he smiles hugely. It isn't a minstrel grin. It's the beam of triumph.

Perhaps I mistimed my discovery of that smile. Only someone who had seen false cheer squeezed out of a black man could have marveled, as I did, at LeRoy's unforced joy. But in 1994, how many people remembered 1960? Who even knew about Stevenson Democrats?

To me, LeRoy's performance shone like the dawn of the civil rights movement, whose glory had been about to burst over the horizon. Here was a demonstration of what could be done by overlooked people once their creative powers were set free, if only for a day, if only in a make-believe setting. But how would LeRoy look to someone steeped in the ideology of the '90s? At best, he'd serve as proof that black people *should* pull themselves up by their bootstraps. At worst, he'd be made into evidence that Negroes had been happy all along.

But acts of recognition don't always serve the political moment. Just as often, they answer needs so personal that they might be mistaken for vanities, serving purposes that don't exist until we're ready to see them. In that sense, recognition may be compared to a shoeshine—and like a shoeshine, it needs to be renewed from time to time.

For about two years, I managed to keep LeRoy Daniels confined within *The Band Wagon.* Then came a night when I was forced to renew my discovery.

I had gone to dinner with my choreographer friend and the woman I was about to marry. (Apparently, I was *not* going to go by myself, alone.) In celebration, each of us had one drink too many and then rolled out of the restaurant into a chilly New York night, where the sidewalk seemed an ideal site for rehearsing a wedding waltz. The choreographer's notes were simple, on the order of "*That* was grisly." So we shoved her into a cab and made our way down the avenue, toward the fresh-smelling apartment we now shared.

I was feeling as sharp as Fred when he's got Cyd Charisse on his arm. And then, at the corner of Eighty-sixth Street, we ran into Mickey, the chief unofficial doorman from my former building.

A lot of the street people addressed him as Sarge—maybe with an eye toward the fatigue jacket he wore in winter, maybe because of the bulky authority with which he carried himself. We'd known him for years, individually and together, and tended to offer him help that we withheld from others. Sarge was capable of being helped. With his set-back eyes and flattened upper lip, he looked like a street-weathered Mike Tyson, dressed in dark green castoffs. Even when he shook the paper cup, there was nothing servile about him. You wouldn't have described Sarge as a sensualist; but he was clearly an entrepreneur of sorts, and a performer, too, whose act was to chat up donors on the sidewalk. He was also like LeRoy in this: I had looked at him for years without seeing.

"Hey, buddy," he said, as we reached the corner. Once again failing to recognize who was before me, I began to dig in my pocket. I knew his routine; I was ready with my two-dollar evaluation.

But it seems my own act was misjudged. With a nod toward my fiancée, Sarge told me, "You're with a beautiful woman. You got good taste." Then the one true critic on the corner grinned at her and said, "You got good taste, too. But his is better."

FILMOGRAPHY

Note: Running times are approximate.

The Accidental Tourist. 1988. Directed by Lawrence Kasdan. Written by Frank Galati and Lawrence Kasdan, based on a novel by Anne Tyler. With William Hurt, Kathleen Turner, Geena Davis. 121 min.

The Addiction. 1995. Directed by Abel Ferrara. Written by Nicholas St. John. With Lili Taylor, Christopher Walken, Annabella Sciorra, Edie Falco, Michael Imperioli. 82 min.

After Life (*Wandafuru Raifu*). 1998. Written and directed by Hirokazu Kore-eda. With Arata, Erika Oda, Susumu Terajima, Taketoshi Naito, Yusuke Iseya. 118 min.

A.I. Artificial Intelligence. 2001. Written and directed by Steven Spielberg, based on a screen story by Ian Watson and a short story by Brian Aldiss. With Haley Joel Osment, Frances O'Connor, Sam Robards, Jude Law, Brendon Gleeson, William Hurt. 145 min.

All Quiet on the Western Front. 1930. Directed by Lewis Milestone. Written by George Abbott, Del Andrews and Maxwell Anderson, based on a novel by Erich Maria Remarque. With Lew Ayres, Louis Wolheim, John Wray, Arnold Lucy, Slim Summerville, William Bakewell, Ben Alexander, Scott Kolk, Owen Davis, Jr. 131 min.

And Life Goes On . . . (*Zendegi Edame Darad*). 1991. Written and directed by Abbas Kiarostami. With Ferhad Kherdamend, Buba Bayour. 95 min.

An Angel at My Table. 1990. Directed by Jane Campion. Written by Laura Jones, based on the autobiographies of Janet Frame. With Kerry Fox, Alexia Keogh, Karen Fergusson, Iris Churn, Kevin J. Wilson. 160 min.

Arguing the World. 1998. Written and directed by Joseph Dorman. With Daniel Bell, Nathan Glazer, Irving Howe, Irving Kristol, Michael Walzer. 106 min.

Austin Powers: The Spy Who Shagged Me. 1999. Directed by Jay Roach. Written by Mike Myers and Michael McCullers. With Mike Myers, Heather Graham, Mindy Sterling, Verne Troyer. 95 min.

The Band Wagon. 1953. Directed by Vincente Minnelli. Written by Betty Comden and Adolph Green. With Fred Astaire, Cyd Charisse, Jack Buchanan, Nanette Fabray, Oscar Levant, LeRoy Daniels. 111 min.

Belfast, Maine. 1999. Directed by Frederick Wiseman. With the people of Belfast, Maine. 245 min.

The Big Parade. 1925. Directed by King Vidor. Written by Harry Behn and Laurence Stallings, based on a play by Joseph Farnham. With John Gilbert, Renée Adorée, Hobart Bosworth, Claire McDowell, Claire Adams, Robert Ober, Tom O'Brien, Karl Dane. 141 min.

Bill & Ted's Bogus Journey. 1991. Directed by Peter Hewitt. Written by Chris Matheson and Ed Solomon. With Keanu Reeves, Alex Winter, William Sadler, George Carlin. 98 min.

The Birdcage. 1996. Directed by Mike Nichols. Written by Elaine May, based on a screen-play by Francis Veber, Edouard Molinaro and Marcello Danon and a play by Jean Poiret. With Robin Williams, Nathan Lane, Christine Baranski, Dianne Wiest, Gene Hackman, Hank Azaria, Dan Futterman, Calista Flockhart. 117 min.

Black Girl (La Noire de . . .). 1965. Written and directed by Ousmane Sembene. With Mbissine Thérèse Diop, Anne-Marie Jelinek, Robert Fontaine, Momar Nar Sene. 65 min.

Borom Sarret. 1964. Written and directed by Ousmane Sembene. With Abdoulaye Ly. 20 min.

Camp de Thiaroye. 1987. Written and directed by Ousmane Sembene and Thierno Faty Sow. With Ibrahima Sane, Sijiri Bakaba, Camara Med Dansogh. 152 min.

Carmen. 1984. Directed by Francesco Rosi. Written by Francesco Rosi and Tonino Guerra, based on a libretto by Henri Meilhac and Ludovic Halévy, based on a novella by Prosper Mérimée. With Julia Migenes, Placido Domingo, Ruggero Raimondi, Faith Esham. 152 min.

Caro Diario (Dear Diary). 1994. Written and directed by Nanni Moretti. With Nanni Moretti, Renato Carpentieri, Jennifer Beals. 100 min.

Ceddo. 1977. Written and directed by Ousmane Sembene. With Tabara N'diaye, Moustapha Yade, Ismaila Diagne, Matoura Dia, Omar Gueye, Mamadou Dioumé, Nar Modou, Ousmane Camara. 120 min.

The Challenge (La Sfida). 1958. Directed by Francesco Rosi. Written by Suso Cecchi d'Amico, Enzo Provenzale and Francesco Rosi. With José Suarez, Rosanna Schiaffino. 93 min.

Christ Stopped at Eboli (Cristo Si è Fermato a Eboli). 1979. Directed by Francesco Rosi. Written by Francesco Rossi, Tonino Guerra and Raffaele La Capria, based on a memoir by Carlo Levi. With Gian Maria Volonté, Irene Pappas, Lea Massari, Paolo Bonacelli, Alain Cuny, François Simon, Stavros Tornes. 150 min.

Chronicle of a Death Foretold (Croanaca di una Morte Annunciata). 1987. Directed by Francesco Rosi. Written by Tonino Guerra and Francesco Rosi, based on a novella by Gabriel García Márquez. With Rupert Everett, Ornella Muti, Gian Maria Volonté, Irene Pappas, Lucia Bosè, Anthony Delon, Alain Cuny, Sergi Mateu. 110 min.

Chronicle of a Disappearance (Segell Ikhtifa). 1996. Written and directed by Elia Suleiman. With Elia Suleiman, Jamel Daher, Fawaz Eilemi, Fuad Suleiman, Nazira Suleiman, Ola Tabari. 88 min.

Close Up (Nema-ye Nazdik). 1990. Written and directed by Abbas Kiarostami. With Hos-sain Sabzian, Mohsen Makhmalbaf. 100 min.

The Cook, the Thief, His Wife and Her Lover. 1989. Written and directed by Peter Greenaway. With Michael Gambon, Helen Mirren, Alan Howard, Richard Bohringer. 123 min.

Crooklyn. 1994. Directed by Spike Lee. Written by Cinque Lee, Joie Lee and Spike Lee. With Alfre Woodard, Delroy Lindo, Zelda Harris, Carlton Williams, Harif Rashed, David Patrick Kelly. 114 min.

The Dawn Patrol. 1930. Directed by Howard Hawks, Seton I. Miller and Dan Totheroh, based on a story by John Monk Saunders. With Richard Barthelmess, Douglas Fair-banks, Jr., Neil Hamilton, Frank McHugh, Clyde Cook. 105 min.

Dead Man. 1995. Written and directed by Jim Jarmusch. With Johnny Depp, Gary Farmer, Lance Henriksen, Michael Wincott, Eugene Byrd, Iggy Pop, Crispin Glover, Mili Avital, Robert Mitchum, John Hurt, Gabriel Byrne, Alfred Molina. 121 min.

D'Est. 1993. Written and directed by Chantal Akerman. With the people of Eastern Europe. 107 min.

Divorce, Italian Style (Divorzio all'Italiana). 1961. Directed by Pietro Germi. Written by

Pietro Germi, Ennio Di Concini, Alfredo Giannetti and Agenore Incrocci. With Marcello Mastroianni, Daniela Rocca, Stefania Sandrelli, Leopoldo Trieste. 108 min.

Dr. Akagi (Kanzo Sensei). 1998. Directed by Shohei Imamura. Written by Shohei Imamura and Daisuke Tengan, based on a novel by Ango Sakaguchi. With Akira Emoto, Kumiko Aso, Juro Kara, Masanori Sera, Keiko Matsuzaka, Jacques Gamblin. 129 min.

Do the Right Thing. 1989. Written and directed by Spike Lee. With Spike Lee, Rosie Perez, Danny Aiello, Giancarlo Esposito, Roger Guenveur Smith, Bill Nunn, Joie Lee, John Turturro, Richard Edson, Samuel L. Jackson, Ossie Davis, Ruby Dee. 120 min.

The Dreamlife of Angels (La Vie Rêvée des Anges). 1998. Directed by Erick Zonca. Written by Erick Zonca and Roger Bohbot with Virginie Wagon. With Élodie Bouchez, Natacha Régnier, Grégoire Colin, Patrick Mercado, Jo Prestia. 113 min.

Ed Wood. 1994. Directed by Tim Burton. Written by Scott Alexander and Larry Karaszewski. With Johnny Depp, Martin Landau, Sarah Jessica Parker, Patricia Arquette, Jeffrey Jones, Bill Murray, Lisa Marie, George "The Animal" Steele, G.D. Spradlin, Vincent D'Onofrio. 127 min.

Election. 1999. Directed by Alexander Payne. Written by Alexander Payne and Jim Taylor, based on a novel by Tom Perrotta. With Matthew Broderick, Reese Witherspoon, Jessica Campbell, Chris Klein, Molly Hagan, Delaney Driscoll, Colleen Camp. 103 min.

Emitai. 1971. Written and directed by Ousmane Sembene. With Ibou Camara, Ousmane Camara, Joseph Diatta, Dji Niassebanor, Sibesalang, Kalifa, Robert Fontaine, Michel Renaudeau, Pierre Blanchard. 103 min.

The End of St. Petersburg (Konets Sankt-Petersburga). 1927. Directed by Vsevolod Pudovkin. Writeen by Nathan Zarkhi. With Aleksandr Christyakov, Vera Baranovskaya, Ivan Chuvelyov, Aleksei Davor, Vladimir Fogel, Aleksandr Gromov. 88 min.

Erin Brockovich. 2000. Directed by Steven Soderbergh. Written by Susannah Grant. With Julia Roberts, Albert Finney, Aaron Eckhart. 130 min.

eXistenZ. 1999. Written and directed by David Cronenberg. With Jennifer Jason Leigh, Jude Law, Ian Holm, Willem Dafoe, Don McKellar. 97 min.

Faat-Kine. 2000. Written and directed by Ousmane Sembene. With Venus Seye, Mame Ndumbé Diop, Ndiagne Dia, Mariame Balde. 118 min.

The Facts of Murder (Un Maledetto Imbroglio). 1959. Directed by Pietro Germi. Written by Pietro Germi, Alfredo Giannetti and Ennio De Concini, based on a novel by Carlo Emilio Gadda. With Pietro Germi, Claudia Cardinale, Eleonora Rossi Drago, Claudio Gora, Franco Fabrizi, Saro Urzì. 120 min.

4 Little Girls. 1997. Written and directed by Spike Lee. With Maxine McNair, Chris McNair, Alpha Robertson, Shirley Wesley King, Thomas James Bevel, Fred Shuttlesworth, John Cross, Wyatt Tee Walker, Lillie Brown, Andrew Young, Jesse Jackson, Coretta Scott King, George Wallace, David J. Vann, Bill Baxley, Albert Boutwell, Nicholas Katzenbach, Howell Raines, Taylor Branch. 102 min.

Gladiator. 2000. Directed by Ridley Scott. Written by David Franzoni, John Logan and William Nicholson. With Russell Crowe, Joaquin Phoenix, Connie Nielsen, Oliver Reed, Richard Harris, Derek Jacobi, Djimon Hounsou. 154 min.

Grand Illusion (La Grande Illusion). 1937. Directed by Jean Renoir. Written by Charles Spaak and Jean Renoir. With Jean Gabin, Pierre Fresnay, Erich von Stroheim, Marcel Dalio, Dita Parlo. 114 min.

The Great White Hype. 1996. Directed by Reginald Hudlin. Written by Tony Hendra and Ron Shelton. With Samuel L. Jackson, Damon Wayans, Jon Lovitz, Jeff Goldblum, Peter Berg. 91 min.

Guelwaar. 1993. Written and directed by Ousmane Sembene. With Thierno N'diaye, Ndiawar Diop, Myriam Niang. 115 min.

Hands Over the City (*Le Mani sulla Città*). 1963. Directed by Francesco Rosi. Written by Francesco Rosi and Raffaele La Capria. With Rod Steiger, Salvo Randone, Guido Alberti. 105 min.

Hoop Dreams. 1994. Directed by Steve James. Written by Steve James and Frederick Marx. Cinematography by Peter Gilbert. With William Gates and Arthur Agee and their families, friends, coaches, teachers and teammates. 170 min.

I Am Cuba (*Soy Cuba/Ya Kuba*). 1964. Directed by Mikhail Kalatozov. Written by Yevgeny Yevtushenko and Enrique Pineda Barnet. With Sergio Corrieri, Salvador Wood, José Gallardo, Raúl García, Luz María Collazo, Jean Bouise, Alberto Morgan, Celia Rodríguez, Fausto Mirabal, Luisa María Jiménez, Mario González Broche. 141 min.

Illustrious Corpses (*Cadaveri Eccellenti*). 1976. Directed by Francesco Rosi. Written by Tonino Guerra, Lino Iannuzzi and Francesco Rosi, based on a novel by Leonardo Sciascia. With Lino Ventura, Tino Carraro, Marcel Bozzuffi, Max von Sydow, Charles Vanel, Fernando Rey, Tina Aumont, Renato Salvatori. 120 min.

In the Name of the Law (*In Nome della Legge*). 1949. Directed by Pietro Germi. Written by Pietro Germi, Aldo Bizzarri, Federico Fellini, Giuseppe Mangione and Tullio Pinelli, based on a novel by Giuseppe Guido Lo Schiavo. With Massimo Girotti, Jone Salinas, Camillo Mastrocinque, Charles Vanel, Saro Urzì. 101 min.

Independance Day. 1996. Directed by Roland Emmerich. Written by Dean Devlin and Roland Emmerich. With Will Smith, Bill Pullman, Jeff Goldblum, Mary McDonnell, Judd Hirsch. 145 min.

J'accuse. 1919. Written and directed by Abel Gance. With Romuald Joubé, Severin-Mars, Maryse Dauvray, Maxime Desjardins, Angèle Guys, Mancini. Original running time approximately 270 min.

Koker Trilogy [*Earthquake Trilogy*] (see *Where Is the Friend's Home?*, *And Life Goes On . . .*, *Through the Olive Trees*).

Lamerica. 1994. Directed by Gianni Amelio. Written by Gianni Amelio, Andrea Porporati and Alessandro Sermoneta. With Enrico Lo Verso, Michele Placido, Carmelo Di Mazzarelli, Piro Milkani, Sefer Pema. 125 min.

The Last Temptation of Christ. 1988. Directed by Martin Scorsese. Written by Paul Schrader, based on a novel by Nikos Kazantzakis. With Willem Dafoe, Harvey Keitel, Verna Bloom, Barbara Hershey, André Gregory, David Bowie, Harry Dean Stanton. 164 min.

Licensed to Kill. 1997. Written and directed by Arthur Dong. With the convicted murderers of gay men. 80 min.

Lone Star. 1996. Written and directed by John Sayles. With Chris Cooper, Elizabeth Peña, Kris Kristofferson, Joe Morton, Matthew McConaughey. 135 min.

The Lost World: Jurassic Park 2. 1997. Directed by Steven Spielberg. Written by David Koepp, based on a novel by Michael Crichton. With Jeff Goldblum, Julianne Moore, Pete Postlethwaite, Arliss Howard, Richard Attenborough. 129 min.

The Lovers on the Bridge (*Les Amants du Pont-Neuf*). 1991. Written and directed by Leos Carax. With Juliette Binoche, Denis Lavant, Klaus-Michael Grüber. 125 min.

Lucky Luciano. 1974. Directed by Francesco Rosi. Written by Francesco Rosi, Tonino Guerra and Lino Iannuzzi. With Gian Maria Volonté, Vincent Gardenia, Silverio Blasi, Charles Cioffi, Larry Gates, Magda Konopka, Edmond O'Brien, Charles Siracusa, Rod Steiger. 105 min.

Magnolia. 1999. Written and directed by Paul Thomas Anderson. With John C. Reilly, Tom Cruise, Julianne Moore, Philip Baker Hall, Jeremy Blackman, Philip Seymour Hoffman, William H. Macy, Melora Walters, Jason Robards, Melinda Dillon, April Grace, Ricky Jay, Felicity Huffman, Michael Bowen. 188 min.

Mandabi. 1968. Written and directed by Ousmane Sembene. With Makhouredia Gueye, Ynousse N'diaye, Isseu Niang, Serigne Sow, Mustapha Ture. 90 min.

Matinee. 1993. Directed by Joe Dante. Written by Charlie Haas, based on a story by Jerico and Charlie Haas. With John Goodman, Cathy Moriarty, Simon Fenton, Omri Katz, Lisa Jakub, Kellie Martin, Jesse Lee, Lucinda Jenney. 99 min.

The Matrix. 1999. Written and directed by Andy Wachowski and Larry Wachowski. With Keanu Reeves, Laurence Fishburne, Carrie-Anne Moss, Hugo Weaving, Joe Pantoliano. 136 min.

The Mattei Affair (*Il Caso Mattei*). 1972. Directed by Francesco Rosi. Written by Tito Di Stefano, Tonino Guerra, Nerio Minuzzo and Francesco Rosi. With Gian Maria Volonté, Luigi Squarzina, Gianfranco Ombuen, Edda Ferronao. 116 min.

A Moment of Innocence (*Nun va Goldoon*; also known as *Bread and Flower*). 1996. Written and directed by Mohsen Makhmalbaf. With Mirhadi Tayebi, Mohsen Makhmalbaf, Ali Bakhsi, Ammar Tafti, Maryam Mohamadamini. 78 min.

Moulin Rouge. 2001. Directed by Baz Luhrmann. Written by Baz Luhrmann and Craig Pearce. With Nicole Kidman, Ewan McGregor, John Leguizamo, Jim Broadbent, Richard Roxburgh. 120 min.

The Muse. 1999. Directed by Albert Brooks. Written by Albert Brooks and Monica Johnson. With Albert Brooks, Sharon Stone, Andie MacDowell, Jeff Bridges. 97 min.

Natural Born Killers. 1994. Directed by Oliver Stone. Written by David Veloz, Richard Rutowski and Oliver Stone, based on a story by Quentin Tarantino. With Woody Harrelson, Juliette Lewis, Robert Downey, Jr., Tommy Lee Jones. 118 min.

Neapolitan Diary (*Diario Napoletano*). 1992. Written and directed by Francesco Rosi. With Francesco Rosi, Carlo Fernariello. 90 min.

Nights of Cabiria (*Le Notti di Cabiria*). 1957. Directed by Federico Fellini. Written by Federico Fellini, Ennio Flaiano and Tullio Pinelli, with additional dialogue by Pier Paolo Pasolini. With Giulietta Masina, François Périer, Amedeo Nazzari, Aldo Silvani, Franca Marzi, Dorian Gray. 117 min.

Paths of Glory. 1957. Directed by Stanley Kubrick. Writeen by Stanley Kubrick, Jim Thompson and Calder Willingham, based on a novel by Humphrey Cobb. With Kirk Douglas, Ralph Meeker, Adolphe Menjou, George Macready, Wayne Morris, Richard Anderson, Joe Turkel. 86 min.

The Portrait of a Lady. 1996. Directed by Jane Campion. Written by Laura Jones, based on a novel by Henry James. With Nicole Kidman, John Malkovich, Barbara Hershey, Mary-Louise Parker, Martin Donovan, Shelley Winters, Richard E. Grant, Shelley Duvall, Viggo Mortensen, Christian Bale, Valentina Cervi. 144 min.

Public Housing. 1997. Written and directed by Frederick Wiseman. With the people of the Ida B. Wells Homes, Chicago. 200 min.

The Puppetmaster (*Hsimeng Jensheng*). 1993. Directed by Hou Hsiao-hsien. Written by Wu Nien-jen and Chu T'ien-wen, based on the life story of Li Tienlu. With Li Tienlu, Lim Giong, Lin Chung. 142 min.

The Rage: Carrie 2. 1999. Directed by Katt Shea. Written by Rafael Moreu, based on characters by Stephen King. With Emily Bergl, Jason London, Dylan Bruno, J. Smith-Cameron, Amy Irving, Zachery Ty Bryan, John Doe, Mena Suvari. 104 min.

The Railroad Man (*Il Ferroviere*). 1956. Directed by Pietro Germi. Written by Pietro Germi and Alfredo Giannetti. With Pietro Germi, Luisa Della Noce, Sylva Koscina, Renato Speziali, Edoardo Nevola, Saro Urzì, Carlo Giuffrè. 118 min.

Red: see *Three Colors: Red.*

Rosetta. 1999. Written and directed by Jean-Pierre Dardenne and Luc Dardenne. With

Emilie Dequenne, Fabrizio Rongione, Anne Yernaux, Olivier Gourmet, Bernard Marbaix. 90 min.

Run Lola Run (*Lola Rennt*). 1998. Written and directed by Tom Tykwer. With Franka Potente, Moritz Bleibtreu, Herbert Knaup. 80 min.

Rushmore. 1998. Directed by Wes Anderson. Written by Wes Anderson and Owen Wilson. With Jason Schwartzman, Bill Murray, Olivia Williams, Seymour Cassel, Brian Cox, Mason Gamble, Sara Tanaka. 93 min.

Safe. 1995. Written and directed by Todd Haynes. With Julianne Moore, Peter Friedman, Xander Berkeley. 119 min.

Salvatore Giuliano. 1961. Directed by Francesco Rosi. Written by Suso Cecchi d'Amico, Enzo Provenzale, Francesco Rosi and Franco Solinas. With Frank Wolff, Salvo Randone, Frederico Zardi, Pietro Cammarata, Nando Cicero. 124 min.

Seduced and Abandoned (*Sedotta e Abbandonata*). 1964. Directed by Pietro Germi. Written by Pietro Germi, Agenore Incrocci, Furio Scarpelli and Luciano Vincenzoni. With Stefania Sandrelli, Saro Urzì, Aldo Puglisi, Lando Buzzanca, Lola Braccini, Leopoldo Trieste. 115 min.

Shakespeare in Love. 1998. Directed by John Madden. Written by Marc Norman and Tom Stoppard. With Gwyneth Paltrow, Joseph Fiennes, Geoffrey Rush, Judi Dench, Colin Firth. 122 min.

She's All That. 1999. Directed by Robert Iscove. Written by R. Lee Fleming, Jr. With Freddie Prinze, Jr., Rachael Leigh Cook, Matthew Lillard, Anna Paquin. 95 min.

Shoulder Arms. 1918. Written and directed by Charles Chaplin. With Charles Chaplin, Edna Purviance, Syd Chaplin, Jack Wilson, Henry Bergman, Albert Austin, Tom Wilson. 46 min.

Sink or Swim. 1990. Written and directed by Su Friedrich. 48 min.

Spice World. 1997. Directed by Bob Spiers. Written by Kim Fuller and Jamie Curtis. With Melanie Brown (Scary Spice), Emma Bunton (Baby Spice), Melanie Chisholm (Sporty Spice), Geri Halliwell (Ginger Spice), Victoria Beckham (Posh Spice). 89 min.

Star Wars: Episode I—The Phantom Menace. 1999. Written and directed by George Lucas. With Liam Neeson, Ewan McGregor, Natalie Portman, Jake Lloyd, Ray Park. 133 min.

The Sweet Hereafter. 1997. Directed by Atom Egoyan. Written by Atom Egoyan, based on a novel by Russell Banks. With Ian Holm, Sarah Polley, Maury Chaykin, Gabrielle Rose, Peter Donaldson, Bruce Greenwood, David Hemblen, Brooke Johnson, Arsinée Khanjian, Tom McManus, Stephanie Morgenstern, Earl Pastko, Alberta Watson, Caerthan Banks. 112 min.

The Target Shoots First. 2000. Written and directed by Christopher Wilcha. With Christopher Wilcha and the employees of Columbia House. 71 min.

Taste of Cherry (*Ta'm e guilass*). 1997. Written and directed by Abbas Kiarostami. With Homayon Ershadi, Abdolrahman Bagheri, Afshin Khorshid Bakhtiari, Safar Ali Moradi, Mir Hossein Noori. 95 min.

Three Brothers (*Tre Fratelli*). 1981. Directed by Francesco Rosi. Written by Tonino Guerra and Francesco Rosi, based on a story by Andrei Platonov. With Philippe Noiret, Michele Placido, Vittorio Mezzogiorno, Charles Vanel, Andréa Ferréol. 113 min.

Three Colors: Red (*Trois Couleurs: Rouge*). 1994. Directed by Krzysztof Kieslowski. Written by Krzysztof Kielowski and Krzysztof Piesiewicz. With Irène Jacob, Jean-Louis Trintignant, Frédérique Feder, Jean-Pierre Lorit. 99 min.

Through the Olive Trees (*Zire darakhatan zeyton*). 1994. Written and directed by Abbas Kiarostami. With Mohamad Ali Keshavarz, Ferhad Kherdamend, Zarifeh Shiva, Hossein Rezai, Tahereh Ladanian. 103 min.

Time Regained (*Le Temps retrouvé*). 1999. Directed by Raul Ruiz. Written by Raul Ruiz and Gilles Taurand, based on a novel by Marcel Proust. With Catherine Deneuve, Emannuelle Béart, Vincent Perez, John Malkovich, Pascal Greggory, Marcello Mazzarella, Marie-France Pisier, Chiara Mastroianni, Arielle Dombasle, Edith Scob, Elsa Zylberstein, André Engel. 169 min.

To Forget Palermo (*Dimenticare Palermo*). 1990. Directed by Francesco Rosi. Written by Francesco Rosi, Tonino Guerra and Gore Vidal. With James Belushi, Mimi Rogers, Joss Ackland, Philippe Noiret, Vittorio Gassman. 100 min.

Topsy-Turvy. 1999. Written and directed by Mike Leigh. With Jim Broadbent, Allan Corduner, Lesley Manville, Timothy Spall, Martin Savage, Ron Cook, Eleanor David, Kevin McKidd, Shirley Henderson, Dorothy Atkinson, 160 min.

To Sleep With Anger. 1990. Written and directed by Charles Burnett. With Danny Glover, Paul Butler, Devaughn Walter Nixon, Mary Alice, Reina King, Corry Curtis, Richard Brooks, Sheryl Lee Ralph, Carl Lumbly, Vonetta McGee. 102 min.

Touch of Evil. 1958. Written by Orson Welles, based on a novel by Whit Masterson. With Orson Welles, Charlton Heston, Janet Leigh, Joseph Calleia, Akim Tamiroff, Marlene Dietrich, Ray Collins, Victor Millan, Lalo Rios, Valentin de Vargas, Dennis Weaver, Mort Mills. 112 min.

Ulee's Gold. 1997. Written and directed by Victor Nunez. With Peter Fonda, Patricia Richardson, Christine Dunford, Tom Wood, Jessica Biel, Vanessa Zima, Steven Flynn, Dewey Weber. 111 min.

Unforgiven. 1992. Directed by Clint Eastwood. Written by David Webb Peoples. With Clint Eastwood, Gene Hackman, Morgan Freeman, Richard Harris, Jaimz Woolvett, Saul Rubinek, Frances Fisher, Anna Levine. 131 min.

La Vie de Bohème. 1992. Directed by Aki Kaurismäki. Written by Aki Kaurismäki, based on a novel by Henri Murger. With Matti Pellonpää, André Wilms, Kari Väänänen, Evelyne Didi, Christine Murillo, Jean-Pierre Léaud, Louis Malle, Samuel Fuller, Laika. 100 min.

The Way We Laughed (*Così Ridevano*). 1998. Directed by Gianni Amelio. Written by Gianni Amelio, Daniele Gaglianone, Lillo Iacolino and Alberto Taraglio. With Enrico Lo Verso, Francesco Giuffrida. 124 min.

When Mother Comes Home for Christmas. 1996. Written and directed by Nilita Vachani. With Josephine, Sumindra, Suresh and Norma Perera. 109 min.

Where Is the Friend's Home? (*Khane-ye Doust Kodjast?*). 1987. Written and directed by Abbas Kiarostami. With Babek Ahmed Poor, Ahmed Ahmed Poor. 83 min.

Wild At Heart. 1990. Directed by David Lynch. Written by David Lynch, based on a novel by Barry Gifford. With Nicolas Cage, Laura Dern, Willem Dafoe, J.E. Freeman, Crispin Glover, Diane Ladd. 124 min.

Xala. 1974. Written and directed by Ousmane Sembene. With Makhouredia Gueye, Thierno Leye, Dieynaba Niang, Myriam Niang, Iliamane Sagna, Seune Samb, Abdoulaye Seck, Douta Seck, Younouss Seye. 123 min.